CHALLENGING HISTORY

INDUSTRIALISATION AND SOCIETY 1700-1914

Neil Tonge

First published in 1993 by:
Thomas Nelson and Sons Ltd

Reprinted in 2002 by:
Nelson Thornes Ltd
Delta Place
27 Bath Road
CHELTENHAM
GL53 7TH
United Kingdom

02 03 04 05 06 / 10 9 8 7 6

A catalogue record for this book is available from the British Library

ISBN 0 17 435061 9

Designed by Roger Walker
Design formatted on Apple Macintosh by Alphaprint, Alton, Hants

Printed in China by L. Rex

Contents

Editor's Preface

This book offers you the challenge of history. It encourages you to engage with the past in a creative and personal way; it also presents you with the many challenges which the past provides for present-day students. It demands a rigorous and scholarly approach. In return, we expect that you will increase your understanding, improve your skills, and develop a personal involvement in historical study.

The challenge is presented to you through the different components of each chapter:

Preview   Each chapter begins with a presentation which is designed to arouse your interest, and alert you to one or more of the major themes of the chapter.

Text   The text demands an active response from you. The book has been carefully written, designed and fully illustrated to develop your learning and understanding. Photographs, artwork, cartoons, statistical tables, maps, graphs are among the many visual images that reinforce the quality of the text.

Examining evidence   These sections present a wide variety of Historical sources, both primary and secondary. They encourage you to analyse the opinions of others, to assess the reliability of evidence, and to formulate and test your own personal views.

Focus   Focus sections zoom in on, and highlight, particular events, people and issues of the period. They are designed to enable you to see these more clearly and to find your way through the complexity of historical problems.

Talking Points   They are scattered widely throughout the book. By talking and listening, we can all learn about the major issues which translate the past into the present. In doing so, we question our own perceptions, test out our ideas and widen our range of interests.

Questions   Throughout the chapters, questions encourage you to consider what you see and read. They invite your personal response and encourage you to share it verbally with your fellow students, and in writing with your teachers.

Review   Each chapter contains an exercise, often a formal essay or question, which enables you to revise the learning and understanding of the whole chapter. You will find supporting ideas and structures to help you to formulate your answer.

This book offers you many experiences of History. It opens up to you the thoughts and feelings of contemporaries; it classifies the distinctive nature of your period; it places people, events and issues in the context of the flow of History. Just as important, it invites and encourages you to formulate your own personal insights and opinions in a living and developing debate. The Challenge of History is essential to the vitality and well-being of the modern world.

J.A.P. Jones

General Editor

Author's Acknowledgements

In memory of my Dad who died during the writing of this book.

Dedication

Challenging History is dedicated, with affection, to the memory of Vince Crinnion. It was inspired by his humanity, and his vision, and by his belief that the study of history is an enjoyable, creative experience, through which we can challenge both our concept of the past and present, and our understanding of ourselves.

1 Heaven or Hell? The Birth of Industrial Society

PREVIEW

A CRITIC'S VIEW OF THE RAPID GROWTH OF LONDON. 1827.

'If we look back to the condition of the mass of the people as it existed in this country, even so recently as the beginning of this present century, and then look around us at the indications of greater comfort and respectability that meet us on every side, it is hardly possible to doubt that here the elements of social improvement have been at work.'

G.R. Porter, *Progress of the Nation* 1851

'We have purchased a great commerce at the price of crowding our population into the cities and of robbing millions of strength and beauty. Out of the work of millions we have added to a landed gentry an aristocracy of wealth. These, striding over the bodies of the fallen, proclaim with certainty the prosperity of their country.'

L.G. Chiozza-Money, *Riches and Poverty* (1905)

Industrialisation

To study the past is to take a journey to a foreign country. Some customs and features will be familiar; other aspects will appear strange. The intention of this book is to provide you with a series of 'maps' to guide your travels so that you can make sense of the unfamiliar, identify landmarks along the way, appreciate why the landscape has changed and why some features persist to this day.

The foreign country we will visit is Britain between 1700 and 1914. During this period Britain went through a series of changes in industrial technology, organisation of labour, transport, finance and business operations which is commonly called the 'Industrial Revolution'. These economic changes in turn produced a radically different sort of society. Britain played a unique role in this process for she was the first country in the world to emerge as an industrialised society.

How did those living through these monumental changes react? What sort of changes did they think were happening?

Any change to an established pattern of life brings with it anxiety about the future, particularly if a lifetime of skills is washed away by a tidal wave of technological advance or if you are trapped in a prison of poverty by impersonal economic forces. Other members of society view such change as presenting opportunities for social and economic improvement. Whilst fortunes could be made for a minority only, they were made by creating jobs for the many and in this way, ultimately, everyone benefitted. We will meet many of the inhabitants of this 'foreign' country on our way and we may ask them for directions. It will not be surprising if their answers not only vary one from another but, at times, actually contradict previous answers.

Unlike them we have the advantage of knowing the actual routes taken but we must never assume that the pathway was inevitable or that the inhabitants we ask share this privileged information. We must accept that we are the 'foreigners' in their country and that we will never learn to understand them except on their own terms.

Examining the evidence
Heaven or hell? – The views of contemporaries

Industrial change affected not only the physical landscape in which we live but also the 'mental' landscape inside our heads. The way we think, feel and behave is strongly influenced by our basic need for food, clothing and shelter. The manner in which these basic necessities are shared out between people determines the different groups that make up the society in which we live and the differences in attitude we have to one another.

In economic relationships, such as those illustrated below, what will be seen by one group as a hopeful future may be greeted with despair by others. The extracts which follow the illustration were both written at roughly the same time about the same group of workers.

Talking point

Consider technological change in our own times (e.g. automation, micro-electronics) closure of uneconomic firms and businesses. In groups discuss which sectors of the workforce have been affected by these changes. In what ways have they benefitted some and appear to have harmed others? What should government do, if anything, to ease the transition of such changes? How will such individuals regard the change they have experienced? How will these varying attitudes affect the way the history of late 20th Century Britain is written?

Source A: Industrialisation and Social Groups

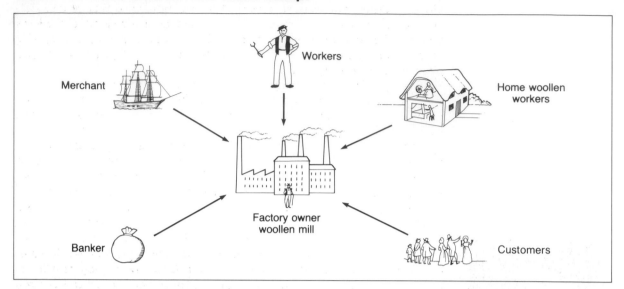

Source B

Debased alike by ignorance and pauperism, they have discovered with the savage, what is the minimum means of life, upon which existence may be prolonged … Long and exhausting labour, continued from day to day, and from year to year, is not calculated to develop the intellectual or moral faculties of man … To condemn man to such severity of toil is, in some measure, to cultivate in him the habits of an animal … He neglects the comforts and delicacies of life. He lives in squalid wretchedness, on meagre food, and expends his superfluous gains on debauchery …

The comparitively innutritious qualities of the basic diet of oatmeal and potatoes upon which they live are most evident. We are, however, by no means prepared to say that an individual living in a healthy atmosphere, and engaged in active employment in the open air, would not be able to continue protracted and severe labour, without any suffering, whilst nourished by this food … But the population nourished on this diet is crowded into one dense mass, in cottages separated by narrow, unpaved, and almost pestilential streets; in an atmosphere loaded with the smoke and exhalations of a large manufacturing city. The operatives are congregated in rooms and workshops during twelve hours of the day, in an enervating heated atmosphere, which is frequently loaded with dust or filaments of cotton, and impure from constant respiration, or from other causes …

… the wages of certain classes are extremely meagre. The introduction of the power loom, though ultimately destined to be productive of the greatest benefits, has, in the present restricted state of commerce, occasioned some temporary embarrassment, by diminishing the demand for certain kinds of labour, and, consequently their price. The hand-loom weavers, existing in the state of transition, still continue a very extensive class, and though they labour fourteen hours and upwards daily, earn only from five to seven shillings per week.

J.P. Kay-Shuttleworth, *The Moral and Physical Condition of the Working Classes employed in the cotton manufacture in Manchester* (1832)

Source C

Good workmen would have advanced their condition to that of overlookers, managers, and partners in new mills and have increased at the same time the demand for their companions' labour in the market. It is only by an undisturbed progression of this kind that the rate of wages can be permanently raised or upheld ...

Ill-usage of children of any kind is a very rare occurrence ...

In an establishment for spinning or weaving cotton all the hard work is performed by the steam engine, which leaves for the attendant no hard labour at all ...

Occupations which are assisted by steam engines require for the most part a higher species of labour than those which are not; the exercise of the mind being then partially substituted for that of the muscles, constituting skilled labour, which is always paid more highly than unskilled. On this principle we can readily account for the comparitively high wages which the inmates of a cotton factory, whether children or adults, obtain ... By reducing the hours of labour, and thereby the amount of subsistence derivable from the less objectionable occupations, they would cause a corresponding increase in the competition for more employment in the more objectionable ones, and thus inflict an injury on the whole labouring community, by wantonly renouncing the fair advantages of their own ...

The factory system then, instead of being detrimental to the comfort of the labouring population, is its great Palladium ...

Andrew Ure, *The Philosophy of Manufacturers, or, an Exposition of the Scientific, Moral, and Commercial Economy of the Factory System of Great Britain* (1835)

Source D: James Philips Kay 1804–1877

JAMES KAY-SHUTTLEWORTH.

After qualifying as a doctor at Edinburgh University he took an active interest in matters of public health, publishing medical pamphlets In 1832, at the height of the Cholera epidemic, he became Secretary to the Manchester Board of Health.

He married in 1842 and adopted his wife's maiden name as an addition to his own. Kay-Shuttleworth, as he now called himself, soon earned a reputation as a social reformer; serving as an Assistant Poor Law Commissioner and later, Secretary to the Education Committee.

In the short book from which this source is taken, he makes a special plea for the adoption of free trade which he regards as the necessary instrument to bring prosperity to all. At the same time he is deeply conscious of the hardship and squalor for many working people and wishes to arouse the rich to accept responsibility for this state of affairs.

Source E: Andrew Ure 1778–1857

ANDREW URE.

Like Kay-Shuttleworth, he too was a qualified doctor but spent most of his career as Professor of Chemistry at Glasgow University. He was particularly interested in the scientific education of working men; an interest which attracted a group of Manchester businessmen to request him to tour and report on factory conditions in Lancashire.

Source F: Legislation to improve working conditions

In 1832 considerable discussion was taking place as to the desirability of an effective factory act which would improve conditions and reduce the hours of work for women and children.

Source G: Mule spinning

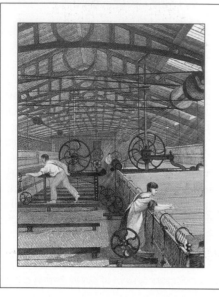

This illustration is from J.R. Barfoot, *The Progress of Cotton*, a book published for the Ladies Society for Promoting the Early Education of Negro Children (1835–40).

Source H: Working conditions and children

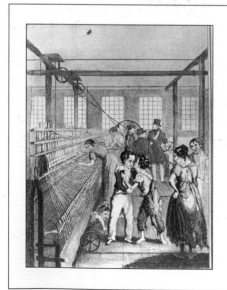

From a novel by Francis Trollope, *Michael Armstrong, Factory Boy* (1840).

Source I: The maltreatment of children

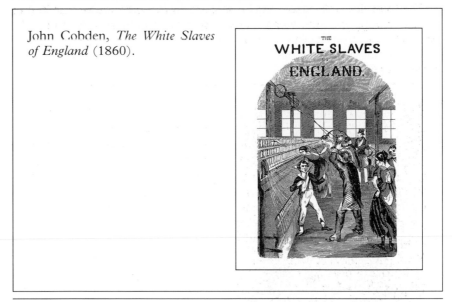

John Cobden, *The White Slaves of England* (1860).

Study source A.

1 What possible attitudes and relationships might develop within and between these groups?

Read sources B and C.

2 Draw up a balance sheet from the information in the sources. Head your answer 'Benefits and Losses of the Industrial Revolution'.

3 From which social group do the writers appear to come? Support your answer with reference to the sources.

4 What sort of audience do the writers appear to be addressing? Support your answer with reference to the sources.

5 The two writers differ in their assessment of the impact of the Industrial Revolution on cotton workers. Does this mean that only one of them is correct?

6 Do both writers accept, reject or present totally opposing views of the benefits of the Industrial Revolution?

7 Study sources G, H and I.

Some writers consciously distort the facts to emphasise the points they wish to make. Others, show their prejudices unwittingly. Compare these three sources. In what ways and for what possible reasons have these illustrations been drawn?

A Journey through Britain in 1700

If we set out to explore industrialising Britain of 1700 we must do so on horseback, along roads which rapidly degenerate into pitted pot-holes the further we travel from the capital. Heavy goods must follow the meandering rivers, hug the coastline in sailing brigs or be packed onto the backs of mules to follow laborious tracks along ridges and across treacherous moors. Trade and population settle ribbon-like alongside the navigable rivers, cluster around sea-ports and market towns or remain, as they have done for thousands of years, scattered thinly in villages following the seasonal cycle of agriculture.

The small population, about five and one-half million, spreads out fan-like from London by way of Hertfordshire into south Norfolk at one edge and by way of Wiltshire and Somersetshire into Devon at the other. Beyond this perimeter lie the less densely populated regions of northern England and Wales, Scotland and Ireland. Here and there are denser pockets of population in the Northumberland and Durham mining districts and the textile areas of Yorkshire and Lancashire.

Agriculture dominates not only the economy but the social and political life of the country. Even those who have won their riches and power through trade yearn for stability and respectability through the purchase of country estates and a noble title. Nor do many of the ancient nobility rest upon their fortunes when, by means of exploiting their mineral and industrial resources, they can provide even more riches for themselves.

The changing industrial landscape

Within this society there are perceptible seeds of change which are taking root and transforming the landscape into a new form, irrevocably different from that which has gone before. The materials to study this transformation are all around you for they shaped, and continue to shape, the environment in which we live.

Before we continue let us pause a while and see how the industrialising process affected one city in England – Newcastle upon Tyne. Of course we cannot, and should not, assume everywhere would be affected in the same way. The regions of England are very different from each other and this was even truer in the eighteenth century when communications were more tenuous.

Newcastle is a typical fair-sized eighteenth century town. It lies at the tidal reach of the River Tyne, the industrial and trading artery for the whole region. The heart of the city is the quayside; a jumbled mass of medieval houses intermingled with warehouses. Everywhere is alive with sound; creaking pulleys, rumbling cartwheels grinding on cobblestones and the cries of all manner of commerce. Baltic timbers lie alongside barrels of salted herring. A forest of masts sway to the slap of water against the lichen-smeared quays. Smaller craft called 'keels' busy themselves like humming insects carrying 'black diamonds' – coal, to the sea-going colliers patiently lying at South Shields at the mouth of the Tyne, unable to journey up-river due to the choking accumulation of silt.

The two banks of the Tyne are linked by a single bridge with houses perched along its length. It can scarcely manage the heavy traffic which crosses it every day. Clouds of smoke hang like hazy curtains from the ironworks and other manufactories which line the muddy Tyne's jagged banks.

TALKING POINT

You could repeat this exercise with an investigation of your own locality. Compare your results with that of Newcastle upon Tyne. What similarities and differences can you note?

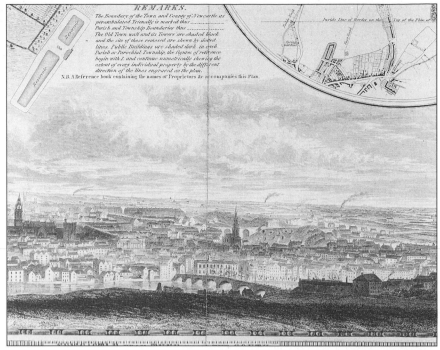

PANORAMA OF NEWCASTLE.

From the quayside the road winds steeply up, past a warren of blind alleyed slums, towards the centre of town and to the old Norman keep and Cathedral which dominate the skyline. A new Playhouse has been opened of which the inhabitants are justifiably proud. Fine mansions belonging to the local gentry reflect the finer side of Newcastle whilst showing up, at the same time, the great social gulf that exists between 'neighbours' not half a mile apart.

Examining the Evidence

Within two hundred years the map of Newcastle was transformed. Compare the three maps of Newcastle, and, as it would be impossible to show all the changes in the city, concentrate on the area known as Elswick.

1 What industrial changes have taken place?

2 What pattern of housing and industry has evolved?

3 In what ways does the pattern of past settlement still continue to impose its imprint on the present?

4 What other types of source would you need in order to more fully understand the nature of change to this area?

Source A: A plan of Newcastle upon Tyne by James Corbridge (1723)

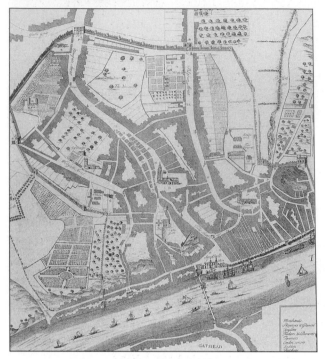

Source B: Elswick in 1844

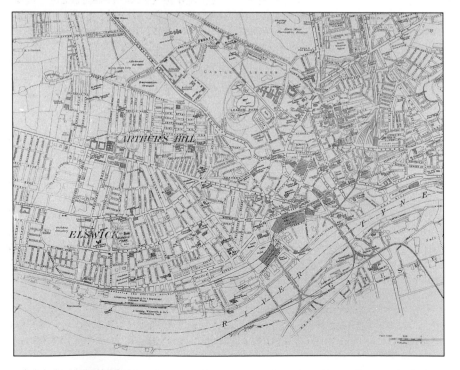

Source C: Newcastle upon Tyne in 1918

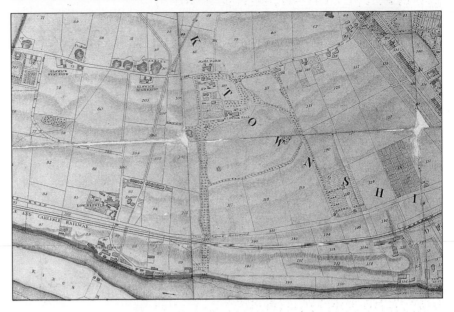

British population and society in the eighteenth century

What was Britain like in the mid 18th century? How many people were there and what was the social composition?

The first census was not conducted until 1801 when it was shown that about ten and a half million people were living in Great Britain. In 1750 the population was around six and a quarter million. Both totals, although showing a marked increase in the last 50 years of the eighteenth century, are small compared to today's total of 54 million.

Without a census we cannot determine exactly how people earned a living or where they lived. Other sources, fortunately, exist. One of the most important of these are the assessment produced by Gregory King, a government official who held a post in the Revenue Department.

The figures in the Focus section show that about 80 per cent of the population were rural and about 50 per cent earned their living from agriculture, supplemented in many cases with earnings from part-time manufacturing. The land provided most of the wealth and most of the jobs. Power and status were also closely bound up with land ownership at a local and national level, for this was the essential prerequisite for possession of the vote and a role in government. New industrial and commercial centres of influence were evolving alongside these traditional ones but it was not until 1820 that industry employed a greater proportion of the workforce and not till 1850 that the majority of the population became urbanised. Nevertheless landowning still played the single most significant factor in determining privilege, power and prestige.

About 160 families belonged to the old hereditary nobility with a further 40 or so owning 10 000 acres of land or more. Their average income was about £3 000 a year compared to the average of £15 per household.

A very few were fabulously wealthy such as The Duke of Newcastle, who had an income from rents of £32 000. A few climbed up the social ladder but for the vast majority a yawning gap existed between rich and poor. Nevertheless an increasing number of alternative routes to prosperity were opening up throughout the eighteenth century.

The family was the most important social and economic group as it had been for centuries. Women played a vital role in the economy as well as the social function of the family, although this was little recognised in either status or earnings. Children, too, from a comparatively young age, were expected to fulfil an economic role. The earnings of both women and children were essential if the family was to be kept above the level of destitution. Gregory King estimated that families would need at least £40 to do so. Considering that less than half did so illustrates the fine balance that existed between desperate poverty and a reasonable but poor existence. The growth of the factory system at the end of the eighteenth century was to bring major changes in the employment of women and children especially. From the earliest factories until well into the nineteenth century, over half the employees were women and children.

The international landscape

'Upon the whole, to sum it up in a few words Trade is the Wealth of the World; Trade makes the difference as to Rich and Poor, between one Nation and Another; Trade nourishes industry, Industry begets Trade; Trade dispenses the natural Wealth of the World, and Trade raises new species of Wealth, which Nature knew nothing of; Trade has two daughters, whose fruitful progeny in Arts may be said to employ Mankind; namely Manufacture and Navigation'. So wrote Daniel Defoe in 1728. By the middle of the eighteenth century Britain appeared to confirm Defoe's observation for she had become a powerful trading nation.

This had not always been so. In 1560 the entire English merchant navy was smaller than that of the Italian trading city states of Venice or Genoa. Only the coal trade and fishing prospered.

Britain hoisted herself to trading pre-eminence by taking advantage of her rivals' conflicts, extending the country's colonial possessions and extending government protection to trade. In the late sixteenth century, whilst the Netherlands fought for its independence from Spain, Britain captured the Dutch dominated Eastern Mediterranean and Baltic trade. The alliance with Holland gave her the required pretext to extend her influence to the Americas.

As Spanish power waned and French power waxed strong Britain found herself in contention for trade and empire with a new enemy. During the Seven Years War (1756–63) much of French sea-power was destroyed and French trading posts captured in India, the West Indies and the whole of Canada. Apart from conquest there was extensive colonisation. By the middle of the eighteenth century the entire eastern seaboard of North America was a British possession.

Jealous of her trade Britain passed a series of Navigation Laws in 1651, 1660 and 1662. These ordered that all products from English colonies must be sent to England before they could be re-exported to Europe. All these colonial goods had to be carried in British ships and the colonists

TALKING POINT

The Navigation Laws were passed in an attempt to nurture British trade. What are the benefits and possible dangers of protecting trade in this way?

themselves obliged to buy only British goods. Sugar-refining and tobacco-curing became important industries in their own right as a consequence as well as an important re-export element in British trade.

By the 1750s Britain was on the verge of a boom that was to greatly influence the economy as a whole on the eve of the Industrial Revolution.

The pattern of trade

Both the southern colonies of North America and the West Indies were of supreme importance to Britain. From the British West Indies came cane-sugar, rum, coffee and mahogany. Virginia sent tobacco, the Carolinas sent rice, pitch, tar and hardwoods.

In return Britian exported her manufactured goods – woollens, cottons, linens, silks, metal goods and leather products. Even the export of people was regarded as a profitable commodity: orphans and criminals from Britain and negro slaves from West Africa. Cargoes of knives, hatchets, firearms, alcohol and textiles were exchanged on the Guinea coast for slaves. As many as 2 million Africans were kidnapped and transported in the holds of cramped slave ships, wretched and manacled in their own filth. As many as one third to one half perished on the voyage alone. But consciences were drowned in money. Slave trading was big business. By the 1750s, planters were paying as much as £40 for a healthy male slave.

Another, but less profitable, triangular trade was situated further north. Liverpool merchants transported Cheshire salt to Newfoundland which was exchanged for cod, which in turn was shipped to the plantation colonies; the ships returning to Britain with sugar and tobacco.

The New England colonies traded fish, furs and ship timber for Britain's manufactured goods – farming tools, textiles, boots, pottery, saws, axes and firearms. In itself this trade was insufficient to produce a balanced budget for the New England colonies and the difference was made up by trade in grain, timber and horses with the plantation colonies.

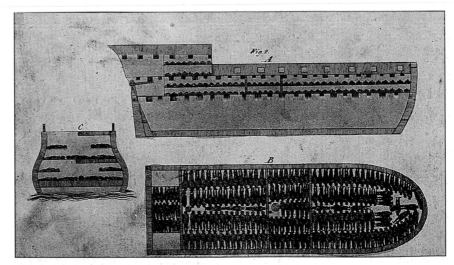

MODEL OF A SLAVE SHIP.

Sources of evidence for the Eighteenth Century

In the 1990s we have considerable statistical information upon which we can make judgements but this is not so for the eighteenth century. In the absence of an official census (the first government census was not commissioned until 1801) the growing demand by historians for precise numerical information can be met, to some extent, by using parish registers, poor law returns, public revenue and expenditure accounts and so on. Deficient as they are, they do at least provide us with a yardstick by which to measure change.

An early estimate of national income made for England and Wales was completed by Gregory King who based his estimates of the size of population upon hearth-tax returns. He assumed each household, on average, contained two parents and four children. Despite the shortcomings of his method his conclusions are generally considered to be reliable.

There is one other often-quoted source for the eighteenth century – Daniel Defoe, the author of *Robinson Crusoe*. During the 1720s he made extensive journeys throughout Great Britain. A description of his observations between 1724–26 was published under the title *A Tour Through the Whole Island of Great Britain*. Defoe is an important source for the economic historian as he wrote on contemporary matters of trade and industry. Clearly, Defoe could not observe everything that was happening and occasionally the vivid imagination of the novelist took over from the objectivity of the reporter. He wrote more fully about the south of England than the north and concentrated his attention on the woollen industry to the exlusion of others.

A Scheme of the Income & Expence of the several Families of England Calculated for the Year 1688

Number of Families	Ranks Degrees Titles and Qualifications	Heads per Family	Number of Persons	Yearly Income per Family		Totall of the Estates or Income	Yearly Income per Head		Expence per Head			Increase per Head			Totall Increase per annum
				£	s.	£	£	s.	£	s.	d.	£	s.	d.	£
160	Temporall Lords	40	6,400	2800	0	448,000	70	0	60	0	0	10	0	0	64,000
26	Spirituall Lords	20	520	1300	0	33,800	65	0	55	0	0	0	0	0	5,200
800	Baronets	16	12,800	880	0	704,000	55	0	51	0	0	4	0	0	51,200
600	Knights	13	7,800	650	0	390,000	50	0	46	0	0	4	0	0	31,200
3,000	Esquires	10	30,000	450	0	1,200,000	45	0	42	0	0	3	0	0	90,000
12,000	Gentlemen	8	96,000	280	0	2,880,000	35	0	32	10	0	2	10	0	240,000
5,000	Persons in offices	8	40,000	240	0	1,200,000	30	0	27	0	0	3	0	0	120,000
5,000	Persons in offices	6	30,000	120	0	600,000	20	0	18	0	0	2	0	0	60,000
2,000	Merchants & Traders by Sea	8	16,000	400	0	800,000	50	0	40	0	0	10	0	0	160,000
8,000	Merchants & Traders by Sea	6	48,000	200	0	1,600,000	33	0	28	0	0	5	0	0	240,000
10,000	Persons in the Law	7	70,000	140	0	1,400,000	20	0	17	0	0	3	0	0	210,000
2,000	Clergy Men	6	12,000	60	0	120,000	10	0	9	0	0	1	0	0	12,000
8,000	Clergy Men	5	40,000	45	0	360,000	9	0	8	0	0	1	0	0	40,000
40,000	Freeholders	7	280,000	84	0	3,360,000	12	0	11	0	0	1	0	0	280,000
140,000	Freeholders	5	700,000	50	0	7,000,000	10	0	9	10	0		10	0	350,000
150,000	Farmers	5	750,000	44	0	6,600,000	8	15	8	10	0		5	0	187,000
16,000	Persons in Sciences & Lib. arts	5	80,000	60	0	960,000	12	0	11	10	0	1	10	0	40,000
40,000	Shopkeepers & Tradesmen	4½	180,000	45	0	1,800,000	10	0	9	10	0		10	0	90,000
60,000	Artizans & handycrafts	4	240,000	40	0	2,400,000	10	0	9	10	0		10	0	120,000
5,000	Naval officers	4	20,000	80	0	400,000	20	0	18	0	0	2	0	0	40,000
4,000	Military officers	4	16,000	60	0	240,000	15	0	14	0	0	1	0	0	16,000
511,586		5¼	2,675,520	67	0	34,495,800	12	18	12	0	0		18	0	2,447,100
															Decrease
50	Common Seamen	3	150,000	20	0	1,000,000	7	0	7	10	0		10	0	75,000
364,000	Labouring People & outservants	3½	1,275,000	15	0	5,460,000	4	10	4	12	0		2	0	127,500
400,000	Cottagers & Paupers	3¼	1,300,000	6	10	2,000,000	2	0	2	5	0		5	0	325,000
35,000	Common Souldiers	2	70,000	14	0	490,000	7	0	7	10	0		10	0	35,000
849,000		3¼	2,795,000	10	10	8,950,000	3	5	3	9	0		4	0	562,000
	Vagrants	–	30,000	–	–	60,000	2	0	3	0	0	1	0	0	60,000
849,000		3¼	2,825,000	10	10	9,010,000	3	3	3	7	6		4	6	622,000
	So the General Account is														
			£	£	s.	£	£	s.	£	s.	d.	£	s.	d.	£
511,586	Increasing the wealth of the Kingdom	5¼	2,675,520	67	0	34,495,800	12	18	12	0	0		18	0	2,447,100
849,000	Decreasing the wealth of the Kingdom	3¼	2,825,000	10	10	9,010,000	3	3	3	7	6		4	6	622,000
360,586	Neat Totalls	$4\frac{1}{20}$	5,500,520	£32	0	£43,505,800	£7	18	£7	11	3	£0	6	9	£1,825,100

SOURCE: Gregory King, *Natural and Political Observations and Conclusions upon the State and Condition of England*, reprinted in *Two Tracts by Gregory King*, ed. George E. Barnett (Baltimore, 1936).

GREGORY KING'S POPULATION ESTIMATES.

A TOUR

Thro' the whole ISLAND of

GREAT BRITAIN,

Divided into

Circuits or Journies.

GIVING

A Particular and Diverting Account of Whatever is CURIOUS and worth OBSERVATION, Viz.

I. A DESCRIPTION of the Principal Cities and Towns, their Situation, Magnitude, Government, and Commerce.

II. The Customs, Manners, Speech, as also the Exercises, Diversions, and Employment of the People.

III. The Produce and Improvement of the Lands, the Trade, and Manufactures.

IV. The Sea Ports and Fortifications, the Course of Rivers, and the Inland Navigation.

V. The Publick Edifices, Seats, and Palaces of the NOBILITY and GENTRY.

With Useful OBSERVATIONS upon the Whole.

Particularly fitted for the Reading of such as desire to Travel over the ISLAND.

By a GENTLEMAN.

LONDON;

Printed, and Sold by G. STRAHAN, in Cornhill. W. MEARS, at the Lamb without Temple-Bar. R. FRANCKLIN, under Tom's Coffee-house, Covent-Garden. S. CHAPMAN, at the Angel in Pall-Mall. R. STAGG, in Westminster-Hall, and J. GRAVES, in St. James's-Street. MDCCXXIV.

TITLE PAGE FOR *A TOUR THROUGH THE WHOLE ISLAND OF GREAT BRITAIN.*

Questions

1 Using your calculators, construct a population pyramid from the information supplied by Gregory King.
What observations can you make about the social hierarchy in England and Wales at this time?

2 Construct a second pyramid graph based on the owner ship of wealth.
What conclusions can you make about ownership of wealth?

3 Why does King divide society into two broad bands in the summary of the table?
What assumptions lie behind this division?

4 Gregory King was an official in a Government department.
What possible reason may have lain behind the compilation of his figures?

5 What appears to have been the motives behind Defoe's publication of the *Tours*?

6 How does Defoe attempt to reassure his readers as to the accuracy of his material?

7 What are the limitations of these two sources as evidence for eighteenth century society?

Daniel Defoe's Preface to the *Tours*

'The preparations for this work have been suitable to the author's earnest concern for its usefulness; seventeen very large circuits … and three general tours over almost the whole English part of the Island; in all which the author has not been wanting to treasure up just remarks upon particular places and things, so that he is very little in debt to other men's labours, and gives but very few accounts of things, but what he has been an eyewitness himself …

It must be acknowledged that some foreigners, who have pretended to travel into England, and to give account of things when they come home, have treated us in a very indifferent manner: As they viewed us with envy, so they have made their account rather equal to what

A TRADING STATION IN MADRAS, INDIA.

The Baltic was an important region of trade. Softwood timber for masts and ship interiors, flax and sailcloth, hemp for ropes, bar-iron from Sweden and potash (used to make alkalis for glass and soap manufacture) swelled British imports. No matter how great the demand for British woollens and coal, however, the Baltic trade remained in deficit.

The Mediterranean proved sound trading ground for British merchants. Spain supplied wine and Portugal sherry at low tariffs under the Methuen Treaty agreement of 1704. The exchange was for the ubiquitous English woollens. Fresh fruit, oranges and lemons were sent from Iberia; currants from the Levant. Iron-ore from Northern Spain was used for the production of high quality goods and wool from the merino sheep was shipped from the Eastern Mediterranean. The trade was decidedly to the advantage of Britain, earning valuable gold and silver bullion. These Mediterranean imports were exchanged for woollen cloth, fish from the Cornish coast as well as Newfoundland cod and herring from the North Sea and, up until the 1780s, grain. Much of the Mediterranean trade was transported in British merchant shipping, adding a vital 'invisible' export to Britain's balance of payments.

Despite the importance of the Americas and the Mediterranean, Northern Europe was by far the single most vital area of trade for Britain. In exchange for woollens, grain from East Anglia, Cheshire salt and Tyne coal, Britain imported linen and silk.

Paying for imports from the East, however, remained a constant problem. Calicoes (cotton printed cloth) and fine muslins were highly prized Indian goods. From China fine porcelain, silk and tea. Pepper came from the East Indies and salt petre from India. Although some of the goods were exchanged for English hardwood the deficit had to be made up with bullion payments and the steady liquid stream of gold and silver became a river.

Eighteenth century statistics are normally unreliable but those from overseas trade are comprehensive and accurate; no doubt due to a zealous government wishing to maximise its revenue from customs duties. The ledgers of the Inspector General of Customs have been scrutinised by many, but most usefully by Mrs E.B. Schumpeter, *English Overseas Trade Statistics* (1960). Different economists have, inevitably, interpreted the figures differently.

Task

Study the sets of graphic information below and answer the questions.

Trade Statistics 1700–1800

1 Draw a large diagram headed 'British Trade 1750' as follows:

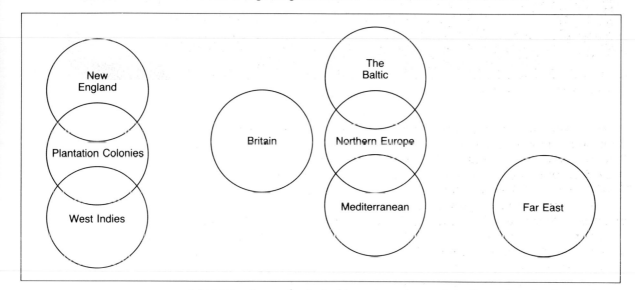

(a) List the items of principal imports and exports to the various trading regions.

(b) Use a colour code to indicate the order of importance of each of these regions.

2 In what important ways did the pattern of British trade change during the eighteenth century?

3 What was the difference between Britain's imports compared to her exports from each individual region?

4 How would you divide the trade statistics 1700–1800 into periods of trade development?

(a) M.W. Flinn, *Origins of the Industrial Revolution,* claims that the figures show four distinct phases.

1700–1735, 1735–60, 1760–85, 1785–1800.

Describe each of these periods as slow, stagnating or rapid.

(b) Phyllis Deane, in *The First Industrial Revolution* divides the century into five periods 1700–1740, 1740–50, 1750–75, 1776–82, 1782–1800. Which of these periods would you describe as slow, stagnating or rapid? What is distinctive about the period 1776–82? What is the difference in interpretation between the two historians? Is the difference a significant one?

Was Britain's economy under-developed in 1700?

It is possible to respond to this question with two contrasting answers. By today's standards the nation was poor, predominantly agrarian and with few towns of any size. Manufacturing was almost exclusively small-scale, labour-intensive and situated in the countryside. Like many third world countries today, it suffered from deep-seated poverty caused by severe under-employment. Poverty operated in a vicious cycle. Low productivity meant low incomes. Low incomes meant few savings which meant, in turn, only limited capital for investment. In this circumstance any increase in population would press hard upon the means of subsistence and threaten starvation.

On the other hand a quite different view can be presented if we compare Britain in 1700 with other countries at the same time. In terms of national income Britain was probably the richest country in the world. Many examples can be cited to support this claim. London was arguably the richest and largest city in the world; Britain had a long lead over her rivals in trade to all corners of the world; she was able to export her surplus of grain; fine town and country houses boasted the wealth of merchant and rural life. By the mid-eighteenth century 80 per cent of Britain's domestically produced exports were manufactured commodities – almost entirely woollen goods.

Whilst England was predominantly an agricultural country her manufacturing capacity was considerable. Farming and manufacturing were not then separate activities. One estimate concludes that less than one half of the labour force was engaged in agriculture and as an economic sector it was contributing little more than one third to the total national income. Even agriculture was developed far beyond a mere subsistence level. Daniel Defoe in his *A Tour through the Whole Island of Great Britain* confirmed that Britain was a national economy. A considerable proportion of agricultural produce was raised for market, and regional specialisation in agriculture and industry was extremely marked. Cash crops and wage labour were additional yardsticks of a national economy.

In addition a number of specialist servicing institutions had evolved. Banks in the provinces, as well as the establishment of the Bank of England in 1697, testify to the growth of credit not only for government but also for commerce. Another example is the growth of joint stock organisation which by the early eighteenth century was dealing in shares. By 1700 insurance and mortgage markets had developed.

This evolving economy was mirrored by an increasingly complex social pattern. A simple pyramid of wealthy privilege at the top supported by a mass of half-starved peasantry will not suffice. The social hierarchy of Britain, whilst undoubtedly possessing fabulously wealthy people at the

What are the characteristics of a developing country today? Do they apply to Britain in 1700?

apex, had a greater number of segments and opportunities for social mobility. Most significant perhaps was the substantial middle group who included not only tenant farmers, bankers, merchants, clothiers, brewery owners, but even some shopkeepers and craftsmen whose businesses had prospered. In some instances merchants had enjoyed such wealth that they were able to buy the prestige of joining the upper ranks through marriage and financial alliances.

Britain in 1700 was by no means a backward country and to compare her economy with a present-day developing economy is a false one. In 1700 Britain possessed an advanced economy compared to her neighbours and competitors. In 1700 Britain had no serious rival to her woollen industry, British shipping was the largest and most powerful in the world and her technological and economic institutions were well-developed.

When did the Industrial Revolution happen?

As we read earlier contemporaries disagreed about the effects of the Industrial Revolution. It would be surprising if historians, reading contemporary sources such as Ure and Kay-Shuttleworth, reached the same conclusions as one another. Historians interpret the sources and in so doing tend to place a different emphasis upon the fragmentary evidence available.

In your study of history you will be heavily dependant upon such interpretations and it is therefore essential that you do not swallow historians' interpretations without question. Always read actively and ask yourself what arguments the historian is using. Does the historian betray bias? Keep this question in mind when you study the Examining the evidence sections.

COTTON MILL IN MANCHESTER.

SIR THOMAS LOMBE'S SILK-MILL, DERBY 1750.

EXAMINING THE EVIDENCE
When did the Industrial Revolution happen?

Despite the assimilation of the term 'Industrial Revolution' into the language of historians, its origin, timing and effects are the subject of intense debate.

Source A

England of the first part of the eighteenth century was virtually medieval, quiet, primeval and undisturbed by the roar of commerce. Suddenly like a thunderbolt from a clear sky were ushered in the storm and stress of the Industrial Revolution.

C. Beard, *The Industrial Revolution* (1901)

Source B

The change was sudden and violent. The great inventions were all made in a comparitively short space of time ... In little more than twenty years all the great inventions of Watt, Arkwright and Boulton had been completed ... and the modern factory system had fairly begun.

H. de B. Gibbons, *Industry in England* (1897)

Source C

Objections were inevitably raised later by some historians who reacted against the notion of a dramatic watershed in history.

The concentration of industrial capital in Great Britain during the periods from 1540 to 1640 and after was caused to a considerable extent ... by the progress of technology ... (an) important cause for the concentration of industrial capital in Great Britain was the general change from a wood burning to a coal-burning economy. The growth in the size of markets, which also promoted industrial concentration, was due partly to the facilities for cheap water transport ... While no different comparison of large scale enterprise in England and the Continent after 1540 can be made until we have more studies – such evidence as is now available suggests that the concentration of capital in mining and manufacturing was more striking in England.

It was probably not, as has been supposed, during the late eighteenth and early nineteenth centuries that the contrast between industrial progress in England and in continental countries was most striking, but of the two centuries preceding the 'Industrial Revolution'.

It gives the impression that the process was especially sudden, when it was in all probability more continuous than in any other country.

James U. Nef, *The Progress of Technology* (1934)

Yet, Thomas S. Ashton, returned in 1948, to the notion of a specific turning point for the Industrial Revolution.

THE FIRST IRON BRIDGE. COALBROOKDALE.

COALBROOKDALE AT NIGHT.

Source D

After 1782 almost every available statistical series of industrial output reveals a sharp upward turn. More than half the shipments of coal, and mining of copper, more than three quarters of the increase of broad-cloth and nine-tenths of the exports of cotton goods were concentrated in the last eighteen years of the century.

Thomas S. Ashton, *The Eighteenth Century* (1955)

Source E

Professor W.W. Rostow has been even more emphatic, narrowing the 'take-off' of the Industrial Revolution to the period 1783–1800. His article, *The Take-off into Self-sustained Growth* in the *Economic Journal LXVI* (1956) and the book which developed from his argument, *The Stages of Self-sustained Growth* (1960), have had an enormous impact on the debate.

You must remember, however, that Professor Rostow was an economist first and an historian second. In other words he was attempting to find general rules that explained why industrialisation happens at all. Of course he used the British experience to establish his ideas but essentially, he was more concerned with the creation of a model of industrial change which could be applied to the whole process of industrialisation.

He likened the economy of a country to an aeroplane, gathering speed along the runway and then, when the acceleration reached a critical point, taking-off into self-sustained flight. The critical factors for an economy to take-off into industrialisation he defined as:

1 A rise in the rate of productive investment from about 5 per cent to over 10 per cent of the national income.

2 The development of one or more substantial manufacturing sector with a high rate of growth, for example cotton or iron.

3 The existence or emergence of a political, social and institutional framework which exploits the impulses to expand in the industrial sector, for example the emergence of a politically powerful group of businessmen or the adoption of an economic system which favours the growth of industry.

W.W. Rostow, *The Stages of Economic Growth – A non-Communist Manifesto* (1962).
(Paraphrased by the author)

Source F

The reaction of many historians to Rostow's economic model have been sceptical to say the least. They find the neatness and precision of his theory does not neatly fit with the facts of British industrial development. As a consequence, some economic historians turned away from the attempt to establish an abstract model to explain the timing of the Industrial Revolution and instead sought to accumulate as much statistical evidence from the period in question. In this way they hoped the statistics themselves would indicate the 'watershed', if such existed.

TALKING POINT

"The Industrial Revolution marks the most fundamental transformation of human life in the history of the world."

Eric J. Hobsbawn, *Industry and Empire* (1968)

"The changes were not merely 'industrial', but also social and intellectual."

Thomas S. Ashton, *The Industrial Revolution* (1949)

Do you agree with the conclusions of these historians?

Return to these comments after completing this volume.

Source G

There is little evidence of growth in the first four decades in the century, but beginning in the 1740s there was a marked upward trend in absolute totals though little real improvement in the rate of growth in incomes per head until the last two or three decades. A considerably sharper upward trend appears in the 1780s and 90s ... Real national output is estimated to have grown at about 0.3 per cent per annum over the period before 1745, 0.9 per cent between 1745–85 and 1.8 per cent over the last two decades of the century.

Phyllis Deane and W.A. Cole, *British Economic Growth 1688–1959* (1964)

Caution must always be exercised when attempting to arrive at conclusions based on inadequate eighteenth century statistical information. There was no collection of such information by the government at that time unless it was for taxation. Many of the figures are based on estimates only.

How are we to make sense of these apparently opposing positions. Historians must constantly review and possibly revise their opinions in the light of new evidence and discussion with colleagues. Most recently, W.W. Rostow has modified his position.

Source H

Narrowly, however, the surge of industrial expansion that began in Britain after 1783 was preceded by a set of prior economic developments that quite technically prepared the way:

... improvements in agricultural method which were not quite sufficient to permit Britain to remain a grain exporter ..., but which did permit a growing and urbanising population to be fed, with a manageable level of grain imports;

... a marked acceleration in the scale of inventive effort, from 1760 forward, including significant improvements in cotton and textile manufacture, iron manufacture with coke as fuel, and the efficiency of the steam engine – all critical for the British 'take-off';

... a wave of enterprise in canal and road building, which rendered Britain a more tightly knit and efficient market;

... an environment of expanding international commerce which ultimately permitted Britain's precocious break through in cotton textile manufacture.

W.W. Rostow, *The World Economy* (1978)

REVIEW
When did the Industrial Revolution happen?

Introduction • Simplistic interpretation of the Industrial Revolution

Development • The complexity of the Industrial Revolution.

• Short and Long term factors – The interpretation is dependant upon which factors particular historians choose to emphasise.

- The unreliability of statistical information.
- The factors in the debate – long and short term.

Conclusion • Reconciling long and short term factors.

Many historians have made bold claims for the significance of the Industrial Revolution. The term 'watershed' is often used by historians to denote a time of significant change.

Whilst historians often wish to highlight periods of accelerated change, such labels often disguise much that continued to be the same or similar. Attaching the term 'watershed' to a period of history may also suggest a more abrupt change than actually occurred since the event may have evolved over a long period of time or its effects may be still evolving.

As you work through this book bear this in mind and decide whether such changes amount to a 'watershed'.

2 An Agrarian Revolution?

A CRITC'S REVIEW OF THE EFFECTS OF THE EIGHTEENTH CENTURY REVOLUTION IN AGRICULTURE.

'Revolutionary changes in agricultural productivity are an essential pre-
condition for industrial "take-off".'

W.W. Rostow, *The Stages of Economic Growth*

'Slow change, gradual diffusion, regional variations: these are the hallmarks of agrarian change in industrialising Britain.'

M. Falkus, *Britain Transformed – An Economic and Social History 1700–1914*

The agrarian revolution in the eighteenth century

For centuries before 1700 the fluctuating fortunes of harvests and the disastrous consequences of crop failure and famine had underlined the utter dependence of human beings on agriculture. It is easy to be misled by the phenomenon of the Industrial Revolution into making the conclusion that the role of agriculture in the economy was minor. Nothing could be further from the truth. In 1700, as well as 1800, agriculture remained the single most important sector of the economy. Not until 1820 did industrial output exceed that of agriculture and not until 1850 did agriculture cease to be the biggest employer of labour.

Furthermore, agriculture was more than simply the means by which society subsisted. It was the hub around which the British political and social wheel revolved. Changes in agriculture however were making possible the emergence of a new society; a society which was to eventually sever its rural roots. Such was the dimension of change that historians in the past spoke of an 'agricultural revolution' during the eighteenth century. The accomplishment of the 'revolution' was credited to the work of a few improving landlords, who introduced new crops, new rotations of crops, new machines and improved breeds of animals. These innovations, it was argued, were made possible by the rapid speed of dismembering the traditional and wasteful open-field pattern and re-assembling the land into blocks of consolidated holdings.

Whilst the majority of the population benefited from improved production as well as the ability to sustain an increased urbanised workforce, some historians were at pains to highlight the losers from these changes. Principal amongst the victims, it was claimed, were the small farmers, the backbone of Old England, who, unable to afford the legal and conversion costs, were cast adrift to become either landless labourers or anonymous fodder for the factory. The illustration of the farmer supervising the skeleton ploughman represents an extreme reaction against agricultural change.

Perhaps the most important issue is the precise relationship between farming and industrialisation. Did increased agricultural productivity stimulate an industrialised economy, or did increasing industrialisation provide the stimulus for agricultural improvement?

TALKING POINT

In 1700 one person engaged in agriculture could feed 1.7 persons. By 1800 one person could feed 2.5 people. What factors could have contributed to this increased productivity?

EXAMINING THE EVIDENCE
The importance of agriculture to Britain's economy in the eighteenth century

Such claims and questions should not go either unchallenged or unanswered. Your task is to examine the evidence and reach a working explanation. It is important to remember that any conclusion is provisional; a working hypothesis which may need to be revised or replaced as new evidence comes to light.

Source A: The percentage contribution of agriculture to the national income

	1688	1770	1801	1821	1851
Agriculture	40	45	32.5	26.1	20.3
Manufacture, mining, building	21	24	23.4	31.9	34.3
Commerce	5.6	13	17.4	15.9	18.7
Housing	5	3	5.4	6.2	8.1
Government, domestic, professional, others	28.4	15	21.3	19.9	18.6
Total	100	100	100	100	100

P.F. Speed, *The Growth of the British Economy*

Source B: Population dependence on agriculture

1688	68% (Gregory King's estimates).
1811	66% (Deane and Cole – *The Growth of the British Economy*).
1851	For the first time the census reveals that the percentage of the labour force is less than that for industry.
1871	20% of the labour force still employed in agriculture.

Source C: Exports of wheat

1670s	300,000 quarters = sufficient to feed 150,000 people.
1732	675,000 quarters = sufficient to feed 340,000 people.
1784	Britain becomes a net importer of grain.

Source D: Price rises (1700 = 100)

1700 = 100

1760 = 117

1780 = 142

1800 = 250

Source E: Net outputs (000s of quarters grain) Population

England / Wales

1760	15,265	6.66 million
1770	15,617	7.12
1780	16,706	7.58
1790	17,884	8.21
1800	18,991	9.16
1810	21,988	10.16
1820	25,086	12.00

Deane and Cole, *British Economic Growth 1688–1959*

Source F: Industrial crops in the eighteenth and nineteenth centuries

Malting, barley and hops

Rape seed for oil

Madder, woad and weld for dyes

Wood, flax, timber, hides, tallow, fodder straw thatch

Source G: Industrial and Agricultural Output

Index numbers of output of homes

Industrial and wheat prices (1700–100)

Home industries			Wheat prices
1700	100	–1700	100
1710	98	1700–1710	105
1720	108	1710–1720	109
1730	105	1720–1730	99
1740	105	1730–1740	84
1750	107	1740–1750	84
1760	114	1750–1760	101
1770	114	1760–1770	117
1780	123	1770–1780	136
1790	137	1780–1790	142
1800	152	1790–1800	196

Dean and Cole, *British Economic Growth 1688–1959*

Source H: Agricultural specialisation

Wiltshire – Wye Hill.

... The sheep sold here are not for immediate killing, but are generally ewes for store sheep for the farmers, and they send for them from all the following counties, Berks, Oxford, Bucks, Bedford, Middlesex, Kent, Surrey and Sussex ...

In Suffolk.

The county around Ipswich, as are all the counties so near the coast, is applied chiefly to corn, of which a great quantity is continually shipped off for London, and sometimes they load corn here for Holland ...

Weybridge, Suffolk.

... considerable market for butter and corn to be exported to London ... The butter is barrelled, or often picked up in small casks, and sold, not in London only, but I have known a firkin of Suffolk butter sent to the West Indies ...

Cheshire.

... in such quantities, and so exceeding good, that as I am told from very good authority, the city of London only takes off 1 400 ton every year; besides the 8 000 ton which they say goes every year down the Rivers Severn and Trent ... besides the quantity ship'd both here, and at Liverpool, to go to Ireland and Scotland ...

Halifax, West Riding.

... their corn comes up in great quantities out of Lincoln, Nottingham and the East Riding, their black cattle and horses from the North Riding, their sheep and mutton from the adjacent counties everyway, their butter from the East and North Riding, their cheese out of Cheshire and Warwickshire, more black cattle also from Lancashire ...

A Tour Through The Whole Island Of Great Britain (1726)

Source I: Social status and land

(In 1790) agriculture was still much the largest single occupation of the people. The wealthiest individual landowners were generally regarded as the richest men in society, though individuals with fortunes more precariously based on sugar, Indian operations politely obscure in their details, or city operations of cunning and lucrative simplicity, could already rival them in income. Above all, the structure of politics was weighted in favour of the landed interest. And yet by halfway through the period, by about 1850, all these conditions had ceased to exist.

D. Thompson, *English Landed Society in the Nineteenth Century*

The possession of land was virtually essential for the aristocracy. (As late as) 1873 only 60 of the existing 585 peers and peeresses held no land. So strong was the mystique of land ownership that in 1847–48, Disraeli had to be set up by his political friends with 750 acres at Hughlenden, in order to make him respectable to the Tory party.

T. May, *An Economic and Social History of Britain 1760–1970*

1 What appears to have been the principal reasons for the increase in the net output of grain?

2 How was agriculture organised during the eighteenth century?

3 A considerable amount of statistical information has been included. What is the value and limitations of the evidence presented? Compare this type of source with that of Daniel Defoe. In what ways does it differ?

4 How important was agriculture to the British economy during the eighteenth and early nineteenth centuries?

5 To what extent had its importance lessened by the early part of the nineteenth century?

Farming in pre-industrial Britain

It is possible to step into the past by making a journey in the present to the village of Laxton, Nottinghamshire. There is much of the village and the communal method of stip-field farming that remains today which reverberates as an echo of former times.

In 1635 there were a couple of things which made this village slightly different from its neighbours. At 3 853 acres, it was about twice the size of the average Midland Plain village and its nucleated settlement lay on the northern boundary rather than at the more usual centre. Even today many of the farmhouses retain their traditional pattern – side by side, each with its associated buildings of yard, paddock and garden.

PHOTOGRAPH OF PRESENT DAY VILLAGE.

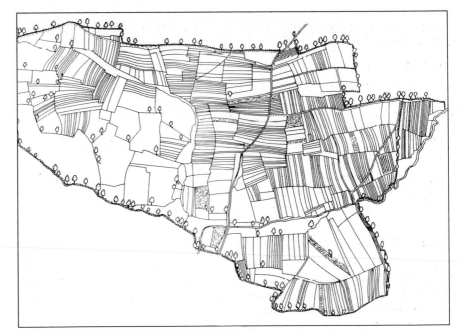

SKETCH MAPS OF OPEN FIELD VILLAGE OF LAXTON.

TALKING POINT

Many new crops and
farming improvements
came from Holland. Why
might this be so?

In a time when communications were poor it was essential that each
community strove to be self-sufficient. The best sites would be on a well-
drained escarpment for grazing, with fertile tillage in between that and
water-meadows deep in the valley. The site of Laxton is more level but
the land was still divided into arable, meadow and pasture.

The village's arable land comprised three large open fields which were
not separated by hedges, fences or ditches. Although consolidated blocks
appear, the vast majority resemble strips. Each farmer in the village had
his strips scattered throughout all three fields. In an earlier age when the
whole community was required to assist with ploughing, sowing and harvesting the arrangement was sound. The inconvenience was partially
avoided when an opportunity arose for farmers to exchange strips for
neighbouring ones. In this way wider blocks of land could be built up.
Inevitably such opportunities came only gradually and as a consequence
the process of consolidation was slow.

If an individual farmer could acquire sufficient land it might be worth
his while to enclose the land by putting a fence around it. Common grazing rights on the land after harvesting, however, had to be respected. A
great impetus toward enclosure (called 'closes' of land) came in the
Tudor age when the high price of English wool stimulated farmers to
convert arable to pasture. It was, of course, sensible to keep sheep in
enclosed blocks rather than open strips.

At the end of harvesting, animals were allowed to graze on the fields.
This not only fattened the animals for winter but the animals themselves
provided valuable manure. Dung contains plant food, makes humus and
holds moisture. Farmers frequently penned or 'folded' sheep and cattle
for the night on arable land; moving the position of the pens so that the

fields could become systematically manured. But this form of regenerating the soil was insufficient by itself. Each year one field was left fallow (empty) in order to recover its fertility; the following year the fallow field was used to grow a fodder crop. In the third year is was used to grow wheat.

Fodder crops were essential in order to keep the livestock through the winter. This was usually in the form of barley, although they also had clover at Laxton. Livestock also needed grazing and about one-tenth of the arable land was set aside as meadow for this purpose. Beyond the lush meadows additional grazing could be found on the commons. A few fortunate farmers had closes where they practiced what is called 'convertable' or 'up and down husbandry'. This meant that they alternated over several years between using the land for grazing and tillage.

It was estimated that a family needed about 30 acres of 'virgate', of land to support itself. By the seventeenth and eighteenth centuries, however, disparate sizes of holding had become commonplace.

The cycle of agriculture and all the social regulation that was necessary to operate the system smoothly was governed by well-established customs. Dates for agricultural activity were hallowed. Disputes and interpretation of custom were handled by the Manor Court, originally under the jurisdiction of the Lord but now run by the landowners themselves. Nevertheless, the Lord of the Manor, who was frequently the local J.P. was not a figure to take lightly. In 1635 Sir William Couten, a London merchant, owned 2181 acres. Much of his land he rented out to Laxton farmers, at an average of about 7 shillings an acre.

It was in this context of a largely non-commercial communal farming and a rigid separation of arable and pasture land that the seeds of change were planted.

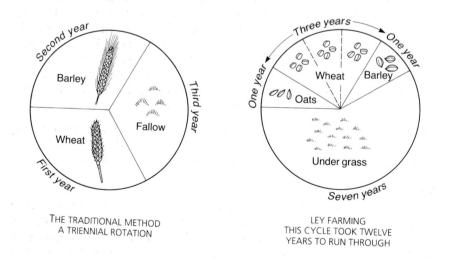

THE TRADITIONAL METHOD
A TRIENNIAL ROTATION

LEY FARMING
THIS CYCLE TOOK TWELVE
YEARS TO RUN THROUGH

Changes in farming in the eighteenth century

New crops and rotations

The catalyst for change in eighteenth century farming was undoubtedly the increase of population pressing upon agricultural resources. As more and more arable land encroached upon pasture, the feeding of livestock became an increasing problem. The following new crops became increasingly popular.

NORFOLK FOUR COURSE ROTATION
A FOUR YEAR ROTATION

- **Turnips** These were the most famous of the new root crops which were introduced from Holland about the middle of the sixteenth century. The new crop was greeted with varying degrees of enthusiasm. Its popularity was given a considerable boost when Lord 'turnip' Townshend demonstrated the benefits of the vegetable as winter fodder with the additional bonus that the crop could be grown in land previously left fallow. By the 1850s new rotations of crops using turnips were becoming common.

- **Swedes and manglewurzels** Turnips were susceptible to a variety of problems. They would often blacken in extremes of cold and were vulnerable to pests. The Swedish turnip strain (Swede) and manglewurzel provided a hardier, if smaller, alternative.

- **Leaf crops** Trefoil, lucerne and sanfoin were leguminous plants introduced from Holland about the same time as turnips. Sanfoin was particularly valuable for it will grow on exhausted soil and at the same time enrich it with deposits of nitrogen through its root nodules.

- **Rape** This plant not only makes fodder but its seeds give oil. The tap root of the plant penetrates deeply and assists in the aeration of the soil.

- **Clover** Clover is natural to the British Isles but new strains from Holland and its systematic cultivation were new departures. Farmers began growing the crop in the 1600s and by the end of the century to 'be in clover' was a popular saying. It makes the best quality fodder and hay. There were problems, though, for by itself it is too rich a crop. Animals can suffer agonies of wind. The land can also become 'clover-sick' by the fifth year of cultivation. The best results were obtained by mixing the clover with other legumes, particularly rye-grass.

- **Water-meadows** These originated in Italy and were imported during the sixteenth century. The land was flooded, then drained and sown. Grass grows abundantly on the heavy, moist, and enriched soil.

Convertible husbandry

Convertible husbandry became increasingly common during the sixteenth century. In this method the land was either ploughed 'up' or remained 'down' in grass leys. Converting grass land to tillage had to be gradually achieved by the use of other crops until wheat was sown as the last crop in the cycle.

There were many other complicated crop rotations but in general they were merely variations of convertible husbandry. It is important to emphasise that the Norfolk four course crop rotation was only suitable to favourable soil conditions and did not become common until the nineteenth century.

Improving the soil

The following methods of fertilising the soil were increasingly used:

• **Dung** This was the most ancient and common of the manures. Occasionally 'town manure' was used although this contained too many unpleasant surprises for the farmer and was not used extensively. Dung contains plant food, makes humus and holds moisture.

• **Drainage** In Medieval times farmers dug ditches at either side of ploughed fields. If the land becomes too water-logged the soil will remain cold and resist germination and growth. Under-drainage began in the seventeenth century but was none too common until the nineteenth. Early drains were filled with stones. Tiles were not used in drains until mass production was introduced about the middle of the nineteenth century. Even then drainage schemes were quite expensive at around £12 per acre.

• **Marling** This was the name given to the practice of mixing clay with sandy soils in order to assist water retention. Marling was quite expensive at around £12 per acre.

• **Lime and chalk** The use of lime and chalk also improved the quality of the soil. The ruins of lime kilns in apparently lonely spots in the countryside are an archaeological reminder of this valuable mineral for farmers.

Improving livestock

The growth of winter-fodder crops was a vital link in the improvement of livestock for both meat and wool. Fodder crops alone, however, will not produce better animals – selective breeding of animals is required.

EXAGGERATED ILLUSTRATION OF IMPROVED PIG.

• **Sheep** The most famous of the sheep breeders was Robert Bakewell of Dishley Grange in Leicestershire but he was not the only one nor the most successful. Joseph Allen, Major Hartopp and Captain Tate testify to a widespread interest in selective breeding and much had already been done in improving the Midland sheep. In the 1780s John Ellkman and Jonas Webb bred the highly successful Southdowns sheep. Nevertheless, Bakewell's animals were much in demand. In 1789 he made 6 200 guineas from the sale of sheep; one ram alone earning him 1 000 guineas in one season. (1 guinea = 105p). Bakewell was proud of his success and kept open house for all who came to marvel at his achievement. His entertainments were so lavish that he eventually bankrupted himself.

Bakewell Sheep
The fleece was heavy and long but coarse.
Delicate constituion.
Useless on poor soils.
Mutton fat and watery – poor flavour.

ILLUSTRATION OF BAKEWELL SHEEP.

• **Cattle** There were three varieties – Shorthorn, Middlehorn and Longhorn which in varying degrees of importance provided meat, milk and labour on the farm. Of these, meat was the least important as Lord Ernle put it, "The pail and the plough set the standard: the butcher was ignored."

Meat   Improvement began on the Midlands plains with the adoption of floating meadows and new fodder crops. Charles and Robert Collings of Darlington were the most successful in breeding Durham shorthorns. These animals were small boned but well-fleshed and the cows were good milkers. When they sold one of their prize bulls 'Comet' it fetched 1 000 guineas.

THE SHORTHORN BULL.

Herefords too were being improved. Previously they had been used as draught animals for about six years before being sent to market for slaughter. By the nineteenth century the Hereford was being kept purely for meat and was fattened for market in a little under two years. Although the Hereford breed spread over the country their advance was stopped by the Shorthorns, which proved to be better milkers than the Herefords. Shorthorns, however, needed lush grass.

HEREFORD BULL.

Dutch cattle were imported in increasing numbers throughout the eighteenth century although for rich creamy milk nothing could compare to the Channel Island breeds. Much of the milk was made into butter and cheese. In general, dairy farmers were less efficient than beef farmers. Most dairy farms were small. Very few were larger than 100 acres and had herds of less than twenty cows. Frequently single cows were owned by small owner-occupiers who desired fresh milk all year round. Insufficient fodder crops could well result in the milk cow drying up.

SHORTHORNS.

• **Other livestock** The horse began to replace the ox. Although the ox is a powerful animal he cannot be hurried. Draught horses, particularly the Suffolk Punch, proved the most successful in sustaining work over long periods. Throughout the Middle Ages it was usual for pigs to forage freely in the forest. As a consequence they were poor specimens. In addition to developing indigenous breeds during the eighteenth century, Chinese pigs were imported and cross-bred with English pigs. Feeding pigs well on barley and meal and giving them shelter added to the meat producing quality of the animal.

Improving Farm machinery

The improvement of farm machinery made slow progress. In the sixteenth century farming equipment consisted of ploughs and hand tools such as scythes and flails. And so it remained until a spate of appliances were developed during the eighteenth century. It was not until after 1850, however, that their adoption was widespread. Indeed, until the development of cheap iron and a railway network, mechanisation was extremely difficult to achieve.

- **The seed drill** Jethro Tull's seed drill was the most famous. The 'drilling' of seed into rows rather than scattering broadcast represented a sound economic invention. His horse hoe was able to cultivate the soil more deeply than the hand hoe. Few of these machines, however, were in use even into the nineteenth century.

- **Threshing machines** These made their appearance during the Napoleonic War. The most successful was invented by Andrew Meikle but such machines were expensive particularly if powered by either water or steam. In the early nineteenth century they cost about £750 which was the equivalent of a labourer's wage for twenty-five years.

- **Ploughs** These had not been designed scientifically but had developed with custom and practice. For example the mould board was often no more than a straight piece of wood and little use was made of iron. In 1730 Foljambe took out a patent for his Rotheram plough, which was probably derived from a Dutch model. This plough sliced through the soil easily and the re-designed mould board turned the soil over efficiently. In 1770 John Bond produced another development with his Suffolk iron plough which, being made entirely from iron, was stronger and lighter. The spate of these inventions should not lead us to the conclusion that they were adopted everywhere. As late as 1850 oxen teams could be seen ploughing on the Sussex Downs using wooden ploughs.

TALKING POINT

These illustrations are obvious exaggerations. What might have been the intention of the artist?

JETHRO TULL'S SEED DRILL.

ILLUSTRATION OF A THRESHING MACHINE.

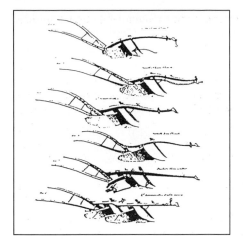

IMPROVED IRON PLOUGHS.

TALKING POINT

What would be the difficulties in the way of spreading technological improvements during the late eighteenth and early nineteenth century?

Eighteenth century enclosures

Of all the characteristics which constituted the 'new' farming the movement towards enclosure was arguably the most vital instrument for improvement. The enclosing of open fields, common lands, meadows and wastes was not a process new to the eighteenth century. During the sixteenth century land had been enclosed to produce sheep runs as profits in wool exports were high. Voluntary agreements continued but towards the latter part of the eighteenth century the pace of enclosure; particularly enclosure by Act of Parliament, quickened. Interpreting the impact and effects of enclosure has aroused much discussion amongst historians. How widespread was the movement and how quickly did it take place? Who lost and who gained from the process?

Arthur Young, the greatest of the New Farming propagandists, was in no doubt as to the backwardness of open-field farming. On the 17 July 1791 he wrote,

'Taking the road from Cambridge to St. Neot's, I viewed for six or seven miles the worst husbandry I hope in Great Britain. All in all, the fallow system, and the loss of time, and the expense submitted to, without the common benefit, these fallows were overthrown with thistles ... all the way from Cambridge, must be classed amongst the ugliest counties in England. The lands mostly open fields, at 6s. an acre. The management very bad, much strong clay, and some fallows not yet ploughed.'

A. Young, *A Month's Tour to Northamptonshire, Leicestershire (1791)*

In the eyes of Arthur Young all the evils of inefficient farming could be summed up in the practice of 'open-field' farming. Conversely, his remedy was equally simple – open fields must become enclosed. Here is his solution:

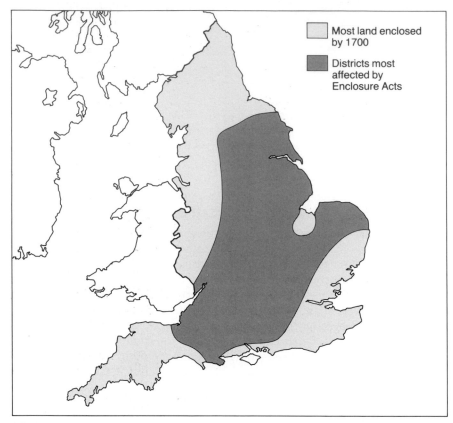

Most land enclosed by 1700

Districts most affected by Enclosure Acts

AREAS AFFECTED BY ENCLOSURE ACT.

"Great improvements have been made by the following circumstances:

First. By inclosing without assistance of Parliament.

Second. By a spirited use of marl and clay.

Third. By the introduction of an excellent course of crops.

Fourth. By the culture of turnips well-hoed.

Fifth. By the culture of clover and rye grass.

Sixth. By landlords granting long leases.

Seventh. By the county being divided chiefly into large farms.

A. Young, The Farmer's Tour through the East of England (1771)

It has been difficult for historians to avoid the strong influence of such polemics as Arthur Young. It is common to read a long list of the defects of the open field system. There is little doubt that it was harder to achieve experimentation with new crops and rotations by the need to achieve

Enclosure by Act of Parliament

Owners of three-quarters of the land could petition Parliament. In many cases the petition was signed by only one landowner. The advantage of enclosure by Parliament was that everyone, including those who had not petitioned, were obliged to abide by the re-allocation of land holdings.

After 1774 it was necessary to give public notice to the rest of the community.

A Committee of the House of Commons received the proposals. Opponents had to present their arguments to the Committee. This was only successful if a large number of landowners were involved.

If the opposition failed the Act was passed.

Enclosure Commissioners were appointed to re-allocate the lands into blocks.

The cost of the enclosure had to be met by all who had land involved in the enclosure. Costs included Commissioners' fees, legal fees incurred in obtaining the enclosure, fencing the land and compensation to the Church in lieu of tithes.

What would appear to be the major obstacles in the way of obtaining enclosure by Act of parliamentary.

common consent but this should not lull us into concluding that farming development had been stagnant for centuries.

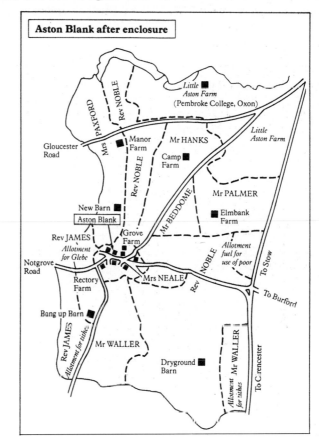

Aston Blank after enclosure

Of course, there were intrinsic difficulties with open field farming. Leaving one-third to one-half of the land fallow was unproductive and the maintenance of commons and wastes inefficient. Time was wasted in moving between widely scattered strips connected by paths which criss-crossed fields. An inconsiderate neighbour could affect others by allowing weeds and plant diseases to spread. Untended animals could trample crops. Above all, the small-scale nature of farming operations produced no benefit from economies of scale nor did they allow selective breeding or the use of machinery.

In the context of the village economy, however, it made sense. Through co-operation the heavy and labour intensive tasks were accomplished. The existence of wastes and commons allowed villagers to supplement their diet and income by keeping livestock. Landless villagers could squat on the common and thereby cease to be a possible drain on the resources of the village economy.

Furthermore, open field methods of farming were not immune from change and re-organisation. Historians have tended to be rather harsh in their judgement. Enclosure had taken place, for example, in Tudor times for sheep runs. Usually this had occurred piece-meal when two or three farmers had swapped strips to achieve blocks of land; at other times a general agreement was reached among all the landowners. Enclosure through Act of Parliament was another alternative, but a costly one. It did, however, provide a comprehensive re-organisation of all the land in the village rather than selected pieces.

Thus it would be mistaken to assume that the countryside was composed of vast tracts of open-fields labouring under antiquated methods of farming. The regional pattern varied considerably throughout Britain as did the number of fields which constituted the village land. Nevertheless by 1750 there still remained a considerable number of arable open-fields. Scotland was virtually unenclosed as was about one-third to one-half of England and Wales. Within England itself, the open fields lay largely in a vast triangle from the Humber to the Avon in the west and the Thames in the south.

It was arable land within this triangle, particularly in the Midlands, which experienced the brunt of enclosure. Before 1750 there were only 64 Acts of Parliament passed for enclosure; the pace quickened between 1760–1780 when 800 were passed and 1000 between 1793–1815. By 1830 virtually all arable land was enclosed and thereafter Enclosure Acts became focussed upon the wastes and commons. Enclosure, by themselves, did not necessarily lead to improvements. Yet it is true to say, as local studies have shown, greater productivity and higher rents from enclosed lands did occur.

EXAMINING THE EVIDENCE
The effects of enclosure upon small farmers

A great deal of concern was expressed at the time of greatest enclosure, and throughout the nineteenth century, over what appeared to be the disastrous fate of the small farmer. It was claimed that he could not afford the costs of enclosure and, as a result, was forced to sell his land and become either a landless labourer or a factory hand. Did the small farmer decline in numbers and, if so, was this due to enclosure?

The Royal Commission of the late nineteenth century which inquired into the problem defined small farmers as owner-occupiers of 30–40 acres. The decline was indisputable. The Royal Commission revealed that a mere 12 per cent remained compared with a little over 20 per cent in 1800 and nearly 30 per cent in 1700. One cannot conclude, however, that the decline was due solely, or in part, to the rapid rate of enclosure in the latter part of the nineteenth century.

HARVEST TIME.

Source A

Oliver Goldsmith, *The Deserted Village*

from 'The Deserted Village' 1770 Reprinted in Austin Dobson (ed.), *Poetical Works of Oliver Goldsmith, 1980*

> Sweep smiling village, loveliest of the lawn,
> Thy sports are fled, and all thy charms withdrawn;
> Amidst thy bowers the tyrant's hand is seen,
> And desolation saddens all the green
> One only master grasps the whole domain,
> And half a tillage stints thy smiling plain;
> No more thy glassy brook reflects the day,
> But choked with sedges, works its weedy way;
> Along thy glades, a solitary guest,
> The hollow sounding bittern guards its nest;
> Amidst thy desert walks the lapwing flies,
> And tires their echoes with unvaried cries.
> Sunk are thy bowers, in shapeless ruin all,
> And the long grass o'ertops the mouldering wall;
> And trembling, shrinking from the spoiler's hand,
> Far, far away thy children leave the land.

Oliver Goldsmith, *The Deserted Village (1770)*

Source B

Enclosure is the theft of state lands ... a systematic robbery of the communal lands.

Karl Marx

Source C: A farmer and labourer

A CRITIC'S VIEW OF THE EFFECTS OF ENCLOSURE.

Source D

The first period of decline occurred between 1650 to 1750 when agricultural products were receiving low prices due to a generally static market and to the imposition of wartime taxes (1688–1715) which the small farmer felt most keenly. The Continental Blockade during the Napoleonic Wars and an expanding population stimulated farming prices and the small farmer was able to prosper. Shrinkage occurred after 1815 due to a depression in agricultural prices but in no way was their decline particularly serious in the early part of the nineteenth century.

A.J. Johnson, *The Disappearance of the Small Farmer*

Source E

In the late eighteenth century the average cost of an enclosure by Act of Parliament was estimated by the Board of Agriculture at about 28s. per acre. This figure included approximately 8s. 6d. per acre for obtaining the Act, 10s, for the fees of the commissioners and the expenses of surveying and valuing, and 9s. 6d. for the cost of fencing. Where the enclosure involved new farmhouses and roads, however, the total outlay could be easily three or four times as much. It is not surprising, therefore, that in many enclosures there was no attempt to rebuild farmhouses or lay down new roads, and that as a consequence the new farms were often remote from the farmers' dwellings, yards and barns. For this reason, where the farmhouses remained in the centre of the village it was sometimes the practice to give the small farmers allotments near at hand, and to allot the more distant fields to the wealthier owners who could afford to rebuild. In general, the rent of open-field land varied from about 5s. to 10s. per acre in the later eighteenth century; after enclosure from about 10s. to 20s. or more. Perhaps a doubling of rents, from about 7s. to 15s. per acre, was the common result of enclosure in the Midlands.

J.D. Chambers and G.E. Mingay, *The Agricultural Revolution*

Source F

A study of enclosures in Lincolnshire of 70 Parliamentary enclosures revealed that 82% of the owners post-enclosures owned less than 50 acres.

T.H. Swales, *Parliamentary Enclosures of Lindsey. Lindsey Archaeological Society reports (1936)*

Source G

Where enclosures took place the process was often lengthy and that full scale enclosure was usually only the final act. Mutual exchange of strips and even the division of the common land had been taking place since the Tudor Age. Enclosures did not create any greater inequality than had existed before.

W.G. Hoskins, *The Midland Peasant (1957)*

Source H: Enclosure and farming changes

Enclosure did not necessarily lead to changed or better farming – and especially was this so if the soil did not lend itself to the cultivation of turnips or clover, or if the farmers were conservative. Marshall was one of a number of authorities who held summer-fallowing to be essential on heavy soils, and it is clear from the country Reports that bare fallows continued in many different areas. In Cambridgeshire Vancouver found enclosed parishes still following the rotations of open-field parishes, and Young noticed the same thing in Lord Chesterfield's new enclosures in Buckinghamshire. In Lincolnshire and Bedfordshire Stone and Batchelor saw only few signs of improvement, and at Knapwell in Northamptonshire Young found the husbandry so bad that he was at a loss to know why the proprietors had troubled to enclose.

J.D. Chambers and G.L. Mingay, *The Agricultural Revolution*

Source I

There is little evidence that the small landowner was opposed to enclosure when there were sufficient small landowners to prevent enclosure taking place. Opposition usually came from absentee landowners who had let out their rights to the commons and thus were left with an uneconomic unit. In some areas graziers resisted enclosure as they benefitted financially if there was a shortage of grazing areas in the neighbouring parishes ... Furthermore some large landowners were selling land to pay for enclosure. During the reign of George III private estate acts were half as numerous as parliamentary enclosure acts and some of this land was sold to the small farmer.

E. Davies, *The Small Landowner 1780–1832 in the light of Land Tax Assessments, Economic History Review (1927)*

Source J: The role of commissioners

... the commissioners did not take a strict view of the legal validity of claims but often gave favourable consideration to claims for compensation based on custom or equity rather than on legal right. Even the Hammonds conceded that the squatters who had settled on the waste and were suffered in the village as 'poor aliens' were sometimes treated fairly,

William Ellis and Arthur Young –

◆

In 1748 the
Swedish botanist Peter Kalm
described his visit to the village of
Little Gaddesden in Hertfordshire, the home
of the farmer and agricultural propagandist,
William Ellis. He inquired of a local farmer.

Source A

"Who is the owner of this field, which to a great extent stands under water, and is so ill-cultivated?

"A Mr. Ellis as he is called."

"Mr. Ellis", I asked, "you must have forgotten yourself, or is there more than one Mr. Ellis … is it the same Mr. Ellis who is celebrated for the many beautiful works he has published on rural economy."

The man answered that it was the very same, and that as for Mr. Ellis, (he) *"sits at home in his room and writes books, and sometimes goes a whole week without getting into his ploughed fields."*

More famous than Ellis as a propagandist Arthur Young dominates the late eighteenth century and provides a treasure house of source material on agricultural change. Young made no secret of his support for enclosure and agricultural change. Yet he too was a failure as a practical farmer. How was it possible for two failures to have had such an impact on agricultural improvement?

◆

successful failures?

SOURCE B:

ARTHUR YOUNG'S CAREER

1767   Began his famous tours writing detailed observations on the state of agriculture and promoting the 'new' farming.

1771   Published Southern, Northern, and Eastern tours.

1784   Became editor of the 'Annals of Agriculture' which promoted and discussed improved methods of farming.

1788   Inherited the family estate at Bradfield in Suffolk where he began to experiment with different farming methods. His estate became a centre for thousands of interested visitors.

1793   Young became Secretary to the Board of Agriculture. This office had been set up with the express purpose of intro-ducing the improved methods of farming. It was not officially backed by the government, how-ever, and this caused it to limp along with insufficient funds.

SOURCE C

People that devote their time to writing cannot act or execute; his (Arthur Young's) sheep are scabbed, his cattle ill-chosen and worse managed; in short he exhibits a sad picture of mismanagement.

SOURCE D

It is incredible how intelligent farmers are, even the small farmers ... I have seen a hundred of them talking with Mr. Young on the principles of their calling, making suggestions and recounting their experiences for three quarters of an hour or an hour; they never fail to win Mr. Young's admiration, though he was well used to it.

This chapter has several examples of Arthur Young's agricultural writing. Re-read these extracts and take particular note of the language, tone and style of the extracts.

1 Upon what does Ellis and Young's reputation rest? Are they:
- Practical farmers
- Enthusiasts for farming improvements
- Successful farmers by example
- Communicators • Others?

2 What would you say were the strengths of Young as a writer?

3 (a) To whom did Ellis and Young address their writing?
(b) Why was this audience likely to be receptive to their ideas?
(c) What other conclusions can you draw about Young and Ellis's audience considering their method of communication?

4 Why did the apparent contradictions in Young and Ellis as agricultural improvers make little difference to their reputations?

SOURCE E

HAYMAKERS

some with more than 20 years standing as occupiers being allowed to keep their encroachments, and those of a lesser standing being allowed to purchase them. 'Taken as a whole', said Gonner, 'the work of division and apportionment appears to have been discharged conscientiously and fairly.'

A more recent investigator, Mr W.E. Tate, has endorsed this conclusion. A remarkable feature of eighteenth-century enclosure, he has said, was the 'care with which it was carried out and the relatively small volume of organised protest which it aroused.' On the basis of his evidence he found that the instances of enclosures deliberately rigged against the small man, which the Hammonds quoted, were 'in the highest degree exceptional ...', and that it would be quite unfair to suppose them typical of the country in general. Ultimately, of course, the enclosure commissioners relied for their employment on the large proprietors, and were bound to satisfy them.

---

1 In what period/s did the decline of the owner/occupier occur?

2 (a) Which sources suggest an immediate decline?

(b) How reliable are these sources as historical evidence?

(c) How useful are these sources as evidence?

3 Discuss the following statements in your class:

(a) "Enclosure was fatal to three classes; the small farmer, the cottager and the squatter?" J.L. and B. Hammond.

(b) "Enclosure was the theft of state lands." Karl Marx.

(c) The costs of enclosure were prohibitive for the small farmer.

(d) Enclosures were sweeping and national in character.

REVIEW
Agricultural change and the Industrial Revolution

The importance of agriculture to the national economy in the eighteenth and nineteenth century was crucial. At the same time Britain began to industrialise and eventually this process was to over-shadow that of farming. The timing of these two developments has led historians to ask the question – "What part did agriculture play in the industrial revolution?" The possible contribution that farming made toward industrialisation can be summarised as follows.

Feeding a growing and increasingly urbanised population
From 1751–1821 the population of England and Wales doubled. Increasingly, this population became urbanised.

No loss of foreign exchange
Despite the population increase the import of corn was insignificant, except in the years of disastrous harvests. If Britain had been obliged to

buy foreign corn then much of our foreign exchange used to purchase cotton and iron ore would not have been available. By contrast, Holland, whose economy was as advanced as Britain's in 1700 became increasingly dependent upon the import of foreign grain. By 1800 the Dutch had been left far behind.

Earning foreign exchange
Until 1756 Britain exported substantial amounts of grain. After 1760 home consumption predominated.

Supplier of raw materials for industry
Agriculture was important to the industrial development as a supplier of many principal raw materials – wool, flax, hides, tallow, timber, oil, barley.

Capital contribution
Landowners frequently developed industries connected with their estates such as timber, coal-mining and iron smelting. Often though the landowner withdrew from direct participation and leased out the industrial undertaking. (For a fuller discussion of the capital contribution made by landowners to industry see chapter three).

Contribution of business talent
Farmers would often assist younger sons in business or they became part-time manufacturers themselves. One of the most famous was Robert Peel who sold his land so that he could concentrate on cotton manufacture.

Contribution of working capital
Rents and profits were often deposited in country banks. The money was then released as loans to businessmen. Of course, farmers themselves needed some of this capital and not all of it was sunk into industrial undertakings.

Investment in transport
Farmers and landowners probably invested as much money in turnpike roads and canals in proportion to their wealth, as any other class. Clearly most were only interested in their direct advantage but once built others could share in the obvious advantages.

(For a fuller discussion see chapters seven and eight).

Supply of labour
When prices fell many farmers in clay areas turned to livestock husbandry which required less labour. As a result many of these workers turned to domestic production of lace, nails and so on. It must be remembered, however, that it was not the changes in farming which propelled people to towns but the overall increase in the rural population for enclosed farms demanded more labour not less.

Demand
Most studies of purchasing patterns at this time suggest the farmers and landowners bought the bulk of manufactured goods. This coincided with the rapid development of industry during the 1780s through to 1815. At

the same time, lower food prices meant that industrialists needed to pay less in wages. This period was one of increasing food prices.

Taxation

The landowning class contributed most to taxation during the Napoleonic Wars (For a fuller discussion see – chapter nine). From 1803–14 taxes levied on incomes from trade and industry rose 10 per cent while taxes on land and agricultural incomes rose by 60 per cent.

Conspicuous spending

On the debit side it must be remembered that many merchants and manufacturers spent income on buying social prestige in the form of country estates. When Richard Arkwright died, for example, he left two and a half million pounds of which two million pounds was in land.

The role of agriculture in industrialisation can be said to fall into three distinct phases. Some factors, of course applied throughout all three periods. Draw and complete the chart below inserting the appropriate factors.

BEFORE 1750	1760–1815	1815

3 The Role of the Cotton Industry

PREVIEW

King Cotton?

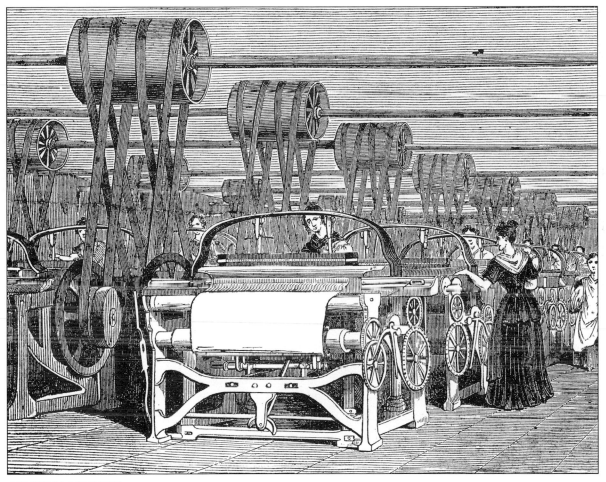

COTTON MILL, LANCASHIRE.

'Cotton was the original leading sector in the first take-off of the industrial revolution.'

W.W. Rostow, *Stages of Economic Growth*

'No single industry played the role of the leading sector. Iron and coal have claims at least as strong as that of cotton.'

P. Deane, *The First Industrial Revolution*

Cotton – the leading sector of the Industrial Revolution?

In the summer of 1784 a consignment of eight bales and three bags of raw cotton were discharged from the hold of an American ship. The receiving Clerk of Customs at the port of Liverpool immediately ordered them impounded for he doubted that, "there is that much cotton in all America". The Clerk of Custom's doubts were shortly allayed by the persuasion of its owner the eminent Liverpool merchant, William Rathbone. Once the cotton was released he offered it to William Strutt of Belper and Samuel Greg of Styal for sampling.

SPINNING WITH DISTAFF.

After the trial shipment of 1784, cotton spinners like Rathbone organised a massive increase in consumption of American cotton by the spinning and weaving mills of Lancashire. By 1833 Liverpool was handling 90 per cent of the cotton grown in America – Greg's company alone consumed nearly 3 per cent. In turn Liverpool became the main port for export shipments, taking Lancashire cotton cloth all over world.

Imported cotton was familiar enough but more usually in the form of printed calicoes, or in its raw form from the Middle East, supplemented by imports from the West Indies, Brazil and Peru. Hence the doubts

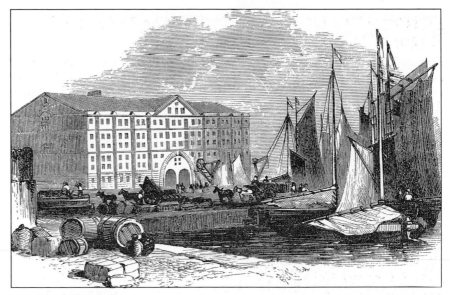

LIVERPOOL, DUKE'S DOCK.

expressed by the Clerk of Customs, yet this particular cargo was to set in train an expansion in cotton manufacture of such magnitude that it became acknowledged as the monarch of British industries.

Imports of raw America cotton in lbs.

1784	3,5000	1801	21,000,000
1787	25,000	1811	62,000,000
1788	97,000	1821	125,000,000
1791	198,000	1831	270,000,000
1794	1,601,000	1841	520,000,000

This dramatic rise in imports of raw cotton not only transformed American agriculture, laid the fortunes of Liverpool and made Manchester into 'Cottonopolis' but, it is argued by some historians, was the principal industry of the Industrial Revolution.

The growth of the cotton industry

Outstanding claims have been made by economic historians for the importance of the cotton industry to the Industrial Revolution.
'Cotton was the original leading sector in the first take-off.'

W.W. Rostow, *Stages of Economic Growth*

'English industrial history (1787–1842) can … be the history of a single industry.'

J.A. Schumpeter, *Business Cycles Volume 1*

'Industrial enterprise on this scale had secondary reactions on the development of urban areas, the demand for coal, iron and machinery, the demand for working capital and ultimately the demand for cheap transport which powerfully stimulated industrial development in other directions.'

W.W. Rostow, *ibid. p.54*

These are outstanding claims and should not go unchallenged.

Wool and cotton consumption (Britain) 1780–1840

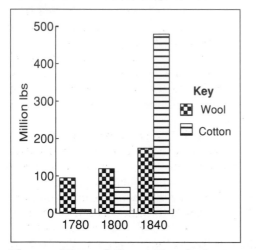

Key
- ▨ Wool
- ▤ Cotton

The position of the cotton industry compared to other textiles

Industry	(a)	(b)	(c)	
			steam	*water*
Cotton	219	110	46	12
Wool	55	5	17	10
Linen	35	0.3	7	4
Silk	31	2	2	1
Total	340	117.3	72	27

	cost per pound		
	1784	1812	1832
(i) Cotton	10p	7½p	3p
(ii) Wool	4p	8p	6p

Cotton's contribution to the national income

1760	one-half million pounds	–	1800 five million pounds
1802	⅚ of total national income	–	1812 ⅞

export value

1760	one-quarter million pounds	–	1800 five million pounds

import value

1780	ten million pounds	–	1840 five hundred million pounds.

There is little dispute that between the periods 1770–1840 cotton was the fastest growing major industry, the fastest growing export industry and the first industry to widely adopt steam power. The rise is even more remarkable when we consider its relative insignificance in 1775. By the turn of the nineteenth century it had become the largest export industry, overhauling the centuries-long dominance of wool. It was to retain this lead until 1914. The census returns for 1841, which gave occupational information for the first time, revealed nearly half a million people working in cotton textiles, compared to 118 000 in coal and 160 000 in woollen and worsteds. The size of the labour force should not lull us into thinking that this phenomenal growth was achieved by an increased labour force alone. By the 1820s virtually all spinning was done by steam power; by 1840, all weaving. The increase in steam power led to greater units of production and a greater concentration of the industry. In the 1770s cotton manufacture was widely scattered throughout rural backwaters around Glasgow and Manchester. By 1838 nearly 86 per cent of all operatives (cotton workers) were to be found within a relatively small radius around Liverpool and Manchester.

Clearly cotton assumed the leading role in the industrialised production of textiles and, in relation to export value, made a significant contribution to the national income, volume of employment and in the extent of mechanisation. How was this achieved?

England had long excelled at textile production and her economic fortune from the Middle Ages to Tudor times had rested upon the export of fine quality woollen cloth. By contrast cotton was tiny to the point of insignificance at the beginning of the eighteenth century and unable to compete with good quality Indian calicoes. Any possible expansion was restricted by the small demand for such home-produced coarse cottons and the slow productivity of spinners who could not supply weavers with sufficient yarn. In common with most other industries production was in the hands of households; the children cleaning and carding, women spinning the yarn, men weaving the cloth. The cloth, often mixed with linen to improve its poor quality and called fustian, had a paltry export value in 1750 of £200 000 whereas wool, by contrast was worth five and a half million pounds.

By the late 1760s, however, significant changes were taking place both in supply and demand. To understand the nature of these changes we must first appreciate the process involved in the manufacture of cotton.

The processes in the cotton industry

Initially cotton products were imported in the form of printed calicoes from India. Despite the tiny imports, the masters in the fustian trade were determined to remove any potential competition and successfully persuaded Parliament to place a high import duty on printed cotton goods. This piece of legislation inadvertently gave a greater stimulus to the manufacture of cotton goods within Britain by increasing imports of the raw material.

Supply and demand were soon to exert a significant influence. If home demand had been the sole instigator for growth then the spectacular rise would not have taken place. Africa presented a ready market for cheap textiles as well as manufactured goods, where conveniently for the profits of British traders, slaves could be bought and transported to the southern plantations of America. India too represented a significant foreign market and the temptation of foreign involvement to protect investment.

COTTON PLANTATIONS IN THE SOUTHERN STATES OF AMERICA.

Imports of raw cotton increased appreciably in the 1780s after the War of American Independence with Britain and was soon to become the principal source of supply. The supply from the United States of America was considerably elastic. The area of cultivation could be expanded almost indefinitely and whilst the cotton plant was subject to some diseases and pests, it did not suffer from the natural limitations that wool production did.

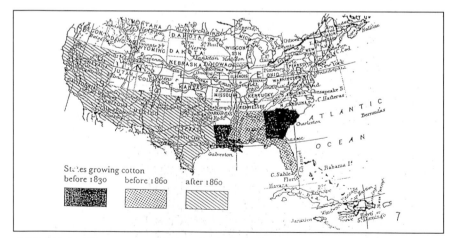

STATES GROWING COTTON.

MISSISSIPPI STEAMER CARRYING BALES OF COTTON.

To understand the technology of the industry we must first examine the processes involved in its manufacture. As you read through make a note of where bottlenecks in the industry occurred.

TALKING POINT

The use of statistics can clearly lend substance to a proposition more effectively than can anecdotes. Averages, mean, medians, percentages refine an argument into an analysis. At the same time statistics are not infallible, for example, those of the growth of the cotton industry.

By altering their scale what different interpretation could they appear to represent?

What objections have been raised by historians to, say the statistics we possess on the growth of the cotton industry?

What is meant by the phrase 'There are lies, damn lies and statistics!'

Processing cotton on its arrival

Blending

BLENDING.

After the bale of cotton was opened it was then blended to achieve a uniform quality. 'Scutching' removed any seeds and dirt whilst 'carding' involved laying the fibres parallel and cleaning the cotton more scrupulously.

Spinning

A SPINSTER AT WORK.

The aim is to produce yarn of a consistent weight and quality per unit length. Whether cotton is spun by machine or hand the same three processes are involved. 'Drawing' or stretching out the fibres, 'twisting' them so they lock against each other. Then 'winding' yarn onto a bobbin so that it can eventually be unwound for use on the weft (the width of the frame) and the warp (the length of the frame).

Weaving

A HANDLOOM WEAVER.

The warp yarn is wound onto bobbins which are then set on a creel, or carriage, depending upon the length of cloth required. The cotton warp is then 'sized' with a starch dressing which gives strength and smoothness to the yarn. This part of the process enables it to bear the strain of weaving. The threads are laid across and between by a shuttle carrying the weft across the warp.

Bleaching, finishing and dyeing

DYEING

When the cloth comes off the loom it is generally in a rough state known as 'grey cloth'. It was usually bought from the mill warehouses in this state. To produce a saleable fabric they then 'put it out' for further processing. The pre-industrial methods of bleaching took several months and tied up much of the merchant's capital. There were several methods of bleaching:

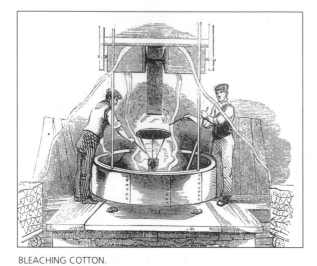

BLEACHING COTTON.

CROFTING. BLEACHING CLOTH IN THE SUNLIGHT.

PRINTING COTTON CLOTH.

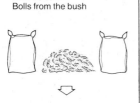

Raw cotton:
Bolls from the bush

Cleaning:
Seeds separated from fibres, made ready for

Spinning:
The fibres are twisted into a continuous thread

Weaving:
The threads are laid across and between, by a shuttle carrying weft across warp

Warp, runs along the length of the cloth

Weft, runs across the width

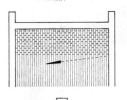

Finishing:
This includes dyeing, bleaching, printing

Soft, lime-free water must be used in dye-vats

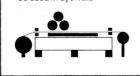

COTTON PROCESSES.

'Bucking': soaking in potash lye.

'Souring': soaking in buttermilk.

'Crofting': spreading the cloth out in fields and repeatedly soaking it.

'Finishing' consisted of a variety of processes to improve the appearance and texture of the fabric of which the most important was raising the nap by means of a rough-textured plant called a teasle. From ancient times to the second half of the nineteenth century fabrics were dyed from natural substances. The main dyes were derived from the following;

plants   –   indigo (blue) birch leaves (yellow)

minerals –   carbon (black) ochre (red)

insects   –   cochineal (red)

shellfish –   (purple)

Printing

Until the late eighteenth century fabrics were printed from wood blocks with raised printed areas. It was slow, labour-intensive and costly.

Questions

Opposite is a summary chart of the main process involved in the manufacture of cotton cloth.

As a manufacturer decide:

1 Where do the most serious bottlenecks occur?

2 What might be done to relieve the pressure at these various bottlenecks?

3 In what ways might your suggested improvements in the manufacture of cotton affect other industries?

The technological revolution in the cotton industry

How then was the cotton industry transformed from an insignificant domestic industry into a so-called 'leading sector'? The answer lies in significant changes that were happening in supply and demand. In the first place the East India Company, which was the chief importer of printed cloth, found it increasingly difficult to maintain its supply at the same time as European demand was increasing. British population growth also swelled demand as did a real growth in incomes. It was not surprising that in the early 1760s a number of prizes were offered to anyone who could improve productivity and the quality of cotton cloth. The response of the cotton industry was a mechanised transformation far more extensive than in any other single industry.

From the survey of the processes involved in cotton manufacture you should have identified 'bottlenecks' which reduced productivity. The following inventions and innovations are presented in chronological order. Read through them first and complete the chart at the end of the descriptions.

John Kay's 'Flying Shuttle'

On average it needed as many as five spinners to maintain a weaving loom in production. John Kay invented his machine in 1733 but it was not widely adopted until after 1750. Even then it provoked furious opposition from weavers who feared redundancy and he was defrauded by manufacturers who refused to pay him royalties.

THE FLYING SHUTTLE.

John Wyatt and Paul Lewis

The expansion made possible by the Flying Shuttle created a demand for a spinning machine. Wyatt and Paul's machine was patented in 1738 but the invention was not a success due to certain design faults. Coupled to their poor business sense they were forced into bankruptcy in 1748.

James Hargreaves 'Spinning Jenny'

Although invented in 1763 the machine was not patented until 1770. The thread produced by this machine was most suitable for the weft and the machine could be used in the home.

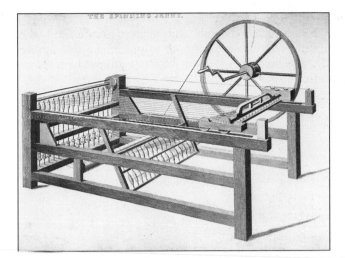

SPINNING JENNY.

Richard Arkwright's 'Water-frame'

Arkwright was one of the most outstanding examples of the business entrepreneur as you will see in the Focus section. Although he claimed to have invented the water frame and other spinning machines a number of inventors successfully won legal battles against him and his patents were withdrawn. His machines were suitable for large scale production in mills. The thread produced by this machine was most suitable as warp and thus the Spinning Jenny and the Water Frame could co-exist.

THE WATER FRAME.

Samuel Crompton's 'Mule'

This machine gradually superseded both the Water Frame and the Spinning Jenny. It combined the qualities of both to produce a fine strong thread. The 'mule' was patented in 1779 but was not adopted for powered factory use until after 1790.

CROMPTON'S MULE.

Edmund Cartwright's Power loom

The series of spinning inventions left only weaving in the hands of domestic production and for a short time the handloom weaver experienced great prosperity as you will see in 'Examining the Evidence' on p.68. The favourable situation for the handloom weaver was ended by the improbable figure of The Reverend Edmund Cartwright and his power loom patented in 1785. His first attempt to exploit commercially his invention ended disastrously. Nor did his competitors who set up power looms fare any better because of determined labour opposition. The invention did not take hold until after the Napoleonic Wars. By the 1830s it was almost universally in use.

Date	Number of power looms
1813	2,400
1820	14,000
1830	69,000
1840	100,000
1850	247,000

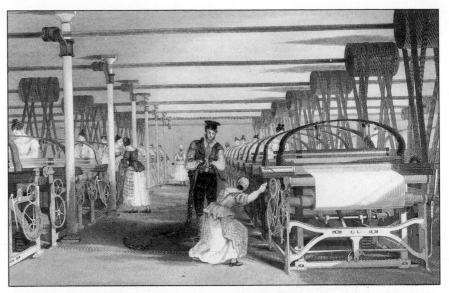

POWER LOOMS, AS INVENTED BY CARTWRIGHT. THEY ARE DRIVEN BY THE BELTS RUNNING FROM OVER-HEAD TRANSMISSION SHAFTS.

Eli Whitney's cotton gin

The turning point in the harvesting of the cotton boll came with the invention of the cotton gin. This machine enabled the seeds to be separated from the fibres and replaced the long process of hand cleaning. One gin could clean and prepare 50 pounds of cotton per day. As a result trade accelerated, prices fell, demand increased and cotton growing on a commercial scale spread southwards from Virginia. By 1860 cotton was the richest industry in America, contributing 66 per cent of United States Treasury funds.

COTTON GIN.

Richard Arkwright (1732–1792):
Heroic innovator or opportunist?

RICHARD ARKWRIGHT.

INTRODUCTION

Richard Arkwright was born into poverty but died a millionaire, honoured by his country with a knighthood. Yet his major invention, the Water-frame was proved to have been substantially 'borrowed' from other inventors. Upon what basis then does the reputation of Richard Arkwright rest?

SUMMARY OF ARKWRIGHT'S LIFE AND CAREER

1750s

Worked as a wigmaker, barber and publican.

1768

Lived in Nottingham where he collaborated with John Kay on the production of a spinning machine. In June he applied for a patent for this machine which he received in the following year.

1769–71

Made further developments to the spinning machine with the help of Jedediah Strutt of Derby – a silk factory owner.

1771

Arkwright built a mill at Cromford Derbyshire using water power to operate the machinery. This led to his 'invention' the water-frame.

1774

Arkwright persuaded Parliament to end the heavy tax on the sale of his cloth of 6d a yard. Arkwright's business prospers.

1775

He obtains a patent to control spinning.

1776–80

Builds new mills at Belper, Chorley and Cromford.

1781–85

Unsuccessfully defends his patents in court where it is proved that John Kay and Thomas Highs had substantially invented the machines to which he laid claim.

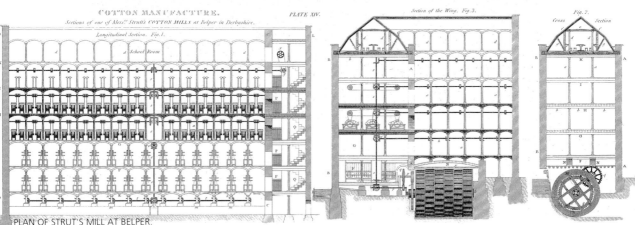

PLAN OF STRUT'S MILL AT BELPER.

ARKWRIGHT AS A YOUNG MAN

'He married your mother, and began business for himself … He was always thought clever in his peruke wig-making business and very capital in Bleeding and toothdrawing and allowed by all his acquaintances to be a very ingenious man.'

An account of Arkwright as a young man in Bolton during the 1750s. It was written by Thomas Ridgeway in 1799 on a request for information from Arkwright's son.

ARKWRIGHT THE INNOVATOR

'I am certain to make the first fraim, I have hands to make three fraims in a fortnet. Richard has hit upon a method to spin woostid with roulers, it is quite sertain, and only altering the shape … Querey, will not cotton make whipcord as good as silk, properly twisted? It may be done at all onst from the bobins. Pray rite to Mr. N. what he thinks best … I ask Mr. Whard to get some let (lead) pipes to bring the water into the mill … It might be brought in the rooms. Would it not be best to fox a crank to one of the lying shafts to work a pump or Ingon (engine) in case of fire.'

A letter from Richard Arkwright to his partner Jedediah Strutt in 1772.

THE MILLS ARE ATTACKED

After an attack on one of his mills by rioters at Chorley the following article appeared in the Manchester Mercury on the 12 October 1779.

'All the gentleman in the neighbourhood being determined to support Mr. Arkwright, in the defence of his works … The spears and battery are always to be kept in repair for the Defence of the Works and Protection of the village, and 5,000 or 6,000 men, Miners etc. can be assembled in less than an hour … determined to the very last extremity, the Works, by which many Hundreds of their wives and Children get a decent and comfortable Livelihood.'

THE PATERNALISTIC EMPLOYER

'… by his conduct appears to be a man of great understanding and knows the way of making his people do their best. He not only distributes pecuniary rewards, but gives distinguishing dresses to the most deserving of both sexes which excites great emulation. He also gives two Balls at the Greyhound to the workmen and their wives and families with a weeks jubilee at the time of each Ball. This makes them industrious and sober all the rest of the year.'

A visitor's remarks after a visit to Arkwright's Cromford mill in 1781.

'… We cannot prevent him from saying ill-natured things nor can we regulate his actions.'

Jedediah Strutt's comment on Richard Arkwright after a quarrel between John Smalley, manager and Arkwright's original partner, with Arkwright.

PATENTS UNDER QUESTION

'... *he has already built a great building for Cotton Works (at Manchester), yet he swears it will never be worked and will sooner let it for barracks for Soldiers, swears he will take the cotton spinning abroad, and that he will ruin those Manchester rascals whom he has been the making of. It is agreed by all who know him that he is a Tyrant ... Surely you cannot think it just that any tyrant should tyrannise over so large a manufactory by false pretences.'*

Matthew Boulton in a letter to James Watt, December 1780, when Arkwright's patents were being fought over in the law courts.

Questions

1 Compare Arkwright's career with the other cotton textile inventors. In what ways was his career more unusual?

2 (a) Where does Arkwright's contribution to the development of the cotton industry rest – as inventor or entrepreneur?

(b) Which role – entrepreneur or inventor – was more important in the development of the cotton industry?

3 What sort of characteristics emerge from these sources which explain the phenomenal success of Arkwright?

THE ROYAL STOCK EXCHANGE, MANCHESTER.

John Roebuck and chemical bleaching

By 1760 the shortage of cheaply-produced chemicals was causing major holdups. In 1764 the use of watered-down sulphuric acid solved the problem of quick and efficient bleaching. In 1775, Claude Berthollet developed the use of chlorine as a bleaching agent.

Roller printing

Roller printing was first started in 1785 at the works of Livsey, Hargreaves & Co. The roller was made of copper with a pattern etched on it.

James Watt and Mathew Boulton's Steam engine

The early mills were water-powered. Indeed, with high installation and maintenance costs, in addition to the relative low horse-power output of the steam engine there was often sufficient reason to retain water power. Of course, there were problems with the unreliability of the water supply. Nevertheless there were only 92 Boulton and Watt steam engines installed in cotton mills by 1800. By 1800 Watt's patent expired and cheaper and more efficient steam engines were available.

The location and sources of power 1838–50

County	Change in number of mills	% decline in water power	% increase in steam power
Cheshire	–21	35	16
Derbyshire	–21	21	65
Lancashire	+49	5	57
Yorkshire	+54	11	143
Totals	+61	16	56

Questions

1 Complete the chart below.

Initial problem in cotton manufacture
↓
Solution
↓
Consequent problem to be overcome
↓
etc.

2 Compare the date of the inventions with the growth of the cotton industry. Does any correlation emerge between the two sets of figures?

3 Which invention/s do you consider to have been particularly significant?

The expansion of the cotton industry

Factors favouring the expansion of the cotton industry were:

1 Cotton was a reasonably new industry and relatively unfettered by vested interests and practices, unlike the woollen industry where apprenticeship regulations, for example, were a disincentive to innovation.

2 The supply of raw material could almost be indefinitely expanded. A raw material that comes straight from the plant, and which does not have to be digested by a silkworm or grown on the back of a sheep has many advantages. The production of cotton can be expanded simply by bringing more land into production and the labour supply can be easily increased by importing more slaves.

3 Established textile workers could readily adapt to the production of the new material for the factory system. The thousands of small men with their jennies and looms allowed an immediate expansion of capacity in response to demand. Skills, such as that of the weaver, were in abundant supply and little capital investment was needed.

4 Cotton products were not new. Indian calicoes had long been in demand and when a British made product could be manufactured to the same degree of quality then it found a ready market, particularly when cotton's price decreased.

5 The cotton industry was highly localised which may have enabled the rapid adoption of technological change. Why it became concentrated in Lancashire is not entirely clear although a damp climate, lime-free water for washing the material, an abundant labour supply and the growth of the port of Liverpool are amongst the explanations offered.

6 Britain was the first to develop machinery for cotton spinning and weaving and could establish a quick lead over any potential competitor. Mechanisation in the early stages was relatively cheap and this initial lead in producing for a mass market could yield high profits.

7 Although prices fell profits did not. In part this was due to continued innovation but perhaps the most important reason was the almost inexhaustible supply of cheap labour. From 1820–45 the output of the industry quadrupled. Whilst average incomes increased by 50 per cent those of cotton workers barely rose at all. Furthermore the factory owner could easily expand or contract hours of work, particularly when the workforce of women and children was so vulnerable. There were few job alternatives for a labour force such as this.

Putting the progress in perspective

On the other hand the undoubted progress of the cotton industry must be kept in perspective. The inhibiting factors were:

1 The transformation of the industry was quite gradual. The spinning jenny, for example, multiplied production in the spinning process and thus maintained the handloom weaver's domestic production. The use of steam power in mills was not widely adopted in factories until after the 1820s.

2 Factories played only a relatively small contribution to output, for most cotton was produced by out-workers. Much machinery, such as the introduction of the power loom, was often delayed for fear of losing money through heavy investment in plant and equipment, particularly when outworkers proved so cheap.

'So eminent a factory owner as John Kennedy was still doubtful in 1815 whether the saving of labour by the power loom was sufficient to counterbalance the expense of power and machinery and the disadvantage of being obliged to keep an establishment of power looms constantly at work.'

Wadsworth and Mann, *The Cotton Trade*

3 The importance of the entrepreneur far outweighed the importance of the run of inventions. It is the process of innovation rather than the invention itself which is the critical factor in industrial development.

4 Technical change in the cotton industry only induced change in other textile industries. It was a long time before cotton production became a consumer of coal for steam power. All textile machinery was made of wood initially and produced at the factory itself. Only after 1850 was a textile machinery industry established.

5 The industry was highly localised and thus its influence on the building and transport industries was confined to a relatively small area.

Examining the Evidence
Handloom weavers – victims of industrialisation?

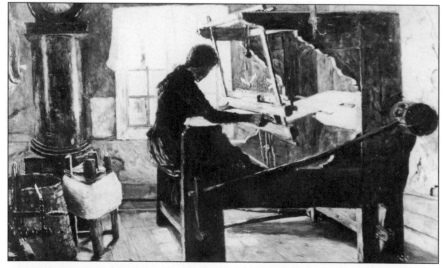

A HANDLOOM WEAVER AT WORK.

Whilst business entrepreneurs such as Richard Arkwright amassed fortunes from cotton, not all shared equally in the prosperity. In the decade 1835–45 power weaving made rapid progress leaving in its wake thousands of displaced handloom workers eaking out a painful existence until extinction overtook them in the 1860s. No other group of workers in social and economic history has elicited so much sympathy as the so-called victims of insiduous industrialisation. Should they enter history as casualties of capitalism or have the facts been misrepresented?

Source A: Power-looms and handloom weavers in Britain's cotton industry

	Power looms	Handlooms
1795	----	75,000
1813	2,400	212,000
1820	14,000	240,000
1829	55,000	225,000
1833	100,000	213,000
1835	109,000	188,000
1845	225,000	60,000
1850	250,000	43,000
1861	400,000	7,000

Open University *Industrialisation and society*

Source B: weekly earnings of a handloom weaving family of six. 1814–33

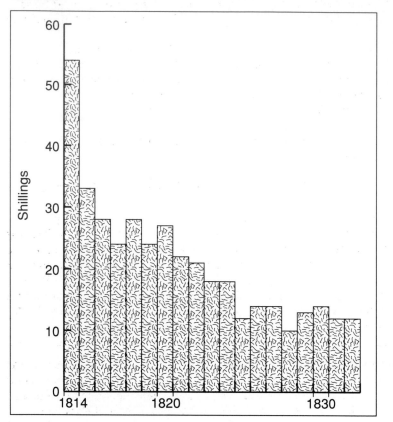

Source C: Evidence given to the Select Committee on Handloom Weavers, 1834 and the Handloom Weavers' Commissioners 1840

An interview with a weaver, called John Brennan. It took place in 1834:

You are a weaver?   Yes
What are your wages?   Seven shillings and sixpence (37½p) a week.
How long have you been a weaver?   Twenty-three years.
What did you earn when you began work?   I was only a boy then, but I could earn 12/- (60p) a week.
How does the fall in wages affect you?   It robs me of all the comforts of life. I can get nothing but the worst of food and less of it than I used to.
What do you do for clothing?   As well as I can. Sometimes I have some and sometimes very little.
What do you do for furniture?   I have never bought any in my life.
How does your wife do for clothes?   Just as I do – quite as bad.
Have your children any stock of clothes?   No, they have just enough to put on clean on Sunday; they have one dress on and one off.
What do you do for cooking utensils?   I have never bought any since I was born. I live in the same place where my father and mother lived; they are dead and the utensils they had, I have still. I never had it in my power to buy any.

Do you belong to any friendly society? No, I do not. I could not pay for it. I have all my children, my wife and myself, in a penny club for burial.

How do you pay the doctor when you are ill? I have to work myself well again.

What do you pay for your church seat? I am not prepared to go. I would if I had got decent clothing. When I was a young man I did get more wages. I had three suits of clothes, and a good watch in my pocket, and two or three pairs of shoes, and one or two good hats.

What does your wife earn? About 5/- (25p) per week.

Does she go to a cotton factory? Yes.

Is it not painful to you to have to send your wife to a factory? Yes, it causes great grief to me.

In 1840 a weaver called John Duce described weavers' lives in the old days, and how things had changed:

When I was young, Monday was generally a day of rest; Tuesday was not severe labour; Saturday was a day to go to the warehouse, and that was an easy day for the weaver. In those times we could afford to go and have balls, and to go and spend money at fairs, and we could afford to take our wives and families to a tea-garden; but it is as much as we can do now, working hard all the week, and sometimes on Sunday besides, to be able to get a bare living; and such as work so many hours destroy their health and strength.

John Duce's evidence to the Handloom Weavers' Commissioners, 1840

There are many complaints of stealing. As proof of this, an employer told me that he had gone to the house of a weaver to ask about some work that was overdue. As the weaver was not at home he went upstairs and the first thing he saw was seven 'widows' hanging over a clothes line.

A 'widow' is the term they use for the unsaleable warp when divorced from the weft, which it is possible to sell and which the weaver had stolen.

Report: Handloom Weavers' Commissioners, 1840

Source D

It is sometimes suggested that the 'evils' of the industrial revolution were due to the rapidity with which it proceeded: the case of the domestic textile workers suggests the exact opposite. If there had been in weaving a man of the type of Arkwright, if there had been no immigration and no Poor Law allowance, the transfer to the factory might have been effected quickly and with less suffering. As it was, large numbers of hand workers continued, for more than a generation, to fight a losing battle against the power of steam. In 1814 the price paid for weaving a piece of calico by hand had been 6s.6d.; by 1829 it had fallen to 1s.2d.

T.S. Ashton, *The Industrial Revolution*

Source E

But, as we have seen, for the power-loom masters it was not a 'battle' but a great convenience to have an auxiliary cheap labour force, as a stand-by in good times and as a means of keeping down the wages of the women and girls (8s. to 12s. Manchester, 1832) who minded the power-looms. Moreover, there was scarcely no 'transfer to the factory'. If the introduction of power had been swifter, then – all other things being equal – its consequences would have been even more catastrophic.

E.P. Thompson, The Making of the English Working Class

Source F

... power-loom weavers have not to buy looms and a jenny to spin for them, or bobbins, flaskets, and baskets; or to pay rent and taxes for them standing; nor candles, or gas and coal for lighting and warming the workshop. They have not to pay for repairs for all wear and tear ... nor have they to buy shuttles, pickers, side-boards, shop boards, shuttle-boards, picking-sticks, and bands and cords. ... They have not to be propped up on the treadles and seatboards ... or have their wrists bandaged to give strength. ... They have not to fetch slubbing, warp their webs, lay up lists, size, put the webs out to dry, seek gears, leck pieces, tenter, teem, dew, and cuttle them; and least of all would they think of breaking wool, scouring, and dyeing it all for nothing too.[2]

J. Lawson, Progress in Pudsey

Source G

The sufferings of the handloom weavers was certainly great ... but it is surely time to discard a number of myths ...

Perhaps the first casualty should be the idea – if it still persists – that cotton handloom weavers were skilled craftsmen whose skill was now to be entrusted to machines which women and children could tend. Cotton handloom weaving was from its earliest days, was an unskilled, casual occupation which provided a domestic by trade for thousands of women and children ...

A second myth which deserves to be dropped is the theory that the deterioration in the material well being of the handloom weavers was simply the result of the powerloom. For it could be argued that they suffered at least as much in the years before 1820, when as we have seen the power loom was of little importance, as they did after that date. Indeed, it is possible to go further and argue that in the reality the power loom was a blessing and not a curse to the handloom weavers, and that their problems were greatest in the earlier period, not because the machine was displacing them, but because it was not displacing them. Certainly there was terrible suffering in some districts in the 1820s, 1830s and early 1840s; but since this was very localised and most of the handloom weavers in the cotton industry were absorbed into alternative employment with remarkable speed and ease, the position in the latter years was far less hopeless than during the wars with revolutionary and Napoleonic France and in the immediate critical post-war period. ... The extension of factory employment which the powerloom, the self-acting mule, and other machines made possible from the early 1820s provided the first escape route from this hopeless dead-end job.

Thirdly, there seems to be need for a substantial revision of the accepted account of the weavers' reaction to a deteriorating economic position. A labour force which contained so large a casual and apathetic element could have hardly represented the 'cohorts of revolution' as Professor Briggs has reminded us.

Finally, there is no need to be melodramatic about the undoubted distress and poverty which many of these unfortunates suffered, particularly those in remote districts. As things worsened many of them were able to take advantage of new employment opportunities offered by an expanding economy … By our own standards, their best was not good enough; for, fatalistically, they accepted some degree of misery as the inevitable result of economic laws which they believed could not be controlled.

D. Bythell, The Handloom Weavers

Source H

… even if the handloom weavers could overcome their deep antipathy towards them (factories) … there were geographical difficulties which are sometimes overlooked, for the earliest power-looms were located outside the old weaving districts which tended to be in rural areas. Secondly, the demand in the mills was mainly for the labour of women and children … Thirdly, there was the suspicion and hostility of workers in other sections of industry who feared for their own jobs, and who were anxious lest employers used handloom weavers as blacklegs. Finally, there were the social factors … There was nothing idyllic about the life of the handloom weaver in his cottage, but … the weaver felt a measure of independence.

T. May, An Economic and Social History of Britain 1760–1970

Source I

I'm a poor cotton weaver as many a one knows,
I've nowt t'eat i' th' house and I've worn out my clothes;
You'd hardly give sixpence for all I've got on.
My clogs they are bursten and stocking I've none.
You'd think it wur hard to be sent to the world
For to clam (starve) and do best that you can …

From 'John O'Grinfield' a popular ballad written shortly after the Napoleonic Wars

---

1 What has been the traditional view of the fate of the Handloom weavers?

2 In what ways, and in which sources, has the traditional interpretation of the handloom weavers been revised?

3 How do sources C and I convey the intensity of the changing fortunes of the handloom weavers?

4 Were the handloom weavers victims of industrialisation or their own inability to adjust to change?

5 Thousands of handloom weavers cannot simply have disappeared. What was their possible fate?

6 Were the handloom weavers beneficiaries or victims of the Industrial Revolution?

REVIEW
Is industrial growth caused by technology?

The expansion of the cotton industry and the rate of technological development was impressive. Was it mechanisation alone that accounted for the claim that the cotton industry took the decisive lead? Clearly there are other factors too:

- Large scale units of production
- Labour saving machinery
- Factory discipline and routine
- Export and import value
- Contribution to the national income
- Employer of labour

Consider

1 How important was supply and demand in explaining the growth of the cotton industry?

2 What was the role of the entrepreneur in the expansion of the cotton industry?

3 Why was Britain specially favoured to develop the cotton industry?

4 A Revolution in Technology? – Iron, Coal and Steam

PREVIEW

The growth of the iron industry

The adaptability and all pervasive use of iron was noted in a song of the 1820s, 'Humphrey Hardfeatures'.

Since cast iron has got all the rage,
And scarce anything's now made without it;
As I live in this cast iron age,
I mean to say something about it.
There's cast-iron coffins and carts,
There's cast-iron bridges and boats,
Corn factors with cast-iron hearts,
That I'd hang up in cast-iron coats.
We have cast-iron gates and lamp posts,
We have cast iron mortars and mills too;
And our enemies know to their cost
We have plenty of cast-iron pills too.
We have cast-iron fenders and grates,
We have cast-iron pokers and tongs, sir;
And we shall have cast-iron plates,
And cast-iron small clothes, ere long sir.

Statistical evidence lends support to the satirical conclusions made by the song writer. At the opening of the eighteenth century iron production was tiny, diffuse and stagnant. By the end of the nineteenth, massive and dominant.

Production of iron		
Date	Annual output of pig iron (in tons)	
1620	35,000	
1700	20,000	
1740	20,000	(30,000 tons imported from Sweden and Russia)
1780	70,000	
1806	250,000	
1823	455,000	
1854	3,070,000	(Russia imports end and Swedish imports tiny)
1884	7,812,000	
1913	10,260,000	
n.b. figures prior to 1854 are estimates only.		

The growth of the iron industry

Statistics show an increase in output of pig iron around 1750 followed by a dramatic acceleration between 1780–1820. But even in the 1780s the industry was by no means major and over half the iron ore used in blast furnaces was imported. Yet the 1780s proved to be a turning point. By 1806 Britain had become a net exporter of iron and the industry contributed 7 per cent toward the national income.

The significance of the growth of the iron industry has led the historian Phyllis Deane to conclude that iron has an equal, if not greater claim, to be the 'leading' sector in the Industrial Revolution.

'… the iron industry played a role in British industrialisation that was both pervasive and stimulating. It provided cheaply and abundantly the commodity on which, more than any other single material except coal, modern industry was to depend for its essential equipment. Nineteenth century industrialisation may have been started by the textile innovations of the end of the eighteenth century. Sustained industrialisation however depended upon the availability of coal and iron, and would have been inconceivable without the steam engine and the technical progress in the iron industry which also took effect in the last three decades or so of the eighteenth century.'

Phyllis Deane, *The First Industrial Revolution*

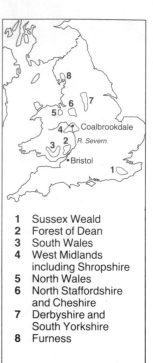

1   Sussex Weald
2   Forest of Dean
3   South Wales
4   West Midlands
     including Shropshire
5   North Wales
6   North Staffordshire
     and Cheshire
7   Derbyshire and
     South Yorkshire
8   Furness

Furthermore the iron industry played a very different role from that of cotton. Cotton developed from domestic handicrafts to large scale enterprises. Iron was already organised on this basis as early as the sixteenth century. Secondly, unlike cotton, iron expanded after 1780 upon the basis of domestic raw material. Thirdly, the innovation of substituting coal for charcoal developed by Abraham Derby around 1709, demonstrates the dependence of the iron industry upon the plentiful supply of another domestic raw material.

There is little doubt that the substitution of coking coal for charcoal was the most significant technological change in the iron industry. Even then its adoption was slow and historians disagree as to the reasons. The fact remains, however, that coke burns much slower than charcoal and, in addition, requires a powerful blast of air to raise it to a satisfactory temperature for smelting. Initially water power was used but it was only with the adoption of the Watt and Boulton steam engine from around 1775 onwards that a sufficiently strong and continuous blast was available to produce pig-iron.

Fourthly, the iron industry was dependent upon the demand of other industries. The effect of this factor meant that the development of the iron industry was intimately connected with the fortunes of other British industries.

Whether a 'leading' sector or not, the rapid rise of the iron industry was due to its ability to develop the technology to meet increasing demand. What were these difficulties which faced the development of the iron industry and how were they overcome?

1   Central Scotland
2   North East
3   Cumberland
4   South Yorkshire/
     Derbyshire
5   North Wales
6   Staffordshire
7   Shropshire
8   South Wales

EXAMINING THE EVIDENCE
Technological change in the iron industry
Source A: Iron production prior to 1760

There were coke blast furnaces only. Experiments using coal were unsuccessful due to the sulphur content of the coal which made the metal brittle.

Pig iron was cast directly but few of the products produced in this way were of good quality.

For superior quality products pig iron was reheated in a forge and hammered to produce bar or wrought iron essential for tools and household implements requiring strength. The hammers were powered by water power.

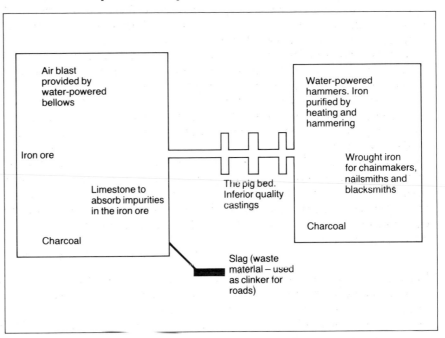

Air blast provided by water-powered bellows

Iron ore

Limestone to absorb impurities in the iron ore

Charcoal

The pig bed. Inferior quality castings

Water-powered hammers. Iron purified by heating and hammering

Wrought iron for chainmakers, nailsmiths and blacksmiths

Charcoal

Slag (waste material – used as clinker for roads)

Source B: Problems facing the iron industry in the early eighteenth century

- Dependence on charcoal fuel.

- British ores contained as much as 50 per cent waste.

- Charcoal difficult to transport over distance as it disintegrates easily.

- Transportation expensive.

- Timber resources increasingly scarce. Only high grade charcoal free from impurities could be used to smelt iron.

- Dependence on water power for blast furnaces forges, hammers and rolling and slitting mills.

Source C: Abraham Derby and coke smelting of iron

About the year 1709 Abraham Derby came into Shropshire in Coalbrookdale ... He here cast Iron Goods in sand out of the Blast Furnace that blow'd with wood charcoal ... Sometime after he suggested the thought that it might be practicable to smelt the Iron ... with Pit Coal... Upon this he first try'd with raw coal as it came out of the Mines, but it did not answer. He not discouraged, had the coal coak'd into Cynder, as is done for drying Malt, and it then succeeded to his satisfaction.

Abraham II Derby's account of his father's iron works at Coalbrookdale

Source D: Slow spread of coke furnaces

The reason for the slow spread (of coke furnaces) was not so much because the Derby family kept their process a well-guarded secret, but because it took several decades for rising timber prices to make the coke smelting an economic proposition. Derby's success was due partly to a particular suitable type of coking coal (made from 'clod' coal) and partly due to his production of a very limited range of specialist products for which his cast iron was specially suitable.

M. Falkus, *Britain Transformed: An Economic and Social History 1700–1914*

Source E: The spread of iron-smelting with coke

There were various reasons why the technique (using coke-fired furnaces) spread slowly. There was the personality of Abraham Derby, who kept the knowledge to himself. Perhaps he was secretive, but, more likely, being a good Quaker, he was not given to boasting. However we can be sure that if other iron masters had been really interested they would have found out what he was doing. There are more convincing reasons.

Derby's coke iron was good enough for cooking pots (but) it contained phosphorous which made it brittle ... It could not convert to wrought iron, so Derby could not sell to forge masters. Secondly, there were, for some time, no great pressures on the industry. From about 1710 to 1740 the economy was quiet, even stagnant and as there was not much demand for iron, no one had any incentive to risk costly failure by trying a new and uncertain technique. Thirdly it is clear that the fuel crisis cannot have been as great as has been suggested ... It is possible that Derby was not so interested so much in fuel saving as in producing high temperatures ...

P.F. Speed, *The Growth of the British Economy 1700–1850*

Source F: Henry Cort and the production of cheap wrought iron

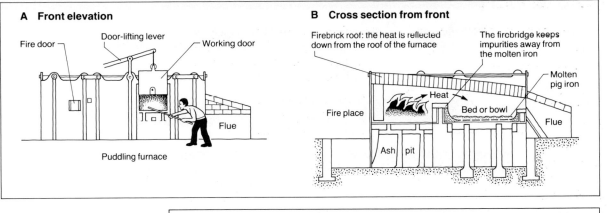

A   Front elevation

Fire door
Door-lifting lever
Working door
Flue
Puddling furnace

B   Cross section from front

Firebrick roof: the heat is reflected down from the roof of the furnace
The firebridge keeps impurities away from the molten iron
Molten pig iron
Heat
Fire place
Bed or bowl
Flue
Ash pit

Problem	• Coal-fired forges introduced impurities into iron which made it brittle.
Solution	• Before1750, high quality wrought iron must be produced from bar iron on charcoal forges.
Problem	• The process of heating and reheating pig iron in the forges to make bar iron was slow, expensive and wasteful of fuel.
Solution	• In 1783/84 Henry Cort took out a patent for a puddling and rolling process which used ordinary coal to produce wrought iron products.

Changes in industrial structure

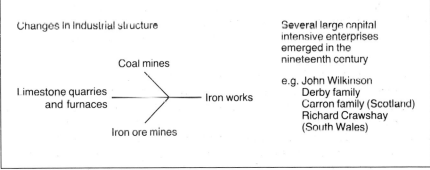

Changes in industrial structure

Coal mines
Limestone quarries and furnaces
Iron ore mines
Iron works

Several large capital intensive enterprises emerged in the nineteenth century

e.g. John Wilkinson
Derby family
Carron family (Scotland)
Richard Crawshay
(South Wales)

1 (a) What materials were used in the process of iron manufacture?

(b) Explain the advantage of Coalbrookdale as a manufacturing site for iron?

2 (a) In what ways do the sources agree and differ on the substitution of coke for charcoal?

(b) In what way did the development of the use of coking coal affect the location of the iron industry?

3 In what way did Henry Cort's process contribute to the development of the iron industry?

The importance of COAL to the British Economy

1 Contribution to National Income

1801	1901
1 per cent	6 per cent

2 The value of coal as an export

Before 1870	After 1870
5 per cent	10 per cent

3 Employer of Labour

1851	1871
one-eighth	one-sixth

4 Mechanisation

1900 – only 2 per cent of coal mechanically cut.
1913 – 8 per cent (75 per cent in U.S.A.)

5 Output 1700–1900 in millions of tons

1700	–	2.9
1750	–	5.2
1775	–	8.8
1800	–	15.0
1815	–	22.0
1830	–	30.3
1854	–	64.7 (first official figures)
1865	–	98.2
1895	–	189.7
1913	–	287.4 (the highest ever)

6 Consumption of coal in Scotland and Britain

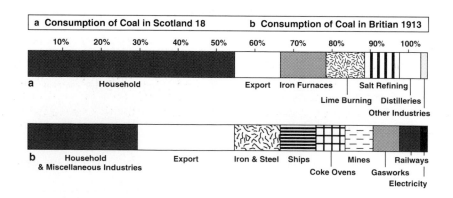

a Consumption of Coal in Scotland 18   b Consumption of Coal in Britian 1913

10% 20% 30% 40% 50% 60% 70% 80% 90% 100%

a Household   Export Iron Furnaces   Salt Refining
Lime Burning Distilleries
Other Industries

b Household   Export   Iron & Steel Ships   Mines   Railways
& Miscellaneous Industries   Coke Ovens Gasworks
Electricity

7 Coal-cutting in the late nineteenth century

COAL CUTTING IN A WIGAN PIT IN THE LATE NINETEENTH CENTURY. TEMPERATURES IN THE PIT COULD
REACH 80°F. BRITAIN LAGGED FAR BEHIND THE USA IN THE INTRODUCTION OF MECHANISED COAL CUTTING.

Questions

1 (a) Of what significance was the coal
industry to the British economy?
(b) In what ways did the nature of
this contribution alter during the
course of the nineteenth century?

2 Production increased despite little
growth in methods of mechanical
cutting? How then is it possible to
account for this increased output?

Coal – the fuel for revolution?

George Stephenson once remarked

'The Lord Chancellor now sits upon a bag of wool; but wool has long ceased to be emblematical of the staple commodity of England. He ought rather to sit upon a bag of coals, though it might not prove so comfortable a seat.'

To George Stephenson Britain's industrial supremacy was based upon the natural resource that this country possessed in abundance and, it is claimed, fuelled the industrial revolution.

● Was George Stephenson's claim for the coal industry justified?

● If so, what role did it play in the Industrial Revolution?

The importance of coal to British industrialisation

Whilst coal was an important industry in its own right it was equally important to many other industries and processes. T.S. Ashton asserts,

'... fuel was basic to the development of most processes of production, and the relatively slow rate of progress in coal mining set the limits to the expansion of British industry in general.'

T.S. Ashton, *The Industrial Revolution*

Consider, for example, the contribution coal may have made to the following industries:

Transport = Canals and Railways

Iron	Steam
Gas Production	Steamships
Distilleries	Salt Refining
Domestic Uses	Glass

Yet the ubiquitous presence of coal should not lead us to exaggerate its importance. Consider the following factors in relation to the coal industry:

● The contribution to the national income was never more than 1 per cent until late into the nineteenth century.

● The industry experienced steady rather than spectacular growth.

● Coal is a primary product which involves no processing or manufacture. Thus there is little value-added factor to the product.

● Mining involves little development of skills which can be transferred to other industries.

TALKING POINT
The causes of industrial growth

Industrial changes often go hand in hand. How would transport changes, developments in coal, new sources of power, all affect the iron industry? What other factors were important?

• The industry is labour-intensive which means returns will diminish as richer coal seams and fields become exhausted, as shown in the figures below:

1850 – 264 tons per man

1870 – 373

1890 – 358

1913 – 260

• The majority of pits were very small concerns. In 1913, 1589 separate companies ran 3289 collieries. This reduced the amount of capital available for technological development

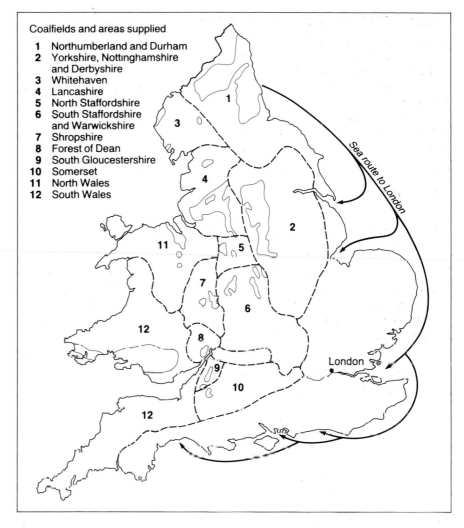

Coalfields and areas supplied

1 Northumberland and Durham
2 Yorkshire, Nottinghamshire and Derbyshire
3 Whitehaven
4 Lancashire
5 North Staffordshire
6 South Staffordshire and Warwickshire
7 Shropshire
8 Forest of Dean
9 South Gloucestershire
10 Somerset
11 North Wales
12 South Wales

Coal production

Coal output by Regions 1854–1913 (millions of tons)			
	1854	*1884*	*1913*
North East	15.4	36.1	56.4
Yorkshire	7.3	19.2	43.4
Midlands	3.9	16.1	38.8
S. Wales	8.5	24.8	56.8
Scotland	7.4	20.4	42.5
Others	22.2	44.2	49.2
Total	64.7	160.8	287.1

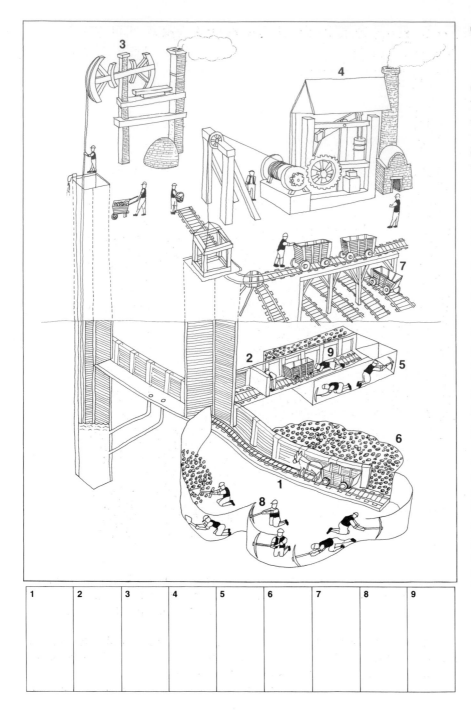

1 Study the picture.

(a) Explain the numbered features in this picture of a Midlands colliery around 1820.

(b) What technical developments had taken place which you can identify in the illustration?

2 'Even if coal was not a leading industry, then at least it was essential for others that undoubtedly were; like iron and cotton.'

To what extent do you agree with this statement?

(a) What do you understand by the term 'leading industry'. Refer to the section 'Cotton – the leading sector' and 'Iron – A revolution in Technology'.

(b) What are the arguments for and against coal being a leading industry in its own right?

(c) What are the arguments in support of coal as a significant contributor to a range of industries?

1	2	3	4	5	6	7	8	9

Powering the industrial revolution
The steam engine

NEWCOMEN'S ENGINE.

'The new form of power, and, no less, the new transmitting mechanisms … were the pivot on which industry swung into the modern age.'

T.S. Ashton, *The Industrial Revolution*

It is a common belief that the Industrial Revolution was also the age of the steam engine … In fact traditional forms of power were important for a long time while steam made only slow progress.

P.F. Speed, *The Growth of the British Economy 1700–1850*

Water power in the eighteenth century

For centuries man has attempted to harness other sources of power to complement human muscle. The eighteenth and nineteenth centuries are particularly important in the history of the human race because they witnessed a major breakthrough in the use of non-human power.

At the beginning of the eighteenth century, industry in Britain was able to draw on three sources of energy – animals, wind and water. Horses could be used to drive machinery and push and pull loads, but there was a limit to their versatility.

Water was of more potential significance and the rapid industrialisation of Britain depended largely on the increasingly efficient and widespread use of water power.

Water wheels

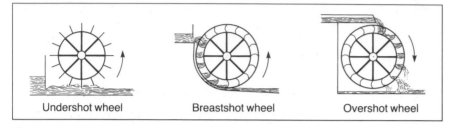

Undershot wheel   Breastshot wheel   Overshot wheel

Which of these water wheels make the most efficient use of water?

'May 29. Another very warm day, and the dry weather is much against us as the river Ribble is very low, in the afternoon our looms go very slow for want of water. August 28. There were 30 mills stopped in Blackburn this week for want of water, and will not start again until wet weather sets in.'

Experiments in the second half of the eighteenth century by John Smeaton helped to establish principles for the construction of the most efficient wheels. i.e. Power = Volume of water x Fall of water. The velocity of the water is not important.

To some extent these problems could be overcome. Quarry Bank Mill at Styal in Yorkshire was one of the earliest cotton factories and demonstrates the increasingly sophisticated ways in which water could be used to drive the mill machinery.

Notice the two diagrams which show the relation of Quarry Bank Mill to the nearby river. Think about the ways could the water source be used efficiently to power the mill.

What local conditions would suit each type of wheel? What problems were connected with the use of water as an energy source?

Phase I   ## Phase II

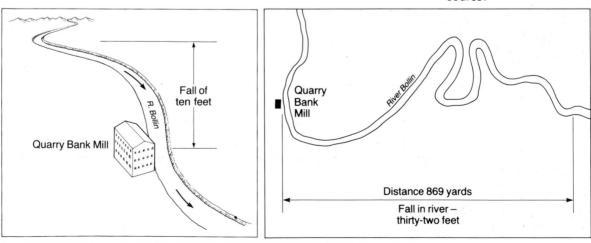

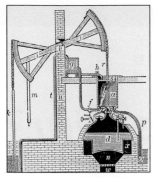

THOMAS NEWCOMEN'S ENGINE.
(32 LBS OF COAL TO GENERATE
1 H.P.)

In 1784 Samuel Greg, the owner of Quarry Bank Mill, had a long head-race channel constructed in order to give a fall to the mill of ten feet. In 1796 Peter Ewart joined Samuel Greg as his partner. Ewart was a gifted engineer and recognised the value of steam power, persuading his partner to buy an engine from the firm of Boulton and Watt. In 1801, a second wheel was installed which required a greater volume of water. This was achieved by the construction of a weir at the large bend in the river.

Between 1817 and 1820 Thomas Hewes, a Manchester millwright, supervised the design and installation of an 100 h.p. iron wheel. Although Ewart had solved the problem of supplying a sufficient volume of water. Hewes needed to double the fall of water. After surveying the river Bollin, a level tunnel was constructed 869 yards from Giant's Castle which provided a fall of 32 feet at the site of the mill.

The development of the steam engine

In 1796 Peter Ewart bought a steam engine for Quarry Bank Mill but only as a supplement to water power. In so doing he had to persuade his partner of the merits of steam compared to water.

JAMES WATT'S ENGINE (9LBS OF COAL TO GENERATE 1 H.P.)

James Watt, the creative innovator behind the development of the steam engine, came from a prosperous Scottish family with a background in mathematics and engineering. In the early 1760s he was employed as a scientific instrument maker at Glasgow university. When he was asked to repair a model of Thomas Newcomen's steam engine, which was used for demonstration purposes by Professor Joseph Black. He began to ponder ways of making it more efficient.

Look at the diagram of Thomas Newcomen's engine, developed during 1705–20, which was employed for pumping water out of mines. Watt observed the engine had particular defects which detracted from its efficiency. Watt discussed possible improvements with members of the University during 1765. During the course of a Sunday morning stroll he hit upon a solution and within a few weeks he made a prototype model. It was to be several years, however, before the technical difficulties of producing a full scale engine were overcome. Alongside Newcomen's engine is the model Watt produced.

JAMES WATT'S ENGINE. SUN AND PLANETARY MOTION PATENTED.

Questions

1 How has Watt modified Newcomen's engine and how would this improve the efficiency of his engine?

2 Study the diagram which shows a further improvement Watt added to his engine.

(a) What has been added to the steam engine?

(b) How would this addition to the steam engine enable it to be used in mills.

Draw up a list of the Advantages and Disadvantages of purchasing a steam engine from the firm of Boulton and Watt.

James Watt:
Inventor or entrepreneur?

James Watt was an outstanding inventor but his genius alone is insufficient to explain the success of the steam engine. During the development of the engine Watt had to survive by earning a living as a surveyor and chartered engineer.

James Watt's career decision

'I had now a choice whether to go on with the experiments on the engine, the event of which was uncertain, or to embrace an honorable and perhaps profitable job with less risk of lack of success – (the building of a canal)'

The canal company went bankrupt. Although Watt was now free to concentrate on developing the steam engine he had little business acumen.

James Watt as businessman

'I can on no account have anything to do with workmen, cash or workmen's accounts … I am not a man of regularity in business and have bad health. I would rather face a loaded cannon than settle an account or make a bargain.'

For several years John Roebuck, owner of the Carron Iron Works, financed Watt's work but was unable to supply the skilled technicians needed. In 1774 Roebuck in the face of financial difficulties, sold his share in Watt's invention to Mathew Boulton of Birmingham.

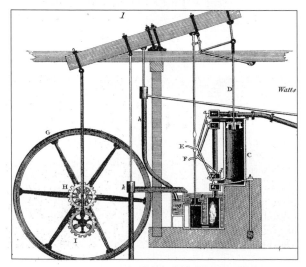

The Watt-Boulton partnership

'I was excited by two motives to offer you
my help, which were love of you and love
of a money getting ingenious project. I
presumed that your Engine would require
money, very accurate workmanship and
extensive letter writing to make it turn out
to the best advantage. The best means to
do the invention justice would be to keep
the engine making out of the hands of the
rule of thumb engineers. They, from
ignorance, want of experience and distance
away would be very likely to produce bad
and inaccurate workmanship … my idea
was to set up a factory near to my own by
the side of our canal. There I would erect
all the things needed for the completion of
engines. From this factory we would serve
all the world with engines of all sizes. By
these means and with your help we would
engage and instruct some excellent
workmen … If a monopoly, it is one by
means of which their mines are made more
productive than ever they were before.
Have we not given over to them two-thirds
of the advantages gained from its use in the
saving of fuel …? They say it is
inconvenient for the mining interests to be
burdened with the payment of engine dues.
Just as it is inconvenient for the person who
wishes to get at my purse that I should
keep my breeches pocket buttoned.'

The partnership was fortuitous. Watt and
Boulton were granted a patent for the sun
and planetary motion which made them sole
producers of the steam engine. The patent
was not granted, however, without
opposition.

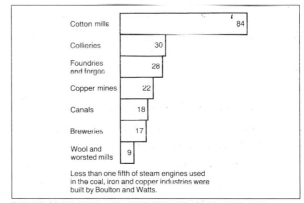

Cotton mills	84
Collieries	30
Foundries and forges	28
Copper mines	22
Canals	18
Breweries	17
Wool and worsted mills	9

Less than one fifth of steam engines used
in the coal, iron and copper industries were
built by Boulton and Watts.

THE USE OF BOULTON AND WATT STEAM ENGINES, 1775–1800.

By 1800 Watt and Boulton's patent expired
and other manufacturers were free to
manufacture their own. In that same year
there were 200 engines in Shropshire alone;
employed in a variety of industries; brick-
works, ironworks, china factories, flourmills
and, of particular importance, cotton mills. By
1840, four out of five cotton mills used steam.

THE BOULTON AND WATT FACTORY AT SOHO, NEAR BIRMINGHAM.

A Revolution in Technology? – Iron, Coal and Steam 91

EXAMINING THE EVIDENCE
The importance of the steam engine

Bold claims have been made for the steam engine's contribution to the Industrial Revolution. Because of the steam engine's later spectacular history there has been a general tendency to see it as the main motive force and to greatly underplay the part played by water power. Up to 1800 it is relatively easy to estimate the influence of the steam engine in British industry for Boulton and Watt held the patent.

The contribution of water power in mills in 1838 was about 26 per cent (12,000 h.p.). By 1850 the proportion had dropped to 15 per cent. But this tells us little as to when the steam engine began to significantly supersede water power.

Local research seems to indicate that the steam engine came relatively late to British industry; the breakthrough probably occurring in the 1820s when fully automatic spinning machinery and power looms became a practical possibility and the economic boom accelerated factory building.

Yet if the contribution of steam power now appears to have proceeded slowly during the Industrial Revolution its ultimate significance was never in doubt.

Source A

In 1785 Boulton and Watt made an engine for a cotton-mill at Papplewick in Notts, and in the same year Arkwright's patent expired. These two facts taken together mark the introduction of the factory system.

A. Toynbee, *The Industrial Revolution*

Source B

The new form of power, and, no less, the new transmitting mechanisms by which this was made to do work previously done by hand and muscle, were the pivot on which industry swung into the modern age.

T.S. Ashton, *The Industrial Revolution*

Source C

The use of a common motive power, and especially of an artificial one, thenceforward imposed general laws upon the development of all industries. The successive improvements in the steam engine reacted equally on the working of mines and of metals, on weaving and on transport. The industrial world came to resemble one huge factory, in which the acceleration, the slowing down and stoppage of the main engine determines the activities of the workers and regulates the rates of production.

P. Mantoux, *The Industrial Revolution*

Source D
Steam power in the cotton industry

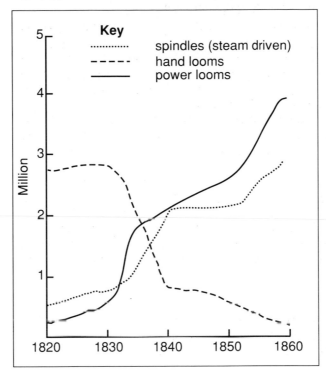

Key
- spindles (steam driven)
- hand looms
- power looms

Source E

As the traditional forms of power were slow to decline, so steam was slow to grow. Steam-engines were unknown in many industries, and rare in certain parts of the country. Apart from breweries, there were few in London, because most of its industries were handicrafts. It must have distressed Boulton and Watt to know that, outside their own Soho works, there were only two of their engines in the whole of Birmingham. Here, also, handicrafts were common. By the time their patent expired in 1800, Boulton and Watt had erected some 500 engines. Their average was only 15 h.p. and between them they gave a mere 7500 h.p. Today, a single turbo-generator produces twenty times as much. There were Newcomen engines as well, but probably there were no more than 1200 steam engines in all, giving together less than 20 000 h.p. The table shows the growth of steam power through the nineteenth century:

	1800	1850	1870	1907
horsepower	20 000 (estimated)	300 000	1000 000	9 700 000

It is clear from this when the steam revolution took place in industry as a whole.

There are, however, important qualifications. In the first place these figures do not include steam locomotives and they were vital for the development of the railways. However, they were not too numerous until the late 1840s, while the railways themselves did not make a significant contribution to the economy until well after 1850.

More important during our period were the colliery engines, and they are not included in any of the figures in the table, save the estimate for 1800. Though the smaller coal-mines made do with horse gins, the larger ones had to have steam, and most employed at least two engines. Usually one was of the Newcomen type, for pumping, while the other was a rotative engine, for winding.

Finally, much of the steam power in manufacturing industry was concentrated in cotton:

Growth of Power in the Cotton Industry

	Steam horsepower	Water horsepower	Imports of raw cotton (millions of pounds)
1838	47 000	13 000	400
1850	71 000	12 000	620
1856	88 000	9 000	800
1870	300 000	8 000	1100

Clearly then, the importance we attach to steam power must depend to quite an extent on how highly we rate the contribution of cotton to the Industrial Revolution.

P.F. Speed *The Growth of the British Economy 1700–1850*

Source F

Industry	Engines installed by 1800	
	No.	H.P.
Cotton Mills	84	1382
Foundries and Forges	28	618
Copper Mines	22	440
Collieries	30	380
Canals	18	261
Water Works	15	241

Source G
Factors when comparing steam and water power

Maximum size of engine	Steam 80h.p. Water 105h.p.
Cost of Fuel	Cost of machinery
Maintenance costs	Reliability

Source H
Iron output at Coalbrookdale

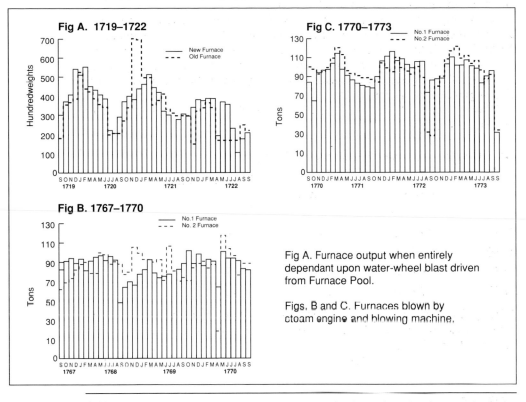

Fig A. Furnace output when entirely dependant upon water-wheel blast driven from Furnace Pool.

Figs. B and C. Furnaces blown by steam engine and blowing machine.

1 Why has so much importance been attached to the development of the steam engine?

2 (a) What problems were associated with adopting steam engines as a form of power for mills?

(b) What advantages did steam engines possess compared to alternative sources of power?

3 When and for what reasons did steam engines become widely adopted?

Review
Which industry can justifiably be described as the 'leading' sector?

The question as to which industry played the role of the 'leading' sector in the Industrial Revolution has been a theme to which constant reference has been made in this and the previous chapter.

1 (a) Briefly outline the competing claims that have been made for cotton, coal and iron.

(b) Which particular industry do you consider to have been more important than the other two?

(c) Justify your choice.

2 (a) Instead of considering each industry in isolation it may be more helpful to consider the ways in which these industries were inter-related.

(b) In what ways were the developments of these industries dependent upon one another?

(c) At what period of time did many of these developments occur?

(d) What role was played in the development of these industries by Britain's expanding trade?

3 Which of the two theories regarding industrial development do you find more accurate:

(a) One industry performing the role of a 'leading' sector, or,

(b) A cluster of industrial innovations which assisted the overall development of industrial growth?

5 Financing the Industrial Revolution

PREVIEW

'If we seek – it would be wrong to do so – for a single reason why the pace of economic development quickened about the middle of the eighteenth century, it is to this we must look. The deep mines, the solidly built factories, well constructed canals and substantial houses of the Industrial Revolution were the products of relatively cheap capital.'

T.S. Ashton, *The Industrial Revolution*

'Looking at the country as a whole … the crucial years at the end of the eighteenth century investment probably increased by no more than one and one-half per cent of national income. Certainly there were dramatic changes in the economy before there was one in the level of investment.'

P.F. Speed, *The Growth of the British Economy*

AN EXPLOSION OF JOINT STOCK COMPANIES. A SATIRICAL COMMENT BY HOGARTH.

The investment controversy

Inventions and innovations alone did not and could not produce industrial revolutions. The need for capital to be placed at the disposal of industry coupled to an adequate system of banking and credit facilities were essential pre-requisites.

Present day firms tend to raise money by selling shares to shareholders who delegate the management of the firm to a Board of Directors who, in turn, employ professional managers. In return for their investment shareholders receive a dividend derived from the profits of the company.

This form of business organisation was not available in the eighteenth century for disastrous speculations in the early part of the century had forced the government to pass laws against it. The South Sea Bubble Act of 1720 restricted partnerships to six members, each of whom were liable 'to his last shilling and acre for the debts of the enterprise' – an unlimited liability.

Limited liability was possible but could only be obtained through the formation of a joint-stock company. This organisation was particularly appropriate when large amounts of capital were required and the only way to raise sufficient capital was to offer the sale of shares to the general public. Despite these obvious advantages there was no rush by groups of partners to form joint stock companies. Few firms were large enough in the early eighteenth century to warrant this and the process was particularly cumbersome. Obtaining a charter from either Parliament or the Crown was costly, viewed with suspicion, and usually failed.

If the mobilisation of capital was so restricted by legislation and hostility, how did large amounts of money become available to finance money-hungry projects such as canals and railways?

Eighteenth century financial institutions

The Bank of England

The most important of the new institutions which opened up channels for the flow of capital were the banks. Joint stock banks in London and Edinburgh were established in the 1690s.

In 1694 The Bank of England raised £1 200 000 and loaned it to the government in return for £100 000 interest a year. Anyone who subscribed £500 could become a member of this joint-stock enterprise. In return for this privileged position the bank was not only allowed to accept deposits, make loans and issue notes but by an act of 1709 was the only bank of more than six members free to issue notes.

Thereafter the Bank of England developed in two important respects. As the Government's banker it managed the National Debt and, as it was backed by the government, it became regarded as a precious institution which must never be allowed to fail, because, if it did, national prestige would be damaged.

Secondly, banks throughout the country, realising the special secure status of the Bank of England, began to deposit their surpluses in its vaults. Country banks outside London would deposit their reserves with their London corresponding bank which in turn would use the facilities of the Bank of England.

The government had not desired the special status of the Bank of England but it was difficult to see how this central role could be avoided. Only the Bank of England could weather financial storms that would batter and destroy the less substantial country banks.

London private banks

All country banks needed a London agent to act on their behalf in the London money market and to deal with the Bank of England. Usually one or two of the partners of the London and country banks would be members of each others' Boards.

When the reserves of the country bank in the London bank were large enough it would buy government stock. The return on these 'consuls', as they were called, was usually low at about 3 per cent but at least they were safe because of government backing. If a government failed to honour its debts then no-one was safe.

The London agent could also enter the 'bill-market' where there was the possibility of investment in trading and industrial concerns. This was more risky but at least offered the possibility of greater returns.

Merchant banks

As their name implies they specialised in loans to one particular type of trading activity. As they developed international business relations, they also developed the specialist knowledge to discount international bills of Exchange.

Country banks

The industrialist and farmer required more localised financial assistance and this service was provided by the country bank. As far as is known the first provincial bank was set up in 1716 by James Wood, a mercer and draper of Gloucester, but it was not until after the 1760s that private banks of this kind became general. In agricultural districts the local corn merchants often graduated into banking. As manufacturing developed, industrialists such as Arkwright, Wilkinson, Boulton and Watt established banks of their own. They were probably motivated by the need to obtain cash for wages as well as an outlet for their growing capital. Lloyds and Barclays originated in this way.

By 1793 there were about 400; by 1815 about 900. Despite their rapid growth in numbers they had one major weakness. If their reserves ran low they had to rely on the Bank of England to assist them. Several financial crises between 1793–1825 resulted in the devastation of country banks.

WILKINSON TOKEN COINAGE.

COUNTRY BANK NOTE ISSUE.

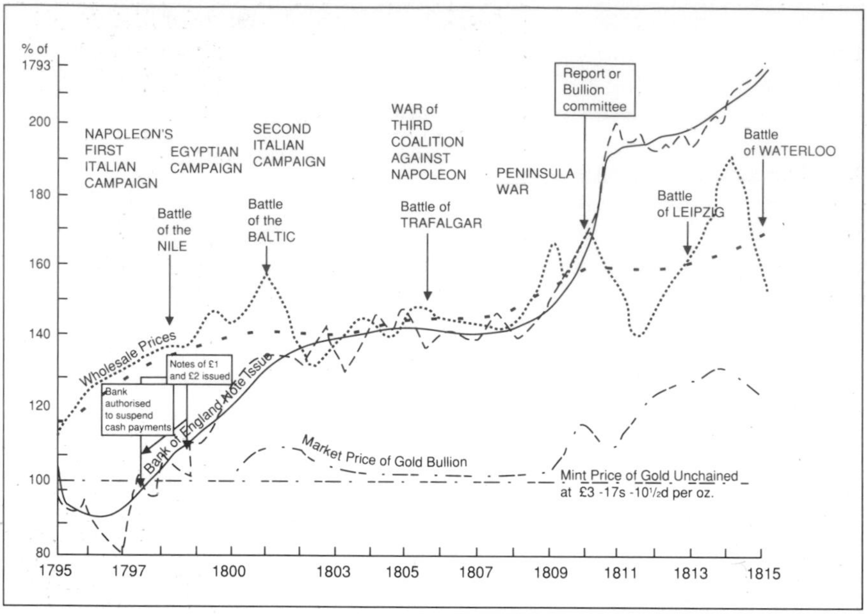
% of 1793
200
180
160
140
120
100
80
1795
1797
1800
1803
1805
1807
1809
1811
1813
1815
NAPOLEON'S FIRST ITALIAN CAMPAIGN
EGYPTIAN CAMPAIGN
SECOND ITALIAN CAMPAIGN
WAR of THIRD COALITION AGAINST NAPOLEON
PENINSULA WAR
Report or Bullion committee
Battle of WATERLOO
Battle of LEIPZIG
Battle of the NILE
Battle of the BALTIC
Battle of TRAFALGAR
Wholesale Prices
Notes of £1 and £2 issued
Bank authorised to suspend cash payments
Bank of England Note Issue
Market Price of Gold Bullion
Mint Price of Gold Unchained at £3 -17s -10½d per oz.

EFFECTS OF BANK RESTRICTION ACT

The stock exchange

Banks normally dealt with relatively short term loans. Longer-term and generally larger loans are more easily met by the issue of shares.

In the late seventeenth century there were already individuals who were making a living out of buying and selling stocks and shares. 'Brokers' bought and sold on behalf of others whilst 'Jobbers' bought and sold for personal profit.

Initially they had been allowed to operate in the Royal Exchange but were ejected because of their noisy behaviour. Thereafter they managed their business from a host of coffee shops which were favourite social meeting places. Jonathan's coffee shop became the most famous.

In 1773 they obtained their own building in Threadneedle Street, moving to larger premises in 1802 at Capel court which still forms part of the present day Stock Exchange building. Its first 'List', issued in 1803, showed that its dealings were no longer confined to Government Funds and the East India Company, but also public utilities and insurance companies. Middle class savings largely went into insurance and those of workers into Friendly Societies, encouraged by the passing of Rose's Act in 1793 which gave legal protection to funds. By 1801 there were over 7 000 Friendly Clubs with a membership of 600 000. It is evident, however, that working class savings of this kind were not large enough to make a substantial contribution to the capital available for industrial and commercial purposes.

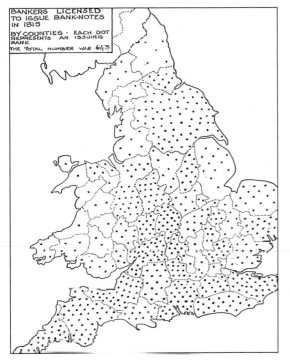

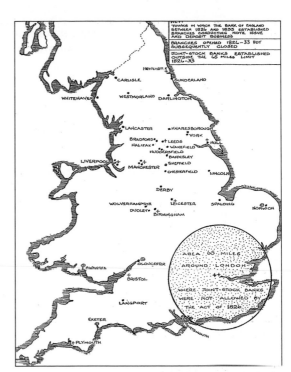

BANKERS LICENSED TO ISSUE BANK NOTES IN 1815.

NEW BANKS OPENED (1826–1833).

Business capital and the industrial revolution

Assignment

Assume you are business entrepreneurs in the latter part of the eighteenth century and wish to set up and develop an industrial project. In small groups consider the following steps by which you will engage in a successful enterprise.

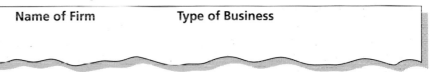

Name of Firm	Type of Business

1 Which form of business organisation will you choose? What are the advantages and disadvantages of each?

- Partnership (Sleeping)

- Partnership (Active)

- Re-invest profit from previous enterprise

- Loan from an individual on security

- Joint Stock Company

2 What will you need capital for?

Expanding industry required two types of capital

Fixed capital	Variable capital (working/circulating)
Machinery	Stocks of raw material
Building	Goods in process of manufacture
	Unsold goods
	Trade credit to customers

To help you decide which type of capital would be of most importance consider the table below of fixed and variable capital compiled by Professor Pollard.

	Fixed Capital	Value of stock material on hand
Ambrose Crowley's Ironworks (1728)	£12,000	£93,000
Bersham Iron Furnace (1735)	£170	£1,245
Llangavelach (Swansea) Copper works (1745)	£5,400	£37,700
Stockport Silk Mill (1762)	£2,800	£13,900

Open University, *Industry and Society*

3 Imagine you have paid off the capital costs of your enterprise – the buildings and machinery. You still have two major outgoings – wages and raw materials, and only one source of income – the sale of your finished product. In what way would you:

- pay for the raw materials you need;
- pay wages?

4 How would the method you use to pay for the raw materials affect your monetary system?

5 If the merchant who supplied you with the raw materials wanted cash, whom would he approach:

- you
- a country banker
- a merchant bank
- a London bank
- the Bank of England?

6 What would the one you have chosen actually do?

7 If the country banker is pressed for cash and can't approach you what then must he do?

What dangers face the country banker at this stage?

8 Imagine you are now in need of capital to expand your industry and you approach a country bank. At the same time there is a disastrous harvest requiring imports of foreign corn. How will this affect your capital requirements and your ability to use the country bank?

Examining the Evidence
The origins of industrial capital

There are two main sources from which additional capital could have been derived. Either there had to be significant changes in the financial habits of the wealthier classes, or there was a need for new social groups whose incomes were growing faster than the average.

In the early years of the industrial revolution most business concerns were owned by families or partnerships of two or three friends.

Source A: Samuel Walker, an early entrepreneur in the iron industry

This year we made about 39 tons of castings; and, as we had occasion, took in raw hands, such as nailors, husbandmen, &c.

This year Saml. Walker, finding business increase, was obliged to give up his school, and built himself a house at the end of the old cottage, then thought he was fixed for life; then we allowed ourselves ten shillings a week each for wages to maintain our families.

NOVEMBER 1746

This year we made 63½ tons of castings; and now, a valuation being made of the effects, the capital amounted to	£400	0	0
Jonathan Walker put into stock	100	0	0
John Crawshaw put into stock	50	0	0
Saml. Walker added	50	0	0
Which made the capital	£600	0	0

Minutes relating to the Proceedings of the Foundry Company
begun by S. and A. Walker (1741)

Source B: Sources of industrial capital

Robert Owen borrowed £100 from his brother and went into partnership with a mechanic who made looms.

James Watt borrowed from his friend Dr. Black and then went into partnership with Mathew Boulton, who had inherited the major share in a family business.

Richard Arkwright began by borrowing from a publican and later went into partnership with the Strutt family.

In the Iron industry the Derbys and Wilkinsons were long established family businesses.

The Carron Ironworks which required £12,000 outlay was financed by three partners and a friend.

Source C: The role of capital in early industrialisation

There seems no reason to suppose that capital accumulation does by itself exercise so predominant an influence on economic development. ... Whatever may have been true in the past, it is now technical innovation – the introduction of new and cheaper ways of doing things – that dominates economic progress. Whether technical innovation, in the sectors of the economy in which it occurs, makes large demands on capital is, how-ever, very doubtful. Many innovations can be given effect to in the course of capital replacement out of depreciation allowances, which, in an expanding economy, may be fully as large as net savings. Others may actually reduce the stock of capital required.

In Britain, the real costs of industrialization were greatly increased by the inevitable misapplication of resources, false starts, errors and rapid obso-lescence inevitable in a pioneer economy. The badly planned towns and transport networks were, perhaps, among the most costly tributes paid to experience.

A.K. Cairncross, The Place of Capital In Economic Progress

Source D: The inter-dependence of industries on capital

'The trade in salt and coal ... helped the flow of money from Liverpool to pay for opening Cheshire salt mines and the south-west Lancashire coal-field ... In turn this led to the making of better transport between Liverpool and its inland area and to the greater use of shipping both coastal and overseas ... The growing town of Liverpool, with its smithies, glassworks, and its salt refinery ... made increasing demands on the col-lieries of south-west Lancashire ... By 1769 the rich coalfield around St Helens was open. By 1771, 90 000 tons of coal were being carried down the canal annually, 45 568 tons to Liverpool.'

F.E. Hyde, The Growth of Liverpool's Trade 1700–1950

Source E: The landed interests and capital

The English landed interest had long accepted the idea that land was an agent of production and not merely an instrument of feudal and social prestige; and through their skilful manipulation of the landlord-tenant sys-tem of management, through, particularly, their employment of able and progressive estate stewards or agents – men whose role in our agricultural development has not been sufficiently appreciated – the more astute landowners were able to get the best of both worlds, the world of political and social prestige which the mere possession of land in sufficient quan-tity conferred, and the world of commercial affluence which the careful selection and encouragement of good tenants could open. The Duke of Bridgewater may have been the greatest of his class who sowed the seeds and reaped the harvest – in his case a fabulous one – of canal enterprise, but he had many imitators, and numerous other landed proprietors made themselves individually responsible for the promotion and completion of canals. Of the £13,000,000 of canal company stock subscribed between 1758 and 1802, mainly from the localities which the projects were designed to serve, a very large proportion must have come from the pock-ets of landed proprietors, many of whom had local development in mind as much as – or more than – mere speculation. Such relatively unknown figures as Walter Spencer Stanhope, with extensive estates in Yorkshire and Derbyshire, interested in coal mines, iron manufacture, the cloth industry and promoter of the bill for the Barnsley Canal, and Joseph Wilkes of Overseal in Leicestershire, improving farmer, canal promoter, banker, cotton manufacturer and creator of the small industrial town of

Measham, show the scope and versatility of the rural capitalist-turned-promoter; and there were many like them. The railway age offers parallel cases of the transference of landed incomes and entrepreneurial leadership to non-rural objectives. Such names as Earl Fitzwilliam in Yorkshire; the Lowthers of Cumberland; Lord Durham and the Marquis of Londonderry; and perhaps particularly the Duke of Devonshire who literally called into being the town of Barrow-in-Furness, are reminders of the aristocratic origin of much of the industrial enterprise north of the Trent.

J.D. Chambers and G.E. Mingay, *The Agricultural Revolution 1750–1880*

Source F: The depletion of capital through conspicuous spending

It was a characteristic of this class (upper) to spend a high proportion of its income above what was required for current consumption on building stately homes. Virtually every landed family built a stately home; some built several; others rebuilt from time to time. Not a few indulged this form of conspicuous consumption to the extent of bankrupting themselves in the process.

A check through half a dozen random volumes of this survey (Durham, Hertfordshire, Middlesex, Northumberland, Nottinghamshire and Suffolk) reveals two broad generalizations that are of interest. First, there were significant regional variations in the chronologies of stately home building; and, second, between 1660 and 1900 there were two major periods of this kind of building – from the 1690s to the 1730s, and from the 1790s to the 1830s. Though there was some revival during the 1750s, '60s and '70s, at no time between the 1730s and '90s did the level reach the peaks of the early decades of both eighteenth and nineteenth centuries. There was relatively little building after the 1830s. This evidence is, of course, far too shaky to serve as a basis for working generalizations, but it may be sufficient to indicate that there were significant fluctuations in this important variable, and that there may possibly have been some reduction in this source of capital consumption in the key half-century from 1740 to 1790 which freed capital for other employment.

M.W. Flinn, *Origins of the Industrial Revolution*

Source G: Capital investment by the landed interests

Where landlords sought industrial employment for their capital, the industries they turned to were generally those most intimately connected with the land – the extractive and metallurgical industries. The Earl of Balcarres, for example, entered a partnership with a Wigan ironmaster, James Corbett, in 1788 to develop the coal and iron resources of his Lancashire estates. Similarly, Lord Penrhyn invested the accumulated rents of his estates to develop the North Wales slate quarrying industry from the 1760s, while in 1777 the Earl of Elgin laid out what was claimed to be the largest private limeworks in Britain on the shores of the Firth of Forth at Rosyth.

The influence of the downward trend in the rate of interest was primarily to stimulate borrowing and investment. It can hardly have acted as a magnet to draw hoardings into the open capital market or to dissuade the wealthy from putting their savings into unproductive stately homes. Yet the fact that the enormously enhanced demand for capital did not lead, except in wartime, to any very serious upward pressure on rates of interest indicates that the new demands were easily met. Thus, the relatively low rate of interest at a time of high demand for capital was not so much the instrument of capital formation, as an indication that the capital already existed and was now being channelled into productive employment.

M.W. Flinn, The Origins of the Industrial Revolution

Source H: Increasing need of industry for greater amounts of capital

In fact, during the Industrial Revolution, it was often the other way round. S.D. Chapman gives these figures for the firm of Coltman & Gardiner, who were stocking manufacturers:

	1783	1792	1800
Fixed capital:			
Warehouse	580	580	580
Frames	186	896	823
Working capital:			
Raw materials, work			
in progress, stock	1319	2305	2967
Customers' debts:	3215	3844	5874

The following shows the fixed and working capital as percentages:

	1783	1792	1800
Fixed	14.7	19.4	13.6
Working	85.3	80.6	86.4
	100.0	100.0	100.0

The more highly developed industries used the factory system, so they had more fixed capital, but it was not excessive. By 1800 only £10 million had been spent in the cotton industry, which amounted to only two weeks of the nation's income. Admittedly it was possible to spend nearly £100 000 on a new, fully equipped, fully integrated cotton factory in the 1830s, but that was exceptional. A water-frame mill cost £5000 at the most, while in the woollen industry even less was needed. An old barn could be converted and the most expensive piece of equipment, the steam-engine, need cost no more than £150. If the textile factory was a modest one, the fixed capital might be a third of the total, rising to a half if the factory were more elaborate. All this meant that a man or a group of partners with moderate wealth could start a business easily enough, and then build it up, provided only they had the self-discipline to plough back their profits.

P.F. Speed, The Growth of the British Economy 1700–1800

---

1 What was the most common form of industrial organisation in the latter half of the eighteenth century?

2 What were the principal sources from which capital was raised for these business enterprises?

3 (a) What type of capital demand was made?

(b) How large were these capital demands?

4 How were these capital demands exaggerated?

5 (a) From which social group could capital derive?

(b) Which social class appears to have made the largest contribution?

6 (a) In what ways was capital diverted from industrial undertakings?

(b) How did this affect the supply of capital at crucial times of industrial development?

REVIEW
What part did capital play in developing industry in the late eighteenth century?

Essay

Write an essay to answer this question. In order to plan your essay, consider the main items you need to include:

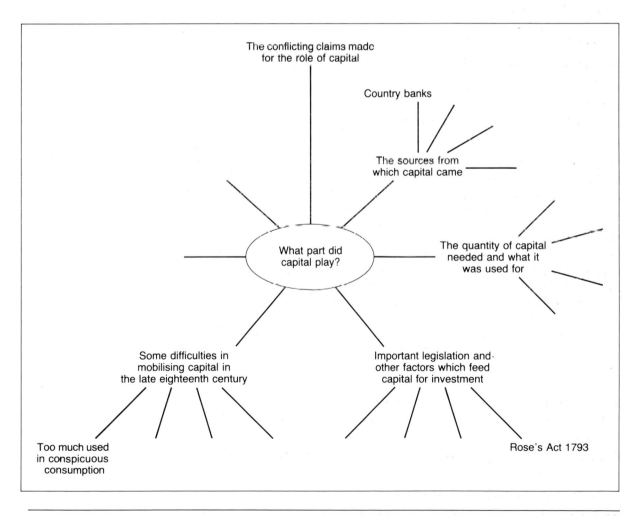

1 Try to complete the rest of these diagramatic notes, perhaps in discussion with a partner.

2 Then use each of the main sections as the paragraphs of your essay.

3 How will you link the paragraphs together? What will you include in the first sentence of each paragraph? What will you include in your final paragraph?

6 Population and Industrialisation

Preview

A COURT FOR KING CHOLERA.

'Move your eye on which side you may, you behold nothing but great riches and yet greater resources ... It is vain to talk of tables of births and lists of houses and windows, as proofs of our losses of people: the flourishing state of agriculture, our manufactures, and commerce, with our great wealth prove the contrary.'

Arthur Young *Secretary to the Board of Agriculture 1780*

'Population increases in a geometrical, food in an arithmetical ratio ... vice and misery ... famine disease and war are the necessary natural agents to curtail the multiplication of numbers of human beings.'

The Reverend Thomas Malthus, *Essay on the Principle of Population (1799)*

The growth of population

In 1700 the population of England and Wales stood at around 5.8 million. In 1901 this number had risen to 35 million and by 1981, 53 million. In addition, life expectancy rose from about 35 in 1700 to 70 today. To maintain such a startling rise in population and living standards is one of the most astonishing features of Britain's economic history.

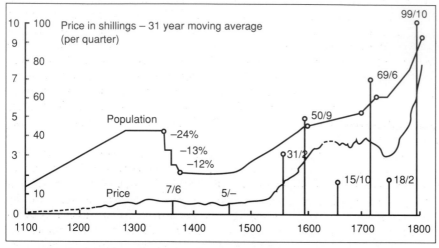

GROWTH OF POPULATION.

1 Divide the graph into phases of:

(a) increasing population

(b) stagnating population

(c) decreasing population.

2 Compare the period 1100–1700 with post 1700. What conclusions can you come to regarding the growth of population between these two periods?

The following figures give detailed information of population trends between 1700 and 1900.

Population of England and Wales in millions

1700	–	5.83	1770	–	7.12	1841	–	15.91
1710	–	6.01	1780	–	7.58	1851	–	17.92
1720	–	6.04	1790	–	8.21	1861	–	20.16
1730	–	6.00	1801	–	9.16	1871	–	22.71
1740	–	6.01	1811	–	10.16	1881	–	25.97
1750	–	6.25	1821	–	12.00	1891	–	29.00
1760	–	6.66	1831	–	13.89	1901	–	35.52

1 Construct a bar graph showing the total population of England and Wales from 1700 to 1900.

2 Calculate the rate of growth for each decade and place the figure above the respective decade to which it refers. This is calculated as follows;

$$\frac{1801 \text{ figure}}{1811 \text{ figure}} \times 100 = \% \text{ increase or decrease}$$

3 Which decades show the biggest rates of growth?

Estimating population before 1801

The first official census in Great Britain did not take place until 1801. Before that date we have only estimates based on a variety of different sources.

Parish registers are a rich source on information. From the middle of the sixteenth century ministers of the Church of England were obliged by law to keep records of births, deaths and marriages in their parish. There are, as one might suppose, a number of difficulties when attempting to draw conclusions based on this evidence. Their survival is uneven and better records exist for the southern counties than the northern. The amount of detail varies enormously; far less in the eighteenth than the nineteenth century. As the population became more urbanised under-registration increased and perhaps as many as one-tenth of all marriages were not registered in church, being referred to as 'irregular unions'. The laxity of ministers who left the documentation to negligent clerks adds to a catalogue of imperfections in the system.

In addition to parish registers, population returns were also made on a limited scale and for other purposes than a census return such as taxation, muster rolls and bills of mortality. The most famous of the tax returns widely used by historians for its accuracy, were the calculations made by Gregory King from hearth-tax returns. Tax returns are variable in reliability depending upon the efficiency of the tax collector. Furthermore the term 'house' and 'family' were used as interchangeable terms and they provide no breakdown of household members into age, sex, occupation and so on.

Even the first returns of the Civil Census between 1801 and 1831 had their weaknesses. Improvements took place after the Civil Registrations Act of 1837/38 when census information became highly accurate. After 1841 the occupations of all householders, not merely the head, were required.

SOME OF THE PROBLEMS FACING ENUMMERATORS AS THEY ATTEMPT TO RECORD THE POPULATION.

These are just some of the difficulties faced by historians when they attempt to interpret the when and how of population change.

How did the population increase?

But how can we explain the rise in population during the eighteenth century? The population of England could have increased because of one of three main factors. The birth rate could have risen, say, due to a change in social conditions which encouraged earlier marriages and a consequent longer period of fertility. Conversely, there may have been a decrease in the mortality rate, for example, by the improvement of living conditions which could have encouraged a greater survival rate amongst babies. In the third instance, migration could have added substantial numbers to the indigenous population. This latter factor we can discount immediately for there was no large influx of population into this country until the Irish immigration of the mid-nineteenth century. The significant factors were therefore a rise in the birth rate or a decrease in the death rate.

A SEVENTEENTH CENTURY MORTALITY LIST.

TALKING POINT

Historians use phrases like 'birth-rate', 'marriage rate' and 'death rate' which are perfectly satisfactory to describe shifts in population size, distribution and structure. The term for population change is known as demography, a highly developed science in its own right. But the terms 'birth rate' and 'marriage rate' would be regarded as imperfect descriptive labels to the demographer.

1 What would you make of the term 'age-specific fertility'?

Take the phrase to pieces and its meaning should become intelligible.

2 Why would this phrase be of particular use to describe the population increase of the late eighteenth century?

3 What would be the advantage of knowing 'age-specific mortality' as opposed to the 'death-rate'?

A fall in the death rate: The case examined

While many historians favour a fall in the death rate as the major cause of population growth, their reasons for doing so vary considerably. Their explanations fall into two main categories. The first are described as autonomous agencies. This explanation refers to any natural forces which improved humankinds' chances of survival, for example, improvement in climate, natural decline in disease. Non-autonomous agencies refers to man-made improvements such as better public health.

The 'Plague'

BURYING PLAGUE VICTIMS.

The most powerful autonomous agency accounting for death was disease. The most sinister and widely feared was the scourge known as the 'Black Death'; the bubonic plague. Spread by an infected flea it first made its deadly entrance in Europe from the Far East in 1348. Between one-sixth and one-third of the inhabitants of Europe died during the first onslaught. Thereafter the disease remained endemic, lashing out periodically with deadly results.

And yet, mysteriously as it had appeared, it began to fade away. The last serious outbreak in England was in 1665 and less seriously in 1686. Thereafter it abandoned Britain. In 1720, after an outbreak around Marseilles the disease no longer struck in Europe.

The disappearance of the disease has led some historians to conclude that this alone is enough to account for a decline in the death rate. On the other hand that explanation is not without its critics as you will see in 'Examining the Evidence' (p117).

Plague was undoubtedly one of the most virulent diseases but there were many alternative infectious diseases capable of cutting swathes through the population. Attempts have been made to relate the generally colder climate which prevailed in Europe from the sixteenth to the eighteenth centuries to the decline of other infectious diseases. There appears, however, to be little correlation between this factor and outbreaks of smallpox, malaria and diarrhoea. This is not to say that severe climatic reversals did not add to the precariousness of life by savagely decimating livestock and crops but such major disasters appear to have virtually ceased from the mid-eighteenth century onwards.

We can now turn our attention to the non-autonomous agencies. Foremost among these explanations are the claims made for an improvement in medical knowledge and treatment. There is no doubt that the eighteenth century witnessed an expansion of hospitals, dispensaries and smallpox innoculation. Hospital provision may have increased but it is important to remember that there is no necessary correlation beween this factor and a decrease in the death rate. Most hospitals, where they existed, were in towns and thus were inaccessible to the bulk of population. Even in towns access to hospitals was not guaranteed and normally required a recommendation from a respectable member of society.

Preventing disease

Preventive medicine is far more potent a force to explain the decline of mortality than treatment in hospital and prescribed medicines. The majority of diseases thrive in an unhealthy environment. There is ample evidence, despite ignorance of the germ theory (not established until the late 1860s/70s), that eighteenth century doctors were beginning to explore the possible association between the environment and disease. In 1720 J. Meade's 'Short Discourse Concerning Pestilential Contagion and the Methods Used to Control It,' advocated better housing, ventilation, disinfection and control of 'nuisances'. A spate of books followed along similar

GILRAY'S SATIRICAL VIEW OF SMALLPOX VACCINATION SHOWING PATIENTS DEVELOPING HORNS AND TAILS AS A RESULT OF THE SMALLPOX VACCINE.

lines such as John Haygarth's survey of Chester's population and the incidence of disease in 1774 and a similar study of Carlisle by John Haysham in 1784. Large studies were completed on London in 1774 and Manchester in 1795. The weight of evidence firmly established the social context of disease.

It did not follow, however, that such a theory was widely accepted let alone implemented. After all there was no scientific proof that such connections existed and advocates of smallpox innoculation, for example, were lampooned by satirists such as Gillray. Even when the empirical evidence was overwhelming it required a change in attitude of government to pass and implement the necessary legislation. Although it proved difficult to pinpoint the reasons, the medical historians McKeown and Brown have concluded,

'Improvements in the environment are therefore regarded as intrinsically the most acceptable explanation of the decline in mortality in the late eighteenth and early nineteenth centuries.'

Of course, different factors as well as combinations of factors, may have been more or less relevant at different times. For example, it would be difficult to sustain the explanation of improved environmental conditions during the nineteenth century. Indeed, it is highly probable that because of rapid and unplanned urbanisation, environmental conditions actually deteriorated in expanding industrial towns. Overcrowding, air and water pollution and lack of effective sewage disposal were problems beyond the capabilities of rudimentary local government to solve. Environmental hazards were compounded by the widespread adulteration of food, both harmless and lethal. For urban dwellers any improvement in health which occurred as a result of better personal hygiene were more than off-set by a disease ridden environment.

NINETEENTH CENTURY TENEMENT SLUMS IN GLASGOW.

Improved nutrition

Many historians have identified rising standards of nutrition as the most significant cause of a decline in mortality. The principle factor sometimes held responsible for the improvement was the introduction and widespread cultivation of the potato. Not all historians agree as to its role in improved nutrition although the food value per acre of cultivation was far in excess of any other vegetable. Certainly the terrible results of the potato blight in Ireland in the mid-nineteenth century when perhaps a million died of starvation and resultant diseases, testify to its growing importance and dependance.

Greater agricultural efficiency and improved transport facilities can largely be dismissed as contributory causes for they were primarily a response to, rather than an initiator of population growth. There is, however, considerable agreement that England experienced a series of good harvests between 1730 and 1750 which, as a consequence, put little strain on distribution facilities. The good harvests also had an impact upon the birth rate which is discussed more fully later in this chapter.

Reduction in infant deaths

There is also considerable evidence of charitable and humanitarian work throughout the eighteenth century which may have cushioned mortality. Birth and early infancy were the most vulnerable period in life. Edward Gibbon, a famous eighteenth century historian from a comfortable background, recounted the practice of christening at least two off-spring with the same forename to ensure the survival of family names. In Yorkshire some children contributed regularly to what was colloquially known as a 'coffin club'. Clearly any reduction in infant deaths would have an immediate and long-lasting effect on population levels. The plight of foundlings in particular was notorious. Many were 'farmed-out' to 'nurses'. The death rate amongst them was staggeringly high.

To combat this social evil Thomas Coram opened the first Foundling Hospital in London in 1745 which, by 1756, was receiving government assistance. Workhouse children, too, often suffered appalling neglect. Josiah Hanway, an ardent reformer, revealed that of 291 children taken in by 11 workhouses in 1763, 256 were dead within two years. Through his influence an Act was steered through Parliament which directed children to be nursed outside of London and a payment made to those nurses whose charges survived beyond nine months.

These institutional improvements, whilst a welcome relief to those in destitution, can have had only a marginal improvement on the death rate.

Increased food supply

Survival on a greater scale could only be possible if the mass of population was receiving better food and thereby increasing their resistance to disease. This would only be possible, in turn, through an increase in real wages.

As has been stated, good harvests between 1730–50 were reflected in low meat and grain prices. Professor Phelps Brown's index of the prices in a 'typical' basket of consumer goods show no price increase between 1730–60 but a rise of nearly 40 per cent between 1760–92. At the same time, it appears wages failed to keep pace with these price rises. Thereafter, real wages did not significantly improve until after 1820.

In any case there is no necessary correlation between higher real incomes and levels of nutrition. Any additional money could well be spent on other things and we have no purchasing patterns in order to assess this factor. Most damning of all, there appears to be little connection between variations of food supply and mortality rates. Despite low grain prices, employment opportunities and high income in the periods 1350–1470, 1650–99 and 1720–50, mortality was not higher in the intervening periods when foodstuffs were in short supply.

EXAMINING THE EVIDENCE

Source A: Decline of the black rat

However, when all is said, an obscure ecological revolution among rodents – the disappearance of the black rat – which we believe to have been responsible for the cessation of the plague in Europe must be given its due.

K.F. Helleiner, *The Vital Revolution Re-considered* Canadian Journal of Economic History 23

Source B: Decline of the plague-bearing flea

The change of rodent species by itself (i.e. from black to brown rat) therefore cannot account for the failure of the disease to spread actively among rural and urban European rats. When, however, the change of rat species is associated with a change in flea species, we have an adequate explanation of the relative immunity of Western Europe from plague in modern times.

L.F. Hirst, *The Conquest of the Plague* Clarendon Oxford Press

Source C: Role of the plague in declining death rate

In relation to the overall decline in mortality since the mid-eighteenth century, however, the role of autonomous agencies must be regarded as modest, even in the hundred years or so before 1850 when its contribution was probably greatest. To see the disappearance of plague as the consequence of a natural rise in human immunity overlooks a variety of considerations: among them, the irregularity of plague outbreaks, fluctuations in the virulence of the infection itself, the fact that recovery from plague does not convey a lifetime immunity from the disease and the fact that the last plague epidemics occurred not in areas which had previously been least susceptible but in those where plague had always been most prevalent. To interpret it as a response to changes in the ecology of rodent populations is equally implausible. Even if the brown rat replaced the black rat, and there is evidence that in reality they co-existed in many areas, the direction and timing of brown rat migrations from Central Asia into Europe do not fit nearly into the geographic pattern of the incidence of plague. In any case, plague can be carried as easily by human as by rat fleas. To see plague's disappearance as the result of a natural diminution in the virulence of the bacillus sits uncomfortably with the major outbreaks of the disease which continued to occur on the Indian continent into the twentieth century. Lastly, to explain it in terms of an increased resistance among rats founders on the difficulties of explaining why rats developed an immunity only from the later seventeenth century, why plague continued to ravage many parts of the world long after it had disappeared from western Europe and why it prevailed longest in cities with the worst historical record of visitation, where the rodent populations ought to have had the greatest opportunity to acquire a natural immunity. On balance, therefore, the causes of the disappearance of plague are more likely to lie in human agency – the substitution of brick for lath and plaster in house-building, the cutting of overland trade routes between the western and eastern worlds by the Ottoman advance into south-east Europe or, the most likely explanation of all, the adoption of more effective measures of public quarantine.

N. Tranter, *Population and Society 1700–1970*

Source D: Hospitals and dispensaries

The eighteenth century witnessed a development of the hospital movement and the beginning of a remarkable growth in dispensaries. Medical and scientific investigations were improved. Sanitary science and right principles in the treatment of such scourges as fever which thrived under insanitary conditions were advanced, though not necessarily for strict scientific reasons. For our purpose, however, the important thing is the reduction in mortality which resulted ... the practice of midwifery improved ... and smallpox was greatly lessened after the middle of the period by vaccination.

G.T. Griffith, *Population Problems in the Age of Malthus*

Source E: Treatment of the sick poor

This is a survey of the treatment of the sick poor in the counties of Berkshire, Essex and Oxfordshire from 1720 to 1834 based on parish records ... The dispensaries might also have made their contribution in the second half of the eighteenth century by providing services for the poor when they had little other assistance ... many sick poor entered hospital as casualties or with non-infectious diseases and were given treatment in conditions which were at least an improvement on their home conditions ... In the urban areas, towns like Chelmsford and Hungerford were making efforts at improving environmental conditions – both in workhouses and in the case of Chelmsford, in general conditions to streets, courts and houses of the poor. Such attempts have at least mitigated some of the unhealthy conditions and contributed in a small degree to the decrease in mortality.

E.G. Thomas, *The Old Poor Law and Medicine*

Source F: Surgery and the death rate

Surgery had an almost inappreciable effect on vital statistics until the advent of anaesthesia and antiseptics which did not occur until the late nineteenth century ... In midwifery, despite the use of forceps and an increase in institutional delivery mortality rates in hospitals were consistently higher than in domiciliary practice and there was only a slight improvement in the hygiene of the labour room … Although the number of drugs available for the treatment of disease was large none were effective as palliatives … Perhaps the only useful contribution made by hospitals was the isolation of infectious patients. Indeed no patient could be reasonably certain of dying from the disease with which they were admitted …

T. McKeown and R.G. Brown, *Medical Evidence Related to English Population Changes in the Eighteenth Century*

Source G

McKeown and Brown's dismissal of improved medical practice and provision is no longer accepted without reservation, particularly when they claim 'it is hard to believe that innoculation can have been responsible for a reduction in the incidence of smallpox. On occasions whole communities were innoculated and vaccinated. … So effective was this that smallpox, which had contributed 16.5 per cent to the total mortality figures was reduced to 1–2 per cent by the mid-nineteenth century.

P. Razzel, *Population Growth and Economic Change in Eighteenth and early Nineteenth Century England and Ireland.*

Source H: Hogarth's anatomy lesson

THE ANATOMY LESSON. MANY SHARED HOGARTH'S LOW OPINION OF THE COMPETENCE OF DOCTORS. IN THIS ILLUSTRATION, HOGARTH IS LAMPOONING THE DISSECTION OF A BODY.

Source I

… it is by no means certain that these factors (which Razzel refers to) had any great effect on levels of human cleanliness. To what extent was the output of increased soap devoted to industrial rather than domestic uses? Were cotton clothes washed any more regularly than the woollens they replaced? Did the sale of portable baths or the use of soap for washing effect more than a small minority of the better-off sections of the community.

N. Tranter, *Population and Society 1750–1940*

Source J: Cartoons of food adulteration

A COMMENT ON THE PURITY OF FOOD. MAGAZINES OF THE TIME FREQUENTLY CONTAINED ADVICE TO HOUSEWIVES ON HOW TO TEST THE FOODS THEY BOUGHT. EVEN THESE WOULD NOT HAVE HELPED VERY MUCH, HOWEVER, SINCE THE TRADESMEN WERE OFTEN EXTREMELY INGENIOUS AND INVENTIVE ABOUT THEIR FAKING. THERE WAS A BRISK TRADE AMONGST SERVING WOMEN, FOR EXAMPLE, IN USED TEA LEAVES.

---

1 (a) What evidence is cited in Source A and B for a decline in the bubonic plague?

(b) How does Source C regard such explanations?

2 (a) What arguments are given both for and against the improvement of the provision of hospitals, dispensaries and medicines as factors in the death rate.

(b) In what way does Hogarth lampoon medical knowledge in the eighteenth century?

(c) Why was it possible for Hogarth to produce such savage satirical attacks on doctors?

3 How effective do the remaining factors appear in accounting for a decline in mortality?

---

4 In what ways is decline in mortality seen as an acceptable explanation of the population growth in the eighteenth century?

A rise in the birth rate: the case examined

The general acceptance of a decline in the death rate should not mean that we automatically disregard the possibility of a rise in the birth rate. As in the case of the death rate, historians differ over the factors they consider to have played an important role in the growing fertility of the eighteenth century.

Average age of marriage

Any reduction in the age at which couples married would have a significant effect on the birth rate. For this to have taken place, however, there must have been powerful incentives to persuade couples to marry at an earlier age.

In the first instance good harvests in the second quarter of the eighteenth century may have encouraged couples to marry earlier. In due course the off-spring of these marriages, should there be no set-back to their maturity, would in turn produce a greater proportion of children. Wrigley and Schofield in 'The Population History of England 1541–1871 – A Reconstruction', have advanced just such a proposition. They claim that the fertility increase was a delayed response to improved conditions in the second quarter of the eighteenth century. This idea can be expressed in the following diagram.

TALKING POINT

How convincing do you find this flow chart? What other factors might influence this sequence of events?

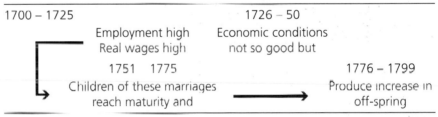

Wrigley and Schofield, *The Population History of England 1541–1871 – A Reconstruction*

TALKING POINT

What do we mean by 'real' wages? Why is it important to determine what 'real' wages were rather than simply an increase in earnings?

'Real' wages

This line of argument rests heavily on the reliability, or otherwise, of real wages statistics. Many of these real wage levels are based on calculations made by Phelps Brown and Hopkins who used the wage rates of building craftsmen in Lancashire and London. M.W. Flinn, however, warns that basing any conclusion on such statistics are built upon 'a terrible frail foundation.'

Poor law and population increase

If there is uncertainty surrounding the 'delayed response' theory then an explanation for increased fertility may lie in other contemporary events. For example, members of the Royal Commission (1834) inquiring into the workings of the old poor law were convinced that generous outdoor relief payment was the principle factor contributing to a rise in the birth rate. The verdict of contemporary critics, who were anxious to make a political point, has come under detailed scrutiny from historians. Mark Blaug, in particular, has questioned the often uncritical assumptions of the Commissioners. (See chapter 12).

New economic opportunities

A more convincing explanation may lie in favourable economic conditions which made possible a rise in fertility. This could have occured in several ways. It has been argued that in the late eighteenth century there were increasing employment opportunities, particularly for women and children. But the evidence to support this notion is by no means conclusive.

Whilst the frailty of basing conclusions on real wages has already been discussed it is possible to approach this factor from another angle. The very fact of money wages in themselves and not the goods and services they bought, may have provided sufficient incentive for an increase in fertility.

Changing patterns of employment

A further variation in the possible relationship between economic conditions and fertility may lie in the decline of lengthy apprenticeships in some manufacturing industries. In other words the advent of mechanisation and the rise of the entrepeneur destroyed the power of the guilds to insist upon long apprenticeships.

In farming a parallel explanation rests upon the notion that a decline of labourers 'living-in' with the farmer removed another possible disincentive to earlier marriages. As farmers became more prosperous they preferred their labourers to live in separate accomodation, albeit in a tied cottage.

Some historians go as far as to claim that the nature of early capitalism itself bore the necessary conditions which fostered earlier marriage by eroding the social position of the peasant farmer and artisan. According to this explanation deferred marriages were of little concern to those who had no skills to develop or property to negotiate a marriage contract. This forms part of a general Marxist critique against capitalism.

Whether one accepts the Marxist interpretation or not there is some evidence that correlates the rate of industrial development with higher fertility. The proposition can be combined with earlier good harvests which prompted an increase in birth rates. Once these off-spring came to maturity the industrial revolution was underway and provided a greater range of job opportunities.

Population increase and industrialisation

Equally the actual increase in population was of just the right magnitude to provide an incentive to industrial demand. If the population increase had been too small or too high this would have been detrimental to the long-term growth of the economy. Thus, it is argued, a fortuitous set of demographic changes in eighteenth century England made the contribution of population change to the industrial revolution a positive one rather than a negative one.

TALKING POINT

Was there a decline in job skills or were the changes in patterns of employment more significant?

EXAMINING THE EVIDENCE:
The birth rate

Source A: A rise in the birth rate; a fall in the average age of marriage

If one takes Gregory King's figures that a number of births per married women was 4.1, a fall of one year in the age of marriage of the mother would increase the size of the family by 8 per cent. If the interval between generations was 25 years, the consequent rise in the annual rate of growth would be about 0.3 per cent ... it suggests that to account for the annual rate of growth of 0.5 per cent, which is the sort of increase which took place in the early nineteenth century over that in the late eighteenth century, one would require a fall in the age of marriage of less than two years.

H.B. Habbakuk, *Population Growth and Development since 1750*

Source B: The old poor law and population increase

If there is considerable uncertainty surrounding the 'delayed response' theory then an explanation for increased fertility may lie in an examination of other more contemporary factors. For example, members of the Royal Commission inquiring into the workings of the old poor law were convinced that generous outdoor relief payments was the principal factor contributing to a rising birth rate.

M. Flinn, *The Population History of England*

Source C: Rates of rural population increase

Rate of rural population increase in counties deemed to have been especially affected by the Old Poor Law, 1801–31.

Group 1 – counties with low or falling rates of rural population increase, and in which more than 50 per cent of sample parishes reported the use of child allowances in 1832.

Group 2 – counties with above average rates of rural population increase, and in which more than 50 per cent of sample parishes reported the use of child allowances in 1832.

Group 3 – counties with above average rates of rural population increase, and in which few parishes used child allowances in 1832.

(S) = designated as Speenhamland county, Select Committee Agricultural Labourers, 1824

	1801 – 11	1811 – 21	1821 – 31	1831 – 41
Group 1	%	%	%	%
Sussex (S)	13.61	14.70	7.13	7.33
Bucks. (S)	7.29	14.83	7.57	7.12
Wilts. (S)	4.23	11.28	7.71	6.42
Berks. (S)	7.35	9.80	7.86	8.21
Suffolk. (S)	8.61	15.13	8.07	4.60
Oxford (S)	6.75	15.47	9.29	1.24
Devon (S)	10.01	13.78	8.59	5.38
Essex (S)	10.63	14.55	8.32	7.97
Northants. (S)	6.43	14.17	7.07	7.71
Group 2				
Huntingdon (S)	10.54	16.71	6.71	10.64
Cambs. (S)	13.73	19.75	12.51	13.89
Somerset	10.52	16.66	14.14	7.59
Group 3				
Notts. (S)	16.34	13.47	19.54	14.20
Lincoln	11.79	18.38	10.96	13.20
Interminate				
Warwick (S)	3.52	15.11	4.46	11.24
Leicester (S)	11.54	12.00	5.60	6.23
Average increases, rural districts of England and Wales	12.11	14.72	10.52	9.69
Average, all areas England and Wales	14.30	18.06	15.81	14.14

Intercensal population increases, rural districts including small towns of less than 2000 inhabitants

	1802		1812		1821		1831	
	s.	d.	s.	d.	s.	d.	s.	d.
Group 1								
Sussex (S)	22	7	33	1	23	8	19	4
Bucks (S)	16	1	22	9	19	1	8	7
Wilts (S)	13	11	24	5	15	8	16	9
Berks. (S)	15	1	27	1	17	0	15	9
Suffolk (S)	11	5	19	4	17	0	18	4
Oxford (S)	16	2	24	10	19	1	16	11
Devon (S)	7	3	11	5	10	8	9	0
Essex (S)	12	1	24	7	20	0	17	2
Northants. (S)	14	5	19	11	19	2	16	10
Group 2								
Huntingdon (S)	12	2	16	9	16	0	15	3
Cambs. (S)	12	1	17	0	14	9	13	8
Somerset	8	11	12	3	9	11	8	10
Group 3								
Notts. (S)	6	4	10	10	9	5	6	6
Lincoln	9	2	10	10	12	3	11	0
Intermediate								
Warwick (S)	11	3	13	4	12	0	9	7
Leicester (S)	12	4	14	8	16	0	11	7

Average per capita relief expenditure on the poor

Source D: The old poor law and the death rate

It is worth noting, of course, that the rate of population growth was no smaller in Scotland and Ireland where earned incomes were never supplemented by the Poor Law Authorities. Most of the Speenhamland counties had fertility ratios above the national average ... but the industrial counties also showed fertility ratios above the national average. In the Speenhamland counties, more generous relief may have worked to reduce the number of infant deaths and in this way increased the registered births. To be sure, this implies that the Old Poor Law did promote population growth, but via the death rate rather than the birth rate.

M. Blaug, *The Myth of the Old Poor Law and the Making of the New*
Journal of Economic History XXIII 2 (1963)

Source E: The old poor law as a response to population increase

A more fruitful model would be to turn this proposition on its head ... the allowance system might be viewed as a reaction to population increase rather than a stimulus ... Although the Malthusian population theory was ideally suited to contemporaries who wished to explain away the problems of poverty by shifting the blame onto the shoulders of the procreating poor, its merit in explaining early nineteenth demographic trends is dubious.

J.P. Huzel, *Malthus, the Poor Law and Population in Early Nineteenth Century England*
Economic History Review XXII 3 (1969)

Source F: Connection between population growth and industrialisation

In earlier periods each such episode had brought with it its own nemesis as over rapid population growth affected standards of living adversely and by symmetry discouraged marriage and reduced or even reversed trends in population growth ... (but) how far children were perceived as potential props in old age, as sources of income ... fuller knowledge is needed.

E.A. Wrigley, *The Growth of Population in England: a conundrum resolved*
Past and Present (1983)

Source G: Money wages and fertility

Possibly, however, the nature of the relationship between income and fertility has been misspecified. In a relatively unsophisticated age, marriage and fertility decisions among the labouring populations were more likely to have been determined by the more tangible and volatile fluctuations in levels of money wages and employment prospects than by an awareness of the amount of goods and services these would buy. Transferring the emphasis from real to money wage variations produces a better fit with fertility trends and a less 'strained' interpretation of the relationship between income and fertility than the 'delayed-response' thesis advocated by Wrigley and Schofield. Looked at in this way the rise in English fertility between the late eighteenth century and the conclusion of the Napoleonic Wars equates neatly with a simultaneous rise in levels of employment and money wages and the post-war decline in fertility with a general depression in employment and money wages.

N.L. Tranter, *Population and Society 1750–1940*

Source H: Patterns of agriculture and fertility

In agriculture communities ages at marriage and proportions celibate were distinctly higher where small, subsistence farming and 'live in' farm servants predominated over larger-scale farming based on non-residential wage labour.

M. Anderson, *Marriage patterns in mid-Victorian Britain* Journal of Family History.

Source I: Agricultural revolution and the birth rate

Capitalist relations of production enlarged the proportion of permanently proletarianised labourers. Just as the material foundations of the traditional economy were undermined by the advent of capitalism, so too were the modes of behaviour that were essential props of the system ... Moreover an increase in the proportion of the population who were proletarianised further lowered the age of marriage.

D. Levine, *Family Formation in the Nascent Age of Capitalism* (1977)

Source J: Industrialisation and the birth rate

In industrial communities ages at marriage and the proportions remaining unmarried fell as the size of manufacturing enterprises and the prevalence of wage labour increased. The scale of the transfer of labour out of agricultural into industrial occupations between the 1780s and the 1820s was certainly sufficient to have left its mark on national average rates of marriage and birth, while the reduced pace of this transfer may well have contributed to the decline of fertility which followed the end of the Napoleonic Wars. This raises the interesting possibility that part of the explanation for the rise in fertility rates during the late eighteenth and early nineteenth centuries may have involved a movement of women out of domestic service into less traditional types of employment, though proof that such a shift occurred is hard to provide.

P. Deane and W.A. Cole *British Economic Growth 1688–1959*

Source K: Agriculture, population increase and industrialisation

... the slow population increase and low grain prices of the 1730s and 1740s produced one type of economic growth and the rapid increase and rising grain prices of the later eighteenth century a different type; and both types of growth, in the order in which they occurred, were necessary for the Industrial Revolution.

H.J. Habbakuk, *Population Growth and Economic Development since 1750*

Talking point

Principal methods used by historians to calculate rates of mortality and fertility before the 1801 Census.

Parish Registers

(a) John Rickman, the initiator of the 1801 Census, required the clergy to also make a return of entries for baptisms and burials for every tenth year between 1700–1780, and marriages from 1754. These results were published under the title of Parish Register Abstracts.

(b) Some historians have by-passed Rickman's calculations and returned to the original registers. They can tell much about the short-range trends in mortality, fertility and nuptiality. This process is termed 'Family Reconstitution'.

Study of British Ducal Families-

This traces the life expectancy and fertility amongst the highest social class because records are particularly complete. Work on this method has been done by T.H. Hollingsworth in A Demographical Study of British Ducal Families.

---

1 Outline the factors which may have caused an increase in the birth rate.

2 Examine extract C. What does it tell you about:

(a) the rate of population growth in relation to the use of child allowance.

(b) the rate of population growth in rural as opposed to urban areas?

3 Which was the more important cause of a rise in the birth rate: the age at which women married or the income bought home by men?

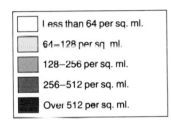

- Less than 64 per sq. ml.
- 64–128 per sq. ml.
- 128–256 per sq. ml.
- 256–512 per sq. ml.
- Over 512 per sq. ml.

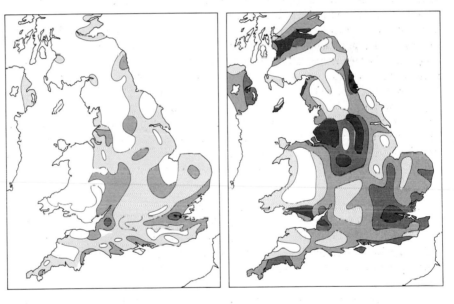

TALKING POINT

How might rates of population growth affect capital formation?

What was the relationship between population growth and industrialisation?

During the latter half of the eighteenth century Britain experienced an industrial transformation. At the same time a cumulative and persistent upward trend in population occurred. The existence of these simultaneous events has led to a search for a possible connection. It is evident from the experience of developing countries that rapid population growth does not result in industrialisation, indeed it may well hinder economic development. Harmful effects of population growth could act on an economy. On the other hand there are a variety of ways in which, at least in theory, population growth may affect economic growth favourably. For example,

The effect of the Reverend Thomas Malthus's 'Essay on Population', and its effect on the future Improvement of Society', in 1798 was immediate, dramatic and destined to leave a legacy which shaped social attitudes and policies for the next fifty years. Malthus's simple yet momentous contribution was 'the principle of population'. He predicted that the rapidly rising population would outstrip food supply. Only the natural disasters of famine and disease could prevent catastrophe unless man regulated his basic desire to procreate by delaying marriage and limiting family size. Such prophecies coming as they did amidst a time of population growth struck a fearful chord within society.

Malthus's influence was immense with politicians such as Pitt and Brougham, economists, Ricardo and both John and James Mill, philosopher Bentham and Macaulay the historian. Some supporters were fanatical in their admiration and hysterical in their proposals. In 1838 two obscure tracts penned by one 'Marcus' suggested that every fourth child born to poor parents

Reverend Thomas Malthus

prophet of population pessimism (1766–1834)

should be gassed at birth and buried in a colonnaded park which would serve as an edification to all classes whilst they took their recreation.

It was not always easy to see where parody began and the serious proposals of his supporters began. Many writers detested what Thomas Carlyle called 'the dismal science' of Malthus and the Political Economists and took to ridiculing his theories.

"What encouragement have the poor to be industrious and frugal when they know for certain that should they increase their store it will be devoured by drones, or what cause they have to fear when they are assured, that if by their indolence and extravagance, by their drunkeness and vices, they should be reduced to want, they shall be abundantly supplied."

Thomas Robert Malthus, *Essay on Population*

"Whence comes all this misery. All this tremendous inequality?
"The misery arises from a deficiency of food …"
"Well: whence the deficiencies of food?"
"From the tendency of eaters

to increase faster than the supply of food."

"But if we can raise more food by cooperation than with it …?"

"Even supposing we could, – unless cooperation also checked the increase in numbers, it could prove no more than a temporary alleviation of our grievances. In my opinion, it would, if it included equality of conditions, leave us in a worse state than it found us, in as far as it would relax the springs of enterprise and industry and, in time bring the community down into a deplorable state of sameness; it would, if perservered in, make us into a nation of half-naked potato eaters; and water drinkers."

H. Martineau, 'For Each and All' Illustrations of Political Economy.

"Mr Malthus … is correct, when he says that the population of the world is ever adapting itself to the quantity of food raised for its support; but he has not told us how much food an intelligent and industrious people will create from the same soil, than will be produced by one ignorant and ill-governed.

Questions

1 What was significant about the full title that Malthus chose for his book?

2 In what way did Malthus question the basic belief in progress?

3 In what ways can you account for the popularity of Malthus's theories?

4 Which of the sources support, and which reject, Malthus's conclusions as to the effects of population increase? In what way do the authors argue their points? Answer with reference to the tone, style, language and audience to which the articles appear to be addressed.

5 As a Malthusian
(a) what role would you think government should play in society?
(b) How would you attempt to convince supporters of humane legislation that they, in fact, were misguided?

For man knows not the limit to his power of creating food. How much has this power been latterly increased in these islands! … Food for man may be also considered as a compound of the original elements; of the qualities, combinations, and control of which, chemistry is daily adding to our knowledge; nor is it yet for man to say to what this knowledge may lead, or where it may end."

Robert Southey, New View of Society (1813)

"Married! Married! The ignorance of the first principles of political economy on the part of these people … A man may live to be as old as Methuselah, and may labour all his life for the benefit of such people as those; and heap up facts on figures … mountains high and dry; and he can no more hope to persuade them that they have no right or business to be married, that he can hope to persuade 'em that they have no earthly right or business to be born. And that we know they haven't. We reduced it to mathematical certainty long ago."

Charles Dickens, 'A Goblin's Story' (1843)

what will be the effect on wages of an abundant supply of labour? And what will be the effect on production, agricultural and industrial, of an increased market?

Thus population growth might either hinder economic growth or act as a stimulant. Capital resources could well have been dissipated in the sole production and ensued if agricultural production failed to keep pace with population.

Various historians have attempted to trace the relationship between population changes and the fortunes of the economy. E.A. Wrigley and R.S. Schofield are merely two amongst many who have come to the following conclusion.

Population changes and the fortunes of the economy

11 –12th centuries	Population increase Urban growth Growth of trade
13 – 14th centuries	Population decline, stagnation = poor economic performance
15 -early 16th century	Population increases Rapid technical and organisational development
Late 17 -early 18th century	Damaged urban economies, low grain prices, high wages, reduction of capital for investment

Mid 18th century – Early 19th century

Successes of earlier innovations adopted	↓ Decreased production costs
↓ Resulted in labour surplus for further industrial expansion	↓ Increased markets ↓ Rising profits
↓ Cheap labour	↓ More investment
↓ Mobile labour	

Whilst this may appear a convincing sequence of events it must also be remembered that there has to exist a society willing and able to sustain this development through a rise in agricultural production.

The controversy over population growth and its relationship to the economy is bound to continue. The evidence is fragmentary and the relationship of so many factors is by no means straightforward. On balance the initial moderate increase of population acted as a stimulant to a developing economy which in turn was sustained by increasing employment opportunities as industry expanded and agricultural production adopted more productive techniques. This appears to be borne out by the distribution of population growth. There were distinct differences between industrial counties such as Lancashire, the West Riding of Yorkshire, Warwickshire and Staffordshire which grew appreciably, while the agricultural counties of the south remained relatively stagnant.

REVIEW

Read through the check list below. Write down whether you consider each of the following factors are;

(a) well substantiated

(b) of some value

(c) repudiated or substantially disproved.

Support your answers with evidence.

Possible factors explaining the decline of mortality in eighteenth century England	
Disease	**Autonomous factors**
Plague – transmitted by fleas. Two forms bubonic and pneumonic.	Climatic changes Growth of natural resistance.
Smallpox – submicroscopic virus. Highly infectious.	**Non-autonomous factors** Medical knowledge and treatment. Medical institutions
Typhus – transmitted by body lice. 'The poor mans' disease.	Public Health Personal hygiene
Malaria – transmitted by the mosquito.	
Diarrhoea – intense intestinal evacuation.	
Nutrition	Alternative foodstuffs Transport and Marketing More nutritious foods
Other Factors-Economic and Social.	Higher real wages Humanitarian

Possible factors affecting a rise in fertility in eighteenth century England	
1 Delayed response to earlier favourable economic conditions.	
2 Generous outdoor relief payments to the poor.	
3 Increased job opportunities	(a) from rural to urban. (b) for women and children.
4 A rise in real wages.	(a) Evidence for a rise in real wages. (b) Expectations and money wages.
5 Changing nature of employment	(a) Decline of long apprenticeships. (b) Decline of 'living-in' system. (c) impact of capitalism system.

Which factors appear to be of more significance than others?

7 Roads and Canals – A Revolution in Transport?

Preview

EARLY NINETEENTH CENTURY TRANSPORT.

'The pavement ceases, the houses disappear; and they are once again dashing along the open road, with the fresh air blowing in their faces, and gladdening their very hearts within them.'

Charles Dickens, Pickwick Papers (1837)

'Nothing more bleak, chilling and miserable, than starting at daybreak of a cold frosty morning, the roads hard and slippery and the cold penetrating through every pore.'

John Cabbell's private diary 1833

Changing transport

"This day an inquest was taken at Ignastone on the body of Richard Aimes, when it appeared that the deceased was thrown from his horse, a little on this side of Ignastone, into a ditch, and was suffocated by mud and filth."

So ran the verdict on an unfortunate traveller in the mid eighteenth century. By no means were such hazards untypical. Arthur Young, who travelled widely in the late eighteenth century commented bitterly on the 'barbarous' and 'execrable' conditions of roads, reserving particular condemnation for a section between Preston and Wigan.

"I know not in the whole range of language terms sufficiently expressive to describe the infernal road. Let me seriously caution all travellers ... to avoid it as they would the devil."

Even in London, the roads were sometimes a gulf of mud. There is the well-known story which, though not true, gives a vivid picture of the state of roads. A beggar with one leg was offered a lift by a passing coach. He is said to have replied, "No, thank 'ee. I can't wait. I'm in a hurry!"

Yet within the space of half a century General Dyott, a retired army officer, wrote this in his diary,

"I should imagine that travelling, as far as speed is concerned, must have reached perfection, from the very fine state of roads ... Lord Angelesey has journied from London to Baudesert in something less than twelve hours: that is one hundred and twenty-five miles."

General Dyott 1827

In this chapter we shall attempt to explain why this transformation took place.

Examining the evidence
Methods of transport in early eighteenth century England
Source A

A PACKHORSE TRAIN (IN MID-EIGHTEENTH CENTURY AVERAGE COST WAS 10d PER MILE).

Source B

WIDE-WHEELED WAGON, 18TH CENTURY.

Source C

COAL DROP AT WALLSEND, NEWCASTLE UPON TYNE.

Source D: Traffic on the River Severn

This river (Severn) is of great importance … Upwards of 100,000 tons of coal are annually shipped from about Broesley and Madeley … also great quantities of grain, pig and bar iron, iron manufactures, and carthen-wares; as well as hops, cyder and provisions are constantly exported to Bristol and other places, from whence merchant goods are brought in return. The freight from Shrewsbury to Bristol is about 10s. per ton, and from Bristol to Shrewsbury 15s., the rates to the intermediate towns being in proportion …

Gentleman's Magazine (1758)

Source E: Poor road conditions

They do not know how to lay a foundation, nor to make the proper slopes and drains. They pour a heap of loose, huge stones into a swampy hole which make the best of their way to the centre of the earth. They might as well expect that a musket ball would stick on the surface of custard.

Gentleman's Magazine (1752)

Source F: Length of overland journeys

Iron from Coalbrookdale Company's Horsehay Works was sent down the Severn to Bristol and then by sea to Chester, the direct and much shorter overland route being ignored.

Mr Philip of Leicester (1828)

STATUTE LABOUR MENDING ROADS, YORKSHIRE. EARLY NINETEENTH CENTURY.

1 Complete the table of information.

Forms of transport available	Type of goods carried	Advantages	Problems/ Limitations

2 What particular form of transport available in the eighteenth century was preferred above others?

3 Why was it of little value to improve the types of carts and wagons?

4 Industrial output in Britain was increasing at 9 per cent per decade after 1780. In what ways would the existing modes of transport inhibit industrial and urban development?

Early eighteenth century travelling conditions

A road map of England in 1700 would have shown an intricate network of roads linking villages and towns, but this appearance of effective communication would have been deceptive. The typical road was a dust bowl in summer, a rutted ribbon of mud in winter. Why was this so?

The most efficient network of roads had been devised by the Romans 1400 years earlier and virtually no new road had been built nor the old ones maintained satisfactorily. The critical change came about when responsibility for road maintenance was removed from central authority to parishes. In the middle ages landowners were theoretically responsible for the highways adjacent to their land. Except for a few roads of strategic importance roadmaking was a matter of local concern and landlords enforced obligations only when it served their interests.

In the sixteenth century regulations were tightened up. Under the Highways Act of 1555 the parish was made responsible for the upkeep of roads. A local 'surveyor' was elected each year to supervise road repairs. He was unpaid, untrained and frequently had to be forced to accept the position. Statute labour was provided for six days a year and local farmers were obliged to use their carts for the hauling of stones. This remained the basis of road-maintenance until 1835.

If the roads could not be made fit then perhaps the vehicles could be adapted to fit the roads. To reduce damage to the surface of the road the Broad Wheels Act was passed compelling wagons to have wheels 9" in width in the belief that broad wheels would cause less damage.

JOSIAH WEDGWOOD (1730–95), POTTER AND FOUNDER OF THE WEDGWOOD COMPANY PRODUCED A DISTINCTIVE STYLE OF POTTERY. AT HIS FACTORY HE PIONEERED MASS-PRODUCTION METHODS. HE WAS A KEEN SUPPORTER OF IMPROVED COMMUNICATIONS FOR THE POTTERIES.

PRIVATE CARRIAGE – EARLY EIGHTEENTH CENTURY. THE PICTURE SHOWS WHY
COACH-BUILDERS IN ANY PARTICULAR AREA ALWAYS KEPT TO THE SAME GAUGE.
IT WAS NOT USUALLY POSSIBLE FOR A CARRIAGE TO GO TOO FAR FROM HOME
BECAUSE A CHANGE OF DISTRICT USUALLY MEANT A CHANGE OF GAUGE.

Turnpiking the roads

Since the government did not take the lead and the parish neglected their
duty, it was left to private enterprise to find a solution. 'Turnpike Trusts'
were groups of businessmen who undertook to maintain the roads (usually on a 21 year lease) in return for which they were allowed to charge
tolls to passing traffic.

Turnpikes probably got their name because tollgate keepers usually
turned a pike or pole to let the traffic onto the road.

Before 1773 a separate Act of Parliament was needed for each new
turnpike. After that date a General Act enabled a great many more to be
built.

Administration of Turnpikes

Purpose
They were not allowed to make profits. Expenses could be deducted from the collected tolls. The remainder was meant to be spent on road maintenance.

Qualification for trustees
They must own property to the value of £100. This was raised to £200 due to the rapid inflation of the Napoleonic Wars.

Type of trustee
Parliament preferred to see JPs on the list. Other useful participants would be local industrialists and prosperous farmers.

Advantages for the trustee
If your farm was near a turnpike then it was possible to command much higher rents. Trustees could lend money to the trusts and charge interest within the conditions of the Usury Laws.

Local businessmen who would benefit from cheaper transport costs
Officials
Clerk   – to record minutes of the Trust's meetings.
Treasurer   – Bankers would be particularly useful.
Surveyor   – to plan the maintenance of the road.
Toll-keepers– could be the weak link in the process as there were many examples of fraud.

Success of the trusts
If well managed a trust would spend 10 per cent of its income on administration, 20 per cent on loans, leaving 70 per cent for road repairs.

Not all were so fortunate. In the 1830s Wiveliscombe Trust was paying 96.8 per cent on interest and spending 7.4 per cent on repairs and heading inevitably toward bankruptcy.

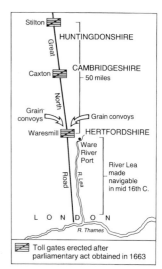

Toll gates erected after parliamentary act obtained in 1663

Early turnpikes
Study the diagram and answer the following questions.

---

1 Why would the villages around Ware complain of the road repairs before the Turnpiking Act of 1663?

2 What different complaint might the villagers have after the Turnpike Act came into operation?

3 Justices of the Peace from the three counties involved in the turnpiked section of the road appointed a surveyor for road repairs. The actual repair however, was still required from parishes.

(a) What new principle of administration did this system embody?

(b) In 1706 an Act of Parliament placed the road from Furnhill to Stony Stratford in the charge of 32 trustees. What was different about the principle of administration in this Act compared to that of 1663?

4 (a) Why do you think three-quarter of all turnpiked roads before 1750 were concentrated within a 40 mile radius of London?

(b) A smaller boom in turnpiking roads occurred in the 1790s in Lancashire. Why should this be so?

Examining the Evidence
The impact of turnpikes
Source A: The number of Turnpike Acts passed for the whole of Great Britain in the eighteenth century

Before 1700	5	1750–1759	170
1700–1709	10	1760–1769	170
1710–1719	23	1770–1779	75
1720–1729	45	1780–1789	34
1730–1739	25	1790–1799	71
1740–1749	37	1800–1899	59

Source B: Reasons for increased turnpiking after 1751
In the early Acts turnpike trusts were given powers for a limited number of years, a renewal at that time being a partial explanation for the great increase in the number of Acts after 1751.

T. May, *An Economic and Social History of Britain 1760–1970*

Source C: An excellent turnpike road
... that from Salisbury, to four miles the other side of Romsey ... is without exception, the finest I ever saw. The trustees of that road, highly deserve all the praise that can be given, by every one who travels it, for their excellent management.

Arthur Young 1768, *A six weeks tour through the Southern Counties of England and Wales*

Source D: An inadequate turnpike road
Fromsthorpe to Coltsworth are eight miles, called by the courtesy of the neighbourhood a turnpike – but in which we were every moment either buried in quagmires of mud, or racked to dislocation over pieces of rock which they term mending.

Arthur Young (1764) Ibid

Source E: Opposition to road improvement
After this description (source D) will you – can you – believe that a Turnpike was much wanted by some gentlemen but opposed by the

numbskulls of this county? I do not imagine that the kingdom produces such an example of detestable stupidity: yet in this tract there are a number of farmers who are perfectly well content with their roads.

Arthur Young (1769) Ibid

Source F: Notice warning against damaging turnpikes

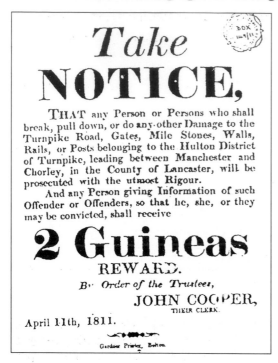

Source H: Increased traffic

About half a century ago, the heavy goods passing through Leicester for London and to Leeds and Manchester did not require more than about one daily broad wheeled wagon each way … One weekly wagon, to and fro, served Coventry, Warwick, Birmingham and on to Bristol and the west of England … At present there are about two wagons, two caravans and two fly-boats, daily passing or starting from Leicester for London … The same number extend the connection to Leeds and Manchester … There are at least six weekly wagons to Birmingham independent of those to Bristol three times a week and the same to Stamford, Cambridge, Wisebeach, and the eastern counties; to Nottingham to the same extent … and at least two hundred and fifty carriers to and from the villages …

J. Phillips, Tour through the United Kingdom (1828)

Source I: Numbers of turnpike roads

… turnpike roads at no time accounted for more than one fifth of the total road mileage of the country. Secondly it is unrealistic to talk of a national turnpike system for there was nothing systematic about the development of trusts, which was left almost entirely to local initiative. Thirdly, the setting up of turnpike trusts merely made an improvement of road conditions possible.

T. May, *A Social and Economic History of Britain 1760–1970*

1 Study source A.

(a) A certain period is known as 'turnpike mania'. When do you think it was?

(b) Can you suggest reasons for the decline in turnpike acts after 1769?

2 Compare source A with B.

How does this information affect your interpretation of the term 'turnpike mania'?

3 Study sources E and F.

(a) In what ways do these sources show a similar attitude toward turnpiking roads?

(b) In what ways do they differ?

4 Study source I.

Do the sources support Trevor May's conclusion?

Indicate which sources are relevant to his argument.

TALKING POINT

The government believed that private enterprise in the form of Turnpike Trusts would enable road improvements to take place. How, therefore, could they justify giving subsidies to road construction?

What modern parallels can you think of on this issue?

The road engineers

Turnpikes by themselves did not necessarily mean an improvement in roads. Nevertheless they provided an incentive for constructing roads of durable quality for their toll-paying customers. Three of the most important engineers who made this improvement possible were John Metcalfe, John McAdam and Thomas Telford.

John Metcalfe 1717–1810

'Blind Jack' of Knaresborough, in Yorkshire, was a remarkable man Although he lost his sight at the age of six as a result of smallpox he became an accomplished musician, general dealer and stage-coach operator, before turning his hand to road improvement.

Metcalf's blindness probably made the development of his other senses more acute. He surveyed routes by means of a stick to test the nature of the ground, often without assistants. He paid particular attention to the foundation of his roads, using broken stones to provide a well-drained base. His roads followed the easiest gradients and thus tended to be rather winding but were nonetheless a great improvement. Metcalfe's first road was a turnpike between Harrogate and Boroughbridge in 1765 and in the next thirty years he directed the construction of many fine roads mostly in Lancashire and Yorkshire. Perhaps his greatest feat was the Huddersfield to Manchester road which crossed a notorious bog in the Pennines. Most people felt the route chosen by Metcalfe was untenable but with the use of bundles of heather for foundations he achieved a serviceable road.

Stage coach travel

By 1840 there were over 35,000 kilometres of turnpike roads in Britain and about 8,000 turnpike gates. Improved roads stimulated road traffic. In the 1820s and 30s there were over 3000 daily coach services in Britain and over 50 per cent of them either started or ended their journeys in London.

Timetables

Timings for stage coach and mail coach services to or from London

1658: Exeter (274 km) 4 days
1706: York (336 km) 4 days
1754: Edinburgh (652 km) 11 days; Manchester (320 km) 4½ days
1757: Liverpool (338 km) 3 days
1784: Edinburgh 2½ days
1797: Exeter 25 hours
1825: Edinburgh 43 hours; Liverpool 27 hours
1836: Exeter 17 hours; Manchester 19 hours; Holyhead (430 km) 27 hours

PASSENGERS AT A COACH INN AT ABOUT 1740.

Length of time for coach travel

1740	London to Birmingham	1 coach per week
1783		30 coaches per week
1829		34 coaches per day
1838	Chaplin and Horne the largest coach proprietors withdraw their services.	

'QUICKSLIVER' PASSING THE STAR AND GARTER INN NEAR KEW BRIDGE IN 1835.

The dangers and decline of coach travel

DANGERS

The getting up was at the risk of one's life. I was obliged to sit just at the corner of the coach, with nothing to hold by, but a sort of little handle fastened on the side. I sat nearest the wheel: and the moment that we set off, I fancied that I saw certain death await me. All I could do, was to take still faster hold of the handle, and to be more and more careful to keep my balance.

The coach now rolled along with prodigious rapidity, over the stones through the town, and every moment we seemed to fly into the air: so that it was almost a miracle that we stuck to the coach and did not fall. We seemed to be thus on the wing, and to fly, as often as we passed through a village, or went down a hill.

Travels in England, 1782, C. Moritz

Questions

1 How would you account for the improved coach timings?

2 How do the extracts support the conclusions reached in question 1?

3 Why did Chaplin and Horne cease operating their coach services after 1838?

4 Explain why these accounts of Stage Coach travel differ?

DECLINE

In London, twenty years ago, the half-hour before the starting of perhaps five or six coaches from any of the large inns was a time of some little excitement. The neat and elegant Telegraph Coach, with its polished boot, in the hinder part of which was painted, in large letters 'The Times' 'The Independent' 'The Wonder', or some such appropriate name: the highly varnished body, the blazing Golden Cross or the Spread Eagle on the door panels: the motley crowd of people, of both sexes and all ranks, from the peer to the humble workman, some anxious to take their seats in or on these delightful conveyances: the well-groomed horses, the harness all in the nicest order: the quantity of packages issuing forth from the booking office: the instructions, not unmixed with a little good natured banter from the booking-clerk, formed altogether a most picturesque scene.

How different the same half-hour in a provincial town today. On approaching the inn not a solitary person did I see. The dingy, half-washed coach stood by itself outside the gates, like a deserted ship; inside the yard there was a dim, dirty place set aside for the office: in it glimmered one poor mutton candle, stuck on a piece of rusty tin, that had served the ostler for a candlestick for years: by its light I entered, and could just perceive a lantern-jawed, melancholy-looking man, whose visage indicated – indeed seemed already to anticipate – the fate that awaited both him and me, leaning with his head upon his hand, inert and heedless, as most men are who have nothing to do – this was the porter. On the other side of the counter, behind an old worm-eaten desk, sat the book-keeper. The usual greeting having passed between us, I took from the desk a long sheet of white paper, which, with the exception of the heading was unsullied – not the name of a passenger or parcel was written thereon!

The Autobiography of a Stage-Coachman, 1861

John McAdam (1756–1836)

He was born in Ayrshire, Scotland and invented a method of road construction which still bears his name. It is shown in the diagram. He claimed that a woman or feeble pauper could break as much stone with a light hammer in a day as two navvies wielding sledge hammers. McAdam's technique became adopted everywhere and in recognition of his service he was given a financial grant by Parliament in 1827.

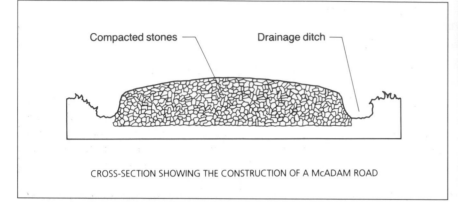

CROSS-SECTION SHOWING THE CONSTRUCTION OF A McADAM ROAD

Thomas Telford (1757–1834)

He contributed to all manner of engineering feats – canals, docks, harbours and bridges throughout Britain and Europe. But it was as a road engineer that Telford really excelled. Working mainly for turnpike trusts, he built nearly 1 000 miles of new road in Scotland, opening up many areas, especially in the Western Highlands and the north of England. The government gave a subsidy for much of this work, as it did for Telford's biggest project, the rebuilding of the road between Shrewsbury and Holyhead to connect with the ferry to Ireland.

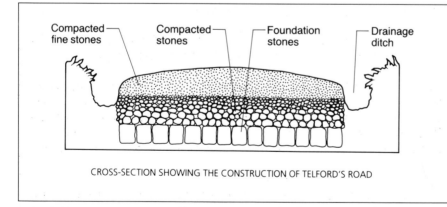

CROSS-SECTION SHOWING THE CONSTRUCTION OF TELFORD'S ROAD

Navigable rivers and canals

Although turnpikes and road improvements were a boon to travellers they were of less value to industry, for even the improved roads were seldom capable of bearing heavy loads for any distance. Furthermore only one-sixth of all roads were turnpiked as late as 1830 and the transportation of heavy goods was torturously slow and difficult. Even as late as 1829 the

normal speed of wagons e.g. between Newcastle and Carlisle was only nineteen to twenty miles per day.

If Britain had had to depend on the roads alone to carry her heavy goods traffic the effective impact of the industrial revolution might well have been delayed until the railway age.

Financing canals

Devising a scheme

↓

Organising a public meeting

↓

Collecting promises of subscriptions for the scheme.

↓

The financing of canals differed from those of turnpike trusts in so far as canals were allowed to make profits. For this reason they were regulated under the joint stock conditions governing the form of share-owning companies. The amount of capital required was enormous and the personal financing of the Bridgewater canal by the Duke was not typical.

↓

Petition Parliament for an act to authorise the construction of the proposed canal. Parliament would define the conditions under which the act would operate e.g. How much toll the company could charge. In return the company was given the right to compulsory purchase the land through which the canal was to pass.

↓

Obtaining the act from Parliament could be an expensive process, particularly if there was powerful opposition to the scheme e.g. turnpike trusts. The hiring of lawyers to state the case for the particular canal before a Parliamentary Committee added to the costs e.g. The Leeds-Liverpool had an authorised capital of £260 000 with a further reserve of £60 000 if required. In the end £1 200 000 was spent on the project.

↓

Selling shares. These would be normally offered at £100 each. Subscription books were placed in local shops for interested investors to sign.

↓

The company calls on the subscribers for cash. If there was an insufficient amount of money then the company would have to obtain a loan. Some companies got into difficulties at this stage e.g. The Barnsley Canal Co. (1808) obtained a further act to make a further demand on subscribers for £60 per share. As a consequence many sold shares quickly, some for as little as £5.

↓

The Company pays dividends. Some projects never got off the ground e.g. Southampton – Salisbury. Some paid huge dividends e.g. The Loughborough Navigation paid a dividend of 154 per cent in its peak-earning year of 1829. The Oxford Canal paid 30 per cent, on average, between 1811–1841. On average early investors who bought shares at par could reckon on a return of between 6–13 per cent. After the 1840s, however, returns were tiny, if dividends were paid at all.

EXAMINING THE EVIDENCE
The construction and importance of canals
Source A: Canals and navigable rivers, 1830

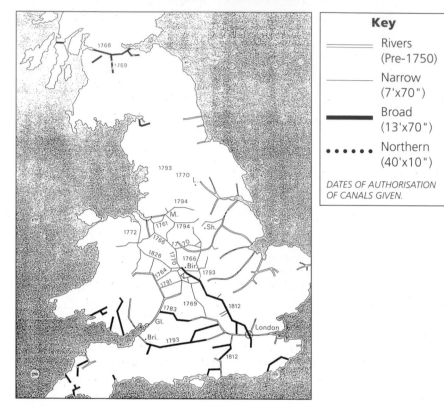

Key

═════	Rivers (Pre-1750)
───────	Narrow (7'x70")
━━━━	Broad (13'x70")
••••••	Northern (40'x10")

DATES OF AUTHORISATION OF CANALS GIVEN.

Source B: Calculation of loads which a horse could transport in 1800

These calculations were made by a group of contemporary engineers.

Transport	Tons
1 Pack horse	one-eighth
2 Stage wagon, soft road.	five-eighths
3 Stage wagon, macadam road.	2
4 Barge on river.	30
5 Barge on canal.	50
6 Wagon on iron rails.	8

Source C: Bridgewater Canal

The original design of the Duke of Bridgewater, was to cut a canal from Worsley, an estate of his Grace's, abounding with coal mines, to Manchester, for the easy transport of coals to so large a market; and, in 1758–9, an Act of Parliament for that purpose was obtained. A later Act enabled the Duke greatly to extend his plan; for he now decided, and with uncommon spirit to make his canal run not only from Worsley to Manchester, but also from part of the canal between both, to Stockport and Liverpool. The idea was a noble one, and ranks this young nobleman with the most useful geniuses of this or any other age.

Arthur Young, *A Six Months Tour through the North of England* (1770)

Source D: Opposition to canals

The petitioners, being Owners or occupiers of Houses and Lands near to or through the said canal is intended to be cut, apprehended that great injury will arise to them ... by the near approach of the said intended Canal to the Houses and Pleasure Grounds of several of the Petitioners, which they have made at great Expence. (sic)

Journal of the House of Commons (23 January 1783)

Mr. Curzon objected to the Ashby-de-la-Zouch canal, and was accused by its promoters of declaring his apprehension that, if the projected canal should take place, Ashby and Measham would become places of as great trade as Manchester and Sheffield.

The Times (16 March 1793)

Source E: The importance of navigable rivers

In Britain there are a number of good rivers. People have travelled and carried goods on them since prehistoric times. Moreover they have improved them by digging cuts to avoid the large bends, building locks and making towpaths. ... The length of this river from Burton on Trent, where it becomes navigable, to the Humber, is about one hundred and seventeen miles and the fall to the low water mark is about 118 feet.

The river, connecting the port of Hull, with a wide extent of agricultural, mining and manufacturing country by means of the various rivers and canals which connect with it, affords an easy means of export for the manufactures of a large district in Lancashire: the salt in Cheshire; the produce of the potteries in Staffordshire: the coal from Derbyshire; and the agricultural produce of Nottinghamshire, Leicestershire and of Lincolnshire. It also opens a link with the sea by way of Lincoln and Boston; through which channels, as well as the Humber, the goods mentioned above are carried: and in return the interior of the country is supplied, either by Hull or Gainsborough, or Boston and Lincoln, with such goods as are required by an immense population.

Joseph Priestley, (Manager of the Aire and Calder Navigation). *Historical Account of the Navigable Rivers and Canals* (1831)

Source F: Josiah Wedgewood's Pottery Works, Etruria, near Stafford

JOSIAH WEDGEWOOD'S POTTERY WORKS, ETRURIA, NEAR STAFFORD. THE TRENT AND MERSEY CANAL RUNS IN FRONT OF THE WORKS. WEDGWOOD NEEDED CHINA CLAY WHICH CAME BY SEA FROM CORNWALL TO LIVERPOOL. HE ALSO NEEDED FLINTSTONES WHICH CAME FROM THE YORKSHIRE HILLS NEAR HULL.

Source G: Increase in canals

England is now crossed in every direction by canals. This is the district in which they were first tried by the present Duke of Bridgewater, whose fortune has been greatly increased by the success of the experiment. His engineer, Brindley, was a man of real genius for this particular type of work who thought nothing but locks and levels, perforating hills, and floating barges upon aquaduct bridges over unmanageable streams. When he had a plan to form he usually went to bed, and lay there working it out in his head till the design was completed. It is recorded of him that being asked why he supposed rivers were created, he answered after a pause – to feed navigable canals.

Robert Southey, *Espirella's Letters from England* (1800)

TALKING POINT

There is an important distinction to be made between sources and evidence. A source is an item surviving from the past. It only becomes evidence when it is used to answer a question about the past. Yet despite the immense range and variety of sources they do not provide all the answers. No matter how dedicated and skillful the historian, sources are fragmentary and imperfect. Sources grouped together in 'Examining the Evidence' sections have been selected by the author and can only represent a part of that fragmentary and imperfect picture.

- How can you check the authenticity of sources?
- Is there anything in history we can say with certainty?
- What forms the better sort of evidence – conscious testimony or unwitting?i.e. What a person deliberately tells us or what the evidence unconsciously reveals about the author's attitudes and feelings?
- Are all the sources of equal value to the historian?

Source H: Acts passed for River Navigations and Canals

Year	Number of Acts	Year	Number of Acts
1750–54	3	1785–89	6
1755–59	7	1790–94	51
1760–64	3	1795–99	9
1765–69	13	1800–04	6
1770–74	7	1805–09	3
1775–79	5	1810–14	8
1780–84	4		

Source I: Number of days the Thames-Severn canal was closed

Year	By frost	For maintenance	Other causes	Total
1809	21	16	14 (Floods)	51
1822	0	127		127
1826	20	26	70[1]	116
1827	19	39	–	58
1828	0	40	–	40
1829	4	63 (Tunnel)	–	67
1830	40	5	35 (Repairs)	80
1839	0	28	–	28

[1] (Construction of Stroudwater Berkley Canal Junction).

Source J: Total trade and coal trade on the Thames and Severn Canal

Year	Total trade Thousands of tons	Coal trade Thousands of tons
1827	56	45
1831	66	48
1838	62	42
1840	84	54 (Railway building Swindon-Cirencester
1843	58	42
1844	70	46 Railway Stroud – Gloucester
1845	80	45
1848	59	45

1 Put sources A–J into categories – primary and secondary, literary and statistical.

2 Then use the evidence available to list the reasons why canals were important to economic development in the eighteenth century.

3 Finally, use all the material in this chapter to plan, write and deliver a speech for or against the following motion:

'Canals were able to remedy the defects of road transport in eighteenth century England'.

REVIEW
Evidence and opinion on canals

Bearing in mind the points made about sources as evidence, study the following statements about canals. For each statement produce a complete box like the one shown in statement 1.

1 The development of canals was a gradual process.

Sources for:	Sources against:	Summary	Adequacy of source
My statement would be:			

2 Canals were a nationally planned network of inland waterways.

Sources for:	Sources against:	Summary	Adequacy of source
My statement would be:			

3 If Britain had had to depend on roads alone to carry her heavy goods the effective impact of the Industrial Revolution might well have been delayed until the coming of the railway age.

Sources for:	Sources against:	Summary	Adequacy of source
My statement would be:			

4 The problems of canal transportation were clearly revealed when competition from railways exposed their weaknesses.

Sources for:	Sources against:	Summary	Adequacy of source
My statement would be:			

5 The opening of the Bridgewater canal in 1761 stimulated widespread construction of canals.

Sources for:	Sources against:	Summary	Adequacy of source
My statement would be:			

6 The benefit of canals was obvious to everyone.

Sources for:	Sources against:	Summary	Adequacy of source
My statement would be:			

8 Railways – A New Age?

PREVIEW

THE RAILWAY JUGGERNAUT OF 1845.

'The people would be smothered in tunnels, and those that escaped would be burned in the carriages.'

Opposition to the Great Western Railway (1834)

'Railroad travelling is a delightful improvement of human life. Man is becoming a bird.'

Rev. Sydney Smith, 1771–1845, (1842)

What is the artist attempting to convey in this picture?

Which of the two quotations support the artist's opinion?

The dawn of a new age?

On 27 September 1825 a huge crowd lined the route from Stockton to Darlington to catch a glimpse of the wonder that appeared to herald the coming of a new age.

'Throughout the whole distance the fields and lanes were covered with elegantly dressed females and all descriptions of spectators ... at one place the passengers by the engine had the pleasure of cheering their brother passengers by stage-coach, which passed alongside, and of observing the striking contrast exhibited by the power of the engine and of horses; the engine with six hundred passengers and load, and the coach with four horses, and only sixteen passengers.'

The historian E.J. Hobsbawm likens the coming of the railways to that of nuclear energy after the second world war: it was the symbol of a new age of speed, economic growth, and widening horizons. Not to have a railway station in a town was a virtual admission of decline. When nearly 50 the novelist Thakray wrote:

'Your railroad starts a new era, and we of a certain age belong to the new time and the old one ... We elderly people have lived in that pre-railroad world, which has passed into limbo and vanished from us. I tell you it was firm under our feet once, not long ago. They have raised those railway embankments up, and shut off the old world that was behind them. Climb up that bank on which the irons are laid, and look to the other side – it is gone.'

quoted in R. Altrick, *Victorian People and Ideas* (1973)

Year	Mileage
1832	39
1833	218
1834	131
1835	201
1836	955
1837	544
1838	49
1839	54
1840	–
1841	14
1842	55
1843	90
1844	810
1845	2816
1846	4540
1847	1295
1848	373
1849	16
1850	7

The importance of the railway

It is argued that change as dramatic as that experienced by Thakray was bound to profoundly affect both the economic and the social life of the country. The impact of the railways upon existing transport systems is an obvious area for investigation. More difficult to calculate, however, is its effect upon industry and agriculture for the contribution railways made is not easy to isolate. Indeed some historians, who describe themselves as 'New Economic' historians, argue that if railways had not developed during this period the economy would have still grown at a remarkable pace.

Whether this latter view can be supported or not, the government found this section of the economy important enough to warrant legislation in 1840, 42, 44, 58 and 71, despite fierce opposition from powerful railway interests in Parliament itself.

In this chapter we shall attempt to answer the following broad questions:

1 How did railways originate prior to the locomotive?

2 By what process were railway companies established?

3 What was the contribution of an individual such as George Stephenson to the process of railway development?

4 What impact did railways have on the social and economic life of the country?

Examining the Evidence
Railways before the locomotive

The following sources illustrate the origins and development of railways between 1600 and 1800. For what purposes were railway tracks built and how did the technology of steam engines develop?

Source A: Early wagonways

When men have pieces of ground between the colliery and the river, they sell leave to load coals over their ground, and so dear that the owner of a rood of ground will expect £20 per annum for this leave. The manner of carriage is by laying rails of timber from the colliery to the river, exactly straight and parallel, and bulky carts are made with four rowlets fitting these rails, whereby the carriage is so easy, that one horse will draw four or five chaldrons of coals, and is an immense benefit to the coal merchants. (A chaldron was about two and a half tons).

Roger North describing the railways on Tyneside in 1676 to his brother Lord Chancellor North. Quoted in J. Francis, A History of the English Railway

Source B: Horse drawn wagons for coal

Source C: Early types of rail

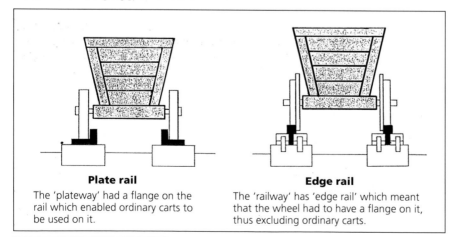

Plate rail

The 'plateway' had a flange on the rail which enabled ordinary carts to be used on it.

Edge rail

The 'railway' has 'edge rail' which meant that the wheel had to have a flange on it, thus excluding ordinary carts.

Source D: Importance of coal to the development of railways

… there is so great a scarcity of wood through out the whole kingdom that not only the city of London, all haven towns and in very many parts within the land, the inhabitants are constrained to make their fires of sea-coal or pit-coal, even in the chambers of honourable personages, and through necessity which is the mother of all the arts, they have late years devised the making of iron. The making of all sorts of glass and burning of bricks with sea-coal or pit-coal.

Edmund Howes, a Jacobean writer on trade in 1630.
Quoted in W.H.G. Armytage, *A Social History of Engineering*

Source E: Coal Wagonways in South Wales about 1810

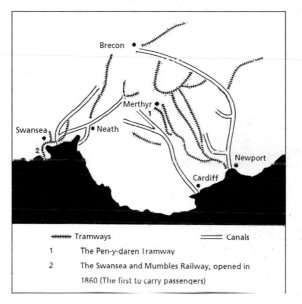

Tramways   Canals

1   The Pen-y-daren Tramway
2   The Swansea and Mumbles Railway, opened in
1860 (The first to carry passengers)

Source F: Scarcity of horses

Horses are scarce and dear, which need not excite wonder, as a foreign slaughterhouse (the war with France) seems regularly appointed for these animals.

Farmers' Magazine (1812)
Quoted in A.H. John, *Farming in Wartime* from Jones and Mingay (eds.)
Land, Labour and Population in the Industrial Revolution

Source G: Canals and navigable rivers in England, 1830

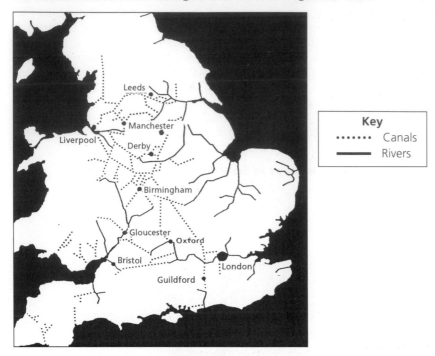

Key
...... Canals
—— Rivers

Source H: Coal shipped from Newcastle 1660–1830

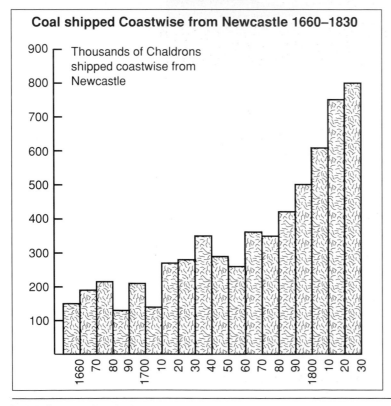

Coal shipped Coastwise from Newcastle 1660–1830

Thousands of Chaldrons shipped coastwise from Newcastle

Source I: Early nineteenth century locomotives

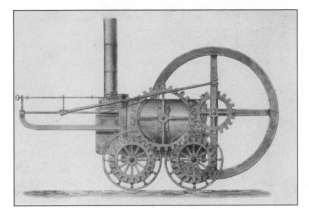

TREVETHICK'S LOCOMOTIVE 'PUFFING BILLY' 1804.

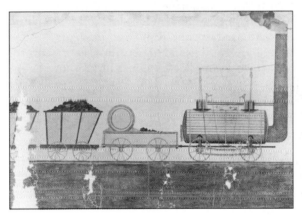

A KILLINGWORTH ENGINE.

1 For what purposes were railway tracks originally built and why were no other transport systems suitable?

2 How did the technology of railways develop to meet increasing industrial demands?

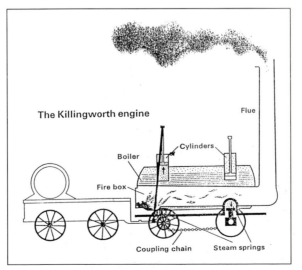

GEORGE STEPHENSON'S LOCOMOTIVE 'KILLINGWORTH'.

The origins and changing technology of railways

The origins of the railway were intimately linked with the fortunes of the coal industry. They remained largely local concerns and frequently acted as feeders for other forms of transport, either canals, navigable waterways or coastal shipping.

In the early 1800s, however, the railways which had remained virtually unchanged for two hundred years faced the challenge of radical change to cater for a rapidly industrialising economy. Edge rails replaced wooden plateways and the carriage of goods was to become exclusive to the railway company itself. Both South Wales and Tyneside were unsuited to the construction of canals and therefore encouraged the development of railways. Wartime demand for horses added a further incentive to the most important technological development of all – the invention of a successful locomotive.

James Watt's steam engine could and was adapted to railway haulage although it was initially easier to use a stationary engine and haul the wagons by cable. On several of the earlier lines, Stockton-Darlington, Liverpool-Manchester, they were used to cope with steep descents.

After Watt's patent expired in 1800 Richard Trevethick, a Cornish mining engineer who had installed several Watt engines in tin mines, constructed the first steam locomotive in 1804. His lead may well have earned him the title of 'Father of the Locomotive' if he had not left England to engineer mines in South America.

Further developments followed as the insatiable demand for domestic and industrial coal escalated. Wrought iron rails replaced those of cast iron. John Blenkinsop produced a rack and pinion cogwheel to ensure purchase between rail and wheel, but this required the expense of specially adapted track. William Hedley adapted his engines to plate rail by distributing the engine's weight over eight driving wheels. But the credit for the most significant development must go to George Stephenson whose locomotives could be successfully used on edge-rail, hauling 70 tons at speeds up to five miles an hour.

How was the railway system created?

The building of the Stockton and Darlington railway coincided with a flood of propaganda on behalf of the railway as a transport network. Yet as we have seen even the Stockton Darlington railway made only a limited use of locomotives. Nonetheless an emerging and successful locomotive gave renewed energy to the campaign.

Thomas Grey's pamphlet

'Observations on a General Iron railway or Land Steam Conveyance; to supersede the necessity of Horses in all Public Vehicles; showing its vast superiority in every respect, over all the present methods of Conveyance by Turnpike, Roads, Canals and Coasting traders. Containing every species of Information relative to railroads and Locomotive Engines' explained its purpose, but more significantly fired the enthusiasm of a wealthy Midlands coal owner and landed gentleman, William James.

Procedure for building a railway

A group of local businessmen meet to consider a proposed railway. After agreement they advertise a public meeting.

↓

The public meeting elects a provisional committee which hires an engineer to prepare a survey of the proposed line.

↓

A subscription shares list is opened for investors.

↓

An application is made to Parliament for an Act to create a Company.

↓

A provisional committee introduces a Bill into Parliament to which objections may be raised.

↓

The Bill may be passed after expensive legal costs.

↓

The Bill is now an Act.

↓

A company with a Board of Directors is now set up and detailed plans are prepared.

↓

Contractors are engaged and work can begin.

Whilst the Stockton and Darlington railway line was being constructed, William James successfully fought a 'campaign' for a railway between the thriving cities of Liverpool and Manchester. In 1824, despite some opposition, George Stephenson was invited to become engineer for the proposed railway.

The first bill in 1826 was rejected largely because of Stephenson's poor performance in face of the Parliamentary Committee but a year later a significant opponent appeared to change his opinion, as shown in a letter from H. Bradshaw, the manager of the Bridgewater Canal to J. Lock, the chief Estate Manager for the Earl of Sutherland.

'The Manchester and Liverpool railroads are certainly going to Parliament again next session. The existing surveyor has just been here to show me their new plans, etc. and ask permission to go over our lands; to which (you will scarcely believe it) I have consented; but the man behaved so fairly and openly that I really could not refuse …

Their new line is certainly a better one and much less objectionable than the former. They avoid Lord Sefton's land entirely and Lord Derby's land as much as possible. They do not cross the river Irwell at all … and they profess their great object to be getting over our canal (which they must cross) with the least possible injury or inconvenience to us. (27th September 1825)'

The construction problems facing Stephenson were immense but he managed to overcome them. The 12 square mile boggy mass of Chat Moss was crossed using a raft of timber and heather foundations; a tunnel into Liverpool and a huge cutting at Olive Mount involving the blasting of half a million cubic yards of rock.

By late 1828 the line was complete but the directors were divided over whether to use locomotives or stationary engines. To settle the controversy it was decided to hold a competition at Rainhill, near Manchester, to which any locomotive could be entered. Their competence was to be determined by three criteria; speed, fuel consumption and mechanical reliability. Stephenson's entry 'Rocket', with its multi-tubular boiler and increased engine efficiency, demonstrated conclusively the superiority of his locomotive.

The Liverpool Manchester railway was an immediate success and stimulated a number of railway projects for which the engineering skills of George, and his son Robert, were in considerable demand. Profits from such ventures were handsome. The Stockton Darlington Railway saw its shares rise from £100 in 1821 to £260 in 1838. The Liverpool Manchester's authorising Act of Parliament limited its annual maximum dividend to 10 per cent which it achieved without effort every year thereafter.

It would be natural to assume as dividends were high in railway companies, then investment would rise as in a spring tide. The situation, however, was not quite so simple.

LIVERPOOL TO MANCHESTER RAILWAY CROSSES CHAT MOSS.

George Stephenson (1781–1848)
father of the railway

There are those who see history as influenced or epitomised by the lives of great men to whom labels are attached to denote the individual's particular significance. This point of view was widely held by historians in the nineteenth century. To Thomas Carlyle, for example, history was made by great leaders, while the common people merely followed. In 'Heroes and Hero-worship' Carlyle concluded that the history of the world is but the history of great men'.

The notion of the 'great' individual moulding history was given an additional dimension in the nineteenth century by those anxious to prove that Victorian industrial society enabled people of humble birth to rise through the ranks of pre-eminence. This philosophy is summed up in the title of Samuel Smiles' most famous book 'Self-help'. In his anxiety to demonstrate his belief in the self-made man Smiles excluded engineers such as Isambard Kingdom Brunel who was not working class and Richard Trevethick who died in poverty.

Diametrically opposed to this interpretation of history is E.J. Hobsbawn, a Marxist historian, who relegates the role of the individual to the prevailing social and economic conditions of the time. In other words the

inventor or innovator does not cause things to happen but sees their emergence as an effect of economic change.

George Stephenson, the son of a colliery fireman, became a respected and successful engineer. He was only semi-literate and spoke with a broad Geordie accent, which on one occasion, when he appeared before a railway commission, required the services of an interpreter. He first acquired attention with his invention of a safety lamp, which he claimed had preceded Humphrey Davey's. His first locomotive was built for the Killingworth colliery where he was employed. By 1825 he had gained such local reputation that he set up his own firm in partnership with his son, Robert. Stephenson's first recognition as a locomotive engineer came with the Stockton Darlington railway; although a stationary engine was also used for part of the track in addition to horses on other stretches. The work of George Stephenson was in many ways less original than other engineers but in the long run more significant.

'The Stockton Darlington railway, of which George Stephenson was the engineer, drew together a number of strands of earlier development and employed steam locomotives from the first, although stationary engines were also used. By 1811 South Wales was estimated to have nearly 150 miles of railways, while it was said that Tyneside had 225 miles before the Stockton Darlington railway was opened in 1825. That was not the first public railway, credit for which must go to the Surrey Iron railway ... Neither was it the first passenger railway, for the Swansea and Oystermouth Railway of 1807 bears that palm.'

T. May, A Social and Economic History of (Britain 1760–1970)

Social aspirations

The Victorians were keen to wipe the coaldust off Stephenson and to cast him in an heroic image as in the illustration.

THE STEPHENSON FAMILY IN AN IDEALISED WORKING-CLASS SETTING. BY THE TIME HE HAD STARTED BUILDING LOCOMOTIVES GEORGE WAS CLOSER IN POSITION TO A COALOWNER THAN TO A MINER. ONE OF HIS 'KILLINGWORTH' ENGINES CAN BE SEEN IN THE BACKGROUND.

Assignment

1 Look at these comments:
  (a) How do the authors differ in their interpretatin of the origins of railways?
  (b) What role in railway development does Trevor May give to George Stephenson?
  (c) To which of the two writers would you consider Trevor May's interpretation to be closely allied?

2 Look at the illustration of the Stephenson family.
  (a) What impression of George Stephenson is the artist attempting to convey in this picture?
  (b) How has the artist attempted to achieve his desired effect?

3 Read the comments again. Can you detect differing views of history in their opinions?

COMMENTS ON THE ORIGINS OF RAILWAYS

'When George Stephenson was struggling to give utterance to his views on the locomotive before the Committee of the House of Commons, those who did not know him supposed him to be a foreigner. Before long the world saw in him an Englishman, stout-hearted and true – one of those master-minds who, by energetic action in new fields of industry, impress their character from time to time upon the age and nation to which they belong.

'I have fought,' said he, 'for the locomotive single-handed for nearly twenty years, having no engineer to help me until I had reared engineers under my own care.' The leading engineers of the day were against him, without exception; yet he did not despair. He had laid hold of a great idea, and he stuck by it; his mind was locked and bolted to the results.

... Watt's invention exercised a wonderful quickening influence on every branch of industry, and multiplied a thousand-fold the amount of manufactured productions; and Stephenson enabled these to be distributed with an economy and despatch such as never been thought possible. They have both tended to increase indefinitely the mass of human comforts and enjoyments, and to render them accessible to all ... it is to be regarded as the grandest application of steam power that has yet been discovered.'

Samuel Smiles, *Lives of the Engineers* (1861)

'Of course, transport needs gave birth to the railway. It was rational to have coal-wagons along 'tram-lines' from pithead to canal or river, natural to haul them by stationary steam-engines, and sensible to devise a moving steam engine (the locomotive) to pull or push them. It made sense to link an inland coalfield remote from rivers to the coast by an extended railway from Darlington to Stockton (1825), for the high costs of constructing such a line would more than pay for themselves by the sales of coal which it would make possible even though its own profits were meagre. The canny Quakers who found or mobilised the money for it were right; it paid two and a half per cent in 1826, eight per cent in 1832–33 and fifteen per cent in 1839–41. Once the feasibility of a profitable railway had been demonstrated, others outside the mining areas, or more precisely the north-eastern coalfields, naturally copied and improved upon the idea, such as the merchants of Liverpool and Manchester. ...'

E.J. Hobsbawm, *Industry and Empire* (1970)

EXAMINING THE EVIDENCE
Railway mania
Source A: Mileage of railway construction

Year	Mileage	Year	Mileage
1832	39	1841	14
1833	218	1842	55
1834	131	1843	90
1835	201	1844	810
1836	955	1845	2816
1837	544	1846	4540
1838	49	1847	1295
1839	54	1848	373
1840	–	1849	16
		1850	7

THE TABLE SHOWS THE TOTAL MILEAGE OF RAILWAY CONSTRUCTION SANCTIONED BY ACT OF PARLIAMENT IN THE 1830s AND 1840s.

Source B

> **The changing railway investor**
>
> Transport schemes required huge amounts of capital for they could not be built up gradually like manufacturing enterprises. Apart from construction, there were legal expenses and compensation e.g. The initial costs for the Stockton Darlington line were estimated to be £82000. By 1826 costs had risen to £169000 of which over one-third came from outside the North-east of England.
>
> ● The huge costs required Joint Stock organisation.
>
> ● Up to 1830 early lines were largely financed by local businessmen.
>
> ● During the 1830s joint stock banks guaranteed the financing. Occasionally some money came from the London banks but by and large they held aloof.
>
> ● In the 1840s and after the London banks came in on railway enterprises on a massive scale.

Source C

A solicitor or two, a civil engineer, a Parliamentary agent, possibly a contractor, a map of England, a pair of compasses, a pencil and a ruler, were all that were necessary to form a railway company.

A Stockbroker recalling the railway mania of the 1830s.

Source D

The most cautious were deceived … and men esteemed good citizens were drawn into acts which averice urged but conscience condemned. They saw the whole world railway mad. The iron road was extolled at public meetings; it was the object of public worship … It penetrated every class; it permeated every household; and all yielded to the temptation.

A contemporary journalist's account in 1838.

1 Study Source A

(a) There were two phases of railway development which historians have referred to as 'mania'. Which do you think they are?

(b) Why do you think railway construction did not progress at a uniform rate? Consider the following points.

Railways took two or three years to build during which time no money was coming in. Costs also rose during construction. What effect would this have on capital required for other schemes?

Railways were still thought of as separate concerns. Link and Branch lines were not considered until later.

Railways had to compete with other investments, particularly government funds. Would investment in government funds be safer? If interest was low why might investors not want to sell?

If industrial costs were rising, say in response to a bad harvest, what capital requirements would this entail and how available would capital be?

(c) Bursts of railway construction co-incided with general economic booms. Why would this be so?

2 Study sources C and D.

(a) How do these sources convey the enthusiasm for railway investment?

(b) How do they differ in their description of railway mania?

3 In what ways might railway mania be regarded as:

(a) wasteful?   (b) beneficial?

TALKING POINT

What impression is the artist conveying in this cartoon? How does he achieve the desired effect?

KING HUDSON'S LEVEE.

The Career of George Hudson

Between 1845–48 some 650 railway acts were passed authorising the construction of nearly 9 000 miles of tracks, yet by 1850, 3500 projected miles had been abandoned. Whilst mania encouraged the proposal of non-viable lines, nonetheless a national network of 7500 miles was laid down in a very short space of time.

Centre stage during the railway mania was the figure of George Hudson. he began his career as a linen draper who, with the help of a £30 000 inheritance and his own joint stock bank, emerged in 1835 as an energetic railway promoter. His first venture was the York and North Midland Railway but he quickly realised the need for amalgamation of other lines. In the following exercise consider carefully what decision George Hudson might make.

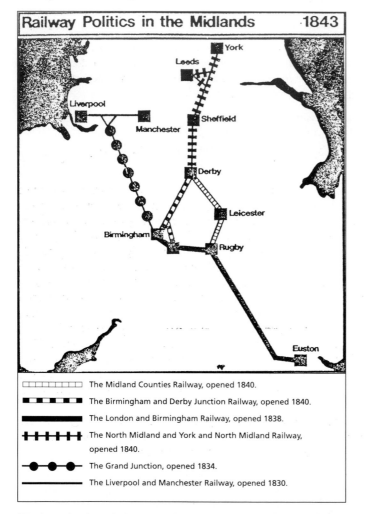

Railway Politics in the Midlands ·1843

The Midland Counties Railway, opened 1840.

The Birmingham and Derby Junction Railway, opened 1840.

The London and Birmingham Railway, opened 1838.

The North Midland and York and North Midland Railway, opened 1840.

The Grand Junction, opened 1834.

The Liverpool and Manchester Railway, opened 1830.

Hudson is the chairman of the York and North Midland Railway. Either of the two lines; the Birmingham and Derby Junction Railway or the Midland Railway will provide Hudson with a link to London.

Note

Canal construction reached its maximum mileage after the coming of the railways. Furthermore they carried their greatest volume of traffic after a railway appeared in the same district. Why do you think there should be this initial increase before the canal's eventual decline?

1 Would you take over both lines?

2 If only one line, which one?

The Midlands Railway is in the red and depends greatly on the goods traffic for the London and Birmingham line with which it competes with Hudson's line. It is presently fighting a savage fare-cutting war with the Birmingham and Derby Junction Railway which it wants to take over.

The Birmingham Derby Junction Railway.

Its stock is even lower than the Midland Counties Railway. It is also dependent on the Yorkshire and North Midlands Railway for traffic. For every £1 the Midland Counties Railway loses it loses £3. What do you think George Hudson should do?

This was precisely the problem George Hudson faced. The company he took, over was the Birmingham and Derby junction railway. So impressive was Hudson's business acumen that he became in great demand as a railway director.

By 1848 Hudson controlled between one quarter and one third of Britain's 5000 miles of railway. A year later he became reviled and despised as his railway empire collapsed about him. As profits fell Hudson continued to pay high dividends to shareholders out of a dwindling supply of capital and by shifting funds from one of his companies to another. As an M.P. (Sunderland) he escaped prosecution for theft but fled abroad in ignominy.

The role of railway development in the economy

The spectacular career of Hudson and the general enthusiasm for railways would lead one to believe that this major transport development must have had profound social and economic effects. A group of historians, some twenty years ago decided to test this basic assumption. They were first and foremost economists who attempted to apply economic models and measurements to this historical phenomenon. At the time they were referred to as 'New Economic historians', although Donald Mc Closky, a leading member of this group, preferred the name 'cliometricians' (from 'Clio' the goddess of history and the Greek word meaning to measure) The name denotes the group's emphasis on statistical evidence. Another important technique they employ is 'counter-factual hypothesising'. This grand term, simply explained, refers to a method of explaining what might have happened if a particular factor had not been present e.g. What would have happened to the British economy if railways had not been developed.

Whether the cliometricians' conclusions can be sustained or not the question of railways contribution to the economy is complex. Its contribution to social change is even more difficult to determine.

EXAMINING THE EVIDENCE
The social and economic effects of railways

Economic effects
1 Railways as an industry in itself.
2 Effect on capital and labour supply.
3 Demands on other industries.
4 Effect on other transport systems.

Social effects
1 Communications.
2 Urban life.
3 Mobility.

Use these headings to summarise the impact railways had.

Source A: Capital invested and total revenue

Year	Capital 1m	Track Mileage	Revenue 1m	Passenger Revenue %
1830		98		
1842		1 938	4.8	65
1850	235	6 084	12.7	52
1860	327	9 069	24.4	46
1870	503	13 562	42.9	43
1880	695	15 563	62.8	41
1890	860	17 281	76.8	43
1900	1 136	18 680	101.0	43
1912	1 290	20 038	124.0	42

The Liverpool Manchester Railway, one of the most profitable railways, averaged 10% on its capital – others averaged about 6%

Source B: Railways as an important investment
Railway property is a new feature in England's social economy which has introduced commercial feelings to the firesides of thousands.

The Economist (1845)

All the above from P.O. O'Brien, *The New Economic History of Railways*

Source C

Opening of provincial stock exchanges
1844 – Glasgow and Edinburgh
1845 – Leeds. Bristol, Birmingham and Leicester

Source D

Labour requirements on the railways			
Year	Mileage under construction	Labour employed as total of labour force	Wages
1839	1 000	50 000 1%	£2m–2.5m
1847	3 500	250 000 4%	£16m
Average number employed 1831–70: 60000			

Source E

Permanent employment by railway companies	
1850	56 000
1856	100 000
1875	250 000
1890	350 000
1910	600 000

Source F

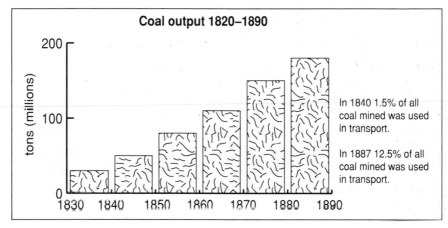

Coal output 1820–1890

In 1840 1.5% of all coal mined was used in transport.

In 1887 12.5% of all coal mined was used in transport.

Source G

Pig iron output 1820–60	
1820	400 000 tons
1830	650 000 tons
1840	1 396 400 tons
1850	2 250 000 tons
1860	3 802 920 tons

Source H: The impact of railways on farming

Fifteen years ago there was no railway communication between Norfolk and London. Cattle and sheep for the Smithfield Monday market had to leave their homes on the previous Wednesday or Thursday week. Such a long drift, particularly in hot weather, caused a great waste of meat. The heavy stall-fed cattle of East Norfolk suffered severely. The average loss on such bullocks were considered to be 4 stones, while the best yearling sheep are proved to have lost 6 lbs of mutton and 4 of tallow; but beasts from the open yards and old sheep, with careful drovers, did not waste in like manner. Stock now leave on the Saturday and are in the salesman's layers (enclosures or large sheds) that evening, fresh for the metropolitan market on Monday morning. The cost of the rail is considerably more than the old droving charges; but against that there is the gain of 20s. a head on every bullock a Norfolk farmer sends to town, to say nothing of being able to take immediate advantage of a dear market.

Source I

EFFECTS OF THE RAILROAD ON THE BRUTE CREATION.

Source J

Canal charges per ton, Hull to Manchester		
	Before railways	*After 1840*
For corn, flour, etc.	£1 4s 0d (120p)	13s 0d (65p)
For cotton twist	£1 12s 6d (152½p)	£1 0s 0d
For manufactured goods	£2 5s 0d (225p)	£1 4s 0d (120p)

Source K

Goods Carried	Rail	Carts, wagons and vans
1851	60 million tons	106 million tons
1900	410	671

Source L: Continued importance of horse-drawn transport

Without carriages and carts the railways would have been like stranded whales, giants unable to use their strength, for these were the only means of getting people and goods right to the doors of houses, warehouses, markets, and factories, where they wanted to be.

P.L.M. Thompson, *Victorian England: The Horse-drawn Society*

Source M: Social Effects

Railroad travelling is a delightful improvement of human life. Man is become a bird; he can fly longer and quicker than a Solan goose. The mamma rushes sixty miles in two hours to the aching finger of her conjugating and declining grammar boy. The early Scotchman scratches himself in the morning mists of the North, and has his porridge in Piccadilly before the setting of the sun ... Everything is near, everything is immediate – time, distance, and delay are abolished.

Sydney Smith, *H. Pearson, The Smith of Smiths*

Source N: Educating the working class

... Railways have accomplished what the far-famed SOCIETY FOR THE DIFFUSION OF USEFUL KNOWLEDGE, with its long train of noble and ignoble patrons and its penny magazines and penny encyclopaedias ... could never have effected; they have taught the thorough-bred Londoner ALMOST to discriminate between a plough and a harrow, and to recognise a potato by its stem.

Railway Times (1837)

Source O: Railways and the working class

... carried on by most lines in the manufacturing districts of Yorkshire and Lancashire, in the coal districts of the North, and in Scotland. These lines are in great measure dependent upon third class passengers, who are conveyed by all or nearly all the trains at fares averaging from 1d. to 1s 2d per mile. ...

In fine weather respectable tradespeople, clerks, etc., avail themselves of the third class carriages to a considerable extent; but the bulk of the half million third class passengers who are carried on this railway in the course of the year are strictly the working classes, weavers, masons, bricklayers, carpenters, mechanics and labourers of every description, some of whom used formerly to travel by carts, but the great number by foot. ...

In one respect a remarkable use has been made of the facilities afforded by railway communication. On the occasion of several strikes, when there was press of work, bodies of workmen have been engaged in London and carried to Manchester. ...

Upon these main lines of communication it is questionable whether the interests of the proprietors will ever induce them to encourage the development of a large third-class traffic. It is satisfactory, however, to find that there is a growing disposition among railway companies, thus circumstanced, to afford the accommodation of at least one train a day by which the poorer classes may be conveyed at reduced fares.

Report of the Officers of the Railway Department to the President of the Board of Trade, Feb. 1842, *Parliamentary Papers*, XLI

Source P: The 'New Economic historians' and the Railways

More than a decade ago trumpets heralded new economic history onto the academic stage ...

The achievement is impressive. Their research on railways exemplifies all the virtues now recognised as the hallmarks of new economic history.

Hypotheses are well specified and logically consistent; measurement is careful and sophisticated and substantial amounts of new data are generated by collection, collation, and by way of imaginative inference based upon economic theory.

The broad conclusions of the new economic history of railways will surely endure and historians can no longer exaggerate the contribution of railways to economic development. Single innovations, even the accelerated growth of particular industries cannot now be described as leading an economy towards 'take-off' or a 'drive to maturity'. Nineteenth-century growth is once again perceived as multi-factoral and complex; as a process in which no one input can be described as necessary or indispensable. Hyperbole and mono-causal explanations have certainly been checked.

Within the history of transport we now understand more clearly the mechanisms through which a decline in the cost of haulage saved real resources, widened markets, promoted local and regional specialisation and provided producers with access to natural resources. In all these ways railways carried forward a process that probably achieved a decisive breakthrough with canals. In fact one of the most interesting hypotheses thrown up by economic history is that for Western Europe, Russia and the United States natural and artificial waterways probably made a greater contribution to long-term economic progress than their more publicised mechanical rival and that railways made the greatest contribution in substituting for overland transport.

Patrick O'Brien, *The New Economic History of the Railways* (1977)

TALKING POINT

What would be the advantages and disadvantages of a railway network created by:

a) Private enterprise?

b) State control?

Some Points to consider:

● Cost of system.

● Standardisation of lines etc.

● Military use.

● Bureaucracy.

● Any Others?

1 What areas of British society and economy were affected by railway development?

2 What problems confront historians when evaluating the sources presented in this examining the evidence section?

3 Why might the role of railways to economic development and social change have been exaggerated by historians as well as contemporaries?

4 What contribution have the 'New Economic Historians' made to our understanding of the role of railways in mid nineteenth century Britain?

5 What methodological difficulties face the 'New Economic Historians'?

Railways and the State

Britain was unique compared to other modern industrial nations in that its railway system was created by private enterprise and not state control. Each method has advantages as well as drawbacks.

Despite Britain's reliance on private enterprise several factors persuaded Parliament that they could not allow such giant monopolies to operate without some form of regulation. Railway legislation, however, was not enacted without fierce opposition. In 1847, 178 M.P.s were railway directors; in 1867, 275. Such impressive railway interests in Parliament guaranteed a difficult passage for regulatory legislation.

Motives for the regulation of railways

Two motives determined the movement to regulate railways. Study the following evidence and determine what they were.

"The payment of legal tolls is only a very small part of the arrangement necessary to open railroads to public competition; any person with the mere authority to place an engine or carriages on a railway would be practically unable to supply his engine with water, or to take up and set passengers down … The Safety of the public also required that upon every railway there should be one system of management under one superintending authority. On this account it is necessary that the company should possess a complete control over the line of road although they should thereby acquire a monopoly."

Select Committee on Railways (1839)

1 (a) Why, in the opinion of the government, does it appear necessary that railway companies operate as a single company?

(b) What principle are they prepared to sacrifice in order to accomplish this objective?

(c) How does this proposal differ from that in practice on turnpike roads and canals?

2 In what ways does the Punch cartoon appear to differ in opinion from that of the select committee?

Legislation centred on two facets of railway operation – the need to regulate in the interests of public safety and measures to prevent railways abusing their monopolistic advantage.

RAILWAY AMALGAMATION—A PLEASANT STATE OF THINGS.

Passenger. "WHAT'S THE MATTER, GUARD?"
Guard (with presence of Mind). "OH, NOTHING PARTICULAR, SIR. WE'VE ONLY RUN INTO AN EXCURSION TRAIN!"
Passenger. "BUT, GOOD GRACIOUS! THERE'S A TRAIN JUST BEHIND US, ISN'T THERE?"
Guard. "YES, SIR! BUT A BOY HAS GONE DOWN THE LINE WITH A SIGNAL; AND IT'S VERY LIKELY THEY'LL SEE IT!"

PUNCH MAGAZINE.

Representation of railway interests in parliament

There are eighty-one directors sitting in Parliament; and though many of those take little or no part in the affairs of their respective railways, many of them are the most active members of the boards to which they belong. We have but to look back a few years, and mark the unanimity with which companies adopted the policy of getting themselves represented in the Legislature, to see that the furtherance of their respective interests – especially in cases of competition – was the incentive. How well this policy is understood among the initiated, may be judged from the fact, that gentlemen are now in some cases elected on boards simply because they are members of Parliament.

H. Spencer, 'Railway Morals and Railway Policy', reprinted from the Edinburgh Review, (1855)

The railway interest as political pressure group

Of all the nineteenth-century pressure groups, the railway interest was the most infamous. It had little in common with the landowning and farming interests, with whom it was often in dispute; was not a professional body, like the lawyers; and was often in conflict with other business interests. The railway interest represented big business at its most ruthless and at its most highly organised. The railway companies played a crucial part in the industrial development of the United Kingdom. The rise and fall of railway shares was regarded as barometer of the country's economic state.

… in the period before 1868 the unity and strength was more apparent than real. … Companies planned together only in emergencies and, as governments were generally reluctant to interfere with them, such emergencies arose infrequently. Indeed the United Railway Companies' Committee of 1867 might have lasted no longer than previous ad hoc committees which had withered away after a few years existence. That this did not happen was due to a stream of hostile legislation, actual or projected, which demonstrated the need for a permanent structure to protect company interests.

The steady growth of state intervention in the railway industry after 1868 was not the result of a carefully prepared plan, but sprang piecemeal from the efforts of all governments to deal empirically with different problems of railway administration.

G. Alderman, *The Railway Interest* (1973)

1 Why should the railways wish to have their interests represented in Parliament?

2 According to Spencer how effective was the railway interest in Parliament?

3 What does Spencer mean when he writes 'especially in cases of competition'?

4 How does Alderman define the nature of the railway interest in Parliament ?

5 Why does Alderman describe the railway interest as 'infamous'?

6 How does Alderman suggest the importance of the railways to the economy?

7 Why did the railway interests combine more closely after 1868?

Railway legislation

Year	Legislation	Year	Legislation
1840	**Railway Regulation Act:** a) Companies must inform the Board of Trade of any new lines which had to be inspected. b) Toll rates and accident figures must be submitted.	1846	**Gauge Act:** Stephenson's 4 feet 8 and a half inch gauge was made the standard width for all railway lines.
1842	**Second Railway Regulation Act:** The board of Trade could delay the opening of any new line until satisfied that its construction was satisfactory.	1854	**Railways and Canals Act:** It was forbidden for railway companies to give any special favours or privileges to any particular individual or company.
1844	**Cheap Trains Act:** a) Newly opened lines must provide cheap 3rd class travel on at least one train per day. The train was also required to stop at all the stations on the line. The fare was fixed at 1d per mile and the trains became nick-named 'Parliamentary Trains'. b) A more biting proposal involving state ownership was weakened by the opposition of Parliamentary interests. As the Act finally took form, the state could only purchase those lines enacted after 1844 and then only after twenty one years of private ownership. This excluded the 2300 miles of main trunk line already open	1858	The Board of Trade could issue 'requirements' to railway companies.
		1873	**The Railway Commission:** This was set up to listen to complaints but it had no powers to prosecute.
		1888	**The Railway and Canal Commission:** Companies were given six months to draw up new rates and charges. (When the companies issued their maximum charges, there was such a public outcry that a further act was passed).
		1894	Charges must not be unduly raised. The general ineffectiveness of this legislation illustrates the power of the railway interests in Parliament.

REVIEW

1	How did the early railways emerge as a major transport system?

- Wagonways.
- Mining industry.
- State of technology.

Stimulus for change:

- Growth of mining – domestic and industrial

Changing technology – advantages over alternative transport systems
Private Enterprise – railway mania – dividends on invested capital.

2 What were the social and economic effects of railways in mid nineteenth century Britain?

- The claims – both contemporary and recent.
problems of interpretation – statistical – diffuse effect of railways.
- Impact on transport – Demise of canals and horse-drawn traffic?
- Impact of industries – Direct and indirect.
- Social impact – the difficulty of measuring qualitive change. Benefits and disadvantages.
- The verdict of the New Economic historians.

3 Why, and with what results, did the State pass legislation affecting railways?

- Phenomenal growth of railways.
- The Role of Private enterprise.
- Government motivation. Detail of the type, range and effectiveness of legislation.
- The Power of the Railway interests.

9 War and the British Economy 1700–1815

PREVIEW

NAPOLEON AND PITT DIVIDING THE WORLD. CRUIKSHANK.

"No people ever yet grew rich by policies, but it is peace, industry and freedom that brings trade and wealth."

Sir Dudley Smith – a late seventeenth century economist in his treatise
The Value of Trade

"The peace has made one general miscontent.
Of these high marked patriots; war was rent!
Their love of country, millions all misspent,
How reconcile? By reconciling rent!"

Lord Byron, *The Age of Bronze*

War and the British economy

Wars waste human life, disrupt trade and destroy industry and capital. Yet Britain's stormy experience of war during the eighteenth century does not seem to bear this observation out. For roughly seventy years of that century Britain was involved in major wars. At the same time the pace of her industrialisation quickened and her overseas trade expanded at an unprecedented rate. Indeed for almost a quarter of a century, 1793–1815, Britain fought against France on a scale not known before. This period also co-incided to a remarkable degree with the most critical stage in the Industrial Revolution.

Summary of major wars involving Britain				
1702–13	1740–48	1756–63	1776–83	1793–1815
Spanish Succession *Dynastic* mainly Europe	Austrian Succ. *Dynastic* mainly Europe	Seven Yrs. Britain acquires Canada and India	American Indep. Britain loses 13 colonies	French Rev. Napol. Wrs

TALKING POINT

Consider the major wars of the twentieth century. In what ways have they benefited society? In what ways have they damaged it? Is it possible to see war as a promoter of progress?

It is therefore tempting to ask: What was the relationship, if any, between war and the process of British industrialisation? Did war actually retard, stagnate or stimulate the economy? And if so, which aspects of the economy were affected most and which least?

TALKING POINT

Let us consider, in a general way, the possible effects war may have had on certain industries. The illustrations will be helpful.

THE BATTLE OF TRAFALGAR – THE SURRENDER OF THE 'REDOUBTABLE' AFTER AN ORIGINAL PAINTING BY CLARKSON STANSFIELD.

TALKING POINT

Secondly, consider the ways the economy as a whole may have been effected by war:

- Trade
- Capital
- Manufacturing
- Labour
- Farming
- Wages
- Prices

CUIRVOSSIERS CHARGING THE HIGHLANDERS IN A SQUARE AT THE BATTLE OF WATERLOO.

18th Century wars and their economic effect

What were wars like in the eighteenth century? How were they fought, and for what reasons? Wars in the twentieth century have been fought with a ferocity and scale unknown in previous centuries which have left the vanquished economically exhausted and frequently the victors depleted of resources. By contrast eighteenth century wars were fought with more limited aims, pursuits and objectives. They were waged by small professional armies and although they had global colonial consequences, they were fought within a limited geographical area.

'In theory and practice eighteenth century wars were of limited liability – about something concrete, rather than earlier wars of righteousness and moral purpose – clashes between rulers, between dynastic states in limited wars fought with limited means and for limited objectives, which ended with a drawing up of a balance sheet.'

E. Robson, *The Armed Forces and the Art of War*
New Cambridge History VII

TALKING POINT

What does E. Robson mean when he refers to 18 Century wars as ones of 'limited liability'?

Note

In America today almost 80 billion dollars is spent on the armaments industry. In addition the collapse of the Soviet Union and the Eastern bloc is partially explained in terms of huge defence expenditure.

The prevailing evidence suggests that at least until the War of American Independence in 1776, Britain's economy appears to have been stimulated by the wars she fought. In the first place these wars occurred at an important point in the history of technological advance. Ideas which had earlier been the subject of experimental interest, were rapidly applied and developed for industrial purposes. These advances were of particular importance in the heavy metal industries and the early stages of steam power. These developments, in turn, led to the opening up of new sources of raw materials and to subsequent reductions in cost. Government demand for arms and ammunition contributed substantially to this growth.

The stimulating impact of war can be clearly seen in its effect upon the iron industry. Whilst Britain was at peace between 1714–1740 the iron industry was languishing but during subsequent wars, 1740–48, and particularly the Seven Years War (1756–63) production accelerated. These wars also had an important effect on demand in so far as wars extended overseas markets. This had a direct effect on the demand for British goods.

Professor W.W. Rostow is most emphatic about the beneficial effects of war on the British economy.

'In the long run unquestionably, the eighteenth century wars paid in a world of competing economies, … It is most unlikely that the total volume of world trade, in the long run, was greater because of the wars between 1700–1815, although the proportionate volume of British trade was undoubtedly greater than it would otherwise have been.'

W.W. Rostow, *The Process of Economic Growth*

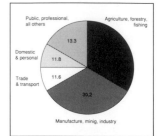

1 DISTRIBUTION OF THE LABOUR FORCE, 1811 (AS A PERCENTAGE OF TOTAL OCCUPIED POPULATION).

The American Declaration of Independence from British rule in 1776 however, marked a down-turn in Britain's fortunes. Hitherto Britain's colonial expansion had proceeded without impediment and the expansion of her trade had grown apace. The war wavered to and fro until the entry of France on the side of the American colonists tipped the balance against the British forces. By 1783 Britain was vanquished – her 'New World' Empire lost. Such a loss was bound to have disastrous consequences for Britain.

A.H. John concluded;

'Considerable counter-balancing factors occured to the wartime expansion of industry which, on the whole, probably negatived the advances of the war. During the years 1776–1783, for example, the financing of government demand was balanced by a contraction of investment in other branches of activity; and there was a fall of employment in the export industries, particularly those supplying the North American market.'

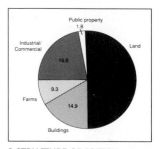

2 STRUCTURE OF BRITISH NATIONAL CAPITAL, 1812 (AS A PERCENTAGE OF TOTAL NATIONAL CAPITAL).

The statistics for English foreign trade indicate a more dramatic set-back than a mere cancelling out of advantages and drawbacks as A.H. John claims.

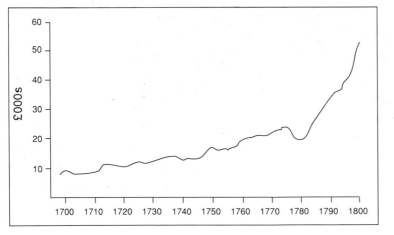

ENGLISH FOREIGN TRADE IN THE EIGHTEENTH CENTURY (NET IMPORTS PLUS DOMESTIC EXPORTS; OFFICIAL VALUES). NOTES:
(1) THE STATISTICS ON WHICH THIS FIGURE IS BASED ARE TAKEN FROM DEANE AND COLE (1967: 48 AND APPENDIX 1).
(2) THE STATISTICS ARE FOR OFFICIAL VALUES OF IMPORTS AND EXPORTS, AS EXPLAINED IN THE TEXT. THEY ARE THEREFORE A ROUGH APPROXIMATION TO A SERIES OF THE VOLUME OF TRADE.
(3) THE STATISTICS ARE FOR ENGLAND, 1697–1774, AND FOR GREAT BRITAIN, 1772–1800. A THREE-YEAR MOVING AVERAGE HAS BEEN COMPUTED FROM THE ORIGINAL SERIES.

Certainly the American War of Independence slowed down the expansion of the British economy and the downward plunge of the trade figures at the end of the war illustrate the subsequent recession. Those industries not heavily dependent upon the import and export trade, however, do not tell the same story of stagnation.

The war with France 1793–1815

The lengthy wars with France, however, were of much greater magnitude than either the War of American Independence or any previous war that Britain had fought in the eighteenth century. No previous political upheaval, however violent, had aroused such passionate enthusiasm. The ideal of the French Revolution was not merely to change the French social system but to regenerate the whole human race.

An atmosphere of missionary fervour was generated with the objective of overthrowing 'corrupt' monarchist regimes and to replace them with virtuous republics. The dynamics of revolution spilled over frontiers and in the hands of Napoleon Bonaparte, the inheritor of the revolution, the Republican ideal became a rationale for conquest and ultimately, Empire. By 1812, France was at the hub of an Empire around which subservient and client states revolved. Such a massive shift in the balance of power was bound to affect the British economy.

Annual averages	Total gross public expenditure (£m)	Total value domestic exports plus ½ re-exports (£m)
1781–5	30.8	15.0
1786–90	19.6	21.0
1791–5	29.4	27.1
1796–1800	59.0	35.0
1801–5	61.5	42.2
1806–10	77.5	44.3
1811–15	101.1	45.8
1816–20	60.7	42.5
1821–5	55.8	38.9
1826–30	54.2	37.2

Sources. Basic public expenditures and export data from Mitchell and Deane, *Abstract of Historical Statistics*. Estimates of market value re-exports 1796–1830 from A.H. Imlah, *Economic Elements in the Pax Britannica*. Gross public expenditure 1781–1800 based on national addition of 20 per cent to net public expenditure figures. Estimates of market value of exports and re-exports 1781–95 based on relationship between official and market values for domestic exports and re-exports respectively over average of period 1796–1800.

Who lost and who gained by these wars? In the first place to wage war Britain required vast funds. Could this have diverted capital from industrial use into government expenditure? The table tells its own story.

Principal sources of government finance 1781–1830				
	Budget deficit	Customs duties	Excise duties	Income, assessed and land taxes
As percentages of: % Net public expenditure G.B.	%	%	%	%
1781–5	46.7	12.6	23.7	10.2
1786–90	–	23.3	43.8	18.0
1791–5	24.2	15.8	35.7	12.1
1796–1800	46.7	10.6	21.7	9.2
Gross public expenditure U.K.				
1801–5	24.9	17.2	31.4	14.8
1806–10	13.4	17.3	34.1	26.0
1811–15	26.2	13.9	27.7	21.8
1816–20	–	21.2	43.7	18.1
1821–15	–	25.8	49.2	12.0
1826–30	–	36.0	38.4	9.6

Source. Based on public income and expenditure accounts summarised in Mitchell and Deane, *Abstract of Historical Statistics*. Since Irish customs and excise duties were not separately returned for the period 1801–6 (though they are included in gross public income) they have been estimated for this table by analogy with their proportion to the corresponding British totals for the period 1807–10.

TALKING POINT

What are the principles which underlie taxation today? Why is it important to know which group of people were paying higher taxes?

As Chancellor of the Exchequer in 1784, William Pitt was faced with a huge financial deficit at a time when Britain's public revenue was a chaotic collection of customs, excise duties and legal stamp duties. He vastly improved the revenue yield by introducing 'assessed taxes'. These were collections of graduated taxes so that the wealthy bore the brunt of the main charges. For example, Pitt's taxation package included a tax on servants, carriages, house windows and so on. In this way he managed to produce a budget surplus in 1787 which enabled him to set up a 'sinking fund'. This novel idea was designed to provide capital for investment from budget surpluses upon which interest would accumulate and, in due course, could be used to pay off the national debt. The diagram below will help you to understand how this was meant to achieve Pitt's objective.

TALKING POINT

Which countries today have massive national debts? What is the danger to those countries of mounting debts?

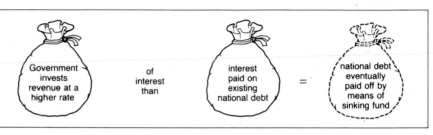

These taxation measures may have enabled Pitt to 'balance the books' but in the process did he take capital away from those groups of people who may have put it to good use by investing in industry? To answer this question we need to know the answers to several related questions, for example; what proportion were of the assessed kind and which groups in society paid the largest share?

Whilst income tax prevented a runaway budget deficit the single most important contributor to government revenue continued to be Customs and Excise. If we take the war years as a whole;

TALKING POINT

What does it mean to 'budget deficit'? Is this always a disadvantage to a country?

Sources of government finance 1793–1815	
Income tax	11%
Land assessed tax	11%
Customs	18%
Excise duties	31%
Borrowing (budget defeciting)	29%

Accepting that the contribution of income tax to the overall budget is small might the demand have fallen more heavily on groups more likely to have invested in industry? The Income and Property taxes initiated by William Pitt in 1799 were levied in five schedules.

Public expenditure financed from income tax 1803–15		
Schedule A:	Tax on rents	6%
Schedule B:	Farmers' capital profits	2%
Schedule C:	Interest from funds	
Schedule D:	From trade, commerce, professions	2%
Schedule E:	Income from offices, pensions	1%
Total revenue from income tax		11%

Of course it would be wrong to ascribe one particular group as being potentially more likely to invest in industry than another, for example landowners invested in developing mineral reserves on their estates and transport improvements. On balance, although some excise duties on paper and glass may have depressed industrial expansion or disrupted the flow of raw materials and manufactured goods to markets, the actual financing of the war from income tax did not bear down heavily on those groups principally active in financing the process of industrialisation.

Industrial development and war demands

Certain key industries were probably boosted by government expenditure on war materials. The iron industry, in particular, clearly would have been affected by the demand for arms and ammunition. The table below shows this to have been the case.

Year	No of Furnaces	Estimated annual production 000s tons
1788	85	68
1796	121	126
1806	225*	243–258
1815	–	344–373
1818	–	300–325
1820	170	368–400
1823	266	455
*55 of these were out of blast in 1806		

FROM A. BIRCH, THE ECONOMIC HISTORY OF THE BRITISH IRON AND STEEL INDUSTRY, 1784–1879, CASS, 1967.

Iron production in the decade 1796–1806 was just under three times that of pre-war years. Although it is impossible to divorce strategic from non-strategic uses of iron, we must attempt to evaluate the contribution

TOKEN COINS CARRON IRON WORKS, FALKIRK.

TALKING POINT

Why would industrialists, like Wilkinson, need to produce their own coinage? What effect might this have on the economy as a whole?

government war expenditure may have made in increasing iron production. One indication of its importance is the decline in output immediately at the end of hostilities in 1815. A few years later, however, industrial needs begin to surpass that of war demands.

From the opening of the war, to around 1796, the price of iron remained fairly steady due to rising industrial demand. Rising demand was met through a combination of increased domestic output and rising imports from Sweden and Russia.

After 1796 the price of foreign iron rose by about 30 per cent and a boom in home production took place. Advertisements for labour strongly imply the difficulty of keeping pace with a rush of orders. New businesses arose and all existing works were extended. Among the causes which led to increased productivity the demand by government for Ordinance must be paramount. The brief peace of Amiens in 1801 was so short that it carried the iron industry through the gap in demand.

Indeed, the prosperity of many major works was founded upon the profits of the manufacture of weapons and ammunition alone. South and North Wales, the Black Country, Shropshire, Yorkshire and Derbyshire shared in the general increase of demand. Nowhere, however, is this dependancy on arms and ammunition better illustrated than by the famous iron works of Carron near Falkirk. These works, founded in 1759, concentrated on the production of cannon and shot. John 'Iron-Mad' Wilkinson, (1728–1808), an engineer employed at these works, developed cannon-boring techniques which were the most advanced of their day and the Works built up a remarkable reputation for powerful and effective carronades.

The one complete year of peace, 1801–1802, (The Peace of Amiens) was a peak of economic activity for the country generally but not at Carron. For the first time total sales fell below £100 000 due to the fall in sale of shot. With the resumption of war a rise in demand took place. By 1804 the sales of shot and carronades reached a new record in total sales.

Initially, however, the war was a double-edged sword for the iron industry. Whilst the war increased demand, supplies and markets diminished due to the conquests of Napoleon and the consequent disruption to trade. Much of the bar iron imported into Britain, for example, came from the Baltic for the ore was free of phosphorous and capable of easy smelting and the manufacture of superior bar-iron. Nevertheless, the necessity of war subsequently improved both the quality and quantity of British iron and by 1812 she had become a net exporter of iron.

Post war decline was avoided by an enormous upsurge in the home market. Iron water pipes came into general use in London in 1810 and Liverpool expanded her docks with iron rather than with wood. 'Iron-Mad' Wilkinson did much to popularise the wider use of the material – iron houses, iron chairs and even iron coffins! More seriously, due to his developments in furnace operations, he produced iron which was less likely to fracture and it was therefore suitable for a potentially vast market of machine production.

We can conclude that, at least in respect of the iron industry:

- Wars greatly accelerated demand in the form of munitions and armaments.
- The course of war greatly favoured the iron trade.
- The continued growth of the home market prevented a damaging recession in the industry at the end of the war.

The impact of the French wars on other industries

The iron industry is an obvious example of how the stimulus of war increased production and assisted a developing technology. But what of other key industries in Britain at this time? Unfortunately information is somewhat sketchy although excise and trade returns can at least give us an indication of trends. Study the table below and answer these questions.

Selected industrial growth rates
Compound rates per cent per annum calculated between quinquennial averages centred on years specified

	1783–93 (%)	1793–1802 (%)	1802–15 (%)	1815–25 (%)
Glass	3.7	0.4	decline	2.9
Bricks	n.a.	decline	0.6	6.4
Paper	2.8	1.6	2.3	2.9
White tin	2.7	decline	decline	6.2
Tallow candles	1.6	1.5	1.2	3.3
Beer	1.5	decline	0.3	1.1
British spirits	9.2	decline	1.8	3.3
Soap	2.1	1.6	2.3	3.4
Hides and skins	1.1	0.3	1.3	1.3
Scottish linens	2.0	0.2	1.9	n.a.
Yorkshire woollens	4.0	3.1	1.6	6.9
Printed goods	6.9	7.2	3.9	5.3
Raw cotton imports	8.7	8.9	2.9	6.9

SOURCE. BASIC QUANTITY DATA FROM MITCHELL AND DEANE, ABSTRACT OF HISTORICAL STATISTICS. MOST OF THESE RELATE TO EXCISE RETURNS AND SOME ARE BASED ON WEIGHTED AVERAGES OF THE ORIGINAL DATA. NET RAW COTTON IMPORTS EXCLUDE RE-EXPORTS.

1 In general terms how did the different phases of war affect particular industries?

2 Which industry appears to suffer the worst set-back during the war? What reasons may account for this?

3 It is usual, during war-time, for inflation to increase rapidly. Why should this be and how might it affect industry?

It seems probable that those industries particularly dependant upon the export trades, for example cotton, benefited from the first phase of the war but coal and timber may have had their growth inhibited by high interest rates due to the inflation of the war years. In short, wars may have brought a short-term stimulus to the economy at a critical period in the Industrial Revolution but only peace could offer long term expansion.

Are final conclusions possible?

Would the pace of industrial growth have been faster if there had been no war or did the war itself play an important role in quickening the momentum of industrial change? There is, of course, no answer to such a 'counter factual proposition'. We can only tentatively assess what might have happened to the British economy if there had been no war at all.

'In the end, however, it must be admitted that a full and accurate reckoning of the costs of benefits might tip the balance of the account one way or another. The accessible evidence, taken as a whole, does not support the view that the war of 1793–1815 exerted a serious brake on British industrial progress. Even in years when public defence expenditure depended most heavily on loan finance, for example in the second half of the 1790s, there seem to have been adequate investment funds available to the private sector to maintain an unprecedently fast rate of capital accumulation in the leading industries of the industrial revolution (particularly cotton and iron) and in the transport facilities (e.g. canals, docks and harbours) which constituted the essential overhead capital needed for sustained industrialisation. When in the second phase of the war the expansion of overseas trade was restricted by the way the conflict developed, British merchants still found it possible to find new markets for and sources of raw materials and the increase in public expenditure was more than enough to maintain a high level of domestic demand for British industry. In the last analysis, and leaving aside the intractable hypothetical questions, it would appear that the war of 1793–1815, prolonged and expensive though it was, does not seem to have caused more than superficial fluctuations in the pace and content of the British industrial revolution.'

P. Deane, *The Industrial Revolution*

The post war situation

The effects of wars live on after hostilities cease. With the return of peace in 1815 there was a short and hectic boom as exports rushed to markets previously blockaded but the extravagant hopes of free access to the Americas and Europe came to an end in 1818 as recession set in.

'Great Britain, though victorious, suffered acutely. Mismanagement was largely responsible for her sufferings – mismanagement of or rather complete indifference to problems of demobilisation; mismanagement of taxes (the income tax was abandoned at the clamour of interested parties, and the interest on the huge debt paid mainly from indirect taxes which bore heavily on the poor): mismanagement of food supplies, by the imposition

Agriculture and the war economy

The structure of the national capital of Great Britain, 1798–1927

(as percentages of the total national capital)

Circa	1798	1812
1. Land	55.0[3]	54.2[3]
2. Buildings	13.8	14.9
3. Farm	8.7	9.3
4. Overseas securities	—[2]	—[2]
5. Domestic railways		
6. Industrial commercial and financial capital	20.8	19.8
7. Public property[5]	1.7	1.8
8. Total national capital[1]	100.0	100.0

Notes:

1 Excluding national debt and moveable property (furniture, plate, etc.).

2 No estimate available: probably negligible.

3 Excludes standing timber which is included in the industrial capital.

5 Excluding roads and military property.

DIAGRAM AND TABLE FROM P. DEANE AND W.A. COLE, *BRITISH ECONOMIC GROWTH 1868–1959* (1967).

CONSIDER

1

What was the importance of agriculture to the national economy?

2

In what way might agriculture exert an even greater effect than is indicated in these tables?

Estimated percentage distribution of the British labour force, 1801–1951

(as percentages of the total occupied population)

	Agriculture, forestry, fishing	Manufacture, mining, industry	Trade and transport	Domestic and personal	Public, profession and all other
1801	35.9	29.7	11.2	11.5	11.8
1811	33.0	30.2	11.6	11.8	13.3
1821	28.4	38.4	12.1	12.7	8.5
1831	24.6	40.8	12.4	12.6	9.5
1841	22.2	40.5	14.2	14.5	8.5
1851	21.7	42.9	15.8	13.0	6.7
1861	18.7	43.6	16.6	14.3	6.9
1871	15.1	43.1	19.6	15.3	6.8
1881	12.6	43.5	21.3	15.4	7.3
1891	10.5	43.9	22.6	15.8	7.1
1901	8.7	46.3	21.4	14.1	9.6
1911	8.3	46.4	21.5	13.9	9.9

STRUCTURE OF BRITISH NATIONAL PRODUCT 1811

	£m	% total national income
Agriculture	107.5	35.7
Trade and Transport	50.1	16.6
Manufactures, Mining and Building	62.6	20.8
Housing	17.2	5.7
Government and Defence	32.4	10.8
Domestic, professional and all other	31.4	10.4
Total National Income	301.1	100

The boxed data hides possible further conclusions. The pie chart refers only to the labour force not the total population. If dependants are added to these totals agriculture nearly encompasses half the total population of Britain in 1811. You should have noted in the earlier chapter 'Financing the Industrial Revolution' how dependent mining, trade, transport and manufacturing were on capital from agricultural profits. Government at this time must have been very dependent upon agricultural interests to finance the war as well as being a provider of food stuffs.

TASK

Study the table of Enclosure Acts and answer this question.

How does this help to explain the fortunes of agriculture during the war period?

ENCLOSURE ACTS 1793-1815

	Mainly commonfields with commonable land		Commons and wastes and common pasture only		Total	
	Acts	Acreage	**Acts**	Acreage	**Acts**	Acreage
1793 - 1795	*156*	274.354	*47*	64.672	*203*	339.026
1796 - 1798	*142*	245.987	*59*	59.544	*201*	305.534
1799 - 1801	*188*	322.837	*76*	149.871	*264*	472.708
1802 - 1804	*169*	265.552	*84*	134.893	*253*	400.445
1805 - 1807	*146*	208.545	*95*	124.510	*241*	333.061
1808 - 1810	*190*	287.534	*119*	161.892	*309*	449.435
1811 - 1813	*190*	283.403	*169*	212.109	*364*	495.512
1814 - 1816	*104*	143.583	*124*	122.820	*228*	226.403

FROM A.H. JOHN, 'FARMING IN WARTIME': 1793–1815, IN E.C. JONES AND G.E. MINGAY, *LAND, LABOUR AND POPULATION IN THE INDUSTRIAL REVOLUTION* EDWARD ARNOLD, 1967.

All farm prices were high throughout the war with grain prices showing a particularly steep climb. This factor encouraged more and more marginal land to be taken into cultivation, thus hastening the process of enclosure. Costs as well as prices rose; the tenant farmer paid high rents, labourers' wages rose and they were much more heavily taxed than before. For the first time, on any sizeable scale new farming methods were introduced and numerous patents were taken out to increase the mechanisation of agriculture.

Over the whole period 1793–1815 more than three million acres were brought under enclosure, in addition to a further unknown acreage, by means of private arrangements. It was a time, in short, of rising prices and prosperity for agriculture. Agricultural interests fought to preserve this advantage at the end of the war when continental competition threatened their unrivalled prosperity.

of the Corn Law; and so on. But suffering due to international economic dislocation following war could not have been avoided by management however good.'

J.H. Clapham, *Europe after the Great Wars, 1816–1920 Economic Journal, Vol. 30, (1920)*

TALKING POINT

J.H. Clapham asserts that many problems were created by government mismanagement. Is this a reasonable historical conclusion to come to?

EXAMINING THE EVIDENCE
The Continental System

'The elephant cannot fight the whale but we must find a means to subdue the sea to the land.'

Napoleon Bonaparte

The Continental System was a plan devised by Napoleon to defeat Britain economically and to replace her dominance with French commercial supremacy. He believed that British dependence upon overseas commerce made it possible for her to be brought down if only she was cut off from her markets by blockade.

In this way Britain's financial prosperity would be damaged and her power destroyed. In Britain's wake, French economic supremacy would rise behind protective walls of preferential tariffs.

The Berlin and Milan Decrees (1806–1807) were orders issued by Napoleon to institute the economic blockade of England.

- Britain to be in a state of blockade with every European port closed to British shipping.
- France and her allies forbidden to trade with Britain.
- Neutral ships not to call at British ports otherwise they would be confiscated.
- All British merchandise on the continent to be destroyed.
- Italy, the German Ruhr and Holland were to become economic satellites of France.

Orders in Council (1806–1807) Britain's Response

- France and her allies blockaded.
- Neutral ships on route to Europe would be diverted to British ports.

Source A: The Plumb-Pudding in danger – or State Epicures taking un Petit Soupe

The great globe itself and all which it inherit, is too small to satisfy such insatiable appetites.

CRUIKSHANK.

Source B: Industry and war

No foreign war of great expense or duration could conveniently be carried on by the exportation of the rude produce of the soil. The expense of sending such a quantity of it to a foreign country as might purchase the pay and provisions of an army would be too great. It is otherwise with the exportation of manufactures.

In the midst of the most destructive war the greater part of manufactures may frequently flourish greatly; and, on the contrary, they may decline on the return of peace.

A. Smith *An Enquiry into the Nature and Causes of the Wealth of Nations*

Source C: War and British industrial progress

The war itself, when it had extended its ravages over Europe, to Asia, and to America, seemed but a new stimulus to draw forth our exhaustless resources; ... Thus our country possessed, at the conclusion of the war, a productive power, which operated to the same effect as if her population had been actually increased fifteen or twenty-fold; and this had been chiefly created within the preceeding twenty-five years. The rapid progress made by Great Britain, during the war, in wealth and political influence, can therefore no longer astonish: the cause was quite adequate to the effect.

Now, however, new circumstances have arisen. The war demand for the production of labour having ceased, markets could no longer be found for them; and the revenues of the world were inadequate to purchase that which a power so enormous in its effects did produce.

Robert Owen. *Report to the Committee for the Relief of the Manufacturing Poor* (1817)

Source D: Balance and loss of war: Great Britain and France

War abstracts from productive employment not only capital, but likewise labourers; that the funds withdrawn from the remuneration of productive labourers are taken from production, to man the army and navy, the labouring classes are not damaged, the capitalists are not benefitted, and the general produce of the country is diminished by war expenditure. Accordingly ... though true of this country, (it) is wholly inapplicable to countries differently circumstanced; to France, for example, during the Napoleonic Wars. At this period the draught on the labouring population of France, for a long series of years, was enormous, while the funds which supported the war were mostly supplied by contributions levied on the countries overrun by the French arms. In France, accordingly the wages of labour did not fall, but rose; the employers of labour were not benefitted but injured; while the wealth of the country was impaired by the suspension or total loss of so vast an amount of its productive labour. In England, all this was reversed. England employed comparatively few additional soldiers and sailors of her own, while she diverted hundreds of millions of pounds of capital from productive employment to supply munitions of war and support for her continental allies. Consequently her labourers suffered, her capitalists prospered, and her prominent productive resources did not fall off.

John Stuart Mill, *Principles of Political Economy with some of its Applications to Social Philosophy*

Source E: Damaging effects of the war on the French economy

From the Baltic to the Archipelago nothing but despair and misery to be seen. Grass is growing in the streets of this city. Its beautiful port is deserted except by two Marblehead fishing schooners and three or four empty vessels which still swing to the tide.

American Consul at Bordeaux, March 28, 1808 quoted by F.E. Melvin, *Napoleon's Navigation System; A Study of French Contro. During the Continental Blockade*

Source F: War and the disruption to trade

The impact of the wars upon the long run development of industry ... was felt mostly through the dislocation of international trade ... in which economic warfare played a prominent part. These dislocations were at work during the whole war period and not only during the Continental blockade ... in fact most of the developments which were thought of as characteristic of the blockade years (1806–13) had started much earlier, so that a longer term view is needed to set the problem into perspective.

Three main factors worked during the Napoleonic Wars towards disturbing traditional trading relations: maritime blockade by the British, 'self-blockade' imposed by the French, and lastly the large scale redrafting of Europe's political map.

The balance sheet of the Napoleonic wars for the Continent as a whole might therefore be something like this: collapse of the 'maritime' industries, decay of the linen industries, stagnation of the primary iron industry, modest growth of the wool, silk and secondary metal industries, relatively fast progress of the cotton industry, and a modest increase in overall industrial output. This was certainly smaller than the rise that had taken place meanwhile in Britain – though recent research has come to the conclusion that the Napoleonic Wars had a retardative effect upon British industrial growth and investment in industry. So on the whole the impact of the wars was more unfavourable to the Continent than to England and made more serious its time-lag.

The shift of industry from the seaboard to the heartland of western Europe (Rhine and Northern France) ... the Napoleonic Wars made most European industries inward looking and geared first and foremost to the national market.

F. Crouzet, *Wars, Blockade and Economic Change in Europe 1792–1815*
Journal of Economic History Vol. XXIV 1964

Source G: Industrial competition between Britain and mainland Europe

Despite the retardation in Britain's industrial development registered in recent research – notably Crouzet's – the Continental industrial sector appears to have been still further behind Great Britain in 1815 than it had been in 1790.

The impression of the period is a relatively familiar one. Crouzet, however, has suggested that the process of adjustment to new markets had a significant positive side ... an accumulation of manufacturing skills, techniques, capital and locations which laid the foundations of subsequent industrial development. Crouzet's key example concerns the development of the textile industry ... Unfortunately Crouzet presents little evidence here which would support this argument: were they as 'large-scale', 'mechanised' and 'integrated'? Not by comparison with British firms. Moreover much of the new manufacturing edifice ... proved unrenumerative after 1814 when faced with British competition.

At least several centres of Continental textile development, one thinks of the German Rhineland, though it was not alone in this respect, – owed much of their buoyancy and success in the 1830s to their trans-oceanic trading connections. Furthermore, if we admit the importance of export agriculture (which the Crouzet paper ignores) the picture of the inward – orientated continental economy, at least for the first third of the nineteenth century, becomes less plausible.

Richard Tilley's discussion of Crouzet's Papers, *Journal of Economic History Vol. XXIV 1964*

Source H: A summary of the impact of the continental system

Britain	France
• Exports remained high to the European mainland.	• French cotton and sugar beet industries relatively prosperous.
e.g. 25%–42% of total exports	• France dominated European economies.
• New markets developed overseas particularly the Americas.	
• Seized about 3840 neutral merchant ships.	• About 480 British ships sunk.
• Total revenue increased 1805–£103,000 1080–£120,000 1811–£131,000 1814–£162,000	• British suffered most through shortage of raw materials; wool–Spain and Germany iron–Sweden corn–Baltic
• Established bases at Malta and Heligoland to smuggle goods into Europe.	• French colonial trade almost at a standstill – never regained 1789 level.

L.W. Cowie, *Eighteenth Century Europe*

---

1 Who were the economic winners and who were the economic losers as a result of the Napoleonic Wars?

2 Why can the effect of wars on the economy not merely be felt during the duration of the war alone? Refer to the impact of the Napoleonic Wars.

3 '...the Continental System became closely connected with the existence of Napoleon's empire and was an important cause of its collapse.' To what extent would you agree with this statement?

4 What are the limitations and advantages of these sources to a student studying the effects of the Continental System?

5 'The greater the industrialisation of the country the greater the chances that country will survive a war of long duration.' How accurately may this statement be applied to Britain's struggle against France?

The 19th Century French economic historian Lefebvre remarked that to understand the past 'Il faut compter' – it is necessary to count.

What did he mean by this apparently simple instruction? Is it sufficient in the study of history merely to 'count'? How appropriately could Lefebvre's instruction be used to measure the impact of the French and Napoleonic Wars on the European economy?

Economic History emerged from the fusion and application of economic theory to the study of history, becoming, arguably, one of the most important sub-histories to emerge. However, the science of economics has become a vast and weighty subject, with mathematics dominating economic theory. What difficulties and opportunities present themselves from the merger of economic theory and the study of history?

Review
What impact did war have on the British economy between 1793–1815?

Introduction: General impact of war – inflation, disruption of trade and industry

Development: (a) Characteristics of eighteenth century wars.
Britain's colonial expansion.
Setback to American War of Independence.

     (b) The scale of Napoleonic Wars.
Continental System as economic warfare.

     (c) Impact on British Trade – new trading patterns.

     (d) Impact on specific industries.

     (e) Impact on British agriculture.

     (f) Post-war Britain.

Conclusion: General gain but important to stress impact upon different industries and at different phases of the war.

10 The Standard of Living Controversy

PREVIEW

Working class poverty or a Golden Age?

'In fifty years of the Industrial Revolution the working class share of the national product had almost certainly fallen relative to the share of the property-owning and professional classes. The 'average' working man remained very close to subsistence level at a time when he was surrounded by the evidence of an increase of national wealth.'

E.P. Thompson, *The Making of the English Working Class* (1963)

'Consumption statistics before 1850 ... indicate modest but fluctuating increases. Import statistics are the most accurate of the measures ... and these show important long term gains ... During the 'hungry forties' there were increases in the average per capita consumption ... Misconceptions existed about England before the industrial Revolution, for example that rural life was naturally better than town life, that working for oneself was better and more secure than working for an employer, that child and female labour was something new, that the domestic system was preferable to the factory system ... and so on, in other words the myth of the golden age.'

R.M. Hartwell, *The Rising Standard of Living in England 1800–1850, Economic History Review 2nd Series XIII* (April 1961)

The difficulties in tackling the question

Great wealth was created by the Industrial Revolution but did all share in the prosperity? One of the hardest fought debates amongst historians is whether the standard of living of the labouring classes rose or fell between 1780 and 1850. It is also one to which no final answer has been reached.

Historians, such as E.P. Thompson, believe that the condition of the mass of working people deteriorated between 1780–1840 and hence they are dubbed 'pessimists'. Ranged against them are the 'optimists', like Hartwell, who argue that a slow but perceptible improvement took place.

Why has an answer to this question proved so elusive? Firstly, there are an enormous number of factors which we need to take into account when measuring the standard of living: consumption of foodstuffs, nutrition, public health and so on. At best, measuring changes in the standard of living depends upon fragmentary and unreliable statistics, of which real wages (money wages adjusted to prices i.e. what money wages will actually buy) and price indices (changes in the price of goods relative to what people earn) are the most important. Both these sets of statistics are fraught with difficulties of compilation and interpretation. Most of the data on money wages tends to come from the south of England and represent the wages of skilled workers. Rarely do they show what the whole family earned which would be more the norm at this time. Shopping baskets of typical goods, upon which price indices are based, often omit important commodities and fail to show regional variations.

Secondly, there is a confusion of terms. 'Standard of living' is often used as if it were interchangeable with 'quality of life'. A sense of progress is very subjective and relative to the individual. New working conditions or changes in life-style, may seem to the individual to be a backward step despite the possible increase in material comfort. Such perceptions are impossible to measure numerically.

Thirdly, historians who 'joust' with one another do not always make it clear which time-span their arguments cover. Some refer to the century in which the full impact of the Industrial Revolution occurred, 1750–1850; others to a more limited period, namely the war period and its aftermath 1790–1830; others to the first 50 years of the nineteenth century.

Fourthly, all historians have political beliefs, whether they belong to a particular party or not, and these can consciously or unconsciously colour their interpretations. Marxist historians, like E.P. Thompson, fiercely denounce the denigration of workers by the capitalist system. Equally, 'liberal' historians point to the ultimate benefits of capitalism and thus, if they admit hardship to workers in the short term, reconcile them in the long term.

Fifthly, it is impossible to isolate industrialisation as the sole cause of fluctuating economic fortunes. For twenty-three years of the period under scrutiny, 1793–1815, Britain was at war, population rose rapidly, urbanisation accelerated and there was a series of poor harvests. All of these factors must have played a part, in varying degrees, to the raising or lowering of the standard of living of working people.

Sixthly, we must be clear about which workers we are discussing. It would be misleading to see all workers as either suffering or benefiting

TALKING POINT

Consider how we might arrive at some measure of the standard of living today. What factors would you include?

Note

In the first years of the twentieth century A.C. Bowey stated that people's perception of progress is largely psychological and relative. He remarked 'People are apt to measure their progress not from a forgotten position in the past but towards an idea which, like a horizon, continually recedes.'

TALKING POINT

Should historians have their own political beliefs and should these colour their history?

'CAPITAL AND LABOUR'. A VIEW OF THE STANDARD OF LIVING IN EARLY NINETEENTH CENTURY ENGLAND. PUNCH MAGAZINE 1893.

DID MACHINERY ENHANCE OR ENSLAVE WORKERS?

from the industrial revolution equally. In the cotton industry alone, for example, the 1841 census enumerates 1225 subdivisions, of which the mule spinner headed the list.

The issues in the debate

The debate ranges over many factors and it would be useful to clarify the issues over which historians disagree. Firstly we need to be clear as to the period under discussion. Successful harvests and lower food prices coupled to low levels of population growth prior to 1770 indicate a general improvement in the standard of living for the mass of people. Additionally, general prosperity was enhanced by the rising home market for industrial goods.

There is even less doubt about the period after 1840, particularly after the deep depression which ended in 1842. There is substantial evidence to show an improvement in real wages, at least up until the 1870s, with a further acceleration in the last quarter of the century as prices fell steeply. The quality of life too improved. Working conditions were generally better and hours were reduced. The environment of towns became healthier as major outbreaks of disease diminished and sanitary reforms became widespread. Thus the specific period of the controversy relates to the period between 1780 and 1840.

There is little dispute that this period was one of extreme economic fluctuations. The long wars with France (1793–1815) induced hyper-inflation which bore down heavily upon the working poor. In the wake of the war, depression, and a series of cyclic catastrophes followed as the economy plunged into a series of depressions: 1815, 1819, 1832 and

TALKING POINT

Why would the quality of harvests be such a critical factor in the debate on the standard of living?

1842. Often, the relative gains during better times were wiped out by widespread and lengthy unemployment during bad times. Nowhere is the pendulum of fortune and misfortune better described than in the Manchester novels of Elizabeth Gaskell.

Of course different workers were affected in different ways. Unskilled and semi-skilled suffered most. Skilled workers, such as engineers, dubbed the 'aristocracy of labour' fared best. Worst-off were the agricultural labourers of the southern counties where the alternative of factory work was not available. Even so, not all benefitted from factory work. Advancing technology, such as that occurring in cotton weaving, displaced large groups of workers such as the handloom weavers. In other instances rapidly expanding industries such as cotton stole markets from linen and wool; railways from canals and coaching.

Yet despite all these variations historians must attempt to generalise whilst accepting that there will be exceptions and modifications to the overall picture. If we are to provide some answer, no matter how tentative, to the question, 'Did the standard of living of the working class rise or fall?', we must deal in averages of real wages, and average consumption of foodstuffs. This latter factor is of particular relevance when we appreciate that a worker in the early part of the nineteenth century spent some 70 per cent of his earnings on food.

Whilst historians define the period under review as a coherent one for the purposes of the debate it is by no means clear that this is the case. Applying the principle of an average of real wages to the period 1780–1840, it appears that the pessimists have a strong case, whilst after 1840, the balance of argument is tipped in favour of the optimists.

Alternatively, if we take consumption of foodstuffs as the yardstick of our measurement the case for improvement looks bleak. Meat consumption, considered to be the principal arbiter of the standard of living at this time (before the age of wholefoods and high fibre diets) seems to show a decline between 1780–1840.

The major source of information we possess for meat consumption consists of the Returns for Smithfield market, the most important meat market in London. Quite apart from the fact that other meat markets were gaining in importance there is a further difficulty attached to the interpretation of these figures. Whilst the Returns tell us the total number of beasts brought to market they do not tell us the weight of these animals. Even if we accept that the weight of cattle and sheep increased it would be wrong to conclude that it kept pace with demand. Furthermore, the meat returns exclude pigs which were often reared by workmen in backyard sties which provided a more staple part of his diet than butchers' meat. Other basic commodities, such as tea, sugar, beet and tobacco show no signs of increased consumption until after the 1840s.

Whilst it would be foolish to suggest a golden age of rural contentment prior to the Industrial Revolution there can be little to recommend the pestilential towns or the dangers of factory and coalmine to health. The self-regard of independent craftsmen cannot have been enhanced, argue the pessimists, by being dragooned into factories. Cyclical unemployment caused by periodic booms and slumps were a depressing characteristic of factory work. Furthermore, prosperity did not return immediately with a resumption of work. Debts had to be honoured and small savings slowly accumulated once more.

And throughout the period population was growing fast. Between 1801 and 1841 there were seven million more mouths to feed and jobs to create. The fact that there was no famine to wipe out this advance indicates an overall increase in production of foodstuffs. Of course, this in no way mitigates the undoubted hardship that many suffered.

What then are we to make from the conflicting interpretations of sources? Definitive conclusions may escape us at present but at least we must endeavour to acknowledge both the problems and issues in the debate – Are historians referring to the same period of time? Have they slipped from discussing the material comforts of life into more impressionistic accounts of the quality of life? How sound is the statistical evidence they employ in their arguments?

TALKING POINT

Make a list of the types of evidence available on this issue. For each type of evidence, examine its uses and limitations.

EXAMINING THE EVIDENCE
The historiography of the Industrial Revolution and the standard of living controversy

The phenomenon of the Industrial Revoltuion was quickly recognised by contemporaries and their successors as a significant break with the past. Historians identified and attempted to explain not only the nature of the change but who had lost and who had gained from the process. In their interpretation of evidence they were often influenced by the times they lived through and their own political outlook.

Toward the middle of the nineteenth century the system of capitalism itself was blamed as directly responsible for the plight of the poor.

Source A: Friedrich Engels and Karl Marx
Revolutionaries who attempted to explain the mechanics of social change argued that social class arose out of who controlled the means of production. The present social classes of proletariat (workers) and bourgeoisie (bosses), they argued, would come into inevitable conflict. From the clash of classes there would emerge a classless or communistic society.

'Under normal conditions, large capital and large landed property dominate society. The middle classes must increasingly disappear until the world is divided into millionaires and paupers … Competition has penetrated into all human relationships and it has brought complete bondage in all its aspects.'

F. Engels, *Outlines of a Critique of Political Economy* (1844)

KARL MARX

'Our epoch, the epoch of the bourgeoisie, possess, however, one distinctive feature: it has simplified the class antagonisms. Society, as a whole is more and more splitting up into two great classes directly facing each other: Bourgeoisie and Proletariat.'

F. Engels and K. Marx, *Manifesto of the Communist Party* (1848)

Source B: Arnold Toynbee 1852–1918
Toynbee pioneered the study of the Industrial Revolution. He stressed the importance of this period as a fundamental break with the past. He was

not a member of any political party but was a fierce critic of the dogmas of political economy. His work had a great influence on his contemporaries at Oxford.

'The new class of great capitalist employers made enormous fortunes, they took little or no part personally in the work of their great factories, their hundreds of workmen were individually unknown to them; and as a consequence the old relations between masters and men disappeared, and a 'cash-nexus' was substituted for the human tie. The workmen on their side resorted to combination, and Trade Unions began a fight which looked as if it were between mortal enemies rather than joint producers. The misery which came upon large sections of the working people at this epoch was often, though not always due to a fall in wages ... But they suffered likewise from the conditions of labour under the factory system, from the rise in prices, especially from bread before the Repeal of the Corn Laws, and from those sudden fluctuations of trade, which, ever since production has been on a large scale, have exposed them to recurrent periods of bitter distress. The effects of the Industrial Revolution prove that free competition may produce wealth without well-being. We all know the horrors that ensued in England before it was restrained by legislation and combination.'

A. Toynbee, *Lectures of the Industrial Revolution* (1884)

Note

Malcolm Thormis in 'The Town Labourer and the Industrial Revolution (1971) has written that the Hammonds books' are passionate and committed ... which features all the villains ... the capital owners of factories and mines.

Source C: J.L. and B. Hammond

A growing interest in working class movements motivated the husband and wife team of the Hammonds to investigate the impact of industrialisation upon sections of the labouring poor. Their pioneer works; 'The Village Labourer' (1911), 'The Town Labourer' (1917) and the 'Skilled Labourer' (1919) became classics of working class history.

'Thus England asked for profits and received profits. Everything turned to profit. The towns had their profitable dirt, their profitable slums, their profitable ignorance, their profitable despair ... For the new town was not a home where man could find beauty, happiness, leisure, learning, religion, the influences that civilise outlook and habit, but a bare and desolate place, without colour, air or laughter, where man, woman and child, ate and slept ... The new factories and the new furnaces were like Pyramids, telling of man's enslavement rather than of his Power, casting their long shadow over the society that took such pride in them.'

J.L. and B. Hammond, *The Rise of Modern Industry* (1925)

Source D: J.H. Clapham 1873–1946

Described as a 'giant' among twentieth century historians, Clapham began his life's major work, 'An Economic History of Modern Britain', in 1921, published in three massive volumes between 1926–38. In this work he challenged certain widely accepted interpretations of the industrial revolution; in particular the legend that everything was getting worse for working people, down to some unspecified date between the drafting of the Peoples' Charter and the Great Exhibition.

'All estimates of the welfare of the labouring population are defective – industrial or agricultural – which are based only upon the earnings of the principal bread winner ... Typical industrial towns such as Manchester or

Leeds provided opportunities for relatively considerable family earnings. But whether the representative parent of the mill child was a spinner, or one of the new engineers or, on the other hand, a despairing handloom weaver or irregularly working Irish labourer.'

J.H. Clapham, *An Economic History of Britain* (1938)

The current debate

Clapham had dented the notion of the 'down-trodden masses' suffering unrelieved cruelty as a consequence of industrialisation. He revealed that the standard of living debate was obscured by inadequate statistical information and political bias. Since Clapham's time the controversy has continued with current historians dividing into two camps.

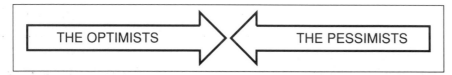

THE OPTIMISTS   THE PESSIMISTS

The Defence and Prosecution cases draw upon the following areas of evidence.

- Real wages
- Mortality and health
- Nature of Employment
- Unemployment
- Nutrition

Source E: Real Wages

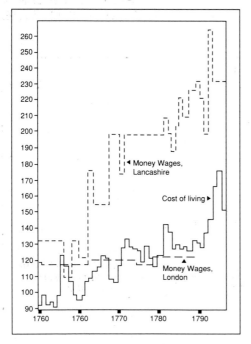

Source F: Cost of living

Compiling a cost of living index is equally beset by difficulties. Among the most widely used by historians is that compiled by Dr. N.J. Silberling. An extract is shown below.

Food (42 points):			Fuel and Light (6):		
	Wheat	15		Coal	4
	Mutton	6		Tallow	2
	Beef	6	Clothing (8 points):	Wool	3
	Butter	5		Cotton	3
	Oats	3		Flax	1
	Sugar	3		Leather	1
	Coffee	1			
	Tobacco	1			
	Tea	2		Total 56 points	

Source G: Birth and death rates

There is little reliable data on health for the statistical evidence that exists can scarcely be described as representative. For example, historians have used military and army recruitment records and friendly society information.

We are therefore left with mortality rates from which to draw conclusions. The limitations of this source of evidence has already been discussed in the chapter on population.

There was particular cause for alarm in those towns experiencing a rapid growth. The death rate in Liverpool, for instance, rose sharply from 1000 in 1831, to 35 per 1000 in 1841. For many urban dwellers, at least, any improvement of health which occurred as a result of advances in standards of personal cleanliness was more than outweighted by the evils of the environment in which they had to live as the chapter on Public health illustrates.

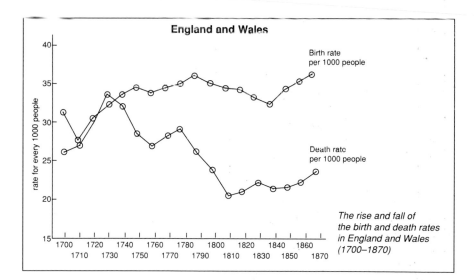

The rise and fall of the birth and death rates in England and Wales (1700–1870)

Source H: Employment and unemployment

Before you consider this aspect of the problem you need to be aware that there are different forms of unemployment. Re-read chapter six on population to help you recall that there were three types of unemployment caused by a) _____ b) _____ c) _____. The most serious form of unemployment in the early nineteenth century was _____.

Few studies have been made on the incidence of unemployment during this period, for most of the employment data refers to the skilled artisan or factory operative. At the most desperate end of the social scale, however, we must consider the almost permanent core of poverty, namely the extent of pauperism. Consider the information below on poor rate expenditure.

Poor rate expenditure		
	Receipts	*Expenditure*
1783–5	£2,168,000	£2,004,000
1803	£5,348,000	£4,268,000
1813	£8,647,000	£6,656,000
1823	£6,898,000	£5,773,000
1833	£8,807,000	£6,791,000
1843	£7,086,000	£5,208,000
1853	£6,522,000	£4,939,000
1863	£9,175,000	£6,527,000

Source I: The 'quality' of life introduction

Despite the introduction of the 'less-eligibility' principle the inmates of the workhouse were not necessarily the worst-off section of the population, and nor can this widespread poverty be purely measured in terms of material deprivation of food and clothing.

It is entirely illegitimate to reject the half million or more handloom weavers of 1830 or the army of seamstresses ... But for the Industrial Revolution most of them would not have been there, or at any rate their life would have been very different ... poverty and dirt alone are not the issue. The change from one way of life to another is equally at stake ... As is often the case, the poets saw things the vulgar economists did not ... The historian forgets at his peril that the problem of the social impact of the Industrial Revolution is not whether men live by white or brown bread, no meat or roast beef, but that it was inhuman.

E.J. Hobsbawm, *'The Standard of living during the Industrial Revolution: A Discussion'*
Economic History Review, Vol 16, August 1963

Source J: Types of unemployment

The impact of structural unemployment cannot be measured, but the largest group, well known and documented are the half million handloom weavers who may have represented, at least in the 1830s, one and one quarter million people in total.

More evidence is available on the impact of cyclic slumps, although caution must be exercised for the worst periods and the most depressed areas attracted the most attention.

(a) Unemployment in some towns, 1841–2				
	Fit for	Employed		Unem-
Town	work	Fully	Partly	ployed
Liverpool,				
Vauxhall	4,814	1,841	595	2,378
Stockport	8,215	1,204	2,866	4,145
Colne	4,923	964	1,604	2,355
Bury	3,982	1,107	–	–
Oldham	19,500	9,500	5,000 (half-time)	5,000
Accrington (textiles)	3,738	1,389	1,622	727
Wigan	4,109	981	2,572	1,563

(b) Unemployment in Bolton 1842			
	Total employed	Total employed whole or part-time	Percentage
Trade	in 1836	in 1842	Unemployed
Mills	8124	3036 (full time)	60
Ironworkers	2110	1325 (short time)	36
Carpenters	150	24	84
Bricklayers	120	16	87
Stonemasons	150	50	66
Tailors	500	250	50
Shoemakers	80	40	50

Source: H. Ashworth, 'Statistics of the present depression of trade in Bolton', Jour. Stat. Soc. V (1842), p/4

All we can say with some certainty is that cyclical and underemployment in addition to structural unemployment was much higher before the 1840s than after, for trade union figures, which became available after 1850, show nothing like the same catastrophies occurring.

Source K: Literature as evidence
The disparity between these 'good' and 'bad' times was vividly described by the contemporary novelist, Elizabeth Gaskell, the wife of a Unitarian minister who worked amongst the poor in Manchester.

(a) The 'good' times
Run, Mary [Barton's daughter] dear, just round the corner, and get some fresh eggs at Tipping's (you may get one apiece, that will be fivepence); and see if he has any nice ham cut, that he would let us have a pound of.'
    'Say two pounds, missis, and don't be stingy', chimed in the husband.

'Well, a pound and a half Mary ... and Mary ... you must get a pennyworth of milk and a loaf of bread – mind you get it fresh and new – and, and – that's all, Mary.'

'No, it's not at all', said her husband. 'Thou must get sixpenny-worth of rum, to warm the tea: thou'll get it at the 'Grapes'.

(b) The 'bad' times

And by-and-by Mary began to part with other superfluities at the pawnshop. The smart tea-tray, and tea-caddy, long and carefully kept, went for bread for her father. He did not ask for it, or complain, but she saw hunger in his shrunk, fierce, animal look. Then the blankets went, for it was summer time, and they could spare them; and their sale made a fund, which Mary fancied would last till better times came. But it was soon all gone; and then she looked around the room to crib it of its few remaining ornaments. To all these proceedings her father said never a word. If he fasted, or feasted (after the sale of some article), on an unusual meal of bread and cheese, he took all with a sullen indifference, which depressed Mary's heart. She often wished he would apply for relief from the Guardian's relieving office; often wondered the Trades' Union did nothing for him. Once when she asked him as he sat, grimed, unshaven, and gaunt, after a day's fasting over the fire, why he did not get relief from the town, he turned round, with grim wrath, and said, 'I don't want money, child! D–n their charity and their money! I want work, and it is my right. I want work.'

Deeper and deeper still sank the poor; it showed how much lingering suffering it takes to kill men, that so few (in comparison) died during those times. But remember! We only miss those who do men's work in their humble sphere; the aged, the feeble, the children, when they die, are hardly noted by the world; and yet to many hearts, their deaths make a blank which long years will never fill up. Remember, too, that though it may take much suffering to kill the able-bodied and effective members of society, it does not take much to reduce them to worn, listless, diseased creatures, who thenceforward crawl through life with moody hearts and pain-stricken bodies.

E. Gaskell, *Mary Barton (1848)*

MRS ELIZABETH GASKELL

Source L

(a) Decennial percentage increase in London population, beef and sheep at Smithfield, 1801–51						
	Animals	Index figure			Decennial increase		
Census date	ave. of	Popu-lation	Beef	Sheep	Popu-lation	Beef	Sheep
1801	1800–04	100	100	100			
1811	1810–12	119	105	119	+19	+5	+19
1821	1819–22	144	113	135	+25	+8	+16
1831	1830–34	173	127	152	+29	+14	+17
1841	1840–43	202	146	176	+30	+19	+24
1851	1850–52	246	198	193	+43	+42	+17

Consumption of food

We have already examined some of the attempts to draw up a cost of living index. When we attempt to calculate the standard of living through consumption we are faced with similar statistical problems. There are at least five problems that historians have encountered when trying to calculate working class consumption. Next to each factor below explain how they may affect the conclusions reached.

- Old and new types of diet.
- Measuring average working class consumption.
- Trends in types of foodstuffs.
- Actual quantities consumed by the working class.
- Nutritional value of the food.

What was a working class diet? This is an almost impossible question to answer. Much of the debate, however, centres upon the returns from the principal meat market in London, Smithfield.

(b) Yield of Excise on Hides and Skins in London and Rest of Country 1801 (1800–1 for Excise) = 100

Date	Population	Country yield	London yield
1801	100	100	100
1811	114.5	122	107
1821	136	106	113
1825	150	135	150

1 Study sources A, B, C, D.

Complete the information in the table below.

Author	Date of writing	Pessimist/ Optimist	Possible reasons for interpretation

2 As late as 1850 more people worked at home or in small workshops rather than factories. Over a million were domestic servants and a fifth were still employed in agriculture. How would this information affect your evaluation of the pessimistic claim of Toynbee that the Industrial Revolution fundamentally changed the employer/employee relationship?

3 Study source E

(a) What is meant by the term 'real wages'?

(b) How does London compare with Lancashire over this period?

(c) How might you attempt to explain the difference between the two regions?

(d) What problems are there in using this information to reach conclusions about real wages in Lancashire?

(e) Explain what probably happened in the years 1756–58 and 1768–70.

(f) What information do you consider necessary in compiling a cost of living index?

4 Study source F

(a) What conclusions can you reach about the relationship between the different items of expenditure?

(b) What is the major item of food expenditure?

How will this make the existence of a workers' family precarious?

(c) What two important items of expenditure are missing from the cost of living index?

5 Study source G

Look back to the earlier chapter on Population and Industrialisation and review the factors given for a decline in mortality.

6 Study source H

(a) What do the figures suggest about the rate of pauperism in the early nineteenth century?

(b) In 1834 there was a fundamental change in the administration of the poor law (see 'Poverty and Policy'). How might this affect your interpretation of the data? i.e. that pauperism appeared to decline because of lower expenditure between 1833–1843.

7 Study source I

(a) What area of the debate on the standard of living does Hobsbawm highlight?

(b) How is this particular aspect of the controversy difficult to determine?

8 Study source J

(a) What impact would these levels of unemployment have upon working class communities?

(b) How might this evidence alter possible conclusions on real wage indices?

(c) What reserves would the majority of workers possess in order to cope with periods of unemployment?

(d) Why would such periods of unemployment have such lasting effects?

(e) The 1842 depression was one of the most severe of the first half of the nineteenth century. How does this information affect your evaluation of this source?

(f) Most of this information was collected by businessmen for poor relief purposes and propaganda for the Anti-Corn Law League. How might this affect your interpretation of the source?

9 Study source K

(a) What type of unemployment is Elizabeth Gaskell describing?

(b) What are the value and limitations of this work of fiction to the historian?

10 Study source L

(a) What conclusions can you draw from these figures?

What does it indicate about the demand for, and the supply of, meat?

(b) What would you expect to happen to the price of meat over this period?

(c) What would be the result of these price movements on the standard of living?

(d) What limitations are there with this evidence when historians use it to generalise about the living standards of the labouring classes throughout the country?

(e) What conclusions can you make about meat consumption outside London?

EXAMINING THE EVIDENCE
The debate about food consumption and diet
Prepare a large double page chart to look like this.

Aspects of Debate	Arguments for Optimism	Arguments for Pessimism
Meat consumption		
Cereals and potatoes		
Fish		
Food adulteration		
Tobacco, tea and sugar		
Summary		

As you read through the arguments of the two main historical protagonists, summarise their views in your chart. Which do you think seems the most convincing?

Eric Hobsbawn is a Marxist and Professor of History at London University.

Ronald Hartwell is a Fellow of Nuffield College, Oxford.

Meat consumption
Arguments for Pessimism The chief weakness of the Smithfield series is that it does not comprise all the meat sold in London, since it neglects pork, and both home and county-killed meat which was sold mainly at Newgate. It is doubtful whether even in the 1850s Smithfield had lost much ground to other markets.

Railways made an even bigger difference ... but in 1842 these had not affected supplies very much.

It has been argued that there was a supposed increase in the average size of beasts but there is no evidence for this ... 668 lbs. in 1821, 630lbs. in 1836 640lbs. in 1842.

Arguments for Optimism Smithfield, between 1800 and 1850, the slaughter of cattle increased 91% and sheep 92% … there were other fast growing markets, Newgate, Leadenhall, Farringdon and Whitechapel. … only two thirds of fresh meat went through Smithfield.

Certainly the railways much increased the supply of country killed meat to London.

Nor, of course, was the increased supply confined to London … increasingly Birmingham and Liverpool provided more.

R.M. Hartwell

Cereals and potatoes

Arguments for Pessimism Wheat production and imports did not keep pace with population, so that the amount of wheat available per capita appears to have fallen steadily from the late eighteenth century until about the 1840s or 1850s, the amount of potatoes available rising at about the same rate … Wheat productivity show fairly stable yields up to 1830, a modest rise of about 10% in the 1830s and a startling large one of 40% after 1840, which fits in with the picture of very rapid improvement … after the effects of the 1842 depression had worn off.

E.J. Hobsbawn

Arguments for Optimism There are unfortunately no adequate statistics for bread and meat consumption … Wheat and bread prices certainly support the view that there was no long term shortage of wheat and flour. Wheat prices fell sharply after 1815 and were relatively stable, though with a discernible trend downwards, after 1822, the yearly average reaching 70s only on one occasion, 1839, before 1850, and the price in 1835, 39s 4d being the lowest price for half a century.

Far less is known about potato consumption … the theory that this increase was not a net addition to total diet, associated after 1815 with the increasing use of allotments by the working class, but a necessary substitute of an inferior vegetable for wheat bread, is based on the doubtful assumptions that bread was declining, and that the potato was an inferior food.

R.M. Hartwell

Fish

Arguments for Pessimism A notable increase is, however, recorded for fish. In Birmingham per capita consumption – negligible in 1829 – had more than doubled by 1835 and continued to grow at a rapid rate until 1840. Undoubtedly this improved the nutritive value of the poor man's diet, though it may not indicate that they felt themselves to be eating better … they may well have moved to fish because they could not afford meat.

E.J. Hobsbawn

Arguments for Optimism By 1840 ice and fast transport were enabling trawlers to fish farther north and were opening new markets in the inland towns ... the supply of fish increased after the abolition of the salt tax in 1825, and, after 1830, with technical innovations in fishing that increased yields, particularly the development of deep-sea trawling and drift fishing.

R.M. Hartwell

Food adulteration

Arguments for Pessimism The growth of adulteration slightly strengthens the pessimistic case. The 'Lancet' inquiry in the 1850s brings the following points out very clearly (i) all bread tasted in two separate samples was adulterated. (ii) over half of oatmeal was adulterated. (iii) all but the highest quality teas were invariably adulterated. (iv) a little under half the milk. (v) all butter was watered.

E.J. Hobsbawn

Arguments for Optimism Similarly food adulteration, which Dr. Hobsbawn seems to think was suddenly discovered in the 1850s was well known to Smollett in 1771, when he complained that, 'The bread I eat in London, is a deleterious paste, mixed up with chalk, alum and bone ashes.

R.M. Hartwell

Tobacco, tea and sugar

Arguments for Pessimism Tea, sugar and tobacco indicate no marked rise in the standards of living, but beyond this little can be deduced from the crude series.

E.J. Hobsbawn

Arguments for Optimism Although consumption statistics before 1850 are inadequate and unreliable they do indicate modest but fluctuating increases. Import statistics are the most accurate of the measures ... and these show important long term gains; for example, in tea, from about 1820 there is a rise; in tobacco a persistent upward trend; and in sugar the trend movement is upward. By 1840 steamships were pouring into England an almost daily stream of Irish livestock, poultry, meat and eggs. During the 'hungry forties' there were increases in the average per capita consumption of a number of imported foodstuffs: butter, cocoa, cheese, coffee, rice, sugar, tea, tobacco and currants.

R.M. Hartwell

Per Capita Consumption of Tea, Coffee, Sugar and Tobacco				
	Coffee (lbs)	Tea (lbs)	Sugar	Tobacco (lbs)
1790	0.10	1.16	–	–
1800	0.08	1.48	15.32	1.24
1820	0.34	1.22	17.74	0.76
1830	0.95	1.23	19.08	0.81
1840	1.08	1.22	15.20	0.87
1850	1.13	1.88	25.26	1.00
1860	1.23	2.67	34.14	1.22

B.R. Mitchell and P. Deane, abstract of British Historical Statistics

'THE CONDITION OF ENGLAND' NOVEL

Historians have always used fiction to illustrate the thoughts, attitudes and feelings of those who have lived in the past in order to recreate what is sometimes called the 'climate of the times'. The historian of mid-Victorian England may use fiction from these times to an even greater extent, for the period spawned an entire genre of novels which explored the 'social question'.

The 'question' which these novels addressed was the state of the lower or working classes under the impact of industrialisation. The authors of such works concluded that England had become irrevocably divided into two nations, poised on the brink of disaster.

ILLUSTRATION FROM HARD TIMES BY CHARLES DICKENS. PRIOR TO WRITING THE NOVEL DICKENS PAID A BRIEF VISIT TO MANCHESTER.

The purpose of these novels was to awaken the conscience of the ruling classes to their responsibility toward improving the condition of the poor in order that the nation might re-unite in common purpose.

A whole host of these novels are now regarded as important literary works. Benjamin Disraeli's 'Sybil' (1845), Elizabeth Gaskell's 'Mary Barton' (1848) and 'North and South' (1855), Charles Dickens's 'Hard Times', and the lesser works of Francis Trollope's 'Michael Armstrong: The Factory Boy' (1839–40) and Charles Kingsley's 'Alton Locke'.

A

TWO NATIONS

Stephen Morley, an Owenite in conversation with Lord Egremont, a young aristocrat

"Say what you like, our Queen reigns over the greatest nation that ever existed."
"Which nation?" asked the young stranger, "for she reigns over two."
The stranger paused; Egremont was silent, but looked inquiringly.
"Yes," resumed the stranger after a moment's interval, "Two nations; between whom there is no intercourse and no sympathy; who are as ignorant of each other's habits, thoughts and feelings, as if they were dwellers in different zones, or inhabitants of other planets; who are formed by different breeding, are fed by different food, are ordered by different manners, and are not governed by the same laws."
"You speak of ..." said Egremont, hesitatingly.
"The Rich and the Poor."

B. Disraeli, *Sybil*

HARD TIMES

They were ruined when they were required to send labouring children to school; they were ruined when inspectors were appointed to look into their works; they were ruined when such inspectors considered it doubtful whether they were quite justified in chopping people up with their machinery; ..

C. Dickens, Hard Times

C Dickens Criticised

It's Dickens delight in grotesque and rich exaggeration which has made him, I think, nearly useless in the present day.

J. Ruskin in a letter to his friend Charles Eliot Norton
just after Dickens's death.

D DICKENS: A TRIBUTE

Dickens has done more to ameliorate the condition of the English poor than all the statesmen Great Britain has sent into Parliament. What other reformers hoped to do by legislation, he did by a supreme act of moral imagination.

D. Webster's tribute to Dickens during the author's
lecture tour of America 1842.

E Types of novels flourishing in the early nineteenth century

The Newgate novel	• tales of crime, imprisonment, escape, recapture and hanging
The Gothic novel	• specialised in the exotic, grotesque and macabre
Silver-fork novels	• tales of aristocratic life, usually containing a lowly-born heroine
Hortatory novels	• morally uplifting tales meant to encourage virtue in the reader. The Society for the Diffusion of Useful Knowledge was the most famous organisation dedicated to this principle.

F Reading for the Masses

We have our penny libraries for debauchery as for other useful knowledge; and colleges like palaces for study – gin palaces where each starving Sardanopolous may revel until he dies.

R.D. Altick, The English Common Reader:
A Social history of the Mass Reading Public 1800–1900

G READERSHIP

It is notoriously difficult to determine which books were read by which classes but some clues are provided by the economics of publishing.

- Three volume novels sold for a guinea and a half.
- Many novels were reissued in a one volume edition for one shilling.
- Many novels appeared in serial form first – Fraser's magazine and Blackwoods were the most respectable and sold for 2s.6d. per issue.
- Lending libraries from about the middle of the century (one year's membership cost about one guinea)
- Mechanics Institutes – there were about 700 by mid century but they would only stock the most famous of the novels.
- Libraries attached to Sunday Schools, Ragged schools and penny lending facilities at railway stations.
- Countless weeklies of a sensational type cost only 1d or 2d. They serialised Dickens, Thackray and Gaskell. In 1840 there were 80 cheap journals in London alone; by 1860 there were 100. The 'London Journal' reached a peak sale of 500,000 copies in 1858. One of its rivals, 'Reynold's Miscellany' sold as many as 200,000 a week.

LITERACY

This is notoriously difficult to estimate and to define. The best overall figure is that in the early Victorian period two-thirds to three-quarters of the working classes had some reading ability.

1. Study the first two sources.
   (a) What messages are the writers attempting to convey?
   (b) How do they achieve this effect? Refer to language, tone and style.
2. Study the next two sources.
   (a) In what ways do they disagree about the value of Dickens social novels?
3. (a) In what ways must a historian differ from the novelist in the way he describes historical attitudes? Use the first two sources as references.
   (b) What other considerations must a novelist take into account when producing his work?
   (c) In what way might a novelist be described as 'shaping reality'?
   (d) How influential could a novel such as Dickens 'Hard Times' be in 'shaping reality'?
4. (a) What different impression would be conveyed if the figures for literacy were reversed and expressed as 'nearly one-quarter of the population could neither read or write.'
   (b) What does the huge circulation of cheap journals suggest as to the standards of literacy of the working classes?
   (c) (i) What is the difference between the actual readership of a Journal and the number of copies sold?
   (ii) What inferences can you draw from this difference?

Wheat and Potatoes Available per Capita 1760–1914

U.K. Wheat		Potatoes	
1760s	1.5 (lbs)		
1770s	1.3	1775	0.35
1780s	1.4		
1790s	1.36	1795	0.40
1800s	1.3		
1810s	1.05	1814	0.47
1820s	0.95		
1830s	0.9	1836	0.67
1840s	0.85		
1850s	0.85	1851	0.70
1860s	1.03	1885	0.80

R.R. Salaman, The History and Social Influence of the Potato (1949) quoted in B.R. Mitchell and P. Deane, Abstract of British Historical Statistics

Summary

Arguments for Pessimism There is thus no strong basis for the optimistic view, at any rate for the period from c.1790 or 1800 or until the middle 1840s. The plausibility of, and the evidence for deterioration are not to be lightly dismissed.

E.J. Hobsbawn

Arguments for Optimism

The failure of living standards to rise much before 1815 was due not to industrialisation but to war. R.S. Tucker's index of consumer good prices – for food, fuel and light and clothing, the most important items in working class budgets – show a downward trend from about 1813–15 to 1845 as also does Miss E.B. Schumpeter's index for 22 articles of food and drink. The conclusion from consumption figures is unquestionably that the amount and variety of food consumed increased between 1800 and 1850.

It is as foolish to ignore the sufferings of this period as to deny the wealth and opportunities created by the new industry. Misconceptions about England before the Industrial Revolution, for example, that rural life was naturally better than town life, that working for oneself was better and more secure than working for an employer, that child and female labour was something new, that the domestic system was preferable to the factory system … and so on, in other words the myth of the golden age.

R.M. Hartwell

E.J. Hobsbawn, *The British Standard of living 1790–1850,*
Economic History
Review 2nd Series X August 1957

R.M. Hartwell, *The Rising Standard of Living in England 1800–1850,*
Economic History Review 2nd. Series XIII April 1961

A Judgement

The social benefits and the costs of industrialisation cannot be neatly summarised on an accounting sheet. Some contemporaries regarded the cheapness and greater availability of some foodstuffs and cotton clothing as a triumph whilst others indicted these same articles as evidence of degradation. How is it possible to reach general conclusions about the labouring poor in total when different groups at different times were affected in different ways? How is it possible to quantify into a single equation such diverse factors as regular but low paid work contrasted with infrequent but highly paid work? How is it possible to measure the benefits arising from government legislation? In what way can we determine the quality of life and in what sense can we weigh it in the balance against material improvement?

Historians still dispute the period of time in question, the reliability and inadequacy of the data, the interpretation of the data and thus the generalisations that can be summed up in terms of a 'rise' or a 'fall' in living standards. The contemporary 'reality' was deeply pessimistic and we must never lose sight of the significance of events as seen by those living through the experience of early industrialisation. More recently historians have attempted to reconcile the optimistic with the pessimistic view. One such attempt has been made by the historian Phyllis Deane, Lecturer in Economics at Cambridge University.

A reconciliation of optimistic and pessimistic views

To sum up, then, what conclusions can we draw from all this? The first is that there is no firm evidence for an overall improvement in working-class standards of living between about 1780 and about 1820. Indeed, when we take into account the harvest failures, growing population, the privations of a major war and the distress of the post-war economic dislocation, we may reasonably conclude that on balance average standards of living tended to fall rather than to rise.

For the period from about 1820 to about 1840 it is difficult to be as definite. Certainly there is no evidence for a substantial rise in real incomes and what we can deduce from the statistics is not strong enough to compensate for the wide margin of error in the data. On the other hand the evidence for a fall in standards of living rests either on presumptions that we cannot empirically check with the information now accessible to us – like the incidence of unemployment, for example – or on data of actual consumption per head of certain not very important commodities whose consumption could as well be attributed to changes in taste or the weight of duties as to a fall in real incomes. Perhaps on balance the optimists can make out a more convincing case for an improvement in the standard of living than the pessimists can for a fall. But either case is based largely on circumstantial evidence and there is one thing that we can take as reasonably certain – and that is that whichever way it went, the net change was relatively slight.

Finally, beginning in the 1840s we find much stronger evidence of an improvement in the average real incomes of the working class, evidence that has been strong enough to convince even some of the remaining pessimists. It does not rest however on a perceptible increase in real wage rates. Habakkuk, for example, observes that 'The inconclusive nature of the current debate about living standards in this period is perhaps a warrant for supposing that a substantial and general and demonstrable rise in the real wages of industrial workers did not occur until the 1850s and 1860s: and it was not until about 1870 that real wages in agriculture began to rise and a steady rise was apparent only in the 1880s.' The argument for an improvement in the average standard of living in the middle of the century rests largely on a change in the composition of the labour force. To quote Hobsbawm, the most recent of the advocates of the pessimistic interpretation of the industrial revolution:

Little as we know about the period before the middle forties, most students would agree that the real sense of improvement among the labouring classes thereafter was due less to a rise in wage-rates, which often remained surprisingly stable for years, or to an improvement in social conditions, but to the upgrading of labourers from very poorly paid to less poorly paid jobs, and above all to a decline in unemployment or to a greater regularity of employment.

This shift in the distribution of the labour force from the traditional highly seasonal occupations characteristic of a pre-industrial economy to the modern sector with its mechanical aids to labour, its disciplined working habits and its continuous intensive use of capital equipment in day and night shifts is the true spirit and essence of the industrial revolution. Agricultural labourers, for example, normally earn less per week than factory workers of equivalent skill; handloom weavers earn less than power-loom weavers; canal bargemen less than locomotive drivers. Thus a shift in the composition of the labour force – a fall in the proportion of workers engaged in the low earning categories and a corresponding rise in the proportion of those in the high earning categories – would raise the average level of earnings per worker even if wage-rates in each occupation remained unchanged. This is the process that seems to have gathered momentum in the 1840s and to have brought with it perceptible improvements in material standards of life for the working classes. It may indeed have begun earlier, but it is not until the 1840s that we can be reasonably certain of its positive effects.

Review
Historiography

Unless you embark on original research you are greatly dependent upon the interpretations of the past made by professional historians. Their objective is to present to the reader a valid account of past events based firmly on a critical analysis of sources. Historians, however, like any other individual, live through particular times and in societies with particular values, attitudes and beliefs. It would be surprising if they were not untouched by their own times and that their writing did not reflect society's perception of itself. Historiography is the rather grand term we use for the study of the writing of history.

It was in fifth century Greece that the application of scientific method to history first began. The greatest of Greek historians was undoubtedly Thucydides (440 – 399 B.C.) who defined his aims as,

'The absence of romance in my history will I fear, detract somewhat from its interest; but if it be judged useful by those inquirers who desire an exact knowledge of the past as an aid to the interpretation of the future, which in the course of things must resemble if it does not reflect it, I shall be content.'

A profound change in the writing of history came with the emergence of Christianity. St. Augustine of Hippo (354 – 430 A.D.) described the purpose of history as an account of the revelation of God in the world and thus a distinction was made between pre- and post-Christian times – B.C. and A.D.

The discovery of the New Worlds and the Ancient Civilisations of the East from the fifteenth century onwards stimulated interest in peoples from non-European and non-Christian societies. Seventeenth century developments in astronomy unseated the accepted Christian view of the earth as the centre of the universe. During this time a number of universal and comparative histories of civilisation were attempted.

In the nineteenth century came the most important step in the development of a critical and scientific historical method. Leopold von Ranke (1795–1886) subjected his sources to rigorous scrutiny, establishing the need for objective ground rules for historical evidence.

---

1 Read Thucydides account of his aims once more.

(a) What does this tell you about the generally accepted notion of history up to the time in which he lived?

(b) Many Greeks believed that the historical process worked in cycles and that eventually history would literally repeat itself. Is there any evidence that Thucydides shared this belief?

2 Why should the expansion of European geographical knowledge and a scientific understanding of the universe shake Christian interpretations of history?

3 'Some scholars take refuge in scepticism, or at least in the doctrine that, since all historical judgements involve persons and points of view, one is as good as another and there is no objective historical truth.'

G. Clarke, *The New Cambridge History I* (1957)

Is it possible to arrive at objective historical truths? What are the problems in so doing?

4 What belief dominates our own age?

Perhaps a belief in progress, regression, cyclic, no discernible pattern?

What evidence would you use to support your point of view?

How might each of these beliefs affect the way in which the history of this age would be written?

Which of these beliefs characterises the writing in this book?

---

11 Government and the Individual in Early Nineteenth Century Britain

PREVIEW

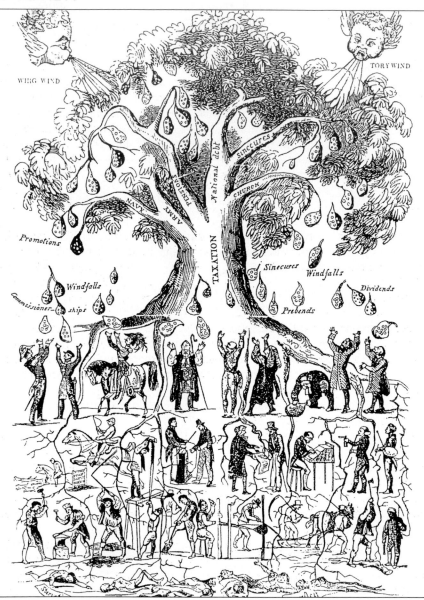

THE TREE OF TAXATION 1832.

TALKING POINT

What view of society is represented by this illustration?

Examine the detail carefully. How does the artist convey his overall impression of society?

How might this picture be representative without being accurate?

Sketch an alternative view of the hierarchal structure of society represented here which would convey beneficial effects to all members.

TALKING POINT

Your teaching group has been set the task of researching this topic. You have also been given the choice of completing the project by yourself or as part of a team. Under which conditions would you choose to work? What are the benefits and disadvantages of both methods of working – collectively or individually?

TALKING POINT

Can you think of any examples of specific laws that guarantee us rights?

Can you think of any laws which restrict our freedom?

In what areas of life do you consider it not legitimate for government to intervene?

TALKING POINT

What arguments could you use to both support and criticise the free market? Is there such a thing as a 'completely free market?'

Individualism collectivism and government

There is scarcely an aspect of our daily lives that is not touched upon by government legislation. Much of this regulation we accept, sometimes reluctantly, as necessary interference by government to protect our individual freedom, our welfare and our environment. On the other hand, some laws we regard as an unnecessary obstacle designed to limit our legitimate freedom of action. Whether we agree or disagree with particular laws we rarely question the fundamental right of governments to pass laws for that is what we consider to be the purpose of government.

The role of Government in the nineteenth century

By contrast with our attitude today, the king's ministers in early nineteenth century Britain were in no doubt about their right to govern. They were equally convinced, however, that the liberty of the individual would be best preserved by a minimum of legislation. To intervene in order to maintain social stability was quite in keeping with accepted and traditional government responsibility. Even the advocates of social reform made social well-being, order and morality and maintaining the status quo the main planks on their campaign platform. Government could act in this traditional way by legislating in such areas of social concern and did so, but with reluctance and a firm eye to social order and the maintenance of a free market economy.

This notion of government's role and the supremacy of individualism was further reinforced because of the wealth generated by the successful entrepreneur. Alongside the accumulation of individual wealth there arose the conviction that those who created this prosperity also possessed moral superiority. Individuals freely pursuing their own self-interest, in competition with others, would benefit all society by providing cheaper goods and increased employment opportunities. It was confidently predicted that 'natural' economic forces alone, free from bungling goverment interference, would achieve social well-being. Those that dared to question these apparently 'self-evident' truths were dismissed as unrealistic dreamers or dangerous agitators.

Individualism – theory and practice

Like most theories, individualism in practice became less clear cut and proponents less sure of their ground when faced with difficult social problems. If people were starving or living in disease-ridden slums it became less tenable to suggest that any help given would only lead to the demoralisation of the recipients. Surely the state could not stand back and refuse to take action on the grounds that they risked robbing the poor of their individual independence.

It was as much this moral dilemma as the uncertainty of measuring particular actions against the yardstick of individualism that propelled government toward the need for collectivist action. It would be a mistake, however to read into this any notions of a welfare state.

Historians prefer to describe the social legislation of this period as creating a 'social service state'. In this context the ruling class saw themselves as adopting a paternalistic role as a father might protect his children from harm. Minimal services could thus be provided without damage to the notion of individual responsibility.

Drawing the line between individualism and even minimal services however was no easier in practice. This uncertainty of whether to act or not goes a long way to explain why an age that espoused the cause of individualism should also have legislated so much collectivist action.

The radical view of government

Other factors were at work helping to soften the harshness of an exclusively individualistic approach. Opposition came from different groups in the name of different interests and ideas – from within both the Tory and the Whig groupings in Parliament.

Some Tories spoke of the rights of the poor and the obligation of the rich to care for and maintain, if necessary, the inferior classes. Large numbers of people spoke and acted in the name of this paternalism, deploring the disappearance, as they saw it, of the old moral ties that bound squire and peasant together. For Tories who thought in this way, industrialism itself had destroyed the very idea of a civilised society.

Tories who supported paternalism of this sort were referred to as 'radicals' and 'ultra-radicals', or in our terms, moderates and extremists. But there were other types of radicals who, unlike the paternalistic Tories, saw universal suffrage as the ultimate form of responsible government. Their adherence to this belief earned them the title of 'popular radicals'.

It is very difficult to categorise radicals as their beliefs tended to be very different from one another. A moderate on one issue (factory legislation) might be an extremist on another (universal suffrage). A distinction between middle-class and working-class radicals is equally difficult to establish as there was no necessary connection between class and extremity of viewpoint.

Sometimes changing circumstances transformed the radical into a pillar of society. In 1830, for example, Colonel T. Perron-Thompson informed the readers of the Westminister Review that, 'the term 'Radical', once employed as a name of low reproach has found its way into high places'. The radicalism to which the colonel referred was 'Philosophic Radicalism' or Benthamite Utilitarianism, of which he was an enthusiastic supporter. (This is discussed in the Focus section).

Yet despite the range of radical opinion, their numbers in the House of Commons after 1832 remained small. This should cause no surprise. The electorate remained a property-owning fraction of the total population and government the perogative of the powerful.

RADICAL VIEW OF THE RIGHTS OF MAN.

Collectivist action

A number of writers attacked the very basis of the power elite and can be described as pioneering Socialists. Among their ranks was Thomas Spence (1750–1814) who believed that there had been a happier golden age based on the free tiller of the soil. If land was brought into common ownership the Spenceans believed the golden age would return. He urged his followers to resume their 'right' to the land. Although the Spenceans were few in number they were tightly organised and dedicated to revolution. They led most of the working-class demonstrations in London between 1816–20 which earned them a reputation as a dangerous force in society. In practical terms, however, they failed to develop as a mass movement and petered out of existence in the 1820s.

Of more importance to collectivist action was the early socialist Robert Owen (1771–1858). A successful industrialist himself, he proposed the setting up of workers' cooperatives in order to harness the productive might of the working classes for their own benefit. These co-operatives, he believed, would grow and develop in such a fashion as to displace peacefully capitalism itself. He was not interested in universal suffrage nor political action, assuming that economic action alone would establish a co-operative utopia. So closely did 'Socialism' (a term first coined in 1827) become identified with Robert Owen that Engels admitted this association had influenced his and Marx's decision to publish their manifesto as 'Communist' rather than 'Socialist'.

Needless to say, socialist theory earned little credibility with the ruling classes and gained no voice in Parliament.

A SPENCEAN DEMONSTRATION.

The power of religion

It is difficult for us living in a more secular age to understand the power of religion which existed in early nineteenth century Britain. Christianity provided the crucible into which society was cast. The established Anglican church its mental mould.

During the first half of the nineteenth century the number of churches expanded rapidly, largely inspired by a group of churchmen who wished for the regeneration of the established church. They wanted to see the Anglican church imbued with a new religious fervour and sense of mission, eager to save souls. Their enthusiasm was often translated into practical action, finding an outlet for their convictions in various reform movements.

The most notable group of evangelical Anglicans was formed at Clapham, near London, and came to be known as the Clapham Sect. Their most influential member was William Wilberforce (1759–1833). He and a group of like-minded members of Parliament became sarcastically referred to as 'the party of Saints'.

The first half of the nineteenth century also saw a remarkable growth in the non-conformist sects, particularly Methodism; an off-shoot from the Anglican church. The movement found many adherents among working class communities and from their ranks emerged lower class leadership.

Some radicals were deeply suspicious of institutional religion which they identified as part of the State's apparatus for brainwashing working class people to accept the status-quo. The churches, they believed, focussed peoples hopes for justice in the next world and a passive acceptance of injustice in this one.

As in any age, no one set of ideas dominated thinking. Points of view were modified in the light of experience or contact with alternative ideas. Time itself transformed opinion from extreme to moderate to established. As you read and listen to these early nineteenth century voices it is important to appreciate, above all else, the need to see them as part of the ebb and flow of their society.

EXAMINING THE EVIDENCE
Political thinkers of the nineteenth century and their ideas

Source A: The responsibility of the state

The State ought to confine itself ... to the public peace, to the public safety, to the public order, to the public prosperity.

E. Burke, *Thoughts on Security* (1795)

Edmund Burke

Edmund Burke (1729-93) entered politics at the age of 36 and was appointed to several posts in the Whig government. At the onset of the French Revolution he became increasingly horrified at the bloody turn of events. In protest he joined the Tory party and wrote an uncompromising attack on the Revolution. He regarded all political change as wrong unless it was in keeping with tradition.

EDMUND BURKE (1729–97).

Source B: Critic of collectivist action

If there be in Mr. Southey's political system any leading principle, any one error which diverges more widely and variously than any other, it is that of which his theory about national works is a ramification. He conceives that the business of the magistrate is not merely to see that the persons and property of the people are secure from attack, but that he ought to be a jack-of-all trades – architect, engineer, schoolmaster, merchant, theologian, a Lady Bountiful in every parish, a Paul Pry in every house, spying, eavesdropping, relieving, admonishing, spending our money for us, and choosing opinions for us. His principle is, if we understand it rightly, that no man can do anything so well for himself as his rulers, be they who they may, can do it for him, and that a government approaches nearer and nearer to perfection, in proportion as it interferes more and more with the habits and notions of individuals.

Thomas Babington Macaulay

Thomas Babington Macaulay

Thomas Babington Macaulay 1800–59 entered Parliament when he was 30 years old and quickly won a reputation as a great orator. Throughout his career in the Whig party, which lasted until 1853, he interested himself in matters of social welfare. In this extract he is replying to a proposal by the radical Robert Southey to set up a public works scheme for the unemployed.

LORD MACAULAY.

Source C: The need to encourage individual enterprise

(i) The uniform constant, and uninterrupted effort of everyman to better his condition is frequently powerful enough to maintain the natural progress of things towards improvement in spite of the extravagances of government, and the greatest errors of administration.

Adam Smith, *An Enquiry into the causes of the Wealth of Nations Book II chapter 8 1776*

(ii) The statesman who would attempt to direct private people in what manner they ought to employ their capital, would not only load himself with unnecessary attention, but assume an authority which could be safely entrusted, not only to a single person, but to no council whatsoever, and which could be nowhere so dangerous as in the hands of a man who had the folly and presumption enough to fancy himself fit to exercise it.

Adam Smith, *ibid. Book IV chapter 2 1776*

ADAM SMITH.

Adam Smith

Adam Smith (1729–90) who was Professor of Political Economy at Glasgow University, comprehensively demolished the then economic system which he termed 'Mercantalism'. The book from which these extracts come was published in 1776 and underwent no less than eight editions over the next twenty years. He attacked the idea that the economy ought to be protected by tariffs and customs duties.

Source D: No state regulation of wages

Wages should be left to the fair and free competition of the market, and should never be controlled by the interference of the legislature. Labour, like all other things which are purchased and sold, and which may be increased or decreased in quantity, has its natural price and its market price.

David Ricardo, Political Economy

TALKING POINT:

Political thinkers – what do their ideas contribute to historical development?

1 The brief extracts and biographical outlines can only give a sketchy impression of those nineteenth century thinkers and writers, shaped and influenced by the age in which they lived. Choose one and:

(a) Give a brief outline of their lives – formative influences – public career.

(b) Consider their system of thought and belief. Was there any change or modification to their beliefs during their lives?

(c) Consider their influence upon other contemporaries and their judgement of others.

In a seminar explain;

(a) What position your individual took on the relationship of the individual and government?

(b) What possible position would your individual take on the suggestion that the government should give assistance to the poor?

Any member of the group can challenge the arguments given in context of the explanation provided. Any inconsistencies voted by the group result in the individual being dismissed.

David Ricardo (1772–1823)

David Ricardo (1772–1823) has been described as the high priest of capitalism (political economy) for like Adam Smith before him, he wished to see a totally free market economy established. Ever increasing wages, he argued, would swallow profits and ultimately decrease capital needed for business expansion. Nassau Senior (1790–1864) was an ardent disciple of Ricardo's and, building upon Smith's theories, established what came to be regarded by many critics as the 'iron laws' of political economy.

DAVID RICARDO.

Source E: Justice for the labouring masses

People who thought only of the child's instant welfare, and not of the consideration of justice and of actual practicability with which the case was complicated, clamoured for a law which would restrict the hours of labour and determine the wages of the persons who should be employed in the cotton and silk mills. Economists had shown how vain had always been, and must ever be, laws to regulate wages. The operative began to see before them a long perspective of legal protection and privilege, by which they as well as their children should obtain the same wage for less and less work, while too few of them perceived that any law which should deprive them of their own labour would steal from their own possession, and in fact a more flagrant oppression than any law had inflicted on their order for centuries.

Harriet Martineau, *Illustrations of Political Economy – A Manchester Strike* (1832)

A SATIRICAL DRAWING OF HARRIET MARTINEAU.

Harriet Martineau

Harriet Martineau (1803–76) won fame at the age of twenty-nine with the publication of 'Illustrations of Political Economy'; a series of books designed to entertainingly instruct readers in the tenets of political economy by means of 'moral' tales. 'Illustrations' was an outstanding success. Sales of the books reached 10,000 per month which compared favourably with the successful novels of Charles Dickens. The work was admired by Queen Victoria and translated into many languages.

The Radical View of government

Source F: Industrialisation and working class improvement

What wonderful accessions have thus been made, and are still making, to the physical power of mankind; how much better fed, clothed and lodged and, in all outward respects, accommodated men now are, or might be, by a given quantity of labour, is a grateful reflection which forces itself on everyone. What changes, too, this addition of power is introducing into the Social System; how wealth has more and more increased, and at the same time gathered itself more and more into masses, strangely altering the old relations, and increasing the distance between the rich and the poor, will be a question for political economists, and a much more complex and important one than they have yet engaged with.

But leaving these matters for the present, let us observe how the mechanical genius of our time has diffused itself into quite other provinces. Not the external and physical alone is now managed by machinery, but the internal and spiritual also. Here too nothing follows its spontaneous course … Thus we have machines for Education … a secure, universal, straightforward business, to be conducted in the gross, by proper mechanism, with such intellect as comes to hand. Then we have religious machines, of all imaginable varieties; the Bible society, professing a far higher and heavenly structure, is found on inquiry, to be altogether an earthly contrivance … a machine for converting the heathen …

With individuals, … natural strength avails little. No individual now hopes to accomplish the poorest enterprise single-handed and without mechanical aids; he must make interest with some existing corporation, and till his field with oxen. In these days, more emphatically than ever, 'to live, signifies to unite with a party, or to make one'. Philosophy, Science, Art, Literature, all depend on machinery.

These things, which we state lightly enough here, are yet of deep import, and indicate a mighty change in our whole manner of existence. For the same habit regulates not our modes of action alone, but our modes of thought and feeling. Men are grown mechanical in head and in heart, as well as in hand. They have lost faith in individual endeavour, and in natural force, of any kind. Not for internal perfection, but for external combinations and arrangements, for institutions, constitutions – for mechanism of one sort or other, do they hope and struggle.

Thomas Carlyle, *Signs of the Times* (1829)

Thomas Carlyle

Thomas Carlyle (1795–1881) was the son of a Scottish stonemason, brought up as a Calvinist (Puritan). Whilst at Edinburgh University he subjected his beliefs to rigorous criticisms from which emerged a highly personal religious belief. Carlyle thundered against the materialism of his age and the mis-use of technology. His influence was widespread in the first half of the nineteenth century, even to people of a very different cast of mind. He wrote in a very vivid and intense style, using Biblical imagery which gave his work the force of an old Testament prophet.

THOMAS CARLYLE.

Source G: The need for reform

I want to see no innovation in England. All I wish for and all I strive for is the Constitution of England, undefiled by corruption. What do we wish for? We wish to destroy no establishment. We want nothing new-fangled. We want no innovation. All we ask for is such a reform as would effectually secure us against the effects of corruption, that is the burden of taxes and the bubble of paper money.

William Cobbett, *The Political Register* (April 15 1816)

Source H: Agricultural utopia

The public mind being suitably prepared by reading my little Tracts ... a few Contingent parishes have only to declare the land to be theirs and form a convention of Parochial Delegates. Other adjacent parishes would ... follow the example, and send also their Delegates and thus would a

WILLIAM COBBETT.

William Cobbett

William Cobbett (1762–1835) was, like Carlyle, a highly individual thinker. Cobbett was probably the greatest political pamphleteer of his age. His weekly Political Register, begun on January 16, 1802, became a widely read journal amongst working men. Cobbett believed England had basked in a golden age before the emergence of factories and this 'paradise' had become corrupted by greedy profiteers. Cobbett blamed industrialism itself for Britain's misfortunes, which he castigated as 'The Thing'.

beautiful and powerful New Republic instantaneously arise in full vigour. The power and resources of War passing in this manner in a moment into the hands of the People … their Tyrants would become weak and harmless … And being … scalped of their Revenues and the Lands that produced them their Power would never grow to enable them to overturn the Temple of Liberty.

Thomas Spence, *Agrarian Justice* (1804)

Source I: Workers unite in co-operatives

The members of this Union have discovered that competition in the sale of their productions is the chief and immediate cause of their poverty and degradation, and that they can never overcome either as long as they conduct their affairs individually, and in opposition to each other.

They are, therefore, about to form national companies of production; each trade or manufacture to constitute one grand company or Association, comprising all the individuals in the business throughout Great Britain and Ireland; but each trade and manufacture to be united to all others by a general bond of interest by which they will exchange their productions with each other upon the principle of equitable exchange of labour for a fair equal value of labour; and all articles, upon a principle of economy and general advantage will be produced, of the best quality only.

The next step in gradation will be the union of master traders and manufacturers with the operatives and manual producers; and when these two parties shall fully understand the value of the union, the Government will not only feel the necessity of uniting with them, but it will also discover the advantages to the whole empire of this national bond of union.

From 'The Crisis', a speech by Robert Owen on the G.N.C.T.U.
(G.N.C.T.U. – Grand National Consolidated Trade Union)

THE RADICAL LADDER.

SUPPORTING CHURCH AND STATE.

THE CLERICAL MAGISTRATE.

Source J: Christianity: the saviour of the masses

Christianity assumes her true character, no less than she performs her natural and proper office, when she takes under protection those poor degraded beings, on whom philosophy looks down with disdain or perhaps with contemptuous condescension. On the very first promulgation of Christianity, it was declared by its Great Author, as 'glad tidings of the poor', and ever faithful to her character, Christianity still delights to instruct the ignorant, to succour the needy, to comfort the sorrowful, to visit the forsaken …

William Wilberforce, *Speech in Parliament on the Emancipation of Slavery,* (June 22 1813)

Source K: False hopes for the masses

Little do these zealous advocates for negro emancipation dream that they are industriously sowing the seeds of anarchy and wild impatience of all government and breaking down the PALE of order. These inflammatory appeals of Wilberforce and his friends, are equally CRUEL, unchristian and unpolitic; cruel to the lower orders of society in engendering and cherishing a spirit of dissatisfaction with their sphere and lot in life, which cannot and ought not to be elevated; unchristian in striking at the very root of every gospel precept of subordination which commands all men to be satisfied with the station and sphere in which they were born.

J.M. Richardson, *Anti-slavery Emancipation* (1824)

---

1 Study sources A to E.

(a) In what areas of social and economic life might the writers of the sources A to E consider it legitimate to legislate?

Area of possible legislation	Source	Argument for or against
Law and order		
Minimum national wage		
Trade tariffs		
Unemployment assistance		
A standing army		

(b) What language, tone, style and argument do each of the writers use in support of individualism?

(c) Who would be the likely readership of these sources and how does this affect the way the authors address their audience?

(d) Study the illustrations that accompany sources A and E. How have the artists conveyed their impression of these two writers?

2 Study sources F and G.

(a) To what extent do Carlyle and Cobbett agree about the impact of industrialisation upon the individual?

Utilitarianism

Historians differ as to how much influence one can attach to individual theories, particularly that of Utilitarianism, a philosophy formulated by Jeremy Bentham. He was credited with great influence during his lifetime and subsequently, by historians. But two questions are now asked.
Did he really have a practical impact on legislation in the first half of the nineteenth century and if so, was his philosophy essentially collectivist or individualistic?
It is easy to exaggerate the role of great thinkers. Theories have to be translated into active policies and in so doing the ideal can become obscure or even contradictory.

THE PRINCIPLE OF HAPPINESS

By the principle of utility is meant the principle which approves or disapproves of every action whatsoever according to the tendency which it appears to augment or diminish the happiness of the party whose interest is in question ... I say of every action whatsoever, and therefore not only of every action of an individual, but of every measure of government ...

It is vain to talk of the interest of the community without understanding what is in the interest of the individual. A thing is said to promote the interest, of an individual, when it tends to add to the sum total of his pleasures: or, what comes to the same thing, to diminish the sum total of his pains.

... A measure of government may be said to be comfortable or dictated by the principle of utility, when in like manner the tendency which it has to augment the happiness of the community is greater than any which it has to diminish it'.

J. Bentham, *The Works of Jeremy Bentham* (Vol 1 1789)
Introduction to the Principles of Morals and Legislation.

Jeremy Bentham 1748–1832. During and after his lifetime several influential administrators regarded Bentham as their inspiration, most notably Edwin Chadwick, The term 'Utilitarianism' which is associated with his name is the notion that government ought to aim to produce 'the greatest happiness of the greatest number'. But how was the happiness of the greatest number to be guaged? Did this give the greatest number the right to decide what was their pleasure even at the expense of the misery of a minority? Who exactly made up the greatest number – those with the greatest power and influence or the whole population?

JEREMY BENTHAM.

Bentham assumed the motivating force of humanity was the pursuit of pleasure and upon this basis he claimed it was possible by 'moral arithmetic' to calculate the greater 'good' of society. Although this ideal could be interpreted as support for representative government it would be a mistake to think Bentham's contemporaries did so. In the electoral system, husbands represented their wives; property owners those without property.

LAISSEZ-FAIRE

Laissez-faire, in short, should be the general practice: every departure, unless required by some general good, is a certain evil. Now any well-intentioned and tolerably civilised government may think, without presumption, that it does or ought to possess a degree of cultivation above the average of the community which it rules, and that it should therefore be capable of offering better education and instruction to the people, than the greater number of them would spontaneously demand. Education, therefore, is one of the things which it is admissable in principle that a government should provide for the people.

John Stuart Mill, *Principles of Political Economy* (1848)

John Stuart Mill 1806–1873 was one of the most ardent spokesmen for Bentham after the latter's death. As a child he was rigorously educated by his father James Mill who taught his son Latin and Greek by the age of 6. By 14, John was widely read in the classics, mathematics and logic. In his early twenties, however, he suffered a breakdown; no doubt partially attributable to his strict academic upbringing. As a consequence of this uncertain period in his life he modified his somewhat simplistic Benthamite stance whilst retaining the basic core of belief.

JOHN STUART MILL.

Questions

1 Upon what idea of human motivation did Bentham base his theories?

2 How might Bentham have explained an individual sacrificing his own personal pleasure for the general 'good' of society?

3 Consider what possible reasons the supporters of Utilitarianism might have given both for and against providing support for the poor?

4 Compare the writings of Bentham and John Stuart Mill.
To what extent does John Stuart Mill support Bentham's ideas?

5 What weaknesses, flaws or contradictions can you identify in the notion of 'Utilitarianism'.

6 Can Bentham be best described as an 'individualist' or a collectivist?

(b) In what ways are the language, tone and style affected by the audience to which they are directed?

(c) The dominant ideology in the age in which Carlyle lived was overwhelmingly one of individualism. How does Carlyle claim that this is not an age of individualism?

(d) What form of government do you think these writers would have found acceptable?

3 Study sources H and I.

(a) What similarities and differences are there in the authors' attitude toward collectivism?

(b) How realistic do you consider the proposals of Spencer and Owen?

4 Study source illustration 11.13.

How do the artists convey their point of view?

To which audience would these be directed?

5 Study sources J, K and illustration 11.14 and 11.15.

(a) According to Wilberforce how may Christianity prompt government into action?

(b) William Wilberforce assisted William Pitt in the passing of the Combination Laws. These laws outlawed early trade unions of working people. How might Wilberforce justify his statement of belief in the extract and his opposition to the combinations of working men?

(c) According to Richardson how does Wilberforce encourage the lower orders to be disatisfied?

(d) Richardson was an admirer of Wilberforce. Why, therefore, does he criticise him?

(e) Both sources claim to portray the Anglican church. Can only one of them, therefore, be correct?

REVIEW
Summary of political and social thinkers

- The theory of Individualism
- Individualism in the context of the Age
- Individualism – theory and practice
- Individualist thinkers and writers
- Form of collectivism
- Collectivist writers
- The power of religion and interventionism
- Utilitarianism

Assignment

(a) Make a list of the nineteenth century political thinkers you have come across in this chapter.

(b) Summarise very briefly the ideas of each.

(c) Why are these ideas so important to the period? What do they contribute to the development of nineteenth century Britain?

12 Poverty and Policy

PREVIEW

The plight of Oliver Twist

OLIVER TWIST ASKING FOR MORE: CRUIKSHANK'S FAMOUS ILLUSTRATION FOR DICKEN'S NOVEL PUBLISHED FOUR YEARS AFTER THE POOR LAW AMENDMENT ACT WAS PASSED.

'The members of this Board were very sage, deep, philosophical men; and when they came to turn their attention to the workhouse, they found out at once, what ordinary folks would never have discovered – the poor people like it! ... 'Oho!' said the Board, looking very knowing; we are the fellows to set this to rights; we'll stop it in no time'. So they established the rule, that all poor people should have the alternative of being starved by gradual process, or by a quick one out of it (The Workhouse) was rather expensive at first, in consequence of the increase in the undertakers' bills, and the necessity of taking in the clothes of all the paupers, which fluttered loosely on their wasted, shrunken forms, after a week or two's gruel. But the number of workhouse inmates got thin as well as the paupers; and the Board were in extasies.'

Charles Dickens, *Oliver Twist* (1838)

TALKING POINT

Of what use are novels to
historians of nineteenth
century England?

The problem of poverty

The plight of Oliver Twist at the mercy of an unrelenting poor law cannot but fail to stir our sympathies while we shudder at the apparent
inhumanity of the Board of Guardians. Prison workhouses and ghostly
paupers haunt the pages of Dickens. But does a work of fiction, such as
Oliver Twist, convey an accurate historical picture of nineteenth century
attitudes to poverty and its treatment?

To this day people tend to adopt different attitudes toward poverty and
the best means of attempting its eradication. Some believe market forces
can create the wealth to remove poverty, others that state intervention is
essential if the cycle of poverty is to be effectively broken. Most take up
their stance between these two positions.

Should the poor be helped at all? If they are, does this dependence rob
them of the initiative to change their lives? Should some types of poverty
be helped and not others? If some of the poor are to be helped, then by
how much? These are not easy questions to answer today. They were less
easy to answer in an age that was undergoing tremendous change.

We must also be aware of the danger of making judgements on those
of a past age whose values, attitudes and beliefs were different from our
own. Often, we are barely conscious of our own bias. It is essential that
we try to understand how contemporaries saw the problems they faced
and hence the way in which they tried to solve them. In short, it would be
foolish to see nineteenth century poverty and the attempts to cope with it
through the spectacles of twentieth century British assumptions about
democracy and the welfare state.

The Old Poor Law

Both central and local government in early nineteenth century Britain was
controlled, as it always had been, through small privileged elites. Poverty
too had always existed. What transformed poverty into a serious social
problem was its concentration in the mushrooming towns and cities of the
industrial revolution and the willingness of society to see it as a problem.
The new and growing pauperism caused greater anxiety to the better-off
who increasingly judged the existing poor laws as incapable of coping
with the problem. It is important to remember that whilst central legislation had been enacted it was largely left to the parish authorities to adapt
this to their own needs. Thus methods of poor relief had evolved from a
patchwork of legislation and local practice.

Nevertheless there were general characteristics which can be identified
from the piece-meal legislation which constituted the old poor laws. The
parish was the main unit of administration which, because of its small
size, possessed only limited resources and relied entirely upon unpaid
non-professional administrators. Secondly, parishes employed their own
methods of dealing with poverty and hence there was no uniform practice
throughout the country. Legislation frequently followed, rather than created, systems for poor relief. The form of relief given often reflected the
particular areas dependence upon particular types of agriculture, trade
and industry. Thirdly, swings of public opinion found general expression
in the implementation of the poor laws. The seventeenth century tended

to be very strict whereas the latter eighteenth century was more lenient. Fourthly, there was an attempt to distinguish between deserving and undeserving poor.

WHIPPING A BEGGAR IN THE REIGN OF ELIZABETH.

These general characteristics were shaped by a number of important acts of legislation. The Elizabethan Poor Law of 1601 is regarded as the foundation for state action for poor relief. The act had been passed out of the fear of growing pauperism and vagabondage. The principal provisions of the Act laid down that the infirm were to be maintained but the able-bodied should be provided with work. A poor rate was levied on all property owners and an Overseer appointed annually to supervise the distribution of assistance.

The Act of Settlement in 1662 reinforced the principle of parish responsibility for the poor. An Overseer could send a pauper to his birth-place rather than suffer the expense; provided that the claimant had not moved to the new parish for an apprenticeship or had worked there less than one year and one day.

Diversity of practice make generalised remarks difficult. Consider, for example, the two extracts below.

'Margaret Roe (aged 10) refuseth to depart with the said infant (her sister) out of the said parish to Burselm ... That upon the ninth day of this instant August she, the said Margaret Roe, was openly whipped and punished as a vagabond ... and is hereby assigned with the said infant forthwith to parish from parish by the Officers the rest straightway to Ince

TALKING POINT

Was the distinction between 'deserving' and 'undeserving' poor a sensible one? What would be the practical difficulties of deciding which would be which?

... in the county of Lancaster where as she, the said Margaret Roe, confessed she and the infant were born.'

Burselm parish minutes, Staffordshire (1679)

'Item paid for sending out of town Cripples Jane Atkinson and Nicholas Harrison who had her leg cut off and was sent by pass from one constable to another until she came home. 12s.2d

Item to a poore body that fell in the street of falling sickness. 0s.4d

Item to Robert Boulton for new clogs and mending her stockings, she having nothing to put on. 0s.6d

Item paid January 18th to a lame soldier. 0s.7d

Ormskirk Quarter Sessions (1691)

In 1679 the Settlement Act was modified to allow a worker to leave the parish to seek employment elsewhere provided he obtained a certificate of good character signed by the local magistrate. But quarrels still erupted between parishes when the responsibility was unclear. Sometimes judgements in these disputes bordered on the bizarre. In Clerkenwell Sessions the following ruling was made in the case of the destitute pauper Henry Robinson, whose bedroom straddled two parish boundaries;

'The court held the pauper to be settled where his head, being the nobler part, lay, though one of his legs at least, and the greater part of his body, lay out of the parish'.

It was the undeserving poor, however, that successive Acts attempted to identify and teach a salutary lesson. In order to curb expense on those considered to be able but unwilling to work the Workhouse Test Act of 1723 introduced an element of compulsion. If such undeserving poor refused to enter the workhouse then they received no assistance.

The cost of providing a workhouse for the undeserving as well as the deserving was expensive. Gilbert's Act of 1782 made it easier for parishes to form 'unions' in order that the cost of building and maintaining workhouses could be shared between them. Gilbert's intention was that such workhouses were to be places of refuge for the old, the sick and orphans rather than institutions of correction for the undeserving. All others who needed assistance would receive it in the form of 'outdoor relief' – they would not be obliged to enter the workhouse but could remain in their own homes and receive help from the parish.

By 1795 war inflation was causing severe hardship, particularly in the agricultural southern counties. In order to cope with the resultant increasing pauperism a group of Berkshire magistrates met at the Pelican Inn in the village of Speenhamland to decide on a formula for poor relief. Bread was basic and a substantial part of the diet of the farm workers and so the price of a 4lb. 'gallon' loaf coupled to the number of dependents was used as the basis of outdoor relief.

Expenditure on Poor Relief in England and Wales	
1750	£700,000
1785	£2,000,000
1803	£4,300,000
1818	£7,900,000
1825	£5,800,000
1832	£7,000,000

The Old Poor Law under attack

Attacks upon the effectiveness and lack of uniformity of the Old Poor Laws increased in the first quarter of the nineteenth century. An urgency was injected into the criticisms by the increase of numbers of paupers and the mounting expense of providing relief.

At the opening of the nineteenth century the vast majority of the population were dependent upon agriculture for their livelihood. Arable farming, in particular, required heavily seasonal input and in less busy seasons many workers supplemented their income with alternative employment. Bad harvests could reduce the availability of work still further and, at the same time, force up food prices. In such circumstances parish relief remained the only life-line for the destitute.

Additional strains were being placed upon a system more used to the limited form of relief described above. The towns were beginning to experience cyclic unemployment; periods of prosperity then sudden and deep depressions. There seemed every indication that the patch-work of old poor law relief was creaking under the pressure of both traditional and new forms of poverty.

What should be done with the poor?

But what should be done? Many solutions were offered. The Reverend Thomas Malthus was among the more strident critics of any form of poor relief. To be generous to paupers, he argued, merely delayed the day of reckoning. The more they were given the more they would demand until the time arrived when there would be insufficient funds to meet the needs.

'I say that the power of the population to reproduce is infinately greater than the power of the earth to produce subsistence for man ... By that law of nature which makes food necessary to the life of man, the effects of these two unequal powers must be kept equal. This implies a strong and constantly operating check on population from the difficulties of subsistence. No fancied equality, no agrarian regulations in their utmost extent can remove the pressure even for a single century.

The poor laws of England tend to depress the general condition of the poor in two general ways ... a poor man may marry with little or no prospect of being able to support a family in independence. They may be said in some measure to create the poor which they maintain. Secondly, the quantity of provisions consumed in a workhouse upon a part of society, that cannot be considered as the most valuable part, diminishes the share that would otherwise belong to the more industrious, and more worthy members.'

Reverend Thomas Malthus, *Essay on Population* (1798)

Others echoed Malthus's call for the abolition of all forms of poor relief.

'The wisest legislator will never be able to devise a more equitable, a more effectual, or in any respect a more suitable punishment, than hunger for the disobedient servant. Hunger will tame the fiercest animal ... Unless the degree of pressure be increased, the labouring poor will never acquire

What other factors, apart from the increase in the number of paupers, could account for the rise in poor relief expenditure?

the habits of diligent application, and of severe frugality. To increase this pressure the poor's taxes must be gradually reduced ... the poor then might safely be left to the bounty of the rich ... if the whole system of compulsory charity were abolished, it would still be better for the state.'

Reverend Joseph Townsend, A Dissertation on the Poor Laws (1785)

THOMAS ROBERT MALTHUS.

The poor – Victims of oppression?

Not surprisingly, Radicals saw in the poor not a dangerous beast to be starved into submission but rather victims of oppression. They demanded that wages should be equal to the cost of living.

'In the year 1821 I addressed a letter to Mr. Scarlett upon the subject of his bringing in a Bill, founded upon the Malthusian scheme. His assertion was, 'that the poor would devour the whole of the landed property, unless they were put a stop to.' I showed him it was not the poor idlers, who were devouring the property of the country; that the increase of the poor rates was the only proof of the diminution of the just renumeration of labour; that the poor rates were in fact a debt contracted with the working people.'

William Cobbett

WILLIAM COBBETT.

Conversely, some radicals identified government legislation of business and industry as the true enemy of enterprise and prosperity. Economic forces alone would mete out a natural justice to the parasitic poor but, in the long run, business and industry would provide prosperity for all.

'Government should protect the natural liberty of industry by removing all obstacles all bounties and prohibitions, – all devices by which one set of people tries to obtain unfair advantage over another set. If this were fairly done, industry would find its natural rewards and idleness its natural punishment.'

Harriet Martineau, A Manchester Strike (1832)

The almost unshakeable belief in the efficacy of market forces was based upon the political economy of David Ricardo who converted Adam Smith's precepts into an 'iron law'. It was foolish, political economists argued, to ignore this basic reality of life.

'... Like all other contracts, wages should be left to fair and free competition of the market and should never be controlled by the interference of the legislature.

The clear and direct tendency of the poor law is in direct opposition to these obvious principles: it is not, as the legislators benevolently intended, to amend the condition of the poor and the rich, they are calculated to make the rich poor; and while the present laws are in force, it is quite in the natural order of things that the fund for the maintenance of the poor should progressively increase. The nature of the evil points out the remedy. By gradually contracting the sphere of the poor laws, by impressing upon the poor the value of independence, by teaching them that they must look to the systematic or casual charity but to their own exertions for support, that prudence and foresight are either necessary virtues, we shall by degrees approach a sounder and more healthier state.

David Ricardo, *Principles of Political Economy and Taxation* (1819)

To more sensitive thinkers and writers the thought of abandoning the poor to the mercy of economic forces was both unchristian and unjust.

'The care of the poor ought to be the principal of all the laws: for this plain reason, that the rich are able to take care of themselves.
Whoever applies himself to collect observations upon the state and operation of the poor laws, and to contrive remedies for their imperfections and abuses which he observes and digests these remedies into acts of parliament … deserves well of a class of the community so numerous, that their happiness forms a principal part of the whole. The study and activity thus employed, is charity in the most meritorious sense of the word.'

William Paley, *Works* (1797)

Jeremy Bentham, architect of the principle of utility applied to social problems, was not opposed to the poor law providing it met the pre-conditions of the general good.

'Shut up the temple of public charity to promote benevolence – shut up the law courts then, to promote justice. If this does with poor rates, try it upon tithes and call them offerings.'

Jeremy Bentham, *Pauper Management Improved* (1818)

The road to reform – The Poor Law Amendment Act 1834

In 1830 the Whigs came to power promising reform. This platform won them considerable support amongst the industrial middle classes, who exerted pressure on the Whigs to grant them the vote. The country was swept by reform fever. Widespread disturbances and riot punctuated the debate. Prodded into making concessions, the Whigs took the industrial middle class into the fold of enfranchisement, excluding, at the same time, the working class support which had helped them into power. The ideas of Smith, Malthus, Ricardo and Bentham began to exert a stamp upon government policy. As costs for maintaining the poor rose rapidly discontent with the existing poor laws began to mount.

1 The extracts above propose three methods of dealing with increasing pauperism.

(a) Replace or amend the existing poor laws.

(b) Maintain the existing poor laws.

(c) Remove all poor laws.

Place the writers in the appropriate categories (a), (b) or (c).

2 What do the sources reveal about the:

(a) nature of early nineteenth century society.

(b) attitudes toward poverty.

(c) the types of argument used to support their respective positions.

THE REFORM RIOTS IN BRISTOL.

In 1832 the government appointed a Royal Commission to enquire into the existing workings of the poor law. The three principal members of the Commission were;

- Edwin Chadwick – ex-secretary to Jeremy Bentham
- Nassau Senior – an economist of the Ricardian school
- The Bishop of London – a leading member of the Tory party

Examining the evidence
The Royal Commission, 1832–1834.

Twenty-six Assistant Commissioners visited 3,000 parishes out of a total of 15,000. Questionaires were issued from which the Commission received about 10 per cent replies, representing about 20 per cent of the population. After this extensive research the Royal Commission was in a position to report its findings and submit its recommendations to Parliament.

The extracts which follow illustrate some of the principal findings and attitudes toward poverty. Read through them and answer the questions at the end of the extracts.

Source A: Employers abuse the existing Poor Law
The employers of paupers are attached to a system which enables them to dismiss and resume their labours to their daily or evenly hourly want of them, to reduce wages to the minimum of what will support an unmarried man and to throw upon others the payment of a part, frequently the greater part, and sometimes the whole of the wages actually received by their labourers.

Source B: Unfairness of the existing Poor Laws
… consider the case of the labourers with four children for the subsistence of which family (according to the Chelmsford scale) 11s.6d is

Considering who the three leading members of the Royal Commission were what conclusions and recommendations might you expect them to make?

Note

The Poor Law Report was an impressive size. The report was supported by thirteen volumes of appendices of 8000 pages. Yet the historian R.H. Tawney has described it as 'brilliant, influential and wildly unhistorical'.

required. Of this sum the good labourer earns 10s from the parish 1s.6d. The man who does not work, and whom no one will employ, receives the whole from the parish.

Source C: A discouragement to savings

He (William Williams, an industrious labourer) told me (Mr. Hickson, a manufacturer) at the time I was obliged to part with him – 'Whilst I have these things I shall get no work; I must part with all my savings; I must be reduced to a state of beggary before anyone will employ me. I was compelled to part with him at Michaelmas; he has not yet got work, and he has no chance of getting any until he is a pauper, for until then, the paupers will be preferred to him. He cannot get work in his own parish, and he will not be allowed to get any in other parishes.

pages 78/79

Source D: An encouragement for children

Four men were working together near a farmhouse; upon questioning them as to the wages they were earning, one among them who informed us that he was thirty years old and unmarried, complained much of the lowness of his wages, and added, without a question on the subject being put to him 'that if he was married and had a parcel of children, he should be better off as he should have either work given him by the parish or receive allowances for his children'.

Source E: The workhouse: an encouragement of idleness and vice

But in by far the greater number of cases, it (the workhouse) is a large almshouse, in which the young are trained in idleness, ignorance and vice; the able-bodied maintained in sluggish indolence ... and the whole body of inmates subsisted on food far exceeding in kind and amount, not merely the diet of the independent labourer, but that of the majority of the persons who contribute to their support.

pages 53/54

Source F: Bankrupt parishes

... it appears that in this parish (Cholesbury, Buckinghamshire) the population which has been almost stationary since 1801 has steadily climbed ... the poor rates were only £10.10s and only one person received poor relief ... in 1832 when it was proceeding at the rate of £367 p.a. suddenly ceased in consequence at the impossibility to continue its collection.

page 64

Source G: A moral discouragement

Mr Issac Wilis collector of the poor rates in the parish of St. Mary – le – Bow, London ... the independent labourer is comparitively clean in person, his wife and children are clean and the children go to school, the house in better order and more cleanly. Those who depend upon parish relief or on the benefactions, on the contrary, are dirty in their persons and slothful in their ways; the children are allowed to go about the streets in a vagrant condition.

pages 89/90

Source H: Harm to the character of the poor

'Those whose minds', say Messrs. Wrottesley and Cameron,' have been moulded by the operation of the Poor Laws, appear not to have the slightest scruple in asking to be paid for the performance of those domestic duties which the most brutal savages are in general willing to render gratuitously to their own kindred. 'Why should I tend my sick and aged parents, when the parish is bound to do it or if I am to perform this service, why should I excuse the parish, which is bound to pay for it?'

page 96

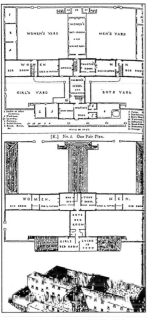

PLAN FOR A WORKHOUSE FOR 200, PUBLISHED BY THE POOR LAW COMMISSIONERS, 1834.

Source I: Conclusions and recommendations

Throughout the evidence it is shown, that in the proportion as the condition of any pauper is elevated above the condition of independent labourers, the condition of the independent class is depressed; their industry is impaired, their employment becomes unsteady, and its renumeration in wages is diminished. Such persons, therefore, are under the strongest inducements to quit the less eligible class of labourers and enter the more eligible class of paupers. The converse is the effect when the pauper class is placed in its proper position, below the condition of the independent labourer. Every penny bestowed, that tends to render the condition of the paupers more eligible than that of the independent labourer, is a bounty on indolence and vice. We have found, that as the poor's rates are at present administered, they operate as bounties of this description to the amount of several millions annually.

It may be assumed that in the administration of relief, the public is warranted in imposing such conditions on the individual relieved, as are conducive to the benefit either of the individual himself, or of the country at large, at whose expense he is to be relieved.

The first and most essential condition, a principle which we find universally admitted, even by those whose practice is at variance with it, is that his situation on the whole shall not be made really or apparently so eligible as the situation of the independent labourer of the lowest class.

page 228

The chief specific measures which we recommended are:

First, that except as to medical attendance, and subject to the exception respecting apprenticeship hereinafter stated, all relief whatever to able-bodied persons or to their families, otherwise than in well-regulated workhouses (i.e. placed where they may be set to work according to the spirit and intention of the 43rd Elizabeth), shall be declared unlawful, and shall cease ...

At least four classes are necessary: – (1) The aged and really impotent (2) The children (3) The able-bodied females: (4) The able-bodied males. Of whom we trust that the two latter will be the most numerous classes. It appears to us that both the requisite classification and the requisite superintendence may be better obtained in separate buildings than under a single roof ...

... Each class might thus receive an appropriate treatment; the old might enjoy their indulgences without torment from the boisterous: the children be educated, and the able-bodied subjected to such courses of labour and discipline as will repel the indolent and vicious.

We recommend, therefore, the appointment of a Central Board to control the administration of the Poor Laws; with such Assistant Commissioners be empowered and directed to frame and enforce regulations for the government of workhouses, and as to the nature and amount of relief to be given and the labour to be exacted in them, and that such regulations shall, as far as may be practicable, be uniform throughout the country.

page 284

Source J

DIET RECOMMENDED FOR ADULT PAUPERS, 1838.

The Enactment of the Poor Law

The recommendations of the Royal commission were enacted with considerable speed. In March 1834 the Report was published. By the following month a bill was introduced into Parliament based entirely on the recommendations. By August the bill had received the royal assent and was law.

Source K: The Poor Law Amendment Act

To effect these purposes we recommend that the Central Board be empowered to cause any number of parishes which they may think convenient to be incorporated for the purpose of workhouse management, and for providing new workhouses where necessary …

… the said Commissioners shall, once in every year, submit to one of the Principal Secretaries of State, a general report of the Proceedings; and every such general Report shall be laid before both Houses of Parliament …

VII ... the said Commissioners shall ... from Time to Time appoint ... Assistant Commissioners for carrying this Act into execution.

VIII ... no Commissioner or Assistant Commissioner shall ... be capable of being elected or sitting as a member of the House of Commons ...

XV ... for executing the Powers given to them by this Act the said Commissioners shall ... make and issue all such Rules, Orders and Regulations for the Management of the Poor, for the government of the Workhouses and the Education of the children therein ... and for apprenticing the Children of poor Persons, and for the Guidance and control of all Guardians, Vestries and Parish Officers, as far as relates to the management or Relief of the Poor.

XXV ... it shall be lawful for the said Commissioners ... to declare so many Parishes as they think fit to be united for the Administration of the Laws for the relief of the Poor, and such Parishes shall be deemed to form a Union ... and ... the Workhouse or Workhouses of such Parishes shall be for their common use.

XXVI ... the said Parishes shall be separately chargeable ... to defray the Expense of the Poor ...

XXVI ... in any Union it shall be lawful ... to direct ... that relief shall be given to any adult Person who shall from Old Age or infirmity of Body be unable to work, without requiring that such Person shall reside in a Workhouse

XXXVII ... where any parishes shall be united ... for the relief of the Poor. A Board of Guardians of the Poor for such Union shall be constituted and chosen, and the Workhouse and Workhouses of such Union shall be administered, by such Board of Guardians: and the Guardians shall be elected by the Ratepayers ...

XLV ... nothing in this Act contained shall authorise the detention in any Workhouse of any dangerous Lunatic, insane Person or Idiot, for any longer period than Fourteen days ...

---

1 What criticisms do the Royal Commissioners make of the existing Poor Laws?

2 If the Commissioners are adamant that the existing Poor Laws are at fault why do they insist on a return 'to the spirit and intention of the 43rd Elizabeth'?

3 What types of poor do the Commissioners identify and what treatment do they recommend?

What principle appears to lie behind their proposals for the treatment of the poor?

4 From the evidence presented here how reliable does the evidence collected by the Commissioners appear to be?

5 Why is the Workhouse thought to be an essential component of the Poor Law Amendment Act?

Why do they consider it necessary to segregate the inmates?

6 What significance lies in the speed with which the Commissioners' recommendations became law?

7 'The Commissioners were steeped in the Malthusian view of Society'. To what extent do you agree with this statement?

8 The Poor Law Amendment Act is often referred to as the 'New Poor Law'. How accurate do you consider this title?

The Poor Law Amendment Act in operation

The bureaucracy for the administration of the poor law was set up with speed. At the centre of the system, three Commissioners were appointed at a salary of £2,000 per annum. Edwin Chadwick, the principal author of the Report, had to settle for the less-influential position of Secretary to the Commission at the more 'modest' salary of £1,200.

The Commissioners began the task of organising the poor law unions. Fifteen Assistant Commissioners, on salaries of £1,500 p.a., set to work implementing the poor law in the southern counties of England. In the first year of the Act 2066 parishes were incorporated into 112 unions and Boards of Guardians elected to govern them. By 1835 a further 5800 parishes were grouped into 239 unions.

By chance the implemention of the poor laws co-incided with improved economic fortunes. The Commissioners were not slow in claiming the improved administration of the poor law was the principal factor in determining this improvement.

When the Commissioners next turned their attention to the northern counties of England they met with considerable opposition as well as hostility as the economic situation deteriorated. To many northern workers the Amendment Act was inappropriate to their circumstances. Unemployment in the growing industrial cities tended to be short term and largely dictated by fluctuating economic cycles. Thus, recipients of poor relief, required only temporary help. Furthermore, to castigate workers at the mercy of trade cycles as able-bodied idle, added insult to injury.

EXAMINING THE EVIDENCE
Opposition to the Poor Law

It was hardly surprising that, particularly in the north of England, opposition to the poor law was vocal and violent. The plaintive voices of protest swelled in volume as outrage fired their anger. The voice of protest was also swelled from voices from many different sections of society.

The pages of the 'Times' and 'Punch' magazine, as well as the novels of Charles Dickens kept up a fusilade of fire at what they regarded as a lack of compassion on the part of government. They warned the general public of what came to be termed 'The Condition of England Question' i.e. The widening gulf between rich and poor. This, they argued, would plunge the country either into an abyss of despair or social revolution. The bleakness of this prophecy could only be avoided if the rich were to show compassion and provide more humane provision for the poor. This line of argument, however, did not lead these writers to conclude that a

How might the factor of an improvement in economic fortunes influence their evaluation of the governments attitude to the Poor Law Amendment Act?

restructuring of power and privilege was necessary. The vote and mass democracy they believed were the elements of chaos. Christian charity was the hope for peaceful change.

In direct contrast, revolutionaries argued that only the rooting-out of corrupt society would assist a new growth of justice to flourish.

A MOB ATTACKS THE STOCKPORT WORKHOUSE.

Source A: The 'milk of human kindness'

A PUNCH CARTOON.

Source B: The cruelty of the workhouse

Since the rich have all the power, the proletarians must submit and have the law actually declare them superfluous. This has been done by the New Poor Law ... The regulation of these workhouses, or as the people call them, Poor Law Bastilles, is such as to frighten away everyone who has the slightest prospect of life without this form of public charity ... the workhouse has been made the most repulsive residence which the refined ingenuity of a Malthusian can invent ...

In the workhouse at Greenwich, in the summer of 1843, a boy of five years old was punished by being shut in the dead room, where he had to sleep upon the lids of the coffins. In the workhouse at Hearne the same punishment was inflicted on a little girl for wetting the bed at night ...

In the workhouse at Bacton, in Suffolk, in January, in 1844, an investigation revealed the fact that a feeble-minded woman was employed as a nurse, and took care of the patients accordingly; while sufferers, who were often restless at night, or tried to get up, were tied fast with cords passed over the covering and under the bedstead, to save the nurse the trouble of sitting up at night ...

As in life, so in death. The poor are dumped into the earth like infected cattle. The pauper burial ground at St. Bride's, London, is a bare morass, in use as a cemetry since the time of Charles II, and filled with a heap of bones: every Wednesday the paupers are thrown into a ditch fourteen feet deep: a curate rattles through the Litany at top speed; the ditch is loosely covered in, to be re-opened the next Wednesday ...

Can anyone wonder that the poor decline to accept poor relief? ... that they starve rather than enter these bastilles.

Frederich Engels, *The Condition of the Working Class* (1844)

The most powerful working class political movement, Chartism was particularly vocal in its opposition.

Source C: Chartist attacks upon the New Poor Law

The Act is an insult to the Rich, a fraud upon the Poor, and a reason against Nature. It is a thief, against which the 'Hue and Cry' should be raised: – a mad dog which should be scouted from hill to hill, and dale to dale.

Fergus O'Connor, *The Northern Star* (January 6, 1838)

Source D: The inhumanity of the New Poor Law

Come you men and women unto me attend,
And listen and see what for you I have penned;
And if you buy it, and carefully read,
'T will make your hearts within you to bleed.

The lions at London, with their cruel paw,
You know they have passed a Starvation Law;
These tigers and wolves should be chained in a den,
Without power to worry poor women and men.

When a man and his wife for sixty long years
Have toiled together through troubles and fears,

And brought up a family with prudence and care,
To be sent to the Bastille it's very unfair.

And in the Bastille each woman and man
Is parted asunder – is this a good plan?
A word of sweet comfort they cannot express
For unto each other they ne'er have access.

To give them hard labour, it is understood.
In handmills the grain they must grind for their feed,
Like men in a prison they work them in gangs,
With turning and twisting it fills them with pangs.

From a broadsheet ballad published in Bradford just after the introduction
of the poor law

Opposition to the Poor Law did not just come from the working class and left-wing politicians. Tory radicals saw little merit in the new industrial society in which the paternalistic bonds of society appeared to be breaking apart.

Source E: The New Poor Law as an attack on liberty

It is possible that your Lordship may enquire: if the state grants relief to the Poor, has she not a right to settle upon what terms that relief shall be awarded? Unhesitatingly I answer NO!! There are certain bounds, limited by the constitution, beyond which the three estates cannot travel, and at the same time retain the present order of society or maintain the present ownership of property. The personal liberty of the subject is not forfeited to the state without crime. The law which interferes with that right is unconstitutional – and every man is justified in resisting it to the death. The right of a husband to the society of his wife is not forfeited because of poverty.

Richard Oastler, *An Open Letter to the Prime Minister, Lord John Russell*

There were also a significant number of those in authority who believed they could oppose the poor law from within the system.

Source F: Guardians refuse to carry out the new poor law

Guardians in many places still paid outdoor relief to able-bodied men and women despite repeated insistence that the workhouse test should be the norm. The Royal Commission found that only 274 unions, about half the total number, were refusing to give outdoor relief to able-bodied paupers, and almost all of these were in rural areas of declining populations.

Norman McCord, *Aspects of Relief of Poverty in Early nineteenth Century Britain*

Source G: The Andover Bastille

THE POOR PICKING THE BONES TO LIVE
See our Leader.

THE COMMISSION OF INQUIRY DISCUSSING THE SUBJECT OVER
A GOOD DINNER.

1 (a) How does the artist and how do the writers convey their opposition to the Poor Law Amendment Act?

(b) What reasons do they give for their opposition to the Poor Law?

(c) In what sense do the various groups represent a united opposition to the Poor Law?

2 Select three members of your group to play the part of the Commissioners. In this role refute the arguments put forward by the opposition.

Supporters of the New Poor Law

Despite the range of opponents to the poor law the Act prevailed. There were many who enthusiastically pointed to the benefits of well regulated workhouses and well regulated paupers. So embedded did the Poor Law provisions become in society that it remained on the statute books until 1929 – well beyond its supercession by other welfare legislation.

The Reverend D. Wrench however spoke for many when he gave his evidence before the Poor law Commissioners in 1836.

'The positive good which has been brought by the new Poor Law is, in the first place, that the public houses and beer shops are, without question, much less attended than before: that drunkeness is decidedly less frequently seen.'

The Poor Law Amendment Act in perspective

The implementation of the Act did not produce the uniform 'well-regulated' workhouse. Scandals broke out from time to time, most notoriously at Andover, where starving paupers, employed in crushing rotting bones for manure were seen to gnaw the putrid scraps of meat still remaining on the bone. The public outcry that accompanied these revelations, fanned almost daily by articles in 'The Times' newspaper, led to a select committee replacing the Commissioners. In 1847 a Poor Law Board was set up which was directly answerable to Parliament.

Furthermore, the cornerstone of the workhouse test and the abolition of outdoor relief, was widely ignored. Both the 1842 and 1844 Outdoor Relief Prohibitory orders only applied to the less populous districts for it was realised by the Commissioners themselves that the insistence upon this prohibition would either be ineffective in the south or lead to riot in the north.

In fact outdoor relief was cheaper to administer and thus more attractive to even the most ardent supporters of the Amended law. Certainly in times of mass unemployment, such as the Lancashire cotton famine of the 1860s, the Poor Law as it stood was totally inadequate to cope with the widespread distress. The passing of the Public Works Act shortly afterwards represented a more realistic approach to the problem of providing the poor with public assistance.

Moreover, the principle of 'less-eligibility' presented the administrators with a moral dilemma. If imposing 'less-eligibility' meant reducing conditions inside the workhouse to near starvation then they could not, at the same time, claim credit as members of a civilised society.

The principles of 1834 gradually became eroded. The workhouse became less and less the scourge of the able-bodied poor and instead became the refuge for the old, the sick, the mentally ill and the young. This was a far cry from the original intention of the law. Even more corrosive to the harsh regulation of the Amendment Act was the slow realisation that other factors than the moral failure of the poor were responsible for poverty.

Since the inception of the Act, supporters and opponents and subsequent historical interpretations have been highly charged and coloured by the writers opinions. The purpose of the historian is to attempt to set the Act within its time and evaluate the significance of it accordingly. Consider the following research conducted by these historians before you reach any conclusions about the nature, intention and operation of the Poor Law Amendment Act of 1834.

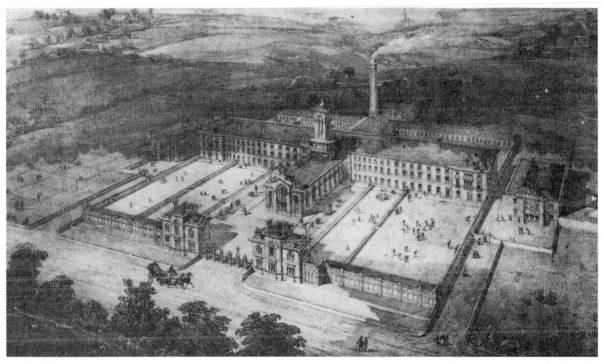

A WORKHOUSE IN MANCHESTER.

EXAMINING THE EVIDENCE

The significance and interpretation of the Poor Law Amendment Act of 1834

Source A: The need for caution

Few aspects of modern British history have aroused so much discussion and disagreement as the record of British society in alleviating poverty during the nineteenth century. The problems involved are complicated, and there is need for more research on both official and unofficial attitudes to poverty and its alleviation. One of the difficulties of these topics is their apparent close relevance to current political problems and questions of social policy. It is an area of historical scholarship in which anachronistic judgements are all too easy to make, and in which it is peculiarly difficult to avoid using 'history' as ammunition in our contemporary political and ideological battles. The snare exists for historians of the right and the left; in this area of historical scholarship it is difficult to achieve a reasonable degree of objectivity.

This could easily be dismissed as a striking example of Whig smugness, yet if these high claims are examined in relation to the full realities of early Victorian Britain it is hard to dismiss them as baseless, especially if, like Macaulay, the reader is prepared to make the two way comparison with earlier as well as later periods.

In a variety of ways, British society in the early nineteenth century was very different from ours, and it is not surprising that there were marked differences in the attitudes and the methods employed in alleviating poverty. The population was much smaller and predominantly grouped in smaller though usually more integrated local communities. For most of the population life was more restricted by local horizons than it is today, and it was in local and private activity that most of the dynamism of that society existed, in the treatment of poverty as in other matters. The society was dominated by small privileged minorities, as it had always been.

... These groups controlled the machinery of central and local government, but in practice derived most of their power from unofficial sources, such as their command of property, employment and education. The point can be simply illustrated by the magistracy, the key office in local government. In early nineteenth century Britain a man did not acquire local influence simply because he was a Justice of the Peace; more accurately, a man who already for other reasons possessed local influence was likely to find himself clothed in addition with the functions and authority of the magistracy.

Norman McCord, *Aspects of the Relief of Poverty in Early Nineteenth Century Britain* (1974)

Source B: The weakness of the royal commission

Whatever their importance in administrative history, the Report of the Royal Commission on the Poor Laws, and the Act which followed hard on its heels, contained weaknesses which severely limited their usefulness in dealing with poverty, or even with pauperism, in the second half of the nineteenth century. In the first place, the Royal Commission had concentrated too much of its attention upon a single problem, that of the able-bodied unemployed, particularly in rural areas, who it feared were being demoralised by ill-conceived grants of outdoor relief. It paid too little regard to the problems of those who were pauperised because of physical or mental health, old age or loss of parents, although these constituted by far the largest proporation of those on relief. The important and complex problem of settlement received only cursory treatment in the Report and was only modified in a few minor details by the Act, and the vital question of rating and the finance of poor relief was dealt with in a cavalier fashion. There were questions which were to harass poor law administrators and social reformers for the next one hundred years. Secondly, the reformers of 1834 focused their attention upon the problem of rural poverty, and produced the machinery to deal with it. Yet the problem of the future was to be the far more difficult one of urban, industrial poverty.

The poor law proved to be ill-adapted for dealing with poverty, and thus was increasingly ignored as a device for social reform ... the oversimplified early nineteenth century view of poverty was broken down by investigation of the causes of poverty, and by changing attitudes towards it, a process which led to the introduction of new methods of treating poverty.

Michael Rose, *The Relief of Poverty 1834–1914* (1979)

Source C: The virtues of the Old Poor Law

The Old Poor Law, with its use of outdoor relief to assist the underpaid was, in essence, a device for dealing with the problem of surplus labour in the lagging rural sector of a rapidly expanding but still underdeveloped economy. And considering the quality of social administration of the day, it was by no means an unenlightened policy. The Poor Law Commissioners of 1834 thought otherwise and deliberately selected the facts so as to impeach the existing administration on pre-determined lines. Not only did they fail in any way to take account of the special problem of structural unemployment in the countryside, but what evidence they did present consisted of little more than picturesque anecdotes of maladministration. Even the elaborate questionnaire which they circulated among the parishes was never analysed or reduced to summary form. No attempt was made to make a census of the poor, and to this day we know more about the nature and composition of the pauper host in 1802 than in 1834. Anyone who has read the Report of 1834 can testify to the overwhelming cumulative effect of the endless recital of ills from the mounts of squires, magistrates, overseers, and clergymen. But as evidence of a social malady it has little value, particularly on the ultimate question of the corrupting influence of lavish relief ... No wonder the 'harsh but salutary Act' fell short, at nearly every point, of effecting sweeping reform.

Gradually ... the 'principles of 1834' were undermined in practice by the administration of successive governments, while competing public services increasingly took over the functions of the Poor Law.

Mark Blaug, The Myth of the Old Poor Law (Essays in Social History) eds. M.W. Flinn
and T.C. Smout (1967)

Source D: A balanced appraisal

Certainly the Act of 1834, whether Benthamite or Malthusian or neither, was not passed as an intellectual exercise. On the other hand neither was it a mindless reaction to a specific social-economic situation; it emerged from a debate, and not merely a conflict of interests. The debate was complex and many-sided ... The kernel of the debate on pauperism in the years 1790 and 1830 was the rise of abolitionism, by no means a new argument but the one which seemed most relevant and cogent at the time. It did not require originality to see the Poor Law itself as a major cause of pauperism; it required either considerable perspicuity or deeply held prejudices in favour of some other explanation to realise that this was a grave simplification of the truth ... (By the late 1820s) there were few dominating figures in the discussion of pauperism ... the ideas on poverty and its relief which grew to dominate opinion in the early nineteenth century have since gained a bad reputation. The workhouse test was not a generous principle ... it is the literature of protest which is immediately attractive ... But were Cobbett's arguments more cogent than Malthus's in the circumstances of the day? The historian must strive above all to understand how men viewed their world, partial though those views must be. The allowance system on the one hand, and the Union workhouse on the other, can all too easily provide the themes for myths of oppression with which to indict whole generations.

Derek Fraser, The Evolution of the Welfare State (1974)

Source E: The value of the Royal Commission

It should be stressed that it is far too easy to assume that the Commissioners were always and everywhere wrong in their criticisms of the old system. As Dr. Blaug's researches show, the potentialities of the Commissioner's material are very great ... nor should we make the mistake of unduly blaming the leading personalities of the Poor Law Commission for attitudes which were widespread at the time ... It is still more unhistorical to blame the Commissioners for not using modern surveying techniques ... Lacking the data to look forward with hope, and therefore with humanity, the Commissioners looked backward and condemned. It was in fact not difficult to make a convincing-seeming case which appealed to ratepayers, landowners and middle class savants.

(The operation of the Old Poor Law) was not a welfare state in miniature but in some areas it did have the advantage of responding to local conditions such as the higher level of industrial development of Lancashire ... Some Lancashire Poor Law Unions remained without a new type workhouse for two decades.

The Poor Law Amendment Act is associated with the achievement of immediate and visible economies and rapid fall in the cost of relief throughout most of the country. There can be little doubt ... that at least some of the evils it was designed to destroy were in fact exaggerated, ... the economic problems which underlay the high relief bills of the Speenhamland counties were not of a kind which could have been removed by Senior and Chadwick. Wages remained low in those counties long after 1834 ...

On the other hand, the new act is rightly regarded as having heralded an administrative revolution.

J.D. Marshall, *The Old Poor Law 1795–1834*

---

1 Study source A

(a) Why does Norman McCord claim that the study of nineteenth century poor relief is an area in which anachronistic judgements are all too easy to make?

(b) What examples does Norman McCord cite to justify this assertion?

2 Study source B

(a) According to the writer what was the intrinsic fault in the Poor Law Amendment Act?

(b) What major mistake, is it claimed, did the Commissioners make?

(c) Which sections of the poor were apparently overlooked?

3 Study source C

(a) What function does the writer see the Old Poor Law as having provided?

(b) Which mistakes does the writer accuse the Commissioners of making?

(c) Why does the writer consider that the 1834 Report has little value as an accurate social document?

(d) Even if the Report lacked an objective base why might it still be considered as a useful historical source?

4 Study source D

(a) What does the writer mean when he accuses the Commissioners of being obsessed with notions that were no longer entirely relevant?

(b) In what way does the writer warn us against exaggerating the impact of a particular individual upon legislation?

(c) If we are to assume the perspective of historians how must we attempt to understand prevailing attitudes toward poverty?

5 Study source E

(a) How does this author attempt to put into perspective the criticisms made of the Commissioners in source B and C?

(b) What evaluation does the writer make of the operation of the Old Poor Law?

6 Use all the sources in this examining the evidence section to answer these questions.

(a) Compare the historians' interpretations with the evidence presented by the Royal Commissioners.

Do you consider the historians' judgements justified?

Which of the historians appear to be most critical of the Poor Law Amendment Act?

Which historian appears to take the context of the times most into consideration in his interpretation?

REVIEW
How valid were the criticisms made by the Royal Commission of the old poor laws?

Historiographical problems – contemporary value

- Judgements – political stances – the need to understand contemporary perspectives.
- The central problem as perceived by the Commissioners.
- The subsidiary causes of poverty.
- The distinction between poverty and pauperism.
- The Commissioners' evidence.
- Range of methods suggested for the relief of poverty.
- Contemporary criticisms of the Poor Law proposals.
- Advantages and limitations of the provision before and after 1834.
- The difficulty of coping with poverty in an emerging industrialised society.
- Poverty and its alleviation in context of early nineteenth century Britain.

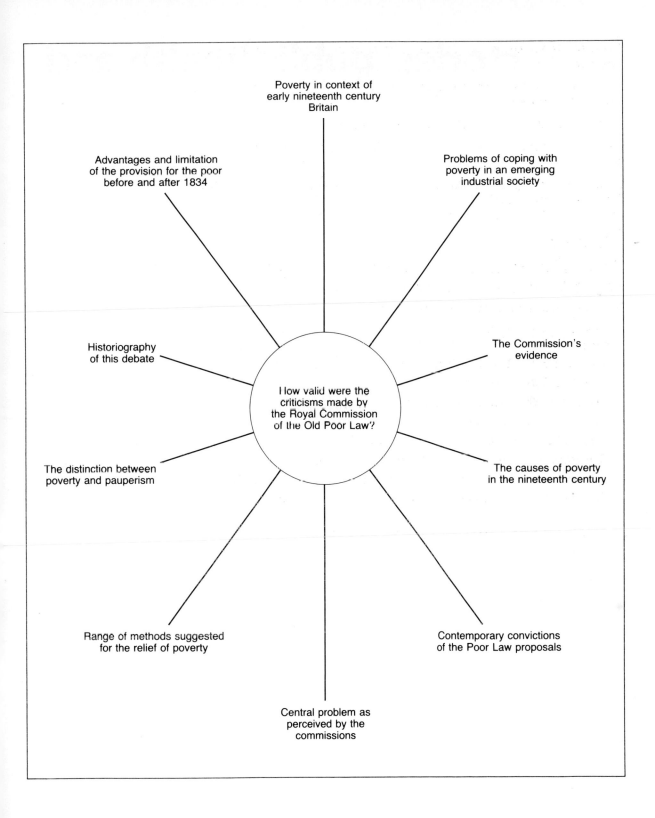

Poverty in context of
early nineteenth century
Britain

Advantages and limitation
of the provision for the poor
before and after 1834

Problems of coping with
poverty in an emerging
industrial society

Historiography
of this debate

The Commission's
evidence

How valid were the
criticisms made by
the Royal Commission
of the Old Poor Law?

The distinction between
poverty and pauperism

The causes of poverty
in the nineteenth century

Range of methods suggested
for the relief of poverty

Contemporary convictions
of the Poor Law proposals

Central problem as
perceived by the
commissions

13 Factories, public health and education

PREVIEW

The factory question

ENGLISH FACTORY SLAVES.

In 1833 Thomas Clarke of Leicester, aged 11, described his working life.

"I was very nigh nine years of age when I first went to work as a piecer. I got 2/6d at first. I think I was a good hand at it. When I had been there half a year I got 3/-d. Badder, the charge-hand used to strap me at odd times. Sometimes he'd catch me over the head, but it was mostly on the back. He made me sing out. He would strap us about twelve times at once. He used to strap us sometimes over our head. I used to sometimes fall asleep when we were on long time ... Castle (another charge-hand in the factory) used to get a rope about us as thick as my thumb, and double it, and lick us with that."

Note

Thomas Clarke made regular appearances at Royal Commission Enquiries on working conditions and received coaching in his responses.

TALKING POINT

Early factory legislation concentrated on cotton mills, the newer form of industrial plant. Why should it have focussed almost exclusively on cotton mills?

The factory question in perspective

Thomas Clarke's story was related to a Parliamentary Commission set up in 1833 to investigate working conditions in the cotton mills. It is easy but mistaken to conclude from such evidence that all nineteenth century factories were dens of capitalist greed which were bent upon extracting the last ounce of work from undernourished and exploited men, women and children.

Abuses there were, but it is unhistorical to judge such incidents from a twentieth century standpoint. In the first place there was nothing new in the notion of children working. It was regarded as perfectly normal that children from the age of five should assist their parents. The family was not merely a social unit but also an economic entity. Child labour was not the creation of the Industrial Revolution but, as with other social problems, the factory tended to concentrate and multiply what previously had been diffuse and hidden from public gaze.

The Industrial Revolution added two strands to child labour – a regimented work discipline and physical danger. Excessive hours produced tiredness and the overlookers were often as much motivated by the need to keep children awake as by their much publicised sadism. Opponents of the factory system were often inclined to exaggerate conditions and to generalise from particular abuses. Much of the verbal evidence taken in the many inquiries was the personal memories of adults who may have embroidered their painful recollections.

At the same time an historical perspective to the factory question should not dupe us into dismissing the harshness of working conditions. Nor should we forget the crusading zeal and popular will of many contemporaries who looked upon these working conditions as a blight upon their society. Despite the newness of the problem, they acted, if but slowly and hesitatingly at first, to remedy the situation through government legislation. Even more surprising, restrictive legislation was passed in the teeth of free market forces which were sweeping all before it. In these circumstances we have to consider very carefully the appropriateness of attaching the label 'Laissez-faire' to this period of British history.

Factory life introduced a new rigid work discipline. 'Time is money' became the slogan of the age. In some factories workers could not go to the toilet without permission and in one case a tub was brought round for the male workers to relieve themselves.

The factory question was not a straightforward issue fought between humanitarians and misanthrops. All too frequently a simplified picture is presented – Tory philanthropic paternalism waging war against heartless Whig political economists – Anglican evangelicanism against selfish capitalists – landed aristocracy against the urban bourgeosie. The movement to reform factories was complex and cut across party and class lines.

Traditionally the triumph of factory reform has been regarded as the sole humanitarian endeavour of one man – Lord Ashley, the seventh Earl of Shaftsbury who pushed an unwilling government towards interventionist legislation in the 1830s and 40s. Increasingly historians have directed attention toward agitation outside parliament.

In the early 1830s Richard Oastler (1789–1861) was the undoubted leader of the factory movement. Oastler, an Evangelical Anglican, was a

'THE SYSTEM THAT WORKS SO WELL.'

land agent for a landowner at Fixby Hall, near Huddersfield. In
September 1830 he visited a wealthy Bradford manufacturer and was horrified at what he learnt of conditions in the worsted mills. Oastler blasted
his indignation onto the pages of the Leeds Mercury under the title of
'Yorkshire slavery.'

Assisted by the emergence of Short Time Committees of working men
the 'Fixby Hall' compact was made in June 1831 to pursue the goal of
factory reform and 'to work together irrespective of political or party considerations.'

Government legislation up to this point had been selective and piece-
meal. The campaign inside parliament was put by Michael Sadler with
renewed vigour. He too was an evangelical Tory who took up the cry of
the 'ten hour day.'

The cause of factory reform was organised as a religious crusade, 'sink
your commerce and rise Humanity, Benevolence and Christianity.' Yet,
despite a petition signed by 130,000 people, Parliament remained
unmoved and instead appointed a select committee with Sadler in the
chair to investigate the issue further.

When Sadler lost his seat in the election of 1832 Lord Ashley
(renamed Lord Shaftsbury in 1851) took over the leadership in the
Commons. The objective was a ten hour day for children. Hours for
adults, however, were a totally different matter. They were regarded as
being capable of looking after their own interests without Parliamentary
help. As a result of pressure from opponents of factory reform, as much
by supporters, Parliament set up a Royal Commission in 1833 under the
chairmanship of Edwin Chadwick.

As a result of the recommendations of the Royal Commission the 1833
Factory Act was passed. The limited nature of the legislation disappointed
many factory reform supporters. Despite repeated pressure for further
reform little was achieved until the Factory Acts of 1844 and 1847.

Note

Sadler's Committee of
Inquiry in 1832 was
almost certainly fixed. No
evidence was given under
oath. When parliamentary
time ran out he published
the evidence of the
reformers only and not
the masters.

TALKING POINT

In which other social movements did Chadwick play a leading role. What does this indicate about his character?

By this time the torch of factory reform had been passed to John Fielden. Lord Ashley returned to Parliament in 1850 to reduce the hours of children and women still further.

By the middle of the nineteenth century the principle and foundations of factory reform had been accepted although such legislation applied only to textile mills. Thereafter there was a lull in agitation until fresh breath was blown into the movement in the 1870s.

Acts of parliament

This sheet outlines the most important Acts of Parliament which affected working conditions that were passed in the 19th century.

Date	Act	Description	Comment
1802	Health and Morals of Apprentices Act.	No pauper apprentices to do night work in textile mills. Day labour limited to 12 hours.	This Act was hardly effective because there was no adequate system of inspection, nor were penalties often enforced.
1813	Owen's campaign to protect factory children..		Select committee chaired by Robert Peel 1816.
1816	House of Lords Committee chaired by Lord Kenyon 1819.		
1819	Cotton Mills and Factories Act.	No children under 9 to be employed in cotton mills. Working hours of young people, aged 9–16, limited to 12 hours a day.	This law proved difficult to enforce and was therefore ineffective.
1825	Act to reduce hours forbade nightwork.		
1832	Royal Commission		
1833	Factory Act (Althorpe's Act).	No children under 9 to be employed. Children, aged 9–13, to work a maximum of 48 hours a week. Young persons, aged 13–18, to work a maximum of 69 hours a week.	The system of government inspectors was started to make the law effective. It applied to all textile factories except silk mills.
1838, 39,40	Unsuccessful 10 hour bills		
1842	Mines Act underground in coal mines.	No children under 10 or women to work.	Inspection of mines was begun.
1844	Factory Act (Graham's Act).	Minimum working age in all textile factories reduced to 8. All children's hours lowered to 6½ per day. Young persons, aged 13–18, and women, to work a maximum of 12 hours a day.	More inspectors were appointed and safety rules passed to fence off dangerous machinery.
1847	Factory Act (John Fielden's Act). (Fielden was a factory owner).	Work of women and young persons, aged 13–18, limited to 10 hours a day in all textile factories.	Long hours for men continued. Women and young persons were forced to work in a shift system.
1862	Children's employment Commission.	Produced five reports by 1866	
1867	Factory and Workshops Act.	Extended the provisions of earlier acts to workshops as well as to factories.	A 'workshop' in the terms of the Act employed 5 or more workers; a 'factory' over 50 workers.
1874	Factory Act– Half time employment		minimum age raised from 8 to 10.
1878	Consolidating Act.	Summed up and made clear the various rules contained in all previous Acts on hours, safety, inspection, etc.	
1880	Employers' Liability Act.	Made employers liable to their employees for damages in cases of accidents.	This was the start of Workmen's Compensation schemes.
1891	Sweated Trades Act.	Attempted to give protection to women working very long hours in trades carried on in back rooms.	The Act was difficult to enforce.

EXAMINING THE EVIDENCE
Factory children – Who was to blame?

Read the following sources and list those people who can be blamed for the abuse of factory children. Who, or what, was most at fault?

Source A

FACTORY PAUPER APPRENTICES FROM ANTHONY TROLLOPE'S BOOK, 'MICHAEL ARMSTRONG'.

Source B: Robert Owen: a supporter of improved working conditions

This evidence was given by Robert Owen to the Select Committee on the state of children employed in manufactories 1816. Robert Owen was a pioneer of improved factory conditions whose mills at New Lanark in Scotland were considered a model of enlightenment.

Questioner: 'At what age do you take children into your mills?'

Owen: 'At 10 and upwards.'

Questioner: 'What are your regular hours of labour per day, exclusive of meal times?'

Owen: '10 and three-quarter hours.'

Questioner: 'What time do you allow for meals?'

Owen: 'Three-quarters for dinner and one half hour for breakfast.'

Questioner: 'Then your full time of work per day is 12 hours?'

Owen: 'Yes.'

Questioner: 'Why do you not employ children at an earlier age?'

Owen: 'Because it would be injurious to the children and not beneficial to the proprietors ... (When New Lanark was bought in 1799) ... I found there five hundred children, who had been taken from poor houses, chiefly in Edinburgh, and these children were generally from the age of 5 and 6, to 7 and 8; they were taken so because Mr. Dale could not, I learned afterwards, ... obtain them at all (except at that age)'.

(Robert Owen then went onto recommend a starting age of 12 years and a working day of 10 hours)

Questioner: 'Do you think if such an arrangement was made in regard to the number of hours, the manufacturers would suffer any loss in consequence?'

Owen: 'My conviction is that no party would suffer.'

Source C: An opponent of reduced factory working hours

Another factory owner, G.A. lee of Manchester, was also examined by the Select Committee.

Questioner: 'How many persons do you employ in your factory?'

Lee: 'Under 10 years of age, 11; from 10–12, 121; from 12–14, 109; from 14–16, 101; above 16, 595. There are none under 9 years of age.'

Questioner: 'Are all whom you employ free labourers?'

Lee: 'They are at full liberty to leave when they please.'

Questioner: 'What are their hours of work?'

Lee: 'From 6 in the morning till 8 in the evening, allowing 40 minutes for dinner and 20 minutes for coming in ... 11 hours on Saturday, in all 76 hours per week ...'

(After being questioned about the length of the working day and week Lee is asked if he would consider a reduction in hours for children)

Questioner: 'The Committee is then to understand that unless any legislative provision takes place to compel you to diminish the hours of labour, you have no intention voluntarily to do so?'

Lee: 'I have no intention to alter the average hours of labour. If I could make them more regular I would.'

Source D: Factory fines

This list of fines was published in a strike pamphlet by the spinners of Tydsley, near Manchester, in 1823. The temperatures inside the mill rarely fell below 80 to 84 degrees. The wages for a spinner at this time would be about £1.10s. 0d per week.

	s.	d.
Any spinner found with his window open	1	0.
Any spinner found dirty at work	1	0.
Any spinner found washing himself	1	0.
Any spinner leaving his oil can out of place	1	0.
Any spinner sleeping with his gas lighted	1	0.

Source E: From the report on the cotton mills of Bolton 1823

In all the above-mentioned mills there are no apprentices employed. In 15 mills out of 28 there is more or less a small number of children under 9 years employed, but the master say this is contrary to their directions, as these children are engaged by journeymen spinners themselves.

Only 14 out of 28 mills have the Act of Parliament or Regulations hung up, and there is not more than one copy in most of those that have it hung up … with two or three exceptions the hours of working are 12 per day, exclusive of meals …

29 October 1823 R. Fletcher H. Richardson

Source F

Richard Oastler to the 'Leeds Mercury', October 16, 1830

Yorkshire Slavery

To the Editors of the Leeds Mercury.

It is the pride of Britain that a slave cannot exist on her soil; and if I read the genius of her constitution aright. I find that slavery is most abhorrent to it – that the air which Britons breathe is free – the ground on which they tread is sacred to liberty.

GENTLEMEN – No heart responded with truer accents to the sounds of liberty which were heard in the Leeds Cloth-hall Yard, on the 22nd. instant, than did mine, and from none could more sincere and earnest prayers arise to the throne of Heaven, that hereafter slavery might only be known to Britain in the pages of her history. One shade alone obscured my pleasure, arising not from any difference in principle, but from the want of application of the general principle, to the whole empire. The pious and able champions of negro liberty and colonial rights should, if I mistake not, have gone farther than they did; or perhaps, to speak more correctly, before they had travelled so far as the West Indies, should, at least for a few moments, have sojourned in our own immediate neighbourhood, and have directed the attention of the meeting to scenes of misery, acts of oppression, and victims of slavery, even on the threshold of our homes.

Source G:
Robert Southey, *a radical view of the oppression of the masses*

But if these children should be ill-used? said I. 'Sir,' he replied, it can never be the interest of the women to use them ill, nor of the manufacturers to permit it.'

It would have been in vain to argue had I been disposed to it. Mr. – was a man of humane and kindly nature, who would not himself use anything cruelly, and judged of others by his own feelings.

… In no other country can such riches be acquired by commerce, but it is one who grows rich by the labour of the hundred. The hundred, human beings like himself, as wonderfully fashioned by nature, gifted with the like capacities, and equally made for immortality are sacrificed body and soul. They are deprived in childhood of all instruction and all enjoyment; of the sports in which childhood instinctively indulges, of fresh air by day and of natural sleep by night. Their health, physical and moral, is alike destroyed; they die of diseases induced by unremitting task work, by confinement in the impure atmosphere of crowded rooms, by the particles of metallic or vegetable dust which they are continually inhaling; or they grow up without decency, without comfort, and without hope, without morals, without religion, and without shame, and bring forth slaves like themselves to tread in the same path of misery.

Source H: A selection of evidence from the 1833 Factories Enquiry Commission

Michael Sadler, leader of the Factory Reform movement in Parliament, was Chairman of the Commission. In the introduction to the factory question you can read the evidence of Thomas Clarke who complained of being beaten by a charge–hand called 'Badder'. Here is Badder's evidence.

In 1825 Ross's built a mill. I went to work at 6 a.m. on Monday and came home at eleven on Tuesday night, and came again at 6 on Wednesday morning, and worked till eleven on Thursday night. Then on Friday morning at 6 till Saturday evening about seven or eight … I was then about seventeen. My parents saw an alteration in me, and wished me to leave; I was then receiving 12/-: that is the rate for nine days. One night I fell asleep, and slipped onto the carding engine when it was running. I ran down off the engine without being hurt …

… I always find it more difficult to keep my piecers awake during the last hours of a winter's evening. I have told the master, and I have been told by him that I did not beat them half enough.

… I know Thorpe (the foreman) has been up before the magistrate half a dozen times or more, on the complaints of the parents. He has been before the bench and I have seen him when he came back, and told the parents they had better take the children away … The master complained that he (Thorpe) was not strict enough. I know from Thorpe that the master always paid his expenses when he was before the magistrate.

I have frequently had complaints against myself by the parents of children for beating them. I told them I was very sorry after I had done it, but I was forced to do it. The master expected me to do my work, and I could not do mine unless they did theirs.

Note:

Another witness, Richard Needham, a Bolton weaver, appeared before no less than four committees between 1803 and 1834.

Source I
This is the evidence of Henry Ross, the factory owner.

I am the owner here. It is nearly a year since I made the change of putting the children under the spinners. The main reason for the change was that they were dissatisfied with the number of piecers we allowed them. They pay the piecers by the week, in the same way I should have done. I don't think there is any difference in the amount. Since the change I have heard that the spinners punished the piecers too much. The overlooker said, 'No sir, not to hurt!' But I think they might do without any, if they always spoke severely to them.

Our last overlooker, (Thorpe) was not a good tempered man; he was honest and hard working, but bad tempered.

Source J
From the Report of Commissioners on the Employment of children in factories (1833).

The weavers are in general idle in the early part of the week, and they afterwards work from eighteen to twenty hours to make up their lost time, during which the draw-boy or draw-girl must attend them. I have known frequent instances of their commencing work at two or three o'clock in the morning (Witness).

In the clothing district both workmen and masters agree in stating that if extra work for extra pay were refused when a press of business comes, the workmen so refusing would lose their situations; both also concur in the statement that it is the constant practice of parents, and even of children themselves to apply for extra work for additional wages, and cases have been detailed in which the children have worked upward of fourteen hours.

It appears that parents encourage their children to make the extraordinary efforts ... by leading them to consider the wages which thus they earn as peculiarly their own, although a cheat is often practised on them even with regard to these extra wages. While all the witnesses agree in the statement, that whatever the child earns by its regular hours is uniformly appropriated by the parents it appears that a large portion of the additional wages earned by extra work also taken by the latter ...

... the Reports of the Commissioners agree in showing that the large factories, and those recently built, have a prodigious advantage over the old and small mills. The working rooms in the large and modern buildings are, without exception, more spacious and lofty; the buildings are better drained, more effectual expedients are adopted to secure free ventilation and to maintain a more equable and moderate temperature.

It is of the old and small mills that the Report pretty uniformly is 'Dirty, low-roofed; ill-ventilated; ill-drained; no conveniences for washing or dressing; no contrivance for carrying off dust and other effluvia; machinery not boxed in; passages so narrow that they can hardly be defined; some of the flats so low that it is scarcely possible to stand upright in the centre of the rooms:' while the account of the recent structures and the large establishments in general is – 'Infinitely better managed in respect to ventilation, height of roofs, and freedom from danger to the workers near the machinery, by the greater width of the passages in the working-rooms, and by the more effectual boxing in of the machinery, than those on a smaller scale.'

TALKING POINT

Why were factory children treated so harshly in the early nineteenth century? Consider this question from both a twentieth century perspective and then a nineteenth century perspective.

How would you prioritise the following factors and how much responsibility would you attach to each one?
- masters
- parents
- workers
- prevailing attitudes to children
- The economic philosophy of free market forces.

What was the point of describing children as 'free labourers'?

How effectively did legislation protect children and women by 1848?

Why was an exception made for these two groups of workers? (and what did this denote about attitudes to women at this time?)

… inquiries have obtained from the children themselves, from their parents, from operatives, proprietors, medical practitioners, and magistrates such statements amongst others as the following: – 'When she was a child too little to put on her ain clothes the overlooker did used to beat her till she screamed again.' – 'Gets many a good beating and swearing. They are very ill-used. The overseer carries a strap.' – 'Has been locked four or five times.' – 'The boys are often severely strapped; the girls sometimes get a clout. The mothers often complain of this. Has seen the girls strapped; but the boys were beat so that they fell to the floor in the course of the beating, with a rope with four tails, called a cat. Has seen the boys black and blue, crying for mercy.' – 'The slubbers are all brutes to the children; they get intoxicated and then knock them about; they are all alike.' – 'Never complained to the master but once to his mother and she gave him a half-penny not to mind it, to go back to work like a good boy. Sometimes he used to be surly and would not go, and then she always had that tale about the half-penny, sometimes he got the half-penny and sometimes not.'

It appears in evidence that in Scotland, and in the eastern part of England where the harshest treatment of children has taken place, the greatest number of bad cases occur in the small obscure mills belonging to the smallest proprietors.

Reports in which corporal punishment is strictly forbidden, and it is proved by the testimony of all classes of witnesses is never inflicted, will be found also in Mr. Mackintosh's Report … 'strapping was more customary in former times than it is now;' 'that he has seen boys severely beaten when he was a young man, but not for a number of years;' 'that he does not use the strap now, though he did formerly …'

In like manner, from the statements and depositions obtained under the present enquiry in the several districts in England, and from all classes of witnesses, it appears that in the great majority of cases, corporal punishment is prohibited by the proprietors, while it is proved on oath by several witnesses that the operatives and overlookers have been suspended or even dismissed from their employment for disobeying this command. It is impossible to read the evidence from Leeds, Manchester, and the Western Districts without being satisfied that a great improvement has taken place within the last few years in the treatment of children.

Source K

In my opinion, and I hope to see the day when such a feeling is universal no child ought to be put to work in a cotton mill at all so early as the age of thirteen years; and after that the hours should be moderate, and the labour light, until such time as the human frame is rendered by nature capable of enduring the fatigues of adult labour … I am aware that many of the advocates of the cause of the factory children are in favour of a Ten Hours Bill for restricting the working of the engines, which in fact would be to limit the use of steam in all cotton establishments (for young persons are, I believe at present employed in every branch of our staple manufacture more or less) to ten hours a day. It has always, however, appeared to me that those who are in favour of this policy lose sight of the very important consequences which are involved in such a principle. Have they considered that it would be the first example of a legislature of a free country interfering with the freedom of adult labour? Have they reflected that if we surrender into the hands of Government the power to make laws to fix the hours of labour at all, it has as good a right, upon the same principle, to make twenty hours the standard as ten? Have they taken into account that if the spinners and weavers are to be protected by Act of Parliament; the thousand other mechanical and laborious trades must in justice have their claims attended to by the same tribunal? I believe it is now nearly three hundred years ago since laws were last enforced which regulated or interfered with the labour of the working classes. They were the relics of the feudal ages, and to escape from the operation of such a species of legislation was considered as a transition from the state of slavery to that of freedom. Now it appears to me, however unconscious the advocates of such a policy may be of such consequences, that if we admit the right of the Government to settle the hours of labour, we are in principle going back again to that point from which our ancestors escaped three centuries ago. Let not the people – I mean the masses – think lightly of those great principles upon which their strength wholly rests ... Am I told that the industrious classes of Lancashire are incapable of protecting themselves from oppression unless by the shield of the legislature? I am loath to believe it. Nay, as I am opposed to the plan of legislating upon such a subject, I am bound to suggest another remedy. *I would, then, advise the working classes to make themselves free of the labour market of the world.*

Cobden to W.C. Hunt October 21st. 1836

The problem of public health

In 1844 Dr. D.B. Reid descended into the dark underworld of a working class district of Newcastle upon Tyne called the Sandgate.

'The streets most densely populated by the humbler classes are a mass of filth where the direct rays of the sun never reach. In some of the courts I have noticed heaps of filth, amounting to 20 or 50 tons, which, when it rains penetrate into some of the cellar dwellings. A few public necessaries have been built, but too few to serve the population. To take a single example of one of the more extreme cases shown to me when visiting them during the day, a room was noticed with scarcely any furniture and in which there were two children of two and three years of age absolutely naked, except for a little straw to protect them from the cold, and in which they could not have been discovered in the darkness if they had not been heard to cry.

Piggeries were also pointed out to me which added their offence to the causes already mentioned.

The absence of dustbins was everywhere a cause of great annoyance, and no such activity horrified me more than the attempt to keep the refuse of privies for the purpose of selling it to neighbouring farmers. The landlords and farmers encourage the practice and the authorities are reluctant to stop it for fear the poor will lose this small source of income.

TALKING POINT

Can an economic philosophy be responsible for the abusive treatment of people?

What were the consequences for factory workers of the market forces philosophy of the nineteenth century?

What are the consequences for unemployed people in Britain in the 1990s of a similar philosophy?

They forget the much larger expense of disease and death which results from this cause.

Stagnant ditches may be seen in the vicinity of most of these houses and part of the ground in the lowest districts is apt to be flooded after heavy rain, and long open sewers cross the public paths. House drains, where they exist, have not been constructed properly and often become choked.

In numerous dwellings a whole family shares one room. But no circumstance has contributed more to the injury of the inhabitants than the tax upon windows.

The lodging houses for the extreme poor present the most deplorable examples to be observed in the whole of the city. They are badly crowded, dirty, badly managed, ill-ventilated, where the sexes mix without control. They are generally favoured by the vagrants and trampers, many without employment, and act as nurseries for immorality as well as being a danger to public health. In one there was neither windows nor fireplace. On entering the lodging house, the occupants were attempting to remove a woman who had been attacked with fever. She was most reluctant to leave without all her clothing, which I was told afterwards had been pawned.

Why was public health a problem?

The most intolerable nuisance is certainly one resulting from a slaughter-house situated in the very centre just off the most fashionable part of the town. It is close to Grey Street: the nuisance consists in the presence of great quantities of animal matter, the offal of beasts heaped up in an ash-pit. There it is left to rot until liquid streams run down High Friar lane and fill the neighbourhood with a fearful odour ... Dense black clouds of smoke from manufacturing prevail to great extent in Newcastle and Gateshead. In the lower parts of the town the amount of black smoke is extremely great and their position renders it prone to retain it and other offensive smells. As much as 20 to 50 tons of acid are discharged into the atmosphere.

Water Co.	Source of water	Type of water	Number of water taps	No. of houses	Houses supplied	Price P.A.
Newcastle Joint Stock Company	River Tyne Carr's Hill Cox's Lodge Town Moor Rain water	soft brackish miry hard sooty	20 public	15,000	1,350	18s. to 30s.

What may seem surprising is why such conditions as those described by Dr. Reid were tolerated.

The spectre of disease had been present from the Biblical fear of leprosy to the scourge of the bubonic plague in the sixteenth century. The contribution of poor environmental conditions to the death toll, however, was not a serious one until the concentrations of urban poor created by the Industrial Revolution highlighted the problem.

Medical science was in its infancy as doctors debated the cause of disease but this had few solutions to offer. The miasmists held sway, arguing

The Mines Act 1842:
The Power of the Picture

(From the Report of the Commissioners on the Employment of Children, 1840. This was the first time illustrations had been used as part of a Parliamentary Inquiry.)

(I) ANN AMBLER AND WILL DYSON BEING DRAWN UP THE PIT-SHAFT.

Source C The cost of living:
A Voice from the Coal Mines, 1825.
Published in Northumberland

Bread, 2½ stone at 2s. 6d. per stone	6	3
1lb. of butcher's meat a day, 7d. per lb.	4	1
2 pecks of potatoes at 1s. per peck	2	0
Oatmeal and milk for seven breakfasts at 4½d each morning	2	8
	15	0

The family need as well to produce comfort:-

2oz. of tea at 6d. per oz.	1	0
2lbs. sugar at 6d. per oz.	1	4
1lb. salt butter.	1	2
1lb. cheese	0	9
Pepper, salt, mustard, vinegar	0	4
Soap, starch, blue, etc.	1	6
Tobacco 1½oz.	0	5½
1 pint of ale a day	1	9
Clothing for five persons	3	0
	£16	3½

(In addition to the above expenditure there was rent, which, in the mining industry, was often deducted from wages, and other deductions for fines and equipment which varied from industry to industry.)

(III) THE COST OF LIVING: A VOICE FROM THE COAL MINES, 1825. PUBLISHED IN NORTHUMBERLAND.

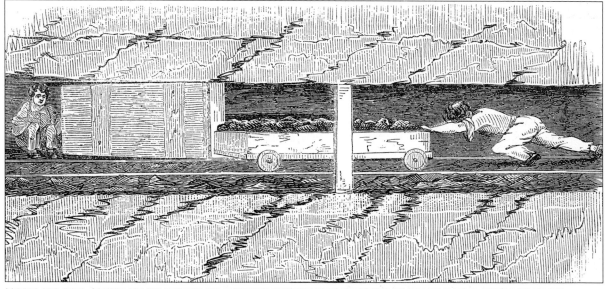

(II) BOYS AND GIRLS, AS WELL AS MEN AND WOMEN, WERE EMPLOYED TO WORK UNDERGROUND IN A COAL MINE, ALTHOUGH ONLY IN SCOTLAND DID THIS PRACTISE PERSIST INTO THE 1830S. THEY OFTEN SPENT LONG HOURS IN SEMI-DARKNESS, DRAGGING TRUCKS ALONG THE NARROW PASSAGES OR OPENING AND SHUTTING VENTILATION SHAFTS. PIT PONIES COULD NOT NEGOTIATE SOME OF THE NARROWER WORKING SEAMS AND IN ANY EVENT WERE REGARDED AS OF MORE VALUE THAN THE CHILDREN.

(IV) A PUNCH CARTOON 'LABOUR AND CAPITAL', 1943.

Policy and Practice – Factories/Public Health/Education 271

'... it appears that the Commissioners have come into this inquiry into mines fresh from the Factory Commission ... expecting to find the same oppression amongst the miners ... examining artful boys and ignorant young girls, putting questions in such a way as to suggest the answers ... and the manner in which the Report is accompanied by pictures ... in some cases scandalous and obscene ... is more likely to excite the feelings than to increase careful judgement.'

(V) THE MARQUIS OF LONDONDERRY PRESENTING A PETITION TO THE HOUSE OF LORDS FROM THE OWNERS OF COLLIERIES IN DURHAM AND NORTHUMBERLAND, 1842.

Assignment

1 What was the significance of using illustrations for the first time in a government report?

2 (a) In what way has the Punch cartoonist been inspired by the illustrations used in the Royal Commission's report?

(b) What is the similarity and difference in intention between the Punch cartoon and the Report's illustrations?

3 (a) What is Lord Londonderry's objections to the illustrations in the Report?

(b) Why does he state his objection to the illustrations in this way?

4 Compare the illustrations with source C. What are the advantages and limitations of this evidence compared to both illustrations?

FOCUS

A NINETEENTH CENTURY FACTORY INSPECTOR.
WHAT IS THE ARTIST ATTEMPTING TO CONVEY IN
THE PICTURE?

THE GIRL ATTENDING TO THE MACHINE IS A 'PIECER'. HER JOB IS TO TIE TOGETHER ANY THREADS THAT BREAK.
A 'SCAVENGER' IS AT WORK BENEATH THE MACHINE. IN THE BACKGROUND AN ADULT MALE SPINNER. WHY IS
IT NECESSARY FOR CHILDREN TO BE EMPLOYED IN THIS FACTORY?

THE LONDON BATHING SEASON.

"COME, MY DEAR! – COME TO ITS OLD THAMES,
AND HAVE A NICE BATH!"

THE ENEMIES OF PUBLIC HEALTH, PUNCH JAN. 1889.

as they did, that the cause of illness arose from decaying matter. Not until the 1860s did Louis Pasteur establish that micro-organisms caused putrefaction and disease and was able to prove that transmission of disease was by infection.

An old town: Leeds

Year	Population
1801	53 162
1811	62 534
1821	83 796
1831	123 393
1841	152 054
1851	171 805

Percentage of total population

Year	Country	Town
1801	69%	31%
1841	54%	46%
1881	32%	68%

A new town: Middlesborough

Year	Population
1801	25
1831	154
1841	5 463
1851	7 431
1861	19 416
1871	39 563
1881	55 934
1891	75 532
1901	91 302

Population Growth in British Cities 1801–61 (in thousands)							
	1801	1811	1821	1831	1841	1851	1861
Birmingham	71	83	102	144	183	233	296
Glasgow	77	101	147	202	275	345	420
Leeds	53	63	84	123	152	172	207
Liverpool	82	104	138	202	286	376	444
Manchester	75	89	126	182	235	303	339
Salford	14	19	26	41	53	64	102
Sheffield	46	53	65	92	111	135	185

Environment and disease

Knowledge of the precise relationship of environment and disease was not necessary for doctors who could observe for themselves the effects of disease in areas of deprivation. Many surveys conducted in the late eighteenth and early nineteenth centuries rooted the incidence of disease in a social context: John Haygarth in Chester 1774, Charles Turner Thackray in Leeds 1831, John Haysham in Carlisle 1780 and Robert Baker in Leeds 1832.

Despite the accumulation of pragmatic evidence little change could be effected without the administrative structure and the will to intervene. Corporations, where they existed, were run for the better-off citizens, whilst the sprawling, newer industrial cities such as Birmingham and Manchester were still administered as village parishes. Central government scarcely stirred unless provoked into action by the visitation of epidemics. Even then, responses in the form of Boards of Health were only temporary, such as the short-lived Board of Health set up to co-ordinate help during the threat of yellow fever in 1806.

Whilst the cholera epidemics appeared to pose the most serious threats other, more insidious, diseases were constantly at work undermining the health of the population. Typhus and tuberculosis (perhaps responsible

Note

Pauperism only affected the lower levels of society but disease respected no social status. In 1861 Prince Albert, the Prince Consort, died of typhoid fever at the age of forty-two.

for a third of all deaths) eked the life from the labouring poor assisted by the vile hand-maidens of scarlet fever, measles and diarrhoea. Only small-pox was removed from the list of killers by Jenner's discovery of innoculation.

Edwin Chadwick (1800–1890)

Of all the campaigners for improved public health, Edwin Chadwick stands monumentally above the rest. Nevertheless without a base of support from which to work little could have been achieved. The creation of the Poor Law Commission (1834), the passing of the Municipal Corporations Act (1834) and the Registrar-General's Office (1837–38) combined to create the foundation upon which Chadwick could build. With the single-minded zeal of a crusader he was drawn into the public health debate through his work with the Poor Law Commission. Reports of the Assistant commissioners constantly stressed the connection between poverty and disease and how such factors could be controlled only through government action.

As a result of the Poor Law auditors refusing to accept the spending of the poor law rate to clean up nuisances in the east end of London, the Home Secretary initiated a pilot study to determine the relationship between environment and disease. Under the auspices of the poor law commission, three doctors were employed to carry out the survey; James Kay, James Arnott and Southwood Smith. The resultant 'fever' report gave Chadwick the pretext for an ambitious national survey. When Chadwick's report 'The Sanitary conditions of the Labouring Population of Great Britain' was published in 1842 it was an instant best seller. The government disassociated itself from the report largely because of the number of influential people that Chadwick had offended; corporations, joint-stock water companies and public figures.

Little was done by the government who commissioned another report to examine Chadwick's conclusion. In order to maintain pressure upon the government a Health of Towns Association was formed in 1844 to agitate for legislation. In this they were bitterly opposed by a coalition of powerful vested interests under the less than salubrious title of the 'dirty party'.

In 1848 a Public Health Board was set up but only on the basis of a reviewed five year lease of life. It survived only two terms with Chadwick himself removed from office in 1854. The mantle of reform passed thereafter to the less effusive figure of Sir John Simon who preferred persuasion rather than force.

A number of acts littered the mid-Victorian years but not until the 1870s were any substantial improvements made. In 1871 the Local Government Board Act gave rise to a major ministry for all local government affairs including public health. The following year the Public Health Act divided the whole country into sanitary authorities. The recommended terms of the 1848 Act now became obligatory. A comprehensive framework for all public health acts was provided for in the 1875 Public Health Act and this remained the basis of public health provision until 1936. The Artisans' Dwellings Act, passed in the same year, empowered local authorities to replace deficient housing. By 1890 loans for working class housing were made easier to obtain.

Note

Edwin Chadwick's Report sold more copies than any other previously published Parliamentary Paper.

Note

Chadwick could be stubborn in his beliefs. He insisted on the value of sewage for agricultural manure even when medical evidence opposed it. On another occasion he insisted on the direct flushing of the London sewers into the river Thames.

EXAMINING THE EVIDENCE
Public health: crusaders and infidels
Source A: Life expectation (average age)

Type of people	Leeds (Town area)	Rutlandshire (Country area)
1 Professional persons, gentry & their families	44 years	52 years
2 Farmers, tradesmen and their families	27 years	41 years
3 Mechanics, labourers and their families	19 years	38 years

Source B: Report on the sanitary conditions of the labouring poor of Great Britain

Chadwick's conclusions from his 1842 Report:

That the various forms of epidemic, endemic, and other disease caused, or aggravated, or propagated chiefly amongst the labouring classes by atmospheric impurities produced by decomposing animal and vegetable substances, by damp and filth, and close and overcrowded dwellings prevail amongst the population in every part of the kingdom, whether dwelling in separate houses, in rural villages, in small towns, in larger towns.

Where those circumstances are removed by drainage, proper cleansing, better ventilation ... the frequency and intensity of such disease is abated.

The formation of all habits of cleanliness is obstructed by defective supplies of water.

That of the 43,000 cases of widowhood, and 112,000 cases of ... orphanage relieved from the poor's rates ... the greatest proportion of deaths of heads of families occurred from the above ... causes.

The loss of working ability ... cannot be less than eight or ten years.

That the population so exposed is less susceptible of moral influences, and effects of education are more transient.

These circumstances tend to produce an adult population short-lived, reckless and imtemperate.

The primary and most important measures, and at the same time the most practicable ... are drainage, the removal of all refuse of habitations, streets and roads, and the improvement of the supplies of water.

Refuse when held in suspension in water may be most cheaply conveyed to any distance out of towns ... and ... pollution of natural streams may be avoided.

All new local public works (should be) devised and conducted by responsible officers qualified by the science and skill of civil engineers.

That it would be a good economy to appoint a district medical officer.

That by the combination of all these arrangements it is probable that ... an increase of 13 years at least, may be extended to the whole of the labouring classes.

Source C

... frequently interested parties are seated at Boards of Guardians who are ready to stop anything which may lead to expenditure for the proper repair of the dwellings of the labouring classes.

Where measures of drainage are proposed and the works carried out by Commissioners of Sewers are found to be defective a cry is raised. Nothing must be done for fear of offending the Commissioners.

When additional supplies of water are called for... one cry raised is 'Oh the interest of the companies is too powerful to be touched'.

Chadwick to Ashley 1844.

R.A. Lewis, *E.C. Chadwick and the Public Health Movement*

Source D

... unquestioning blind passive obedience to the ukase, decree, bull or proclamation of the autocrat, pope, grand lama of sanitary reform, Edwin Chadwick, lawyer and commissioner. He was determined that the British world should be clean and live a century but on one condition only – that they consented to purchase real patent Chadwickian soap, the Chadwickian officially gathered soft water and the true impermeable telescopic earthenware pipe and when they did die, were interred by his official undertakers in the Chadwickian necropolis.

A contemporary caricature of Chadwick. *Punch magazine*

Source E

I have 10,000 pounds worth of property and have been at considerable expense in getting water. My neighbour has the same [but no water] and his property will be considerably benefited by having water brought to it and mine can't possibly be benefited at all – is [it] just that I should be made to contribute a yearly sum towards furnishing his estate with water and increasing the value of his property 15 or 20% [which] taxes me.

Anon quoted in Thoresby Society *Projected Leeds waterworks*

Source F

The legislature has not yet given them the authority to dictate to tradesmen in what way they shall carry out their business, as how often they shall whitewash their buildings and if they are once permitted to usurp such an authority ... such is the spirit of busy officious intermeddling ... that no man's place of business or even private house would be safe.

Leeds Intelligencer (7 July 1838)

Source G

George Hudson (the 'Railway King') spoke:

The country was sick of centralisation, of commissions, of parliamentary inquiries – of all sorts of jobs. The people wanted to be left to manage their own affairs; they did not want Parliament to be so paternal as it wished to be – interfering in everybody's business, and, like all who so interfered, not doing its own well.

Source H

Colonel Sibthorp, MP for Lincoln, spoke against the appointment of paid commissioners:

He objected also to their being salaried, entertaining a strong feeling that if they had not patriotism enough to give their services for the good of their country, they were utterly unworthy of so important a trust. He objected also to the appointment of three inspectors. These things led to a great deal of bribery of a peculiar kind; and he had served long enough in that house to be extremely jealous of all Governments, whether Whig or Tory. They all could, and did, do a great deal behind the scenes; and there was a great deal of secret service money spent.

The Times 1848

Examining the evidence
Public health after Chadwick
Source A

Date	Deaths per 1 000 of population		Deaths of infants under one year per 1 000 (live births)	
	England and Wales	Scotland	England and Wales	Scotland
1858	23.1	23.1	151	121
1859	22.4	20.3	153	108
1860	21.2	22.3	148	127
1861	21.6	20.3	153	111
1862	21.4	21.7	142	117
1863	23.0	22.9	149	120
1864	23.7	23.6	153	126
1865	23.2	22.3	160	125
1866	23.4	22.7	160	122
1867	21.7	21.3	153	119
1868	21.8	21.2	155	118
1869	22.3	23.0	156	129
1870	22.9	22.2	160	123
1871	22.6	22.2	158	130

Source B

No less than 29 sanitary measures have been enacted since the Health of towns Commission of 1846 ... These Acts displayed much redundancy and ... confusion. They had been made at different times, by various hands ... Some were permissive, some compulsory ...

The Times (1875)

Source C: Introduction of the 1875 Public Health Act

... we have endeavoured to pass laws to prevent overcrowding in dwelling houses : We have also passed Acts enabling Corporations to give up their land and borrow money in order to erect dwelling houses for the working classes. We have also passed an Act ... enabling local authorities to pull down such houses as are absolutely unfit for human habitation ... When we remember that the growth of London has advanced during the last twenty years at the rate of 40 000 each year, it is clear that much more must be done if we wish to reach the rest of the evil ...

I would ask [people to remember] that health is actual wealth.

We have ... to ask ourselves whether we can give the children of the working classes an equal chance of growing up to healthy manhood and womanhood. The causes of the present loss of life are not far to seek ... it is not simply that houses are overcrowded ... but districts are over-crowded ...

Source D

CARTOON FROM PUNCH, SHOWING 'MICROBES' IN A DROP OF LONDON WATER.

Source E

THE SILENT HIGHWAYMAN. 'YOUR MONEY OR YOUR LIFE'

Source F: Misgovernment

When contemplating an ugly ill-built town where every little free-holder asserts his indefeasible rights as a Briton to do what he likes with his own; to inflict his own selfishness, ignorance and obstinacy upon his neigh-bours and on posterity for generations to come and where local self-government means merely misgovernment we are apt to wish for a lit-tle wholesome despotism to curb such vagaries.

J. Hole *The Homes of the Working Classes* (1866)

"Health is actual wealth". What prevented governments implementing this proposition in the first half of the nineteenth century?

● The nature of the problem of public health

● The recognition of public health as a social problem

● The lack of a rationale for intervention

● Ideological opposition

- Financial objections

- Technological difficulties

- Political obstacles

Consider each of these factors in turn, in the light of the sources of evidence. Rank them in order of importance in preventing government action.

Educating the poor

So dangerous a notion as the education of the labouring poor provoked this response in the early nineteenth century,

'The scheme would be found to be prejudicial to the morals and happiness of the labouring classes; it would teach them to despise their lot in life, instead of making them good servants in agriculture and other laborious employments to which their rank in society has destined them; instead of teaching them subordination it would render them factious and refactory as was evident in the manufacturing counties; it would enable them to read seditious pamphlets, vicious books and publications against Christianity; it would render them insolent to their superiors."

(A reply by Davies Giddy to the Whitbread's proposed bill for the creation of a state sponsored educational system (1807).

The bill which Giddy opposed, never came to fruition in law. Yet, as is apparent from the extract, the labouring classes could not be kept in total ignorance. The embers of discontent had been set alight by the seditious printed pamphlets of agitators advocating revolution in the crowded industrial cities of the north. Many middle class reformers who supported educating the poor were therefore motivated by a desire to see the 'correct' attitudes and values inculcated among the less fortunate.

Christianity, the basis of nineteenth century morality, appeared to the influential to be the necessary vehicle for the indoctrination of the poor. Education of the poor could thus become an act of Christian benevolence for the improvement of those not fortunate enough to belong to the middle and upper classes and act, at the same time, as an instrument of social control albeit unconsciously.

Nineteenth century christianity, however, did not present a united front. The church was fragmented into a number of different denominations each competing for souls. This competition developed into a bitter confrontation not only for the souls but for the minds of the poor. In 1811 the National Society was founded to promote the educational provision of state Anglican schools as a direct response to the creation of the non-conformist British and Foreign Society in 1808.

Intense competition bred bitter rivalry and fervent champions. The Anglican, Andrew Bell, developed his teaching techniques whilst in India. He introduced these reforms into English schools on his return. Meanwhile, the Quaker Joseph Lancaster, developed an almost identical monitorial system in darkest London. The common approach of using older and abler pupils to teach the younger was based on the common need to provide a cheap form of education.

TALKING POINT

Was Giddy correct when he stated that education would produce discontentment?

Note

The mass of people remained indifferent to religion. In 1899 the Non-Conformist Edward Miall wrote 'the bulk of our manufacturing population stands aloof from our Christian institutions'. Hence the need for the twin targets of religion and education.

Furore ~ Outbreak of public anger or excitement

TALKING POINT

Do you consider the religious competition aided or hindered the development of education?

From now important.

The state came to the assistance of the voluntary system hesitantly and only to supplement educational provision. The Select Committees of 1816–18, chaired by Henry Brougham found that only 7 per cent of the population were attending the voluntary day schools. This revelation, however, failed to win support for his proposed parochial schools' bill of 1820.

In 1833 a small but significant step was taken when a grant by the Chancellor, Viscount Althorp, provided £20,000 in aid to the voluntary schools. Public money had to be accounted for and, in so doing, he took the further step of appointing two Inspectors.

Money alone will not provide an efficient educational system; trained teachers were essential. In order to effect this idea, Lord Melbourne proposed the establishment of non-denominational teacher-training colleges. The suggestion provoked the furore of the Anglicans – state education must be directed by the state church. Their opposition won the day and the idea was dropped.

The Anglicans' hopes were, in turn, defeated by the non-conformists who successfully defeated the education clauses in Gresham's factory bill of 1843. Only the state, it came to seem to many, could hold the ring between the religious contenders. This conclusion propelled the government into further involvement.

James Kay-Shuttleworth (1804–1877)

The agent of change on behalf of the state was Dr. James Kay. He was appointed Secretary to the Education Committee of the Privy Council. His training college at Battersea became a model for others to copy and his inspectors were to prove themselves capable men of vision. By 1846 Kay had gained such pre-eminence and his inspectors were so respected that his championing of state-sponsored teacher training colleges met with little opposition. The Committee of Council evolved a pupil-teaching training system based on a five year apprenticeship beginning at the age of thirteen. From these candidates a few pupils were selected and forwarded to training college on a Queen's scholarship. Costs of training inevitably mounted.

In 1858 a Royal Commission under the Duke of Newcastle was appointed to evaluate the effectiveness of the expenditure. The Commission reported in 1861 and recommended that central government grants be paid to schools based on attendance coupled to a local grant from the rates based upon the achievements of the pupils.

Robert Lowe, Vice-President of the Education Department was determined to implement the recommendations of the Newcastle Commission; as he explained to Parliament,

'I cannot promise the House that this system will be an economical one and I cannot promise that it will be an efficient one but I can promise that it shall be one or the other. If it is not cheap it shall be efficient, if it is not efficient it will be cheap.'

The grant was fixed at four shillings from the state and eight shillings from the local authority per pupil.

Number of certificated Teachers	
1849	681
1859	6878

Costs of teacher training in thousands of pounds			
1833	£20	1856	251
1840	30	1858	669
1842	32	1860	723
1844	39	1862	775
1846	58	1864	655
1848	83	1866	676
1850	113	1868	750
1852	164	1870	895
1854	251		

Industrialisation, Education and Society

It is generally agreed that one of the hallmarks of an advanced industrial society is a high level of literacy. Indeed such societies see investment in education as a necessary requirement to sustain and develop the economy in order to keep pace with competitors. Was a high level of literacy needed in the early stages of industrialisation or did this become a later phenomenon?

Did industrialisation itself bring about an improved educational system or were other factors at work?

4 *Education and religion*

The alphabet

A – is an angel who praises the lord
B – is for Bible, God's most holy word
C – is for Church where the righteous resort
D – is for the Devil who wishes our hurt

Arithmetic

'At the marriage in Cana in Galilee there were six water pots of stone, holding two or three firkins a-piece. If they held two firkins, how much water would it take to fill them? And how much if they held three each?'
John Poole, The Village School Improved, 1813

1 *Literacy is measured by most historians as the ability to sign one's name on a marriage register. A standard form of marriage certificate was instituted by Lord Hardwick's Marriage Act of 1753.*

2 *There was considerable expansion of education in Britain before the Industrial Revolution and the expansion was important in promoting faster economic growth and finally the Industrial Revolution.*
R.M. Hartwell, *Two Services: Education and the Law – The Industrial Revolution and Economic Growth*

5 *Growth of Sunday Schools*
The sunday school movement was founded by Robert Raikes, a Gloucestershire businessman 1780.

Number of schools	**1801**	**1851**
	2290	23 151
Enrolled children	**1788**	**1851**
	59 980	2 000 000

7 *Literacy rates*

	1841	**1851**	**1861**	**1871**
Male	67.3	69.3	75.4	80.6
Female	51.1	54.8	65.3	73.2

6 *'The view that the Sunday Schools were the creation of a working class culture of respectability and self-reliance has been questioned by those who see them as middle class conservative institutions for the reform of working class pupils from above... they probably prevented literacy falling more than it did in areas vulnerable to decline.'*
M. Dick, The Myth of the working Class Sunday School. History of Education Volume 9, 1 1980.

3 *Education and crime*

'It is, indeed, strange that with the facts of daily life before them in the street, in the counting-house, and in the family, thinking men should still expect education to cure crimes. If armies of teachers, regarded with a certain superstitious reverence, have been unable to purify society in all these eighteen centuries, it is hardly likely that other armies of teachers, not so regarded, will be able to do it ... The expectation that crime may presently be cured, whether by State education, or the silent system, or the separate system, or any other system, is one of those Utopianisms fallen into by people who pride themselves on being practical.'
H. Spencer, Social Statics

8 Steam printing of newspaper after 1850 cheapened the process considerably.
- Tax on newspapers was abolished in 1855
- Tax on paper was abolished in 1861
- Price of books was halved between 1828–53
- Public Libraries Act in 1850 allowed the establishment of libraries from the rates.

9 Establishment of schools for the underclasses

Workhouse Schools	1834
Factory Schools	1833
Prison schools	1823

10 A comparative study of literacy rates between urban and rural areas.

	Peak			Trough	
	1750s	1760s	1770s	1810s	1820s
Lancashire (inc. Stockport)					
Bury	69				32
Chorley			61		49.6
Deane		65.7			20.1
Eccleston (St Helens)	66.2				49.7
Kirkham	76.5			51.4	
Preston	72.7				49.6
Manchester	66.5			42	
Stockport	71.1			51.6	
Bolton	66			37.9	
Industrial Lancashire	67.3			43.1	

Other areas		
East Riding	1781-90	1801-10
	67	64
Leamington Spa	1761-70	1781-90
	68	41

Questions

1. What appears to have been the relationship between the provision of education and industrialisation?
2. Did this provision appear to be constant throughout the whole period of industrialisation?
3. What other factors appear to have stimulated the growth of elementary education?
4. Why do the literacy rates for women remain below those of men?
5. In the eighteenth and early nineteenth centuries Britain has frequently been referred to as a collection of regions. How might such a view affect conclusions?
6. What conclusions can you draw about industrialisation and the provision of education?
7. Does the evidence support the notion that industrialised societies need a developed system of mass education?

B The Borough Road school was rebuilt in 1817. Compare this description with source A.
The room for the boys could accommodate 500 scholars. The windows were six feet from the floor. The central part was occupied with desks and forms, fixed by iron supports. Spaces left around were for semi-circular 'drafts' for some eight to ten lads, engaged under Monitors in reading, spelling, or arithmetic.

James Bonwick, *An Octogenarian's Reminiscences*, 1902.

C Monitors did more than teach.
The whole school is arranged in classes; a monitor is appointed to each, who is responsible for the cleanliness, order and improvement of each boy in it.

The proportion of boys who teach, either in reading, writing or arithmetic, is one in ten. In so large a school, there are duties to be performed which simply relate to order, and have no connexion with learning: for these duties different monitors are appointed...The boy who takes care that the writing books are ruled, by machines made for that purpose, is the monitor of ruling. The boy who superintends the inquiries after the absentees, is called the monitor of absentees .... Another is called the monitor of slates, because he has a general charge of all the slates in the school.

Joseph Lancaster. *Improvements in Education*, 1806.

D James Bonwick began at the sand desk.
In front of the row the Monitor held a board on which were plainly printed the capitals and small letters of the alphabet. My little teacher pointed a letter and shouted its name, which we repeated aloud. He then told us to smooth the sand in front of us, and try and make the letter by marking the sand. After this was done, we again shouted the letter.

Bonwick advanced through all the reading, writing and arithmetic classes. He eventually became head monitor and at seventeen the teacher at Hemel Hempstead's British School. The first thing he did was to choose monitors.

EXAMINING THE EVIDENCE
Was 1870 a turning point in state education?

By 1870 the balance was firmly tipped in favour of the right of every child to some form of schooling with the passing of Forster's Education Act. This Act has come to be seen as the fulcrum of nineteenth century educational development. Why should this be and is the claim justified?

Source A: An extract from W.E. Forster's speech introducing the Education bill (1870)

... though we have done well in assisting the benevolent gentlemen who have established schools, yet the result of the State leaving the initiative to volunteers is, that where State help has been most wanted, State help has been least given, and that where it was desirable that State power should be most felt it was not felt at all ... Therefore, notwithstanding the large sums of money we have voted, we find a vast number of children badly taught, or utterly untaught, because there are too few schools and too many bad schools ... Hence comes a demand from all parts of the country for a complete system of national education ...

Our object is to complete the present voluntary system, to fill up gaps, sparing the public money where it can be done without ...

Now I will at once proceed to the main principles ... They are two in number. Legal enactment, that there will be efficient schools everywhere throughout the kingdom. Compulsory provision of such schools if and where needed, but not unless proved to be needed ...

Upon the speedy provision of elementary education depends our industrial prosperity ...

Now that we have given them political power we must not wait any longer to give them education.

Speech by Mr. W.E. Forster introducing the *Elementary Education Bill in the House of Commons, 17th February 1870*

Source B

Literacy Rates: England and Wales	
1700–1775	50–56%
1800	65%
1840	66%
1870	80%

Literacy, at minimum, means being able to write one's name.

Source C: Reasons for the passing of the Education Act in 1870

It is not clear why this act should have been passed at that time, and several reasons have been suggested. The most obvious was the connection between the Second Reform Act of 1867 with its enfranchisement of the urban working class and the need to educate the new electorate. As Lowe put it, "I believe it will be absolutely necessary to compel our future masters to learn their letters." ... A factor sometimes ignored is that there was a healthy economic climate and a feeling that there was money to finance it ... Forster's Act did not provide universal free or compulsory education but it did allow for the glaring deficiencies in English education to be removed.

D. Fraser, *The Evolution of the British Welfare State*

Source D: The significance of the 1870 Act

1870 marked a watershed in two main shifts of emphasis. From 1830–1870 the main thrust of public policy had been the response to social problems created by successful industrialisation, namely the mass education of the working class. After 1870 the aspiration of the working classes themselves rose from the securing of a basic literacy to the desire for some form of secondary instruction.

Secondly, and most importantly, the main effort of educational development shifted towards trying to create an educational system which would not only deal with a social problem at home but which would sustain the economy in the face of competition abroad from the industries of Germany and America.

M. Sanderson, *Education, Economic Change and Society in England 1780–1870*

Source E

Formation of the National Union of Elementary Teachers in 1870.

Source F: The duties of government

(i) What are the duties of government? Generally speaking to maintain the frame of society; and for this end to restrain violence and crime ... it is not the duty of the government to feed the people ... to cultivate their mind, to shape their opinions, or to supply them with religious teachers, physicians, schoolmasters, books and newspapers.

These are the things that the people can and ought to do for themselves.

Edward Baines, *Letters to Lord John Russell on State Education* (1846)

(ii) I confess to a strong distress of government action, a passionate love of voluntary action and self-reliance but now as a practical man I am compelled to abandon the voluntary system.

Edward Baines to Kay-Shuttleworth 19 October 1867

Source G: Punch, 2 July 1870

SCHOOL

"OBSTRUCTIVES."

Mr. Punch (to Bull & Co). "YES, IT'S ALL VERY WELL TO SAY, 'GO TO SCHOOL!' HOW ARE THEY TO GO TO SCHOOL WITH THOSE PEOPLE QUARRELLING IN THE DOORWAY? WHY DON'T YOU MAKE 'EM 'MOVE ON'?"

Source H: Compulsory education

In regard to the compulsory attendance of children at school, 'the provisions of the bill' are tentative and timid. The principle of direct compulsion is admitted; but it is to be applied only in those districts in which a school boards exists, and not necessarily even in them.

The Illustrated London News (26 February 1870)

Source I: Free and compulsory education

By-laws making education compulsory to the age of ten were made obligatory in 1880, (Mundella's Education Act), and the age was raised to eleven in 1893 and twelve in 1899. In 1891 parents were given the right to demand free education for their children, although fees in elementary schools were not finally abolished until 1918. A factor which helped to delay the introduction of free education was the concern felt by the voluntary schools for the income they feared they would lose. The 1902 Act (which saw the replacement of independent School Boards by Local Education Authorities) finally placed the voluntary schools on the rates. Saved from extinction many of them survive to this day.

T. May, *An Economic and Social History of Britain 1760–1970*

Source J

The Act has been called a 'hard compromise'. Forster was forced to steer between the National Education League and the National Education Union, both well represented in Parliament and the Liberal Party itself. The League was secularist and wanted popularly elected Boards to run education on a nationwide basis. The Union was religious and wished voluntary schools to continue with augmented government aid.

Six months grace was given to the church schools ... Nearly 4,000 building applications resulted, whereas the normal annual total was 150, and the churches increased their school properties by a remarkable 30%.

... The debates were long and bitter, as were the school boards elections that followed the passage of the act. The religious issue was solved by the inclusion of a conscience or withdrawal clause – the famous Cowper-Temple clause ... Nonetheless, by 1874, when the Liberal government fell, 5,000 schools had been added to the existing 8,000. There had been an increase in places of one and one-half million places, a third of these in Board Schools. By the end of 1871, as many as 300 school boards were in existence.

D. Fraser, *The Evolution of the Welfare State*

---

1 What factors, independent of the objective of educating the working classes for its own sake, appear to have created the necessary climate for the passing of Forster's Education Act?

2 How justified was the charge that there were gross deficiencies in the educational system prior to 1870?

3 How important was the religious dimension in the creation of a mass educational system for the working classes?

4 What reasons can be used both for and against the notion that the 1870 Education Act represented a major landmark?

REVIEW

The nineteenth century has been described as the age of laissez faire. Consider how convincing this label is with respect to:

- factory conditions
- public health
- education

14 Industrialisation and protest

PREVIEW

Was there a revolutionary threat?

DEATH OR LIBERTY? PUNCH MAGAZINE.

In the years between 1780 and 1832 most English working class people came to feel an identity of interests as between themselves and as against their rulers and employers. This ruling class was itself much divided, and in fact only gained cohesion over the same years because certain antagonisms were resolved (or faded into relative insignificance) in the face of an insurgent working class.'

E.P. Thompson, *The Making of the English Working Class* (1968)

'Our first doubt is whether or not Mr. Thompson has over-dramatised. Was there a revolutionary threat? ... Or has the idea of a revolutionary threat been introduced to prove that the social and political policies of Pitt and his successors were counter-revolutionary? Our second main doubt is whether in 1832 there was one working class ...'

R.M. Hartwell and R. Curie, *The Making of the English Working Class?* quoted in *Popular Politics* Open University A401 11 3–6

A revolutionary working class?

In 1839 the militant working class radical George Harney was in no mood to compromise when he declared,

'Universal suffrage there shall be – or our tyrants will find to their cost that we will have universal misery ... Believe me, there is no argument like the sword and the musket is unanswerable.'

George Harney's vitriolic cry represented one response to industrial change from those who felt themselves to be victims of the process. Change is threatening, particularly if you are on the sharp end. Not surprisingly, reactions ranged from the silent resignation of those living in tuberculin slums to those who passionately held aloft the firebrand of revolution and demanded social justice.

It was already apparent at the height of the Napoleonic Wars that rapid industrialisation was producing casualties. Chronic price rises and periods of unemployment erupted into sporadic food riots in the short term and demands for political and economic equality in the long term. Riots had always stretched the slender law and order resources of the ruling classes but now, set against the backdrop of the French revolution, they appeared to threaten the overthrow of the status-quo. Increasingly repressive measures obliged working people to organise themselves in order to improve or at least maintain their present position. This normally found expression in four ways.

Firstly, by means of self-help groups. As the medieval guilds became obsolete and government ceased to protect wage rates, skilled workmen began to form themselves into infant trade unions called 'combinations'.

Early trade unions were not, as is sometimes supposed, groupings of factory workers but mainly skilled artisans anxious to maintain their status in a time of rapid technological change.

In the hysteria engendered by the French Revolution it was not difficult for the establishment to see, or choose to see, such combinations as thinly disguised efforts to promote revolution. To forestall any potential threat, as they saw it, the government outlawed working mens' organisations by means of the Combination Acts of 1799 and 1800. Promoters of the legislation argued that their reasons for so doing were based on the need for free market forces to arbitrate 'naturally' between labour and capital.

The actual impact of the Combination Laws may have been less than the symbol of working class oppression they came to represent. Besides, most combinations managed to operate discretely as Friendly Societies, ostensibly organised to protect their members from financial hardships through savings contributions.

Frustrated by the general ineffectiveness of Friendly Societies and the illegality of combinations some workers resorted to illegal direct action through riot, industrial sabotage and machine wrecking. Afraid that the spectre of revolution had now materialised, the ruling class resorted to even greater repression.

The end of the Napoleonic Wars did not bring about the hoped-for prosperity and political stability. The British economy in the first half of the nineteenth century lurched between cycles of boom and depression.

On the crest of prosperity trade union activity increased, particularly after the repeal of the Combination Acts in 1825, whilst during the troughs, political demands for the vote dominated.

Chartism was the single most powerful expression for political representation of the working class. In 1832 the Great Reform Act was passed but the electorate was only marginally increased. Working people felt cheated. The resultant demand for universal suffrage and parliamentary accountability contained within the 'Peoples' Charter' were a direct response to the 'betrayal' of the Great Reform Act.

Although Chartism was the single most important movement it was a label which papered over many cracks in their organisation. Its lack of unity was a result of the diverse elements from which the movement sprang. Anti-poor law Associations to demands for currency reform were to be found within its umbrella. Nor was there unity over tactics. One wing demanded a violent overthrow of the government, others argued for

THE MEETING ON KENNINGTON COMMON – FROM A DAGUERREOTYPE.

peaceful persuasion. Frequently both views shaded into one another or changed according to circumstance.

Did these movements constitute a revolutionary threat? Certainly there existed a great fear that English Jacobins would imitate the French Revolution and violently overthrow the existing order. Notable among the claimants that English Jacobins existed is the historian E.P. Thompson who passionately asserts that between 1790–1832 Britain came close to revolution. This threat did not subside until the fiasco of the meeting on Kennington Common in 1848 which provided the last faint echo of revolutionary threat.

Yet no revolution occurred. If the fuse was primed what prevented ignition? In the main, working class leaders aimed at reform, or in extremity, to by-pass the capitalist system by workers' co-operatives.

Weakness and division characterised such attempts. How then do we account for government reaction in the face of what appear to be such timid threats? It may be appropriate to ask whether it was over-reaction or the readiness to believe in revolution in order to maintain their own political survival. In short, to identify reform with revolution was a useful political device in order to stay in power.

If divisions existed within the working class it may have been due to a lack of homogenity in the term itself. Was there a distinctive working class or is it more appropriate to talk of working classes? Is it possible to assert that there is, or could be, a sense of common identity between the factory hand and the skilled craftsman? When did the labouring poor emerge as a working class? The historical debate centres as much on definitions as the interpretation of historical events.

Examining the Evidence
Was there one working class?

To some historians the term class is a useful label, but one which needs constant refinement. It is important to remember each time we use phrases such as the 'working class', 'labouring poor', 'middle class' and so on that we understand the composition and diversity of the groups of which we speak.

Source A: What is class?

The language of 'ranks' and 'orders' which belonged to the writing of Gregory King, Daniel Defoe, Archdeacon Paley and Edmund Burke recognised social inequality and graded men into hierarchy which was linked by 'chains' and 'bonds'. The use of this language implied an acceptance of inequality. Paley accepted these ranks as the will of God ... After 1780 this language was slowly replaced by the language of class, which first appeared among the philosophers Millar and Gisborne. By the 1830s and 40s, 'working class', 'middle class' and 'aristocracy' had become part of the language which recognised social conflict centred on the clash of interests which arose from the distribution of wealth, income and power.

... there are absolutely no correct answers in the study of the history of class. The subject must be written with all the consistency, logic and demands of evidence ... The history of class must be the history of the actual and the concrete, and not just abstractions and theories. The history of class was the history of John Doherty addressing the striking cotton workers with the ideas of Owen buzzing in his head; it was the history of Kay-Shuttleworth working himself to a nervous breakdown at the Education Department with the ideas of the evangelicals, of Swiss theorists, and of the political economists as well as the memories of poverty and violence in Manchester in his mind. But in the end historians must take their own values and perceptions to the past so that the study of the history of class remains a relationship between them and the people of the past.

R.J. Morris, *Class and Class Consciousness in the Industrial Revolution 1780–1850* (1979)

Tom Paine (1737–1809)
Devil or Democrat?

THOMAS PAINE.

In the turbulent years of the French Revolution Thomas Paine became the most powerful representative of Republicanism and the most hated by the ruling class. To supporters of reform he was the principle source of inspiration; to opponents an atheistic monster. Why did he inspire such powerful feelings?

THOMAS PAINE, A BIOGRAPHY

1737	Born at Thetford, Norfolk, son of a Quaker staymaker.
1757	Turned down a possible ministry in the Church of England and settled at Sandwhich as a master staymaker.
1764	Entered Excise Service.
1765	Dismissed for neglecting his duties.
1768	Restored to the Excise Service at Lewes but,
1774	dismissed again for neglecting his duties.
1776	Emigrated to America where he published a pamphlet entitled 'Common Sense' which advocated independence for America.
1776-83	Published a newspaper 'Crisis' which attacked George III.
1787	Returned to Europe where he attempted to interest Parisian Academy of Science in an iron bridge of his own design.
1788	Returned to England where he joined the political opposition.
1791	Thomas Paine publishes his famous 'Rights of Man' as a counter attack to Burkes' 'Reflections'.
1792	Paine is charged with sedition. He escapes from England to France where he is offered a seat in the French National Convention.
1795	Paine publishes a second book 'The Age of Reason' which angers those in power and he is arrested.
1802	Paine manages to survive the Terror in France and emigrates to America.
1809	Paine dies amid lies, scandals, poverty and obscurity.

HOGARTH'S VIEW OF AN EIGHTEENTH CENTURY ELECTION

THOMAS PAINE AND THE RIGHTS OF MAN

Parts 1 and 3 were published as companion volumes to Burke's 'Reflections'. Part 2 was published at 6d per copy with the royalties given to the Society for Constitutional Information, a radical society. Public Readings from the book were widely held. The S.C.I. had distributed 50,000 copies by 1791.

Thereafter Paine allowed complete freedom to publish and distribute his book. It has been estimated that 200,000 were sold.

from The Rights of Man (Part 1)

There never did, there never will, and there never can exist a parliament, or any description of men, or any generation of men, in any country, possessed of the right or the power of binding and controlling prosperity till the 'end of time', or of commanding forever how the world shall be governed, or who shall govern it; and therefore, all such clauses, acts or declarations, by which the makers of them attempt to do what they have neither the right nor the power to do, nor the power to execute, are in themselves null and void. – Every age and generation must be free to act for itself, in all cases, as the ages and generations which precede it. The vanity and presumption of governing beyond the grave, is the most ridiculous and insolent of all tyrannies. Man has no property in man; neither has any generation a property in the generations which are to follow. The parliament or the people of 1688, or of any other period, has no more right to dispose of the people of the present day, or to bind and control them in any shape whatever, than the parliament or the people of the present day have to dispose of, bind or control those who are to live a hundred or a thousand years hence. Every generation is, and must be, competent to all the purposes which its occasions require. It is the living, and not the dead, that are to be accommodated. When man ceases to be, his powers and wants cease with him; and having no longer any participation in the concerns of this world, he has no longer a ny authority in directing who shall be its governors, or how its government shall be organised, or how administered.

I am not contending for nor against any form of government, nor for or against any party here or elsewhere. That which a whole nation chooses to do, it has a right to do. Mr. Burke says, No. Where then does the right exist? ... Mr. Burke is contending for the authority of the dead over the rights and freedoms of the living. There was a time when kings disposed of their crowns by will upon their deathbeds, and consigned the people, like beasts of the field, to whatever successor they appointed. This is now so exploded as scarcely to be remembered, and so monstrous as hardly to be believed: But the Parliamentary clauses upon which Mr. Burke builds his political church, are of the same nature.

Thomas Paine The Rights of Man Part one, March 1791

Whereas divers wicked and seditious writings have been printed, published and industriously dispersed, tending to excite tumult and disorder, by endeavouring to

EDMUND BURKE.

raise groundless jealousies and discontents in the minds of our faithful and loving subjects, respecting the laws and constitution of government ... established in this kingdom ... we do strictly charge and command all our magistrates in and throughout our kingdom of Great Britain, that they do make diligent inquiry in order to discover the authors and printers of such wicked and seditious writings as aforesaid, and all others who shall disperse the same.

Royal Proclamation, 21 May 1792. Parliamentary History Vol XXIX

Edmund Burke

You will observe, that from Magna Carta to the Declaration of Right, it has been the uniform policy of our Constitution to claim and assert our liberties, as an entailed inheritance derived to us from our forbears,

SHOW OF HANDS FOR A LIBERAL CANDIDATE

an estate specially belonging to the people of this kingdom, without any reference whatever to any other more general or prior right. We have an inheritable crown; an inheritable peerage; and a House of Commons and a people inheriting privileges, franchises and liberties, from a long line of ancestors....the people of England well known that the idea of inheritance furnishes a sure principle of transmission; without at all excluding a principle of improvement.

Edmund Burke, *Reflections of the Revolution in France*

All hereditary Government is in its nature tyranny. An inheritable crown, or an inheritable throne, or by what other fanciful name such things may be called, have no other significant explanation than that mankind are inheritable property...

Government ought to be a thing always in full maturity. It ought to be so constructed as to be superior to all accidents to which individual man is subject; and therefore, hereditary succession, by being subject to them all, is the most irregular and imperfect of all systems of government.

Thomas Paine, *No Rights of Man Part II*

Questions

1 Upon what basis does Thomas Paine argue his beliefs?

2 In what way does Paine's reasoning differ from that of Edmund Burke?

3 In what way did Paine appear to become more radical in his views?

4 The Royal Proclamation does not specifically mention 'The Rights of Man'. What circumstantial evidence suggests that the Royal Proclamation was aimed at Thomas Paine's writings?

5 Paine was charged with sedition i.e. advocating the overthrow of the established government. Do you consider this charge to be justified?

6 What indications are there in the evidence that Paine held his views sincerely?

Source B: Definitions of class

... I am convinced that we cannot understand class unless we see it as a social and cultural formation, arising from processes which can only be studied as they work themselves out over a considerable historical period. If we stop history at a given point, then there are no classes but simply a multitude of individuals with a multitude of experiences, but if we watch these men over an adequate period of social change, we observe patterns in their relationships, their ideas and their institutions. Class is defined by men as they live their own history, and, in the end, this its only definition.

E.P. Thompson, *The Making of the English Working Class* (1968)

Source C: Thompson criticised

To make sense of the class thesis, a certain cohesiveness is necessary. Mr. Thompson's working class, however, is rich in conflict; in particular he fails to establish the class identity of artisan and labouring poor. Most of his evidence of the so-called working class comes from the artisan and self-employed, and as he himself says: 'The artisan are a special case – the intellectual elite of the class' (p.716). ... Mr. Thompson's working class, 'united by common experience', remains, even after 850 pages, a myth, a construct of determined imagination and theoretical pre-suppositions.

R.M. Hartwell and R. Currie, *The Economic History Review Vol. XVIII no. 3*
December 1965

Source D: What was the 'middle class'?

The general expression 'middle class' remains useful as a name for a large section of society. Moreover it is important to remember that a belief in the importance and significance of the middle class in the nineteenth century derives from contemporary opinion ... They do not always say clearly who they have in mind, and since the possible varieties are so great a modern writer should follow them with great caution coupling any reference to the middle class with as precise an analysis as possible of what groups are under discussion ... The middle class, however defined, (did not) dominate the country after 1832.

Certainly they were deemed to be politically important at the time of the Reform Bill, and that Bill was passed largely as a recognition of their importance; but after the Bill the final control in politics still lay without question in the hands of the governing classes; the nobility and the gentry. It is sometimes suggested that the repeal of the Corn Laws in 1846 is a sign that by then the decisive political power had passed to the middle classes. Again it is unquestionable that the case for the repeal had been vehemently pressed by what was on any calculation a middle class body, the Anti-Corn Law League; but the actual repeal was carried through by the head of one aristocratic party because he believed it to be desireable with the assent of the other because, at least, he believed it to be expedient ... (but) what is not doubtful is that after the repeal of the Corn Laws as before the final political control still remained in the hands of the old governing classes.

... A poorer man, a wage earner, may have to face simple economic problems, but a historian has no right to infer that he will interpret his economic interest according to the terms of the class war as conceived by someone writing a long time afterwards, or in the confirmed belief that there must be a necessary clash of interests between capital and labour ... Indignation, however, can stimulate research ... But indignation is a dangerous passion for historians. Dislike tends to simplify the men and women disliked and to make it impossible for them to be seen for what they were, complex human beings, creatures of a moment, purblind with prejudices of the time and ignorant of much that it would have been better for them to know.

G. Kitson-Clark, *The Making of Victorian England* (1968)

---

1 In what ways might you sub-divide 'working class' and 'middle class'?

Do these terms have any coherence?

2 (a) How does E.P. Thompson explain the phenomenon of class?

(b) What criticisms does Hartwell and Curie make regarding Thompson's analysis of class?

(c) What reservations does Kitson-Clark express about the operation of class in nineteenth century British history?

3 What are the advantages and limitations of using class as an explanation of change in history?

4 You have been invited to discuss the notion of class largely in isolation of the actual historical events of the nineteenth century. Return to the discussion of the relevance of class as an historical explanation when you have studied the following areas of working and middle class protest. The areas of protest we will examine next will be: radical reform, chartism, trade unionism, Anti-Corn Law league.

Radical reform or revolution

News of the destruction of the Bastille was greeted with almost universal approval in Britain. Charles James Fox, leader of the opposition in the House of Commons, declared, "How much the greatest event it is that ever happened in the world, and how much the best!"

Intellectuals and poets gushed enthusiasm. William Blake began writing his epic poem 'The French Revolution', in which,

'... the valleys of France shall cry to the soldier
Throw down thy sword and musket,
And run and embrace the meek peasant! Her nobles
shall hear and shall weep, and put off
The red robe of terror, the crown of oppression.'

William Wordsworth, an ardent supporter of the Revolution in its early days, was rhapsodic when he declared,

'Bliss was it that dawn to be alive,
But to be young was very heaven!'

The universal praise for the Revolution, including that of the British government, was in measure due to the conviction of many British people

Note

Of all the British poets and writers that eulogised the beginning of the French Revolution only William Blake retained a burning faith in revolution.

SOCIAL CLASS, CHANGE AND HISTORY

We all carry around with us a construct of society as a series of stereotypes. This helps us to generalise about the world around us, and, although we attempt to see people as individuals, we often resort to our stereo-typical viewpoint.

1 Construct a stereotype of a twenty year old working class and middle class male and female. This may include thoughts on dress, name, mode of transport, politics, hobbies, favourite newspaper, food and holidays.

2 What difficulties are there in producing such stereotypes?

As you have already seen historians are divided over whether we can talk of the 'working class' or the 'middle class' as if these groups had a separate identity and shared common experiences. Some find it useful to analyse society in strictly class terms whereas others stress the divisions of interest within social groups thus robbing the term of any coherence.

Opinion today is divided on the issue. Some politicians assert the term 'working class' is redundant whilst others speculate on the changing nature of the working class as defined by the government's socio-economic categories and the emergence of what has come to be termed an 'underclass'.

Consider the illustrations as sources and discuss with your group whether they demonstrate the existence of class in Britain today.

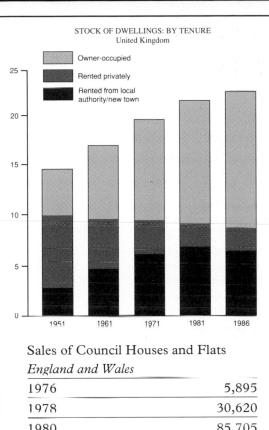

STOCK OF DWELLINGS: BY TENURE
United Kingdom

- Owner-occupied
- Rented privately
- Rented from local authority/new town

Sales of Council Houses and Flats

England and Wales

1976	5,895
1978	30,620
1980	85,705
1982	207,365
1984	107,485
1986	90,820

Social Class and Housing Tenure (1985)

	Owner Occupied (%)	Council Housing (%)
Class 1	87	4
Class 2	79	10
Class 3NM	67	20
Class 3M	66	28
Class 4	46	41
Class 5	33	58

(Other forms of tenure not included)

Source: Social Trends 17, 18 (HMSO, London, 1987, 1988)

COUNCIL/PRIVATE/PRIVATELY RENTED HOUSES.

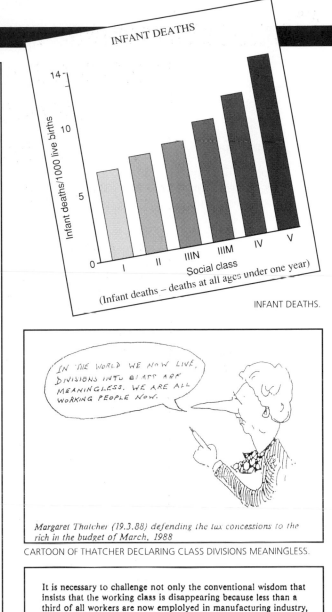

INFANT DEATHS

Infant deaths/1000 live births

Social class: I, II, IIIN, IIIM, IV, V

(Infant deaths – deaths at all ages under one year)

INFANT DEATHS.

IN THE WORLD WE NOW LIVE, DIVISIONS INTO CLASS ARE MEANINGLESS. WE ARE ALL WORKING PEOPLE NOW.

Margaret Thatcher (19.3.88) defending the tax concessions to the rich in the budget of March, 1988

CARTOON OF THATCHER DECLARING CLASS DIVISIONS MEANINGLESS.

It is necessary to challenge not only the conventional wisdom that insists that the working class is disappearing because less than a third of all workers are now employed in manufacturing industry, but also those Marxist formulations which declare that sellers of labour-power remain doomed to discover the true nature of their situation. Thus, even as the 'traditional' working class shrinks from year to year, so that coal miners, for instance, now constitute one tenth of their number fifty years ago, it is constantly being augmented by new categories of worker which capitalism is calling into existence. This is happening with the reconstitution of large sections of the working class in the interest of 'service industries' that new and unfamiliar manifestation of something age-old, a subordination that descends directly from that of those unfortunate people called to be hired annually at the Michaelmas mop as farm servants, or to be carried off into the Victorian suburbs as little more than children to scour the steps and polish the brass and blacklead the grate in rambling redbrick villas.

Source: Trevor Blackwell and Jeremy Seabrook *A World Still to Win* (Faber & Faber, London, 1985)

TREVOR BLACKWELL AND JEREMY SEABROOK.

that France was merely attemtping to achieve the constitutional success that the British had achieved 100 years earlier. Other, more malevolently, were glad to see France plunged into confusion and apparent helplessness.

A minority, however, were convinced that France was overtaking Britain in achieving a complete overthrow of the aristocracy and the remnants of the feudal system. Thomas Paine, the most infamous British radical in the eyes of the government informed Thomas Jefferson, the American President;

'The people of this country speak very differently on the affairs of France. The mass of them, so far as I can collect, say that France is a much freer country than England ... there are as yet in this country, very considerable remains of the Feudal System which people did not see till the Revolution in France placed it before their eyes ... and they now appear to be turning their eyes towards the Aristocrats of their own Nation.'

Quoted in M.D. Conway, *The Life of Thomas Paine* Vol I p.267

By 1792 opinion had shifted and attitudes had soured toward the Revolution. This was due to two factors. As France was torn apart those that attempted to steer the Revolution to open waters suspected traitors everywhere. The September Massacres and the butchering of the King's Swiss Guards during 1792 were outpourings of a psychotic need to see and destroy enemies of the Revolution. The ideas and hopes of the Revolution appeared to be descending into a bloody pit from which the fearful spectre of Republicanism would emerge to haunt Europe. Samuel Romilly, initially enthusiastic for the Revolution, was disillusioned by 1792, 'one might as well think of establishing a republic of tigers somewhere in Africa as of maintaining a free government among such monsters.'

The most outspoken and consistent critic of the Revolution was the Irish peer, Edmund Burke. He had supported the American colonists in their revolution against British rule but as early as August 1789 he was expressing doubts over the direction of the revolution. By November he was convinced that the Revolution represented a threat to liberty everywhere. A year later his fears were expressed in his book 'Reflections on the Revolution in France'. Burke declared that the British 'Glorious Revolution' of 1688 had been inspired by the need to restore traditional rights whereas the French Revolution was imposing new restrictions on the freedom of the individual. The book sold well and by the end of November had sold 12,000 copies.

The Nore mutinies

In 1797 a more serious threat to the government occurred. In February, General Tate with a French Legion of 1200 men landed at Newquay in Wales. Although they failed to recruit local support it was a serious breach of Britain's defences.

In April an even greater calamity. On the fifteenth of that month English seamen commandeered their warships at Spithead. Their discipline throughout was impeccable. On the twelfth of May they were joined

ONE VIEW OF THE 'GAGGING ACTS'.

by the fleet at Nore which proceeded to block the Thames estuary. The government assumed that the Corresponding Society's radical infection was spreading and Britain's vital naval defences were threatened.

At Spithead the government agreed to the mutineers demands but not to those of the Nore. These mutineers, after running short of provisions surrendered. 412 seamen were court-martialled of which 59 were sentenced to death. 29 were actually executed.

Luddism

Apart from isolated examples the cause of political reform was not to emerge as a serious campaign until after the Napoleonic Wars. Nevertheless, below the surface of suppression and despite legislative enactments other forms of political and industrial protest simmered. One such threat came from direct and violent attacks upon masters who attempted to install new machinery in their mills.

Luddism was industrial in its origins and its objectives but, as its tactics were to destroy machines that were making workers redundant, then it appeared to forbode revolutionary intent. Machine breaking by groups of skilled workers began in the lace making industry in Nottinghamshire in 1811 and spread to the woollen industry in Yorkshire and Lancashire in the years 1812–13. The Napoleonic Wars and the Continental Blockade had brought acute distress to many workers. Deprived of their right to combine, it was felt by some skilled workers, that there was little alternative for them but to take direct action. Eric Hobsbawm, the historian refers to this direct action as 'Collective bargaining by riot'.

The government was quick to pin the blame for the disturbances against underground cells of Jacobin agitators or covert trade unions. E.P. Thompson has claimed that an organised network of dissension existed; other historians stress the localised and specifically economic aims of the Luddites. Whether one accepts the notion of mass conspiracy or localised disturbances, the Luddite attacks were well planned. To the authorities, ill-equipped to cope with civil disturbances, this represented an organised attempt to overthrow the ruling classes. The deployment of 12,000 soldiers alone indicated the seriousness with which the government viewed Luddism. It also put an extra strain on resources needed for the war with France.

TALKING POINT

Does the Luddite movement have any significance for us today? How should we react today if technological advance forces redundancy?

EXAMINING THE EVIDENCE
Were the Luddites revolutionary?
Source A

Synopsis of Luddite disturbances
1811: Stocking frames were smashed throughout Nottinghamshire.
1812: February – Meetings of Yorkshire croppers resulted in the breaking of frames in the Spen Valley. Manufacturers formed the Committee for the Supression of Disturbances.

1812: (March): Almost daily attacks. The Committee offers 1000 guineas for information. The Home Office is petitioned for military support.

1812: (April): Edmund Cartwright's well defended mill is attacked but they are driven off. On the eighteenth Cartwright is shot at but not hit. A militiaman who refuses to fire on the Luddites is flogged. On the twenty-eighth April, William Horsefall, owner of Ottiwells Mill is shot on his way home from Huddersfield Market, and later dies of his wounds.

1812: (May): Government spies report the drilling of armed men. Spencer Percival the prime minister is assassinated at Westminster.

In June the Orders of Council were recinded. A slow trade revival begins but is set back by the outbreak of war with America. During the summer the area around Huddersfield was virtually under martial law.

In October the tide turned against the Luddites and many arrests followed.

1813 (January): Trials of Luddites take place before a Special Commission. Three men responsible for Horsefall's death are publicly hung and fourteen others are transported. Some bodies are returned to their families, others are sent for dissection.

THE SHOOTING OF MR. HORSEFALL.

Source B: A warning letter from the Luddites

Sir,

Information has just been given in, that you are the holder of those detestable Shearing Frames, and I was desired by men to write to you, and give you fair warning to pull them down, ... that if they are not taken down, I shall detach one of my lieutenants with at least three hundred men to destroy them, ... and if you have the impudence to fire at any of my men, they have orders to murder you and burn all your Housing ... by the last returns there were 2782 sworn heroes bound in a bone of necessity, either to redress their grievances or perish in the attempt, in the army of Huddersfield alone, nearly double sworn men in Leeds ... the weavers in Glasgow will join us ... the Papists in Ireland are rising to a man ... the immediate cause of this beginning was that rascally letter of the Prince Regent to the Lords Grey and Grenville which left us no hope for a change for the better ... but we hope with the assistance of the French Emperor is shaking off the yoke of the Rottonest, wickedest and most Tyrannical Government that ever existed ... and we will be governed by a just Republic ... we will never lay down our arms till the House of Commons passes an act to put down all machinery hurtful to the Commonality and repeal that to the Frame Breakers – but we petition no more, that won't do, fighting must.

Signed by the General of the Army of Redressers.

Ned Ludd

Clerk.

From a letter to a Huddersfield master, 1812. Home Office Papers 40/11 quoted in
G.D.M. Cole and A.W. Filson (eds) British Working Class Movements pp. 114–5 1951

Source C: 'Machinery Destroyed' 29 February 1812 The Leeds Mercury

The depredators, or to use the cant terms, Luddites, assembled with as much privacy as possible, at the place marked out for attack and divided themselves into two parties, the more daring and expert entered the premises, provided with proper implements for the work of destruction, which they accomplished with astonishing secrecy and dispatch. The other party remain conveniently stationed ... to keep off intruders ... As soon as the work of destruction was completed, the Leader drew up his men, called over the roll, each man answering to a particular number instead of his name, they then fired off their pistols (for they were armed) and marched off in regular military order.

Source D: General Maitland Prescot to Richard Ryder (Home Secretary) 23 May 1813.

General Maitland was in charge of the military operations against the Luddites.

It gives me great satisfaction on considering the whole of the situation of this District (County of Chester), and after weighing in my mind everything that has actually occurred since I came here, to be able to state to you my decided Conviction that those who may be concerned in any real

Revolutionary Object, are by no means in so considerable number as is generally credited by many; and Believing as I do their numbers to be small, I am equally convinced their plans and Objects, such as they may be, are Crude and Indigested.

I have not a doubt that their great supporter was Fear. The operation of which induced many nominally to join them, who the moment they saw themselves protected against them, deserted their Cause, and though undoubtedly the Present Price of Provision and Labour, must press upon the Lower Orders; I do not believe that Disatisfaction will get any Head, or that the real mischief will increase to any extent, provided a vigilant eye be kept over them.

Home Office 40.1 (1812)

Source E: A letter from William Chippendale to Richard Ryder (Home Secretary) 22 May 1812

William Chippendale was captain of the local militia in Oldham and a local Magistrate.

... Of the disturbances which have taken place in this County, of the peculiar political character and desperate Cast of those Wretches who have been the Formentors of them and of the Object to which their diabolic Efforts are directed ... I have lately become acquainted with a Member, and of one of no Common Activity, of the Secret Revolutionary Committee of Royton, a Place in which every Inhabitant (with the exception of not more than five or six) are the most determined and revolutionary Jacobins.

... I have had various interviews with him, in which he expressed strong contrition for the Participation he has had in exciting the People to these Enormities and I have endeavoured to avail myself of the Disposition he has manifested by inducing him to make a Disclosure of their Proceedings and to give Information as would lead to the detection of their Leading Men and this Complete Frustration of their Designs. I regret, however, to say that hitherto I have exerted my Address in vain, ... It is under this impression that I have taken the liberty to trouble you on this occasion and to suggest to your Excellency the propriety of trying him with a small sum of money or proposing to engage him in a contrived service at certain wages.

Home Office (1812)

Source F

If ... you were taking the larger view, and looking for a larger purpose, you would need your Luddites to have aims that extent beyond machine breaking and encompassed perhaps some plans to change government and society as a whole. And to achieve such aims you would need to find evidence of organisation beyond the need to perform the limited local exercises of selective machine breaking ... their (Luddites) political actions are not easy to establish but that does not necessarily mean they did not exist ... The expressed fears of revolution seem to me to be more understandable in the context of 1812, but they tell us what people were afraid of, not what was happening. The testimony is rarely first hand and where it comes from those supposed to be implicated themselves, they are supplying information for profit or for saving their skins. The arms stores, the Jacobin cells, the armies, were never found, perhaps because they never existed, the rumour, gossip, the imagination and exaggeration of the panic stricken and over-zealous, all these rather than the actual state of affairs, were perhaps the origin of the revolutionary scare that accompanied the machine breaking.

M.I. Thomas, *Luddism and the English Working Class. Popular Politics, Open University*
A 401 II Units 3–6

Questions

1 What appears to have been the principal aims of the Luddites?

2 Do you consider such aims to have been revolutionary?

3 Why did some contemporaries see or choose to see the Luddites as revolutionary?

REVIEW

Were the working classes Revolutionary 1790–1830?

Consider the following points in your answer.

● The political and economic climate.

● The difficulty of classifying social groups – was there a distinctive working class?

● The impact of the French revolution on the ruling class consciousness

● Thomas Paine and his influence.

● The fears of the Establishment.

● The aims and influence of the Reform club.

● Government reaction to the reform club.

● The naval mutinies.

● The Luddites – aims and influence.

NB You will need to consider these factors in conjunction with chapter 15.

The Reform Clubs

The Society for Constitutional Information (founded 1780)

Objectives: To educate the ordinary 'free-born' Englishman in his 'rights' and restoring the constitution to the purity believed to have existed in the Anglo-Saxon kingdom of Alfred the Great, subsequently destroyed after the conquest by William. The production of cheap educational pamphlets was designed to inform Englishmen of their rights.

Subscription: 1 guinea

Membership: Obtained only by the ballot of all the members.

Major Cartwright was the principal leader of the Association of the peers of the realm and country gentlemen.

Parliamentary Reform: Their aims were to reduce sinecures and pensions 'the influence of the Crown has increased, is increasing and ought to be diminished' – from John Dinning's opening remarks in the Commons for reform.

April 1780

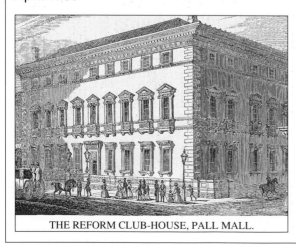

THE REFORM CLUB-HOUSE, PALL MALL.

The London Corresponding Society (founded 1792)

Subscription: 1d per week

Membership: Admission was solely dependent upon a positive reply to the following question, 'Are you thoroughly persuaded that the welfare of these kingdoms require that every adult person, in possession of his reason, and not incapacitated by crimes, should have a vote for a member of Parliament?

Classification of the members of the L.C.S. Division 18 about the end of 1792.

6 shoemakers	1 sailmaker	
1 butcher	1 broker	
6 blacksmiths	1 hairdresser	
1 clockmaker	1 tailor	
3 bricklayers	1 carpenter	1 clerk

Lord Loughborough to Henry Dundas (Home Secretary) 24 April 1792

'Two very intelligent persons with whom I could converse in perfect confidence, ascribe the growth of the Sheffield club to the disorderly habits of the place, the source of which is in its Constitution. The staple manufacture of Cutlery ware is under the restraint of a very strict Corporation. The work is carried on by Apprentices and Journeymen who earn a full maintenance without employing their whole time, and have no inducement to do more, because they do not work for their own account. None of the masters are engaged in this club which they would supress if they durst …

It is very certain that this Sheffield Club was formed by Payne (sic) while he was in that neighbourhood, having picked up two or three men of low condition, but of quicker parts than their companions, who by haranguing at ale houses, were at last encouraged to become the orators of the club. Very few of them can write their own names.'

Scottish Record Office, Melville Castle MSS GD 51/1/17/2)

questioning them with respect to their views, they have always declared, that all they wished was to spread information amongst the lower classes of people, and to convince them of the existence of abuses, in order that they might join, whenever persons of consequence should think it expedient to come forward, by Petition, or any other legal peaceable way, to obtain a Reform in Parliament.

Quoted in Reverend C. Wyvill (ed) Political Papers Vol. V pp.47–9

Report of the Acquaintances of Samuel Shore

Samuel Shore was a property owner in Yorkshire and Derbyshire, and this report was forwarded to Christopher Wyvill in May 1792.

'The Society (in Sheffield) first originated with four or five persons, Mechanics, without having the business in the least suggested to them by anyone. The leading people in it are considered in general as persons of good character … A Parliamentary Reform is their professed object, and the friends of liberty believe they keep this object in view; though timid persons, and those who are alarmed at the mention of a Reform, ascribe widely different motives to them, and assert that they aim at nothing less than confusion. The writer of this has frequently conversed with some of the leading Members, whom he has found men of understanding, with their minds open to information. Upon

Questions

1 What appear to be the principal differences between the L.C.S. and the S.C.I.?

2 Is the term 'working class' appropriate to describe the members of the L.C.S.?

3 What appears to have been the principal inspirer of the L.C.S.?

4 What is the political objective of the L.C.S.?
Does this differ from that of the S.C.I.?

5 Why might the ruling classes regard the L.C.S. with suspicion?

(a) What different views of the Sheffield Society are presented by the authors?
(b) For what possible reasons do they present differing interpretations of the Sheffield Society?
(c) Which of the two texts do you consider to be the most reliable?

15 Trade Unions

PREVIEW

Unions and the Industrial Revolution

PRINTERS VERSUS POLICE AT WAPPING. 1980s.

The Combination Acts 1799–1800

Trade unions were a direct result of the Industrial Revolution. As guilds of masters, craftsmen and apprentices became obsolete and government ceased to regulate wages, skilled workmen felt themselves forced to combine in order to maintain and improve their position. Such combinations of workers were forbidden by the Combination Laws of 1799 and 1800.

The Combination Acts 1799–1800 stir deep-seated passions amongst historians. On the one hand, some regard the Acts as one of the more outstanding examples of repressive class legislation. Others suggest that the penalties were mild and the Act rarely used. Both sides agree that the growth of trade unions was not hampered during this period.

What then is the significance of these Acts?

'Whereas great numbers of Journeymen Manufacturers and Workmen, in various parts of the kingdom have, by unlawful Meetings and Combinations, endeavoured to obtain Advance of their Wages, and to effectuate other Illegal Purposes; and the Laws at present in Force against such unlawful Conduct have been found to be inadequate to the Suppression thereof, whereby it has become necessary that more effectual Provision should be made against such unlawful Combinations ... be it enacted ... That ... all Contracts, Covenants, and Agreements whatsoever, in Writing or not in Writing, at any Time or Times heretofore made or entered into by or between Journeymen Manufacturers or other Workmen, or by persons within this Kingdom, for obtaining an Advance of Wages of them, ... or for lessening or altering their or any of their usual Hours or Times of working, or for decreasing the Quantity of work, or for preventing or hindering any Person or Persons from employing whomsoever he, she, or they shall think proper to employ in his, her, or their Manufacture ...

An Act to Prevent Unlawful Combinations of Workmen (2 July 1799)

... and every journeyman and workman who ... shall be guilty of any of the said offences, being thereof lawfully convicted, upon his own confession or the oath or oaths of one or more credible witness or witnesses, before any two Justices of the Peace ... shall, by order of such Justices be committed to and confined to the common Goal ... for any time not exceeding three calendar months, or ... be committed to some House of Correction ... and ... kept to hard labour for any time not exceeding two calendar months.

Combination Act (1800)

A Contemporary, William Cobbett wrote in 1823 to his friend William Wilberforce:

'Now, you will observe Wilberforce, that this punishment is inflicted in order to prevent workmen from uniting together ... Every man's labour is his property ... The cotton spinners had their labour to sell; or at least they thought so ... The purchasers were rich and powerful and wanted them to sell it at what the spinners deemed too low a price. In order to be a match for the rich purchasers, the sellers of labour agree to assist one another, and thus to live as well as they can; till they can obtain what they deem to be a proper price ... If men be attacked either in the market or their shops; if butchers, bakers, farmers, millers be attacked with a view of forcing them to sell their commodities at a price lower than they demand, the assailants are deemed rioters, and are hanged!

This Combination Act does, however, say that the masters shall not combine against the workmen ... the utmost fine that the two Justices of the Peace can inflict is a fine of twenty pounds! But, and now mark the difference. Mark it Wilberforce; note it down as proof of the happiness of your 'free British labourers': mark, that the masters cannot be called upon by the Justices of the Peace to give evidence against themselves or their associated.

William Cobbett, *Political Register* (30 August 1823)

TALKING POINT

What current legislation affects the activities of trade unions today? Do you regard such legislation as reasonable or unreasonable?

Historical opinion has been varied on the effects of the Combination Laws:

... a far reaching change of policy, producing in the first twenty years of the nineteenth century a legal persecution of trade unionists as rebels.

Sidney and Beatrice Webb, History of Trade Unionism (1920)

... the most unqualified surrender of the state to the discretion of a class in the history of England.

J.L. and B. Hammond, The Town Labourer (1949)

... an odious piece of class legislation.

A. Aspinall, Early English Trade Unions (1949)

... it was in the very years when the Acts were in force that Trade Unionism registered great advances.

E.P. Thompson, The Making of the English Working Class (1963)

---

1 For what reasons were the Combination Acts passed?

2 In what way did the legislators intend the Combination Laws to be fair?

3 Why did this attempt to be fair not result so in practice?

4 Were the Combination Laws 'pieces of odious class legislation' in theory as well as practice?

The emergence of greater tolerance

As the fear of the French Revolution receded a greater tolerance toward trade unions emerged. The laws themselves appear to have done little to impede the development of trade unions. A strike of spinners in 1810 in Lancashire had as their object 'the equalisation of wages'. It was only defeated after four bitter months of struggle. In 1818 another major strike occurred which involved weavers and spinners and resulted in an attempt to set up a General Union of Trades known as the 'Philanthropic Hercules'. Its life was brief but it served as a landmark of an early attempt to bring about working class unity.

Agitation for the repeal of the Combination Laws took place in a changing climate. Robert Peel, a member of the government, reflected this change when he commented, 'Men who have no property except their manual skill and strength, ought to be allowed to confer together, if they think fit, for the purpose of determining at what rate they will sell their property.' Francis Place, a Benthamite economist, and Joseph Hume, a Radical M.P. spearheaded the assault on the Combination Laws.

In 1825, largely as a result of the skilful management of Hume and Place, the Combination Acts were repealed. Place had assumed that the removal of these laws would lead to the withering away of trade unions in the new climate of 'freedom and trust'. The reverse was the case. Trade unions mushroomed. Strikes increased. Government feared that they had acted too hastily and re-imposed legislation in 1826. The new legislation allowed trade unions to exist but their freedom to pursue their activities was severely curtailed. The Master and Servant Act still applied and the

Note

In 1811, in one of the few recorded actions under the Combination Laws against masters hosiers in Nottingham who had combined to reduce wages, the authorities took no action.

Act of conspiracy could bludgeon them into submission with either prison and transportation.

A SATIRICAL VIEW OF A TRADES' UNION COMITTEE.

The Grand National Consolidated Trade Union

Despite the repeal of the Combination Laws, trade societies in the 1820s remained small and local, although loose federations were emerging amongst some skilled groups of workers such as the engineers. Increased communications by the postal service and the expanding railway network provided the means by which closer links could be established. In 1829, the dynamic trade union organiser John Doherty, founder of the Cotton Spinners Union in Manchester, organised a conference in the Isle of Man. His purpose was to establish a Grand General Union of the Operative Spinners of Great Britain and Ireland. Staffordshire potters and other trade societies were invited to swell the ranks into a National Association for the Protection of Labour. Aspirations alone though could not become the necessary muscle to make the protection of labour a fact. After the failure of the organisation to support a strike by spinners in Ashton under Lyme the N.A.P.L. receded into oblivion.

A parallel General Union of Bricklayers and Carpenters was formed in 1827 which had become known as the Operative Builders Union in 1832. This Union established a twice yearly Builders' Parliament to decide policy for its members.

There were differences, however, between these two major attempts at forming general unions. Doherty's intention was to raise sufficient funds to finance a strike. The Operative Builders' Union, on the other hand, had a more political and social intention, namely, to replace the competitive market forces with workers' co-operatives. This vision failed to survive a bitter dispute. Operatives were required by employers to sign what became notoriously known as 'the document'. The document obliged workers to renounce union membership if they wanted work. The protracted dispute tore the union apart.

Failures on this scale did not prevent further attempts at grand national unions. In 1834 a group of Derby workers appealed to London trade societies for their help in a struggle to prevent wage reductions. A conference was called in order to rally support for the Derby workers. Sympathy was widespread although the bulk of support came from London tailors and shoemakers.

Despite the groundswell of support amongst many sections of workers for the emergent Grand National Consolidated Trades Union it was beset by a number of fundamental weaknesses. Few well-established craft trade societies joined. Builders and Engineers stayed aloof. Nor did it win over the northern unions such as the cotton spinners. Above all, from a claimed one million membership, only 16,000 had paid their dues and thus it had little financial clout.

The test of its power was not long in coming. In Tolpuddle, Dorset, six labourers were sentenced to seven years transportation for taking an oath to form a union. Lord Melbourne, Home Secretary, decided an example had to be made and the 1779 Act against unlawful oaths was invoked.

There was a huge outcry at what was considered to be an excessive use of force. Well-disciplined demonstrations took place in London.
At the height of the protest an ex-factory owner and manager, Robert Owen, was invited to become President of the G.N.C.T.U.

DEMONSTRATION AT COPENHAGEN FIELDS, LONDON, IN SUPPORT OF THE TOLPUDDLE MARTYRS.

The 'New Model' Unions

The survival of trade unions at all was remarkable testimony to the courage of working people. Many jobs were relatively unskilled and the rapid rise of population, supplemented by immigrants from Ireland, created a labour pool which could be used to swamp any industrial action with blackleg labour. Even in skilled occupations, new technology represented a constant threat. Trade cycles of depression and the general hostility of the law represented further stumbling blocks to the growth of trade unions.

Toward the latter end of the 1840s there appeared to emerge much more soundly organised trade societies which some historians have dubbed 'new model'. Not all historians agree that this label is appropriate and suggest that there was nothing 'new' about these older craft unions.

Examining the evidence

New Model Unions?

Source A

The witness stated that the society was formed in 1851 of a number of societies which had previously existed, and it now numbered 33,000 members, with an annual increase of 2,000 to 3,000 a year. There are, he said, 308 branches … All these branches are governed by one code of rules … Each member pays 1s.0d per week and the society has now a fund in different banks, in round numbers, of £140,000. The annual income in 1865 was £88,885, made up, besides subscriptions, of entrance fees, each member having to pay an entrance fee varying from 15s. to 3.10s.

With respect to trade purposes the secretary stated that the average annual payment to members out of work for the 15 years the society had been in existence was £18,000. On being questioned as to what percentage of this money had gone through strikes and disputes, he said: – 'We have only had one dispute which you may call important in our trade since the commencement of the society, and that was in 1852. In the first six months of that year we expended £40,000 … it was the fault of the employers who locked us out …' Mr. Hughes asked: It is very difficult for a strike to happen in your society I believe? What measures have men to take, for example, before they can strike in your society? The witness answered: They have to represent their grievances to the committee of their branch. In a town where there is more than one branch there is what is called a district committee, composed of seven members from the different branches or more in proportion to the number of branches in the district; and instead of the branch committee dealing with the question …

Mr. Hughes: But supposing that the men who wished to go out had got the consent of their branch in their own town, what else would they have to do?

Witness: then they would require to get the consent of the district committee, and the approval of the executive committee.

From 'The Beehive' the trade union newspaper – May 11 Report on the
Trade Union Inquiry

Robert Owen – *Father of Socialism?*

B y any standards of judgement, Robert Owen was a charismatic figure. Born in 1771 at Newton, Montgomeryshire, the son of a postmaster, he rose by his own initiative and a careful choice in marriage, to become the owner and manager of the textile mills at New Lanark, just south of Glasgow. At his mill he began an experiment in new working conditions from which was to emerge a critique of capitalist society. As a consequence of a growing reputation and a number of publications he has been labelled 'the father of British Socialism'. Is the title apt? Did he exert such a pervasive influence over early nineteenth century working class movements that warrants this title?

ROBERT OWEN.

CHRONOLOGY OF OWEN'S CAREER

1800–24:	The New Lanark Period.
1800–16:	Owen proves himself a successful business manager. At the same time he makes improvements in housing, schools and working conditions at his mill.
1816–24:	Owen publishes 'A New View of Society' (1813) and begins to spread his ideas for co-operative communities. He joins the agitation for factory reform. In 1818 he publishes 'Two Memorials on Behalf of the Working Class'. This is followed by 'Report to the County of Lanark' 1821.
1824–34:	Political agitation
1824–29:	Owen attempts to put his ideas into practice by establishing Owenite communities – New Harmony in the U.S.A., Orbiston (1825–28), Exeter (1827) and Rahaline in Ireland (1831–33). Few of these communities survived for very long.
1829–34:	Owen becomes involved with working class movements such as Labour Exchanges, consumer co-operatives and trade unions. In 1834 he became President of the G.N.C.T.U. but this collapses within a year.
1834–58:	Owen returns to his attempts to set up model communities His political beliefs take on increasingly religious overtones.

ROBERT OWEN AND LANARK MILL
'I became the government of New Lanark mill about the first of January 1800. I say 'government' for my intention was not just to be manager but to change the condition of the people … the great majority of them were idle, drunken, dishonest liars.'
Robert Owen, *The Life of Robert Owen* (1857)

A VIEW OF ROBERT OWEN

'Owen deceives himself. He is part owner and the only director of the large establishment at New Lanark Mill: the persons under him happen to be white and are free to leave his place of work, but while in it they are as much under his absolute control as so many negro slaves … And he jumps at once to the monstrous conclusion that because he can do this with 2210 persons, who are totally dependent upon him – all mankind ought to be governed with the same system.

Robert Southey, *Journal of a Tour of Scotland* (1819)

ROBERT OWEN'S SYSTEM OF SUPERVISION

'Most of the innovations were prompted by a desire for improved efficiency, work flows and output … Owen backed up a system of supervision by overseers and spinning masters with his "silent monitor", a four sided wooden block, designed to hang on the machine and coloured white, yellow, blue and black. The colour of the side showing to the front represented the conduct of the individual during the preceding day, white was excellent, black the opposite. Supervisors kept 'books of character' which Owen regularly inspected.'

Ian Donnachie, *Owenite Radicalism* Open University A401 Block II Units 3–6 p. 30 1974

Owen wrote the following after the collapse of an Owenite community at Orbiston in 1828 to Archibald James Hamilton co-founder of the community.

'It will gratify you to learn that the good cause is progressing substantially in all counties, and that your exertions, although not crowned with immediate success at Orbiston, have contributed especially to make the principles known, and to prepare the way for practice in many places.'

Owen to Hamilton. Hamilton Collection. *Letters of Archibald James Hamilton of Dalzell* (1828)

'Robert Owen had little sympathy with political reform and held aloof from all popular movements of the day for political democracy … he sought to permeate the existing governments, whatever they might be, with his 'Rational System', his principles of solidarity of interest.'

C. Tsuzuki, Robert Owen and Revolutionary Politics in S. Pollard and J. Salt, (eds) Robert Owen, Prophet of the Poor p.13 1971.

'Certainly Owen's flirtation with artisan unions was doomed from the start. As the prophet of a New Society he had no real interest in bread and butter issues and was completely intolerant of those who thought in terms of short term economic gains.'

J. Butt, *Robert Owen and Trade Unionism* contained in *Robert Owen: Industrialist, Reformer, Visionary 1771–1858.* Robert Owen, Bicentenary Association p.18 (1971)

Social hymn no. 74 from Social Hymns for the use of the Friends of the Rational System of Society, Manchester (1835) quoted by E. Yeo, Robert Owen and Social Culture in S. Pollard and J. Salt p.84 op.cit.

Oh! may this feast increase
The union of the heart;
And cordial harmony and peace,
To everyone impart.
As one in heart in mind
Just heirs to all the earth
Be each to each humane and kind,
In all our social mirth.

'Robert Owen was a remarkable instance of a man at once Tory and revolutionary. He held with the government of the few, but, being a philanthropist, that the government of the few should be the government of the good. He would revolutionise both religion and society – indeed, clear the world out of the way – to make room for his new 'views'.'

G.J. Holyoak, *Sixty years of an Agitators' Life* T. Fisher-Unwin Vol. I p.117 (1900)

A DEFINITION OF SOCIALISM:

'A system based on collective ownership and administration of the means of production and distribution of goods.'

1. How appropriately do the beliefs of Owen fit this description of Socialism?
2. "For each age there is a new view of Mr. Owen" Professor J. Harrison A New View of Mr. Owen in S. Pollard and J. Salt op. cit.
   What did Professor Harrison mean by this statement?
3. Is the title 'father of socialism' appropriately applied to the career and beliefs of Robert Owen?

Source B

The history of trade unionism in the later 1830s and early 1840s has been inadequately investigated, but there is abundant evidence in the Report of the Select Committee on combinations in 1838, and also in local newspapers and surviving, though scrappy, trade union records, to indicate that a large number of societies remained in existence after 1834. They had to face great difficulties between 1836 and 1842 because of serious trade depression: the burden of unemployment, wage reductions and loss of membership may have caused some societies to collapse, but most of them appear to have survived. These, of course, were of the sectional skilled type – unskilled labourers still remained almost entirely unorganised – and there was no change in the character of trade unionism during these years; when trade revived and the forward movement among trade unions was resumed in the 1840s, it was along the old lines.

A.E. Musson, *British Trade Unions 1800–75*

---

1 Study source A.

In what way does the A.S.E. appear to be a well-organised trade union?

2 Compare the A.S.E. with the G.N.C.T.U. In what ways are they different?

How would these differences affect the operation and success of the A.S.E.

3 In what sense, if any, can one talk of 'new model' unions in the late 1840s and '50s?

'New Model' Unions expanded

The relative prosperity of the 1850s enabled other unions to adopt similar constitutions and objectives as the A.S.E. The Amalgamated Carpenters was formed in 1860 and the Operative Bricklayers Society swelled the ranks of the 'new model' unions. Their influence in London was remarkable but they had little effect on the northern unions. Furthermore the very fact of belonging to a union remained confined to the skilled male artisan. Even the most successful unions contained only a fraction of the total possible number.

By the 1850s, however, the unions had emerged from being industrial outlaws to legal if somewhat suspiciously regarded as members of the industrial community. In the 1860s this limited advance was to be brought into question once more.

Chartism and Political Reform

Agitation for political reform did not die with the defeat of the reform clubs. Membership of the S.C.I. and L.S.C. were relatively small. The issue of reform was kept alive by a small group of radicals; Sir Francis Burdett, Samuel Whitbread, William Cobbett and Major Cartwright. All were anxious to disassociate themselves from the taint of French Jacobinism, especially during the gale of loyalist reaction which swept the country.

A new force for reform also emerged this time which was to be of significance later. In 1809 Jeremy Bentham published his 'Plan for Parliamentary Reform'. The doctrine of Utilitarianism was made manifest. This unrefined set of beliefs underpinned an attack upon aristocratic privileges.

Peace in 1815 only brought a short-lived prosperity. Each class armed with its defences – Burke for those who desired the status quo to remain, Bentham for those in the ruling orders who argued change was essential, and Paine for the lower orders. Economic depression fuelled discontent and demand for reform. Luddism in industrial areas and agrarian riots in East Anglia provided the backdrop for the debate.

By March 1817 Cartwright had founded forty 'Hampden Clubs' for reform in Lancashire. Cobbett's 'Political Register' sold 200,000 copies in two months. Frustrated outbursts of protest, demonstration and violence followed. The Spa Field riots in London in December 1816, the infamous 'massacre' at St. Peter's Field in Manchester 1819 and the March of the 'Blanketeers' in 1817 bore testimony to troubled times. On ninth June 1817 an attempted if somewhat farcical attempt at revolution at Penrtrich led by Jeremy Brandreth ended with three hung and thirty transported.

THE PETERLOO 'MASSACRE' AT MANCHESTER.

A SATIRICAL COMMENT ON THE PETERLOO MASSACRE.

The 'Six Acts'

The government smelt the whiff of revolution in the air. To eradicate the stench the government passed what came to be called the 'Six Acts'.

1 Military training and drilling was banned.

2 Additional powers of search were given to magistrates.

3 Public meetings of more than fifty people were banned unless they had approval of a magistrate.

4 Trial procedures could be speeded up.

5 Increased controls on the press were introduced.

6 A stamp duty was imposed on the press.

The return of modest prosperity in the 1820s reduced the popular clamour for radical reform. Working men turned to trade union activity for in times of full employment they could exercise more influence. 1830, however, brought a sudden slump in the economy and in its wake renewed demands for parliamentary reform.

The 'Swing Riots' were a series of destructive attacks upon landowners property. A revolution in France helped raise the temperature. The ruling Tory Party was split over the issue of Reform and in the resultant general election of 1832 the Whigs, who had fought the election on the issue of reform, triumphed.

But the degree of reform that the Liberals had in mind fell far short of that which the working class radicals demanded. Lord Brougham, principal architect of the Reform bill, made this perfectly clear when he announced, 'By the people, I mean the middle classes, the wealth and intelligence of the country, the glory of the British name.' Lord Grey, who

THE MISFORTUNES OF THE POOR.

introduced the bill was quick to reassure the House of Lords, '... the more the bill is considered, the least it will be found to prejudice the real interests of the aristocracy ... (and that) there is no more decided against annual parliaments, universal suffrage and the secret ballots than I am. My object is not to favour but to put an end to such hopes.'

And so it was. The newly increased enfranchised population rose from a mere 478,000 to 813,000 – only one in seven of adult males. The representation of women was not even considered. Only property, and landed property at that, was invested with political power. Rich businessmen made only slow inroads into this power base and did so largely by 'buying' into the aristocracy through marriage and the purchase of country estates. Little appeared to have changed.

WHIG CARTOON OF REFORM BILL.

Source D: Physical force or Moral force – O'Connor on physical force.

He (O'Connor) had never counselled the people to use physical force, because he felt that those who did were fools to their own cause; but, at the same time, those who decried it preserved their authority by physical force alone … He counselled them against all rioting, all civil war. He hoped and trusted that out of the exercise of that judgement which belonged exclusively to the working class, a union would arise, and from that union a moral power would be created, sufficient to establish the rights of the poor man: but if this failed, then let every man raise his arm in defence of that which his judgement told him was justice.

R.G. Gammage, a Chartist , History of the Chartist Movement (1854)

Source E: General Napier – Commander of Government Forces in the north of England

General Napier was in charge of 4,000 troops in the north of England. 1st December 1839.

An anonymous letter came, with a Chartist plan. Poor creatures, their threats of attack are miserable. With half a cartridge and half a pike, with no money, no discipline, no skilful leaders, they would attack men with leaders, money and discipline, well armed and having sixty rounds a man. Poor men!

A CHARTIST ARMING. PUNCH MAGAZINE.

Source F: Chartist success

It would be great mistake to suppose that the Chartist movement was really fruitless ... It may have looked too much to outward means, and little to inward and spiritual reform; but it was an excellent means of political education for the working class.

Ramsden Balmforth, son of a Bradford handloom weaver and a Chartist himself,
Some Social and Political Pioneers of the nineteenth century (1900)

Source G: Chartism's diversity

A study of Chartism must begin with a proper appreciation of regional and local diversity ... It is impossible to understand either the birth of Chartism or its fluctuating fortunes ... without examining the relevant fluctuating economic indices ... Chartism was a snowball movement which gathered together local grievances and sought to give them common expression in a nationwide agitation ... the pull of early Chartism seems to have been strongest – first in old centres of decaying or contracting industry, like Trowbridge in Wiltshire or Camarthen in Wales, and second, in the new or expanding single industry towns like Stockport ... there were three main groups within the heterogeneous labour force ... superior craftsmen ... factory operatives ... and domestic outworkers.

Asa Briggs, *Chartist Studies*

Source H: Call to arms! Julian Harney's response to revolution in Europe, 1848

Glory to the Proletarians of Paris, they have saved the Republic!

The work goes bravely on. Germany is revolutionised from end to end. Princes are flying, thrones are perishing. Everywhere the oppressors of nations yield, or are overthrown. 'Reform or Revolution' is now the order of the day. How long, Men of Great Britain and Ireland, how long will you carry the damning stigma of being the only people in Europe who dare not will their freedom?

Patience! The hour is nigh! From the hill-tops of Lancashire, from the voices of hundreds of thousands has ascended to Heaven the oath of union, and the rallying cry of conflict. Englishmen and Irishmen have sworn to have THE CHARTER AND REPEAL, or VIVE LA REPUBLIQUE!

'The Paris Proletarians', editorial in the Northern Star, 25 March 1848

Source I: Fear of chartism – real and imaginary

It must be remembered that at that time for many people Chartism aroused very real fears. To the middle and upper class a Chartist rebellion was more than a remote possibility. The Home Office papers contain numerous reports to the Home Secretary from anxious magistrates and Lord Lieutenants passing on rumours of Chartist insurrections. Some of the reports are well founded, others have much less justification ... Certainly it was the fear of mob violence that did much to shape the attitudes of authorities and of sections of the general public to the grievances of the working class.

Nevertheless, it is important to take into account that, for a variety of reasons, fear was sometimes deliberately fostered by the authorities. There was a tendency to ascribe any industrial unrest or disturbance to the work of Chartists and the more violent aspects of these disturbances were often emphasised in order to win the support of the uncommitted. By this means the authorities hoped to produce a united opposition against the rioters or strikers which would help prevent the disturbances … caused by Chartist agitators (and) the authorities often succeeded in obscuring the very real grievances of the strikers.

John Golby, 'Chartism and Public Order' from Popular Politics,
Open University A401 II pp.3–6

THE BRITISH LION IN 1850; OR THE EFFECTS OF FREE TRADE.

Questions

1 How serious a revolutionary threat was Chartism?

2 What factors appear to have influenced the "ebb and flow" of Chartists support?

3 What are the principal reasons why Chartism failed to achieve its political objectives by 1850?

4 How serious a threat did the physical force Chartists present?

5 What limitations did the 'moral force' Chartists have in favouring the aims of the movement?

6 Was Chartism a total failure?

The Anti-Corn Law League

The repeal of the Corn Laws in 1846 marked what many contemporaries saw as a major victory for free trade. It also signified the triumph of the most successful protest campaigns in early nineteenth century Britain.

The Corn Laws had been introduced in the wake of the defeat of Napoleon in 1815. British landowners feared that the unrivalled prosperity that they had experienced during the war years would come to an end as cheap foreign corn came flooding into the country. The Corn Laws represented a barrier behind which the protectionists believed they would be safe and the price of corn stabilised.

This was not to be so. Stable prices did not occur. Corn dealers frequently held back corn in order to raise prices artificially whilst buying in cheaper foreign imports which they could release to their advantage. It was a speculator's market.

By 1828 some of the worst effects were mitigated when Wellington introduced a sliding scale of dues. In 1842 Robert Peel lowered the rates still further. In the meantime a vigorous campaign had been launched from its base in Manchester to remove the laws entirely. The League was led by two energetic activists; Richard Cobden (M.P.) and John Bright (a Quaker cotton manufacturer). From its inception in 1839 it set about arguing powerfully through the medium of meetings, speeches, and pamphlets distributed through the new penny post (1840), posters and

Note

The Corn Laws, although introduced by a government dominated by landed interests represented other interest too. Arguments of the economic and strategic importance of agriculture were voiced. Furthermore, not all landowners supported their imposition.

Why was the Anti-Corn Law League so successful when other protest movements had either failed or only made modest headway?

unrestrained attacks upon their opponents. Cobden was soon joined in Parliament by Bright.

With the threat of famine in Ireland and the need for cheap imports of foodstuffs the stage was set for the League's triumph. In 1846 the Corn Laws were finally repealed and in the process Peel split his party in two.

Examining the Evidence

The Anti-Corn Law League – a successful protest

Source A: The aims of the League

I want the anti-corn Law League to be known as the Free Trade League. I know that the honourable gentlemen opposite think that all we want to do is to take away the corn monopoly. The public mind is urged on by us against the key-stone in the arch of monopoly.

Richard Cobden in a speech to Parliament. *Parliamentary Debates* Series III Vol. LXIX col. 386 15 May 1843

Source B: Free Trade – a moral force for good

I see in the free trade principle that which shall act upon the moral world as the principle of gravitation in the Universe – drawing men together, thrusting aside the antagonism of race and creed and language and uniting us in the bonds of eternal peace ... I believe the effect will be to change the face of the world, so as to introduce a system of government entirely distinct from that which prevails. I believe that the desire and motive for large and mighty Empires; for gigantic armies and navies ... will die away ... when man become one family and freely exchanges the fruits of his labour with this brother man.

Richard Cobden in a speech in Manchester, *Manchester Guardian* 15 January 1846

Source C: Repeal of the Corn Laws defended

Our opponents tell us that our object in bringing about the repeal of the Corn Laws, is, by reducing the price of corn, to lower the rate of their wages. I can only answer upon this point for the manufacturing districts; but, as far as they are concerned, I state it most emphatically as a truth, that, for the last twenty years, whenever corn has been cheap wages have been high in Lancashire; and, on the other hand, when bread has been dear wages have been greatly reduced ...

Now, let me be fully understood as to what Free Traders really do want. We do not want cheap corn merely in order that we may have low money prices. What we desire is plenty of corn, and we are utterly careless what its price is, provided we obtain it at the natural price. All we ask is, that corn shall follow the same law which the monopolists in food admit that labour must follow that 'it shall find its natural level in the markets of the world' ...

To pay for that corn, more manufacturers would be required from this country; this would lead to an increased demand for labour in the manufacturing districts, which would be necessarily attended with a rise in wages, in order that the goods might be made for the purpose of exchanging for the corn brought from abroad ... I observe there are narrow minded men in the agricultural districts, telling us, 'Oh, if you allow

Free Trade, and bring in a quarter of corn from abroad, it is quite clear that you will sell one quarter less in England' … What! I would ask, if you set more people to work at better wages – if you can clear your streets of those spectres which are now haunting your thoroughfares begging their daily bread – if you can depopulate your workhouses and clear off the two million of paupers which now exist in the land, and put them to work at productive industry – do you not think that they would consume some of the wheat as well as you; and may not they be as we are now, consumers of wheaten bread by millions, instead of existing on their present miserable dietary?

Richard Cobden, Speeches I (1870)

Source D: Cobden attacks protectionists

The Landowner and the Factory Child

This is my idea for the factory child and Lord Ashley. Lord Ashley has taken the bread from the first factory child and has broken it in two, and whilst putting the largest share in his pocket and returning the smaller to the child, he lifts up his eyes and in a very sanctamonious tone says, 'I will never rest until the poor factory child is protected by a ten hours bill from the tyranny of the merciless and gripping millowners'.

Richard Cobden, Richard Cobden Papers (1839)

Source E: Corn Law League propaganda

Source F

ANTI-CORN LAW LEAGUE POSTER.

ANTI-CORN LAW LEAGUE MEMBERSHIP CARD.

Source G: Opposition to the Anti-Corn Law League

The House of Lords.

(Repeal of the Corn Laws) will greatly increase the dependence of this country upon foreign countries for its supply of food … rapid and disastrous fluctuations in the markets of this country … it is unjust to withdraw protection from the landed interests of this country, whilst that interest remains subject to exclusive burdens imposed for purposes of general, and not special advantage.

... the loss to be sustained by the Repeal of the Corn Laws will fall most ... severely on the tenant farmers, and through them with ruinous consequences, on the agricultural labourers ... because of free trade in corn a large and unnecessary diminution of national income.

Parliamentary Debates, Series II Vol. LXXXVII pp.961–63 (signed by 89 peers)

Source H: Chartist opposition

Who are the blustering, canting crew,

Who keep the cheap loaf in our view,

And would from us more profit screw?

The League

Who cry 'Repeal the curs'd Corn Law',

And would their workmen feed with straw,

That they may filthy lucre paw?

The Northern Star, (1840)

Source I: Chartist distrust of the Anti-Corn Law League

The outraged feelings of the operative classes enabled the Chartist leaders to thwart the Corn Law repealers in nearly every effort that they made ... The reasons given by various men ... for not going with the League widely differed. With a very large number it was detestation of the social tyranny exercised by manufacturers, which led them to believe that anything coming from such a quarter was not likely to be very favourable to their interests ... the Free Trade under the existing arrangements of society, so far from being beneficial, would rather prove injurious to the producing class ... because they would come down in strength and move resolutions in favour of the Charter, protesting that they were as good repealers as we were but the Repeal of the Corn Laws was more of a manufacturers' question than a working man's, and taking this view a few Chartists unconsciously became protectionists.

James Leach, *Mechanics Institute Birmingham*

Source J: Christian socialist opposition

Next you have the Manchester School, from which heaven defend us; for all narrow, conceited, hypocritical, and anarchic and aesthetic schemes of the Universe, the Cobden and Bright one is exactly the worst ... To pretend to be the workmen's friend, by keeping down the price of bread, when all they want thereby is to keep down wages and increase profits, and in the meantime to widen the gulf between the working man and all that is time honoured, refined and chivalrous in English society, that they make men their divided slaves, that is, perhaps half consciously, for there are excellent men amongst them.

Letter from Charles Kingsley to Thomas Hughes, (1852).
Members of a Christian Socialist Movement

Source L: The Repeal of the Corn Laws, 15 May 1848

Sir, I do not rest my support of this bill upon the temporary ground of scarcity in Ireland ... Now all of you admit that the real question at issue is the improvement of the social and moral condition of the masses of the population; we wish to elevate in the gradation of society that great class which gains its suppoort by manual labour – that is agreed on all hands. The mere interests of the landlords – the mere interests of the occupying tenants, important as they are, are subordinate to the great question – which is calculated to improve the condition, and elevate the social character of the millions who subsist by manual labour, whether they are engaged in manufacturers or in agriculture? ... I wish to convince them that our object has been so to apportion taxation, that we shall relieve industry and labour from any undue burden, and transfer it, so far as is consistent with the public good, to those who are better enabled to bear it.

Robert Peel, *Speeches IV,* pp.689–96

Source M

PEEL'S CHEAP BREAD SHOP. PUNCH MAGAZINES 1846.

Source N

THE PREMIER'S FIX. PUNCH MAGAZINE 1846.

---

1 (a) What reasons are advanced by the League for the repeal of the Corn Laws?

(b) How do they attempt to make their case attractive to potential supporters?

(a) What reasons are given by the opponents of the Anti-Corn Law League?

(b) How do they attempt to persuade people to support their cause?

(c) Does this opposition imply that they supported the retention of the Corn Laws?

3 Why does Richard Cobden attack Lord Ashley's promotion of the ten hours bill to limit the hours worked in cotton manufactures?

---

4 (a) In what specific ways is it possible to account for the success of the anti-Corn Law League?

(b) In what sense was the agitation by the Anti-Corn Law conducted in an atmosphere which was conducive to its success?

REVIEW
Industrialisation and Protest
(Charters fourteen and fifteen)

Protest by working class people concerning political and economic reform had little success unless the government wished concessions to be made. Some of these protest movements were violent in character. E.P. Thompson in 'The Making of the English Working Class' asserts that during the period 1789–1848 Britain came close to revolution by a class-conscious working class. Eric Hobsbawm asserts that no time since the seventeenth century had labouring people been, 'so persistently, profoundly, and often desperately disatisfied.' (Industry and Empire, 1968). The discontent and the sense of class-consciousness, they argue, was a direct product of industrialisation.

A revolution, however, did not happen. It is by no means clear why they do. De Tocqueville made the profound observation on the French Revolution that it occurred in a country that was not the most reactionary, that had attempted reforms and at a time of growing expectations of improvement. More recently Simon Schama in 'Citizens' has stressed that pre-Revolutionary France was dynamic and not the languid effete aristocratic society so frequently portrayed.

Nevertheless the years of political crisis were also invariably periods of economic crisis. This leads to the more complex question of the relationship between the course of the Industrial Revolution and the revolutionary movement. Many made a simple forecast that revolution would ensue, as competition for scarcer resources forced down wages, and as manufacturers were obliged to become more competitive. In general terms, however, the fortunes of the working people began to improve, if hesitantly and slowly. Furthermore the assumption of a single cohesive proletariat is in doubt for a kaleidoscope of aspirations are apparent in different sections of the working class. Rising living standards, particularly for the skilled, detached then from the unskilled. Leaders of radical reform either emerged from the ranks of the middle classes or artisans and rarely from what Marx would have recognised as the proletariat.

The failure of the working class to produce a unified response to industrialisation was the failure to agree on a common ideology. Short term economic advantage, nationalism or religion were all magnets pulling in a variety of directions.

Equally, government proved itself increasingly sensitive to the need for improvement. Factory legislation, public health reform and education bear testimony to the need to legislate to remedy social evils and, to an extent, retain power by defusing discontent. At the same time industrialisation brought into being working class institutions of self-help. Trade unions, friendly societies, co-operative societies and Chartism were manifestations of this phenomenon. The protest movements themselves began to merge into vehicles for an acceptance and identification of interest within the capitalist system.

Questions

1 Was Britain near revolution in the period 1789–1848?

2 Could the various forms of working class protest be construed as revolutionary?

16 The Great Victorian Boom 1851–73

PREVIEW

THE GREAT EXHIBITION OF 1851.

'All the World going to see the Great Exhibition of 1851' Drawn and etched by George Cruikshank.

The Great Humbug Contemporary comment (1851)

The mid-Victorian boom 1850–73

The problems of historians' labels

On May 1st 1851, 'The Great Exhibition of the Works of Industry of all Nations' was opened by Queen Victoria in London, to a rapturous reception. By the time the exhibition was over six million people, about 17 per cent of the total population of Great Britain, passed into the vast iron and glass building and marvelled at the technological and industrial wonders of the world. The Exhibition was international, but there was little doubt that, for most visitors, it symbolised Britain's economic domination of the world which heralded, it is claimed, an unparalleled period of prosperity virtually unbroken until 1873.

Many history textbooks have referred to this period as that of a 'Golden age of prosperity' or even the 'Great Victorian Boom'. Minor disagreements concentrate on the precise dating of the phenomena, but not the central assertion. E.J. Hobsbawn describes 'twenty-five years of inflation' whereas E.V. Morgan locates the period between 1858–73.

Notwithstanding this minor difference of opinion several major questions arise before we can accept this period as one of unrivalled prosperity.

1 Upon what basis did Britain attain such outstanding economic domination?

2 Is there sufficient justification to attach a universal label of prosperity to this period?

3 Assuming there was prosperity did all share in the good fortune?

When did the 'Boom' happen?

Study the graph below showing the course of wholesale prices in Britain, 1815–1913.

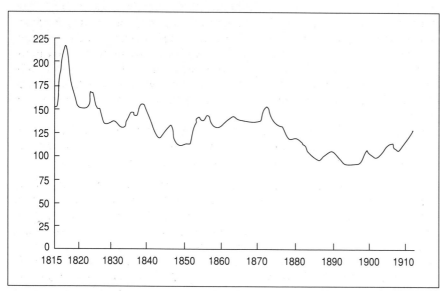

TALKING POINT

All historians tend to label and categorise the past as a convenient shorthand for isolating what appears to be distinctive about an age or period. But there is a danger that such labels may distract from the complexity of historical change. It is particularly difficult when an attempt is made to measure such complex factors as the performance of the economy.

1 What is meant by
'The Dark Ages'
'The Middle Ages'

2 How much do they explain and how much do they obscure our understanding of these periods of history?

3 What title would you give to the period covered by this book? Substantiate your choice.

4 What title would you give to the present age?

Task

1 Into what periods of economic performance would you divide this graph?

2 What difficulties did you experience when attempting to do this?

3 What are the uses and limitations of using wholesale prices to determine Britain's economic performance?

Historians generally identify three broad periods. In the first half of the nineteenth century Britain's growth was impressive but broken by an erratic series of peaks and troughs, eventually plunging into the depression of the 'hungry forties'. On the other side of the great Victorian divide lies the period of Britain's retardation or 'Great Depression'. Between these dark vales the mid-Victorian period appears to stand out as a plateau of stability. It is a possible danger, however by comparing this to what preceded and followed, to exaggerate its prosperity.

Bearing this caution in mind, let us consider which economic indicators we need to evaluate. The answer to this is not simple for it depends very much on what aspect of the economy we are looking at and for what reasons. There are a number of elements which we need to consider in order to examine the validity of the label 'The Great Victorian boom'.

- The rise, or otherwise, of the National Income.
- The growth and composition of imports and exports.
- The rate of industrial and agricultural production.
- The rate of capital investment.
- The development of commercial and business organisation.

The 'Boom'

The key indicator of a country's economic performance is its national income and growth of industrial production.

There is every reason to be cautious when categorising these years as a period of 'boom', for the rates of growth in preceding and subsequent periods do not show a marked difference, nor are they particularly impressive. Furthermore it would be wrong to think of the ordinary working people as living in a golden age. Unemployment and under-employment were constant threats to their standard of living. The American Civil War (1861–65), for example, cut off cotton supplies from Lancashire and threw many cotton workers out of work. Only the cold comfort of the workhouse existed to save the destitute from starvation. Although the nation as a whole was accumulating wealth it was unevenly spread. More than half the total national income went to less than 10 per cent of the population whilst a quarter to one third lived below the poverty line.

However a substantial majority of the population did benefit from a rising tide of exports which were exchanged for foodstuffs from all over the world. Certainly by any standards, the growth of trade is impressive.

Exports were maintained at a high level throughout the period but, on the other hand, their growth was not higher than that of the 1830s and 40s. Furthermore there were inherent weaknesses in the export base. Britain was very dependent upon a narrow range of staples – coal, cotton and iron. These commodities became proportionally cheaper as technological progress was made, particularly in textiles. This moved the terms of trade against Britain for she increasingly had to sell more goods to obtain the same volume of imports. Compared with 1810 Britain had to sell twice the volume of exports in 1860 to obtain the same imports. It thus became

The Great Exhibition of 1851

*T*he whole meaning of the Great Exhibition of the Works of Industries of all Nations in 1851 could not have been better symbolised by what came to be called the 'Battle of the Elms'. During the planning phase it appeared that it might be necessary to demolish some elm trees which would be in the way of the Great Exhibition Hall.

An outcry arose particularly from those who had serious doubts about the value of the Exhibition. They questioned that technological advancement necessarily improved the human condition. Was the Exhibition a celebration of human progress or a dirge to its folly? A compromise was reached and ten of the elm trees were enclosed within the Great Exhibition Hall.

ALBERT! SPARE THOSE TREES.

Whatever the contemporary judgement, it was, nonetheless, a masterpiece of prefabricated design and engineering skill. Standardised factory made parts were dispatched to the site where 2260 men, aided by a whole host of machines, erected the building in less than three months.

The success of the Exhibition was due to three men. Joseph Paxton, who designed the building, began his career as head gardener on the Chatsworth Estates; Henry Cole, a civil servant with a taste for design and the arts, and who had organised previous exhibitions by the Royal Society for the Arts; and finally Prince Albert whose patronage ensured the success of the Exhibition.

COMMENTS ON THE EXHIBITION

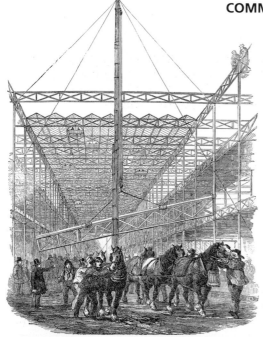

'The Great Exhibition is an augury of good as a means of helping onward the triumphant reign of peace – an opportunity to praise the glory of God, the wonder and enlightenment of the age, a temple of concorde.'
From a contemporary sermon.

'Celestial peace the plan designed,
Her snow white banner she unfurled;
Love oped the gates to all mankind,
And hailed the workmen of the world.'
-Ode to the Great Exhibition.

'But as for doing good to English trade,
I think a slight mistake therein is made;
These foreign gentry sell, but are not sold,
And lack, not English goods, but English gold.'
from Ode to the Great Humbug.

'But the island of the Bees had now become the most powerful of all the world …and the good fairies, Industry, Art and Science, had to spread their powerful influence over all the Island, and, indeed, the whole Universe, that the good queen and her consort resolved to do honour to the fairies, by establishing a gala in their dominions, and inviting the industrious bees of all nations to send their products to this great fête.'

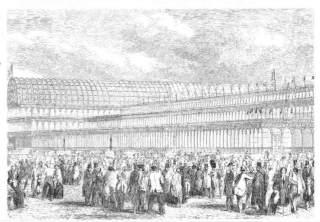

OTHER VIEWS OF THE EXHIBITION

Although the following extracts were not specific comments on the Exhibition of 1851 they represent the views of those who believed that technological progress was not necessarily a hallmark of a civilised society.

'I tell you it is not wealth which our civilisation has created, but riches, with its necessary companion poverty, or in other words slavery. All rich men must have someone to do their dirty work. If competitive commerce creates wealth, then should England surely be the wealthiest country in the world, as I suppose some people think it is, and as it certainly is the richest; but what shabbiness is this rich country driven into.'
William Morris in a speech, 1871. William Morris was a Socialist who advocated a return to greater craftsmanship in Art.

'Men are grown mechanical in head and heart, as well as in hand. They have lost faith in individual endeavour, and in natural force, of any kind. Not for internal protection, but for external combinations and arrangements, for institutions and constitutions – for Mechanism of one sort or other, do they hope and struggle. Their whole efforts, attachments, opinions turn on mechanism and are of mechanical in character.'
Thomas Carlyle, Signs of the Times (1829)

Questions

1   The sources convey a belief about the relationship between technology and progress.
   (a) Which of them support an optimistic and which a pessimistic relationship?
   (b) What justifications do the writers use for the position they take?
   (c) How do the authors convey a sense of commitment to their positions? Refer to language, style and context.
2   Some of the extracts are banal. Does this mean they are of less value to the historian than a serious social comment such as those made by William Morris and Thomas Carlyle?

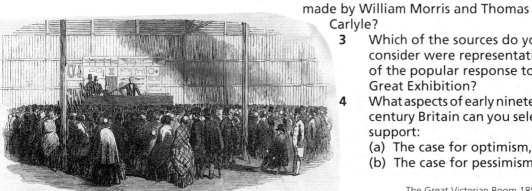

3   Which of the sources do you consider were representative of the popular response to the Great Exhibition?
4   What aspects of early nineteenth century Britain can you select to support:
   (a) The case for optimism,
   (b) The case for pessimism?

Economic rates of growth			
Year	Industrial Production	Real National Income	Real National Income per head
1815–52	3.2	1.9	0.7
1853–73	2.2	2.1	0.9
1873–99	2.2	1.9	0.8

G.H. Wood's Index of real wages 1850=100

1850	100	1857	94	1863	107
1851	102	1858	94	1864	118
1853	100	1859	104	1865	120
1854	97	1860	105	1866	117
1855	94	1861	99	1867	105
1856	95	1862	100	1868	105
				1869	111

'Real wages and the Standard of comfort since 1850' Journal of the Statistical Society p.72

Does this evidence support or refute the notion of this period as one of prosperity?

even more difficult for Britain to obtain an export surplus during the nineteenth century, a goal which, in point of fact, she never achieved.

Indeed the imbalance of trade in these basic commodities would have left Britain in the red if it had not been for the contribution of invisible earnings from shipping and insurance. A healthy return from invisible earnings depended upon the maintenance of a high level of world trade and Britain was particularly vulnerable if foreign countries decided to impose protectionist tariffs.

Invisible earnings became of increasing importance to Britain's economy and this was reflected in the changing composition of exports. The proportion of manufactured goods fell from about 90 per cent of the total in the mid-nineteenth century to about 75 per cent at the turn of the century, although the value of coal exports increased from about 2.5 per cent to 9 per cent in the same period.

It was widely believed at the time that the policy of Free Trade was the instrument by which mid-nineteenth century economic success was achieved. Supporters of the proposition pointed put that 1146 articles which had been liable for duty in 1840 had been reduced to twelve in 1860 and this unfettering of trade had encouraged economic expansion. But only silk carried an appreciable rate of duty at 15 per cent and more important to Britain's economic development was her substantial lead over her competitors.

Many historians have quite rightly pointed out that Britain's strong overall trading position was due to a long and sustained rise in prices. What evidence is there for this?

Study the source in conjunction with the source on p.332 showing the course of wholesale prices.

TALKING POINT

Study the table showing Britain's imports and exports and the questions below.

1 What general conclusions can you make about trade during this period?

2 What particular items appear to have contributed to Britain's trading success?

3 What possible weaknesses were there in the base of Britain's trading position?

What conclusions can you make about price rises and profits during this period?

VICTORIAN BOOM 1851–1873

EXPORTS

Total value in millions of pounds
£97m (1854) ⟶ £256m (1873)

Coal 3.5m tons (1851) ⟶ 18m tons (1872)

Iron 0.5m tons (1851) ⟶ 3.5m tons (1872)

Cotton £30m (1853) ⟶ £80m (1870) ⁴⁄₅ production going abroad

Woollen £10m (1853) ⟶ £27m (1870)

Re: exports most important commodity – cotton, wool and silk

IMPORTS

£133m (1854) ⟶ £297m (1873)

Chief imports in 1850 were raw cotton and wool from the colonies and wheat (¼ of British consumption). By 1870 relative importance of raw materials becoming increasingly replaced by foodstuffs. Imports of raw cotton suffered setback in the 1860s when the American civil war disrupted this trade

Overseas trade as proportion of national income

1855–59	17.9%
1860–64	18.5%
1865–69	21.4%
1870–74	22.1%

Balance of payments in millions of pounds

	1850	1870
Exports	83.4	244.1
Imports	103.0	303.3
Balance of trade	−19.6	−59.2
Invisible earnings	+31.2	+112.1
Surplus	11.6	52.9

Tonnage of merchant shipping (British)

1851 3.6m tons ⟶ 1871 5.7m tons

Transfer to shipping

Tonnage of shipping cleared in British ports in foreign trade

1851 9.8m tons ⟶ 1871 28m tons

Britain's share of world trade – between ⅕ and ¼ 1850–1875

Invisible earnings depended on a high level of world trade. This was made more difficult as countries raised tariff barriers – America (1860s) Russia (1877) Germany (1879)

Export of capital
Overseas investments
£230m (1851) ⟶ £700m (1870)

Nearly 41% of all funds invested in overseas railways. Much of it in North and South America which offered high dividends e.g. USA 7.5% as opposed to 4% in Britain

Much of these loans returned to Britain in purchases of railway construction materials and stock. By 1914 41% of British overseas investment in railways

Source H: Selected Price Indices: 1847–50=100*

	Upland or Middling American (raw cotton)	Cotton Yarn	Piece Goods (plain)	Piece Goods (printed)	Stockings and socks	Flax	Linen Yarn	Linen Manufacturers (plain)
1847–50	100	100	100	100	100	100	100	100
1851–55	99	97	93	96	88	118	110	106
1856 60	122	103	96	94	74	108	123	103
1861–65	342	191	145	121	88	125	140	108
1866–70	211	185	130	117	92	121	147	107
1871–75	156	152	107	109	88	110	142	108

	Lincoln Half Hog (raw wool)	Woollen and Worsted Yarn	Woollen Cloths	Flannels	Stuffs	Carpets
1847–50	100	100	100	100	100	100
1851–55	128	102	86	95	82	96
1856–60	165	123	91	103	88	96
1861–65	210	153	115	128	107	99
1866–70	159	156	128	121	118	114
1871–75	204	157	135	122	104	117

	Hides (river plates, dry)	Leather (crop 30–40 lb.)	Pig Iron (scots)	Iron Bars (common)	Coal (London market)	Coal (export)	Glass (common bottles)
1847–50	100	100	100	100	100	100	100
1851–55	135	120	122	111	110	139	93
1856–60	207	167	123	104	103	121	93
1861–65	169	147	113	95	104	129	86
1866–70	152	147	113	95	104	129	86
1871–75	201	175	177	135	138	199	88

Sources: Prices of British goods delivered at Hamburg collated by A. Soetbeer, in Royal Commission on Precious Metals, Accounts and Papers, XIV, C.5512–1 (1888), app. xvi, pp.236–7. The indices for raw cotton, wool flax, hides, pig iron, bar iron and coals are based on prices quoted by A. Sauerbeck, 'Prices of Commodities and the Precious Metals', Journal of the Statistical Society, XLIX (1886).

* The Rousseaux overall price index for 1847–50 is 101, which suggests that this is a reasonable base period adopted by Soetbeer.

The first difficulty is our dependence on wholesale price trends and only those in leading items. We do not have retail prices which tended to fluctuate less than wholesale prices and would show lower price inflation. What does stand out, is substantial price inflation in the early 1850s, followed by stability thereafter.

Contemporaries needed little persuasion that these price rises in the early 1850s were due to the gold discoveries in California (1848) and Australia (1852). This increase in gold supply inflated the price of goods i.e. the money supply rose because of the newly discovered gold which encouraged a rise in the price of goods and services. The diagram below shows how Britain in particular benefitted from this new flow of gold.

Only in the early part of the 1850s were there price rises inducing higher profits. In the long run there were other factors operating to bring prices down. The most important of these have already been alluded to; namely – technological development which reduced unit costs.

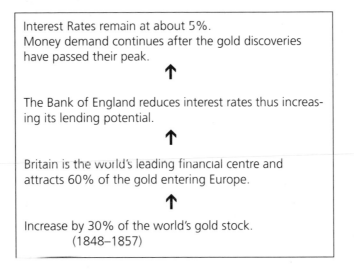

Interest Rates remain at about 5%.
Money demand continues after the gold discoveries have passed their peak.
↑

The Bank of England reduces interest rates thus increasing its lending potential.
↑

Britain is the world's leading financial centre and attracts 60% of the gold entering Europe.
↑

Increase by 30% of the world's gold stock.
 (1848–1857)

Aspects of the economy

Not surprisingly, behind the chief exports were the great industries themselves of which textiles was the leading sector.

Consumption of cotton

Cotton spinning was almost completely mechanised by the 1870s. The self-acting mule, invented in the 1820s, although expensive, became widely adopted. In the woollen industry too, a successful combing machine, invented by Samuel Lister and James Noble, was in widespread use by the 1850s but only in the 1870s did the woollen power-loom triumph. In lace and hosiery the application of powered machinery was still in its infancy whilst flax, jute and hemp were moving rapidly towards complete mechanisation. Thus textiles were the most technically advanced in mechanical invention which contributed not only to an absolute increase in production but an increase per operative.

Year	Consumption of raw cotton
1850	300,000 tons
1870	600,000 tons

Year	Number of power looms
1856	300,000
1886	560,000

Year	Coal Production
1856	65 million tons
1870	110 million tons

Year	Employer of Labour
1851	one-eighth
1871	one-sixth

Coal

Despite the enormous increase in coal production, stimulated by an increasing population, low transport costs and expanding metallurgical, railway and gas industries, technological advancement was slow. Some seams were so narrow that a miner had to crawl out to reverse his pick and were thus unsuitable for mechanisation. Even in larger seams, such as the ten yard seams of Staffordshire, mechanical cutters were rare. As late as 1900 only 2 per cent of coal was cut mechanically. Underground, pit ponies were employed in increasing numbers – 11,000 in 1851 and 70,000 in 1911.

Iron and Steel production

The manufacture of iron and steel witnessed the most important techno-logical developments. A series of three inventions revolutionised the industry by developing mild steel as an alternative to malleable iron.

Iron and Steel output

The life of a steel rail was about thirty times that of an iron one. By 1877 steel rails were most common. By 1877 steel built ships were accepted by Lloyds of London, the Shipping Insurer.

The Bessemer converter

The imperfections in cannon manufacture which came to light during the Crimean War (1854–56) led Sir Henry Bessemer (1813–1898) to develop a cheap process for producing cheap steel. On the publication of his pro-cess there was a rush to adopt the converter but one major drawback prevented its widespread use. The converter required phosphorous-free ores to work successfully, which apart from the domestic source in Cumberland, came from Spain and Sweden. As a consequence the price of steel did not drop dramatically.

Year	Iron Output Steel Output
1850	2 million tons 60,000 tons
1875	6 million tons 2 million tons

Year	Cost of Iron Cost of Steel
1850	£3–£4 per ton £50 per ton
1870	£3–£4 per ton £30 per ton

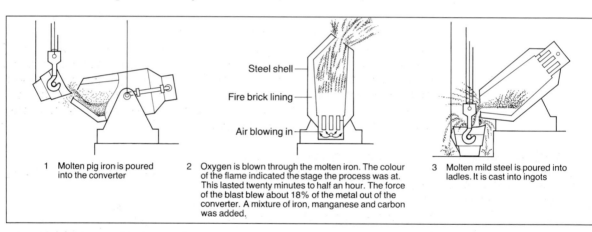

1 Molten pig iron is poured into the converter

2 Oxygen is blown through the molten iron. The colour of the flame indicated the stage the process was at. This lasted twenty minutes to half an hour. The force of the blast blew about 18% of the metal out of the converter. A mixture of iron, manganese and carbon was added.

Steel shell
Fire brick lining
Air blowing in

3 Molten mild steel is poured into ladles. It is cast into ingots

The Open-hearth furnace

Sir William Siemens (1823–1883) developed a furnace which was first used in 1861 for manufacturing glass. Early experiments for steel making proved a failure until 1869. Although Siemen's Open hearth method was a cheaper process than the converter, it still required the use of phospho-rous-free ore. The open-hearth method proved by far the most popular and by the 1870s two-thirds of all British steel was produced in this man-ner.

SIEMEN'S REGENERATIVE OPEN HEARTH.

The Gilchrist-Thomas method

Sidney Gilchrist-Thomas and Percy Gilchrist solved the problem of smelting phosphoric ores in 1879 when the two cousins devised a method of lining furnaces with limestone which absorbed phosphorous. British ironmasters proved slow to adapt to the new process whilst Belgium, France, Germany and the U.S.A., where phosphoric ores were abundant, were quick to utilise this development.

The steam hammer

James Naysmith constructed a superbly accurate machine for delivering precise blows to iron and steel castings.

The development of engineering

Hand in hand with the growth of the iron and steel industry was the development of engineering. Chief among the precision tool makers was the partnership of Joseph Whitworth (1803–87) and the great Tyneside engineering firm of William Armstrong. Whitworth had the largest display of any competitor at the Great Exhibition – twenty-three exhibits of lathes, machines for planning, shaping, slotting, drilling, punching and shearing metal. His greatest contribution to engineering was his crusade on behalf of standardisation. In 1885 every one of his marine and loco-motive engines had the same screw for every given diameter. Britain was slow to standardise parts compared to America where mass production methods were developing over a much more comprehensive range of goods.

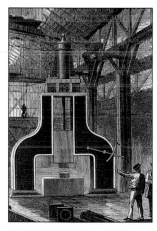

NAYSMITH'S STEAM HAMMER.

The price of mechanical tools, however, remained high and could be prohibitive, e.g. a steam sawing machine cost £700 whereas a pair of sawyers could be hired at the rate of 5s per day. Many new materials were appearing for industrial purposes. Cement began to be more widely used, India rubber and gutta percha (a latex from a species of East Indies tree which quickly became extinct through over-exploitation).

Shipping

Expanding industry required greater transport development. By the 1850s British ship-building wrested the lead from their American competitors although iron tonnage did not exceed wooden until the 1860s. Equally, steam tonnage took some time to establish itself and supersede sail. As late as 1866 only three-quarters of a million tons of shipping was steam driven compared to four and one-half million tons under sail. The development of a steam boiler in 1856, however, hastened the transformation and maintained Britain's lead in shipping well beyond the 1870s.

Employer of labour	
1847	47000
1860	112000
1873	275000

Railways

The development and contribution that railways made to Britain's expanding economy is dealt with more fully in chapter 8. Railways provided an efficient form for the carriage of goods and played a key role in world development, both in terms of capital, equipment and rolling stock.

Year	Mileage
1848	4600
1870	13600

Agriculture

Agriculture in particular basked in a 'golden age' despite the rural population falling as a proportion of the total. The repeal of the Corn Laws had sent anxieties of a great slump in motion which were not realised. The closeness of markets and the development of railways meant farm produce could be carried to markets both rapidly and cheaply.

The farming press, of which James Caird's book, High Farming – The Answer to Protection was the high water mark, experienced a veritable explosion of information on methods of improvement. Farmers' clubs mushroomed. A research station was opened at Rothamstead in 1843 and the Royal Agricultural College at Cirencester three years later.

National income as a percentage of labour		
Year	Income	Percentage
1850	20%	22%
1871	14%	15%

In nearly every case the most important contribution to the adoption of high farming was drainage improvement. In 1845 Thomas Scragg patented a pipe-making machine. Cheap government loans were made available for this particular improvement to cover the relatively inexpensive cost of £3–£4 per acre. Nevertheless the Select Committee of the House of Lords in 1873 stated that only 3 million acres out of a total of 20 million had benefitted in this particular way. To those fields that were well drained could be added a further refinement. Guano (sea-bird excrement) from Peru, although expensive at £10 per ton, could improve yields dramatically.

Not all farms and farmers, however, were able to benefit from such improvements. Some farms were too small whilst insecurity of tenure may have acted as a disincentive to others. Tenants were caught on the horns of a dilemma. If they improved their rented land then they might expect higher rents without compensation for the improvements they had initiated. A statutory right to compensation was not passed until 1875.

The spread of agricultural machinery was slow. Despite the invention of a much improved reaping machine in 1853 and combine harvester in the 1860s, only 47 per cent of the British harvest was mechanically collected as opposed to 80 per cent of the American.

Not all aspects of agriculture shared in the general prosperity. Agricultural labourers wages remained low as the Report on Agricultural in 1867 pointed out,

'It is difficult to expect the landlord to lower his rent in the face of an increasing demand for land and to expect the occupier to raise wages in the face of an increasing demand for rent'.

Any attempt on the part of labourers to form an effective oposition could only be patchy at best.

There were marked regional differences with livestock farmers in general doing best. Nor was the rate of return on agricultural investment encouraging – 3.5 per cent on average compared to the 10 per cent often possible on railway development. Worse was to come after 1870. After that date a grain invasion developed from North America due chiefly to the expansion of steam shipping and transcontinental railways in the U.S.A. which opened up the vast grain growing areas of the mid-west. Neither was pastoral farming in a safe position. In the late 1870s refrigerated shipping brought cargoes of meat to Britain's shores from New Zealand and Australia.

Joint-stock development

Mid-Victorian prosperity, in so far as the label can be usefully employed, was not solely due to technological development. The expanding economy was insatiable in its demand for capital yet much of it was under utilised because of restrictive legislation. Partnerships and joint-stock organisation which would have mobilised large amounts of capital were only possible under the laws of unlimited liability. This meant that investors were responsible to their last penny for any debts incurred by their investments. The Report of the Select committee on Joint Stock companies in 1844 cautiously recommended the adoption of limited liability but this was not put on the statute books until 1856. It took a further two years before limited liability was extended to banks and six years before it applied to insurance companies. Despite the clamour for limited liability there was little rush to form joint-stock companies and it was not until the 1870s that manufacturers began to lose their suspicions of this form of commercial organisation.

The Bank Charter Act of 1844 divided the Bank of England into a Banking Department and an Issue Department. The issue of notes was to correspond exactly to the amount of gold reserves and government securities. It was hoped that this arrangement would eliminate booms and depressions in the value of money. Country banks would lose the privilege if they amalgamated with other banks or let their issue lapse. The number of note-issuing banks declined rapidly thereafter.

The Act did not bring the financial stability intended; indeed the Act had to be suspended in 1847, 1857 and 1866. But the crisis of 1866 proved to be the last of its kind for the Banking Department withdrew from commercial competition to take on the present role of regulating the money market.

Questions

1 Which aspects of the economy contributed to the prosperity of Britain during this period?

2 Is the term 'boom' justified when applied to these industries?

Is the term 'boom' appropriate?

Are historians justified then in referring to the period between 1850–1873 as the Great Victorian Boom? R.A. Church in the conclusion of his book Great Victorian Boom 1850–73, provides a severely qualified affirmative.

'Whilst growth was striking, it is misleading to assume that it was also a period of profit inflation, easy gain and entrepreneurial euphoria. In the largest industrial sector – textiles – price and cost relationships reinforced by intense competition, stimulated innovation, investment, expansion and profit fluctuations. The artificial stimulus of war demands produced similar complex discontinuous development in iron, shipbuilding and coal.'

'Because prices rose spectacularly for a time, because the secular rate of economic growth achieved its nineteenth century maximum, because British expansion and speculation did occur and living standards eventually improved significantly the label contains sufficient truth to conceal their several defects'.

The 'defects' R.A. Church lists are as follows:

1 The difference in economic growth between the preceding and subsequent periods was relatively small.

2 Economic growth was significant but more so at particular times – 1853–56, 1863–65, 1871–73 whilst 1858 was a year of pronounced depression.

3 Different sectors of the economy experienced different price trends and in farming the effect was quite uneven.

4 From 1850–73 there was little industrial euphoria. Share prices rarely rose beyond 3 per cent and only in the 1860s was there a significant speculative boom.

5 Capital exports overseas to primary producing countries certainly generated demand for British goods but it is doubtful whether the policy of free trade assisted in this expansion.

6 The rise of real wages was limited in extent and only showed a particularly marked improvement in the 1860s.

7 The commercial crisis of 1866, if anything, marks a more significant turning point than 1873.

REVIEW

To what extent can the period 1850–73 be regarded as one of prosperity?

Introduction

What has been the traditional interpretation of this period? What doubts have been expressed in describing the period as one of unrivalled prosperity?

Development

- Historiographical problems of labelling.
- Problems of identifying economic cycles.
- Difficulties interpreting statistical data.

Economic indicators

- Gauging the applicability of the term 'prosperity'.
- Exports and Imports.
- Contribution made by free trade.
- Rising prices – rising profits?
- Industrial production and technological development in:

    Textiles

    Coal

    Iron and steel

    Engineering

    Railways and shipping

    Farming

- Contribution made by changing commercial and banking organisation.
- Did all share in the prosperity?

Conclusion

- Was 1850–73 a period of prosperity?
- Is there sufficient coherence in the period to warrant the title?

---

17 The Great Depression 1873–1896

PREVIEW

Did the late Victorian economy fail?

CAUGHT NAPPING!

'Britain was no longer in the van of technological change; instead even the best of her enterprises were usually being dragged in the wake of foreign precursors, like children being jerked along by important adults.'

D.H. Aldcroft and H.W. Richardson, *The British Economy 1870–1939*

'As regards the "Great Depression" itself, surely the outcome of major research has been to destroy once and for all the idea of such a period in any unified sense.'

S.B. Saul, *The Myth of the Great Depression 1873–96*

Contemporaries agreed, and Royal Commissions were directed to investigate, the causes, as they saw it, of economic depression and decline. Were their assessments correct? Does this period deserve the label "Great Depression" and was Britain entering the first phase of her long term decline?

EXAMINING THE EVIDENCE
Statistics for growth or decline?
Source A: The Victorian Boom

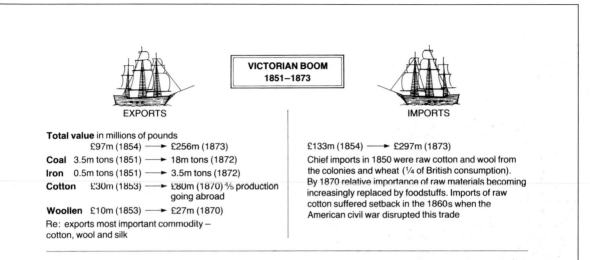

VICTORIAN BOOM
1851–1873

EXPORTS

IMPORTS

Total value in millions of pounds
£97m (1854) ⟶ £256m (1873)

Coal 3.5m tons (1851) ⟶ 18m tons (1872)

Iron 0.5m tons (1851) ⟶ 3.5m tons (1872)

Cotton £30m (1853) ⟶ £80m (1870) ¹⁄₅ production going abroad

Woollen £10m (1853) ⟶ £27m (1870)

Re: exports most important commodity – cotton, wool and silk

£133m (1854) ⟶ £297m (1873)

Chief imports in 1850 were raw cotton and wool from the colonies and wheat (¼ of British consumption). By 1870 relative importance of raw materials becoming increasingly replaced by foodstuffs. Imports of raw cotton suffered setback in the 1860s when the American civil war disrupted this trade

---

Overseas trade as proportion of national income

1855–59	17.9%
1860–64	18.5%
1865–69	21.4%
1870–74	22.1%

Balance of payments in millions of pounds

	1850	1870
Exports	83.4	244.1
Imports	103.0	303.3
Balance of trade	−19.6	−59.2
Invisible earnings	+31.2	+112.1
Surplus	11.6	52.9

Tonnage of merchant shipping (British)

1851 3.6m tons ⟶ 1871 5.7m tons

Transfer to shipping

Tonnage of shipping cleared in British ports in foreign trade

1851 9.8m tons ⟶ 1871 28m tons

Britain's share of world trade –
between ⅕ and ¼ 1850–1875

Invisible earnings depended on a high level of world trade. This was made more difficult as countries raised tariff barriers – America (1860s) Russia (1877) Germany (1879)

Export of capital
Overseas investments
£230m (1851) ⟶ £700m (1870)

Nearly 41% of all funds invested in overseas railways. Much of it in North and South America which offered high dividends e.g. USA 7.5% as opposed to 4% in Britain

Much of these loans returned to Britain in purchases of railway construction materials and stock. By 1914 41% of British overseas investment in railways

Source B

Economic growth (% per year 1850–1913)		
Years	Real Income per head	Exports
1850–60	1.4	5.7
1861–70	2.5	3.2
1871–80	0.8	2.8
1881–90	3.5	2.9
1891–1900	1.2	0.4
1901–10	0.4	5.4

Source C

Growth rate of real gross national product (% per annum)	
Year	Rate of Growth
1858–73	2.8
1873–1900	2.0
1900–10	1.2

Source D

Growth rate of industrial output (% per annum)	
Year	Rate of Growth
1856–73	3.2
1873–1900	2.2
1900–12	1.6

Source E

Growth rates of Britain, Germany and the U.S.A. (1870–1913 % per annum)			
Country	Industrial output	G.D.P. per head	Output per man hour
U.S.A.	4.7	2.2	2.4
Germany	4.1	1.8	2.1
Britain	2.1	1.3	1.5

Source F: The total value of imports and exports

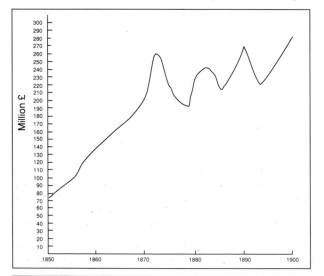

Source G

Britain's balance of payments in millions of pounds 1870–1913			
	1870	*1900*	*1913*
Exports	244.1	354.1	634.8
Imports	303.1	523.1	768.7
Balance of commodity trade	−59.2	−168.7	−133.9
Invisible earnings	112.1	212.7	367.8
Surplus of balance of payments	+52.9	+44.0	233.9

Source H: Selected Price Indices: 1847–50=100*

	Upland or Middling American (raw cotton)	Cotton Yarn	Piece Goods (plain)	Piece Goods (printed)	Stockings and socks	Flax	Linen Yarn	Linen Manufacturers (plain)
1847–50	100	100	100	100	100	100	100	100
1851–55	99	97	93	96	88	118	110	106
1856–60	122	103	96	94	74	108	123	103
1861–65	342	191	145	121	88	125	140	108
1866–70	211	185	130	117	92	121	147	107
1871–75	156	152	107	109	88	110	142	108

	Lincoln Half Hog (raw wool)	Woollen and Worsted Yarn	Woollen Cloths	Flannels	Stuffs	Carpets
1847–50	100	100	100	100	100	100
1851–55	128	102	86	95	82	96
1856–60	165	123	91	103	88	96
1861–65	210	153	115	128	107	99
1866–70	159	156	128	121	118	114
1871–75	204	157	135	122	104	117

	Hides (river plates, dry)	Leather (crop 30–40 lb.)	Pig Iron (scots)	Iron Bars (common)	Coal (London market)	Coal (export)	Glass (common bottles)
1847–50	100	100	100	100	100	100	100
1851–55	135	120	122	111	110	139	93
1856–60	207	167	123	104	103	121	93
1861–65	169	147	113	95	104	129	86
1866–70	152	147	113	95	104	129	86
1871–75	201	175	177	135	138	199	88

Sources: Prices of British goods delivered at Hamburg collated by A. Soetbeer, in Royal Commission on Precious Metals, Accounts and Papers, XIV, C.5512–1 (1888), app. xvi, pp.236–7. The indices for raw cotton, wool flax, hides, pig iron, bar iron and coals are based on prices quoted by A. Sauerbeck, 'Prices of Commodities and the Precious Metals', Journal of the Statistical Society, XLIX (1886).

* The Rousseaux overall price index for 1847–50 is 101, which suggests that this is a reasonable base period adopted by Soetbeer.

Source 1

Prices of iron and steel		
Steel rails	£12.05 per ton (1874)	£5.37 per ton (1883)
Iron rails	£9.90 per ton (1874)	£5.00 per ton (1883)

Study sources A to I.

1 Does the phrase 'Great Depression' i.e. a period of low economic activity marked by a rapid rise in unemployment, appear to be an appropriate label for the period 1873–96?

2 According to these tables what appears to be a growing weakness in the British economy?

3 For each of the sources indicate what they convey about the performance of the British economy.

4 Which of the factors do you consider to be of most significance in the performance of the British economy?

The appropriatness of the term 'Great Depression'

None of these tables show a marked overall slowing down of rates of growth except in relation to other competitors. Indeed in some there is an actual improvement such as a growth in real income per head. Furthermore trends in industrial production and manufacturing productivity continued to improve. The volume of shipping in British ports increased. There was more goods traffic on the railways, more wool and cotton produced, 51 per cent more coal hewn, and the smelting of pig iron doubled. Nor did capital investment at home substantially decline.

Upon what factors therefore has the notion of a Great Depression been founded? Thousands of speeches, hundreds of pamphlets, several government inquiries and the Royal Commission on the Depression of Trade of 1886 attempted to provide the answer. Three elements were defined as the characteristics of the 'depression': a slowing down of the rate of export growth, falling profits and prices and a depressed agricultural sector. Nearly all wholesale prices fell, 40 per cent overall. Yet, as outlined in the previous chapter this was largely due to technological change. Working people benefitted in terms of a real rise in incomes. Thus in these terms the period can hardly be described as one constituting a 'depression'.

Yet there was some cause for concern. Perhaps the most disturbing feature was the failure of Britain to match the growth rates of her principal rivals both in terms of economic production and exports. Now this slower pace should not be confused with a lack of growth. Productivity and the volume of trade increased but not at the same pace as her competitors.

TALKING POINT

Are these factors sufficient to describe this period as the 'Great Depression'?

World manufacturing output		
	1870 %	1913 %
Britain	33	14.1
U.S.A.	25	35.9
Germany	*	15.9
* No figure available		

EXAMINING THE EVIDENCE
A depression in agriculture
Certainly a case can be made for a depression in agriculture.

Source A

Net imports of wheat Annual average	Millions of cwts.	%age of imported wheat consumed in Britain
1840–49	10.7	
1850–59	19.3	about 50%
1860–69	33.7	
1870–79	50.4	about 70%
1880–89	70.3	
1890–1900	85.9	
1900–1909	102.6	

Source B

Numbers employed in agriculture	
18/1	1.6 million
1891	1.4 million
1901	1.3 million

Source C

Gross agricultural output	
1867–76	13%
1894 1903	4%

Source D

Price of meat products
Beef 11% price fall by mid 1890s
Mutton and lamb 8% price fall

Source E

Agricultural rents
Grazing counties of northern England rose by 18%
Arable areas of southern England fell by 30%

Source F

Agricultural productivity compared to Industrial		
	1867–69	1886–93
Agriculture	rose by 15%	
Industry	rose by 23%	

Source G

Share of national income	
1855–59	20%
1870–74	13%
1895–99	6%

Source H

Weather conditions	
Poor years	1873
	1875
	1876
	1879 (worst of the century)
1881–83	Liver rot in sheep Foot and mouth epidemic in cattle

Source I: The Royal Commission Inquiry into the 'Depression'?
Can you explain to the Commission how it is that the fulfilment of these prophecies (of depression in agriculture) have been delayed so long a time, because we have passed through a period of great prosperity since the Repeal of the Corn Laws?

I think I have already stated that the discovery of gold and a series of great wars averted for a number of years the effects of free trade, and it was only when those great wars ceased, and when things were left to find their own level, that the depressive effects of free trade made themselves fully felt in the country.

G.W.P.A. Bentinck M.P. to the Royal Commission on Agriculture 1881

Source J

Crop acreage in Great Britain						
Millions of acres				**Percentage of the total**		
	1872	*1895*	*1913*	*1872*	*1895*	*1913*
Wheat	3.6	1.4	1.8	12	4	5.5
Surface cultivated	13.4	10.9	10.4	44	33	31
Fallow, grass and pasture	17.3	21.8	21.9	56	67	69
Market gardening	0.2	0.3	0.4	0.8	1	1

1 (a) What appears to be the principal reason why British agriculture appears to falter during this period?

(b) Source H shows a period of poor harvests. Normally prices would rise when there was shortage of production. Why, therefore, did the price of wheat not rise during this period?

2 What happens to the importance of British agriculture within British economy during this period?

3 (a) Which sector of British agriculture appears to fare best?

(b) For what reasons do you think this particular sector of British agriculture suffers the least?

4 Two Royal Commissions inquired into the state of British farming. Many of the witnesses were large landowners from the Midlands. How would this affect the weight of evidence and the judgements made by the Commissioners?

A 'Depression' in agriculture?

The effect of the Depression was felt very unevenly in agriculture. From around 1875 the combination of railway and steamshipping were making an impact on foreign food imports, particularly supplies of American wheat which supplanted the traditional Russian supply. From the 1880s cheap refrigerated meat began to arrive from New Zealand and Argentina although this meat was destined for the cheaper end of the market. Wheat

TALKING POINT

The impact on farming was very diverse. Is it possible, therefore, to come to a general conclusion?

prices markedly fell from £2.70 a quarter ton to £1.35 in the 1890s, as did the acreage under wheat. Australian wool too, severely dented home production.

Grain farmers suffered the most whilst those specialising in meat, dairy products and market gardening fared better due to a number of internal factors. Population rose by 5 million between 1870–90, urbanisation spread and a real rise in incomes contributed to increased demand. Furthermore the importation of cheap grains reduced the cost of fodder crops for livestock farmers.

Considerable restructuring of farming took place during this period in order to cope with changing conditions. Farmers could either diversify or switch to alternative produce where possible. Fresh milk never suffered a price decrease and nor did cheese. Orchard acreage increased from 150,000 acres to almost 250,000.

Thus the notion of a general depression throughout agriculture is untenable. E.P. Thompson concludes that perhaps a third of farmers, mainly in the western counties, enjoyed moderate to unmistakeable prosperity, whilst a further third maintained their position and a final third, mainly in the Midlands and East Anglia experienced a depression.

Examining the Evidence
A slower rate of growth

Is there any more substance to the charge that industry experienced depression? Before we examine the evidence the student of this period must be aware of the following pitfalls.

Note

In 1853 the Americans held their own Great Exhibition in New York. Joseph Whitworth, the great engineer was sent by the British government. He remarked the Americans showed an amount of ingenuity, combined with undoubted energy which we could do well to imitate if we meant to hold our position in the great markets of the world.

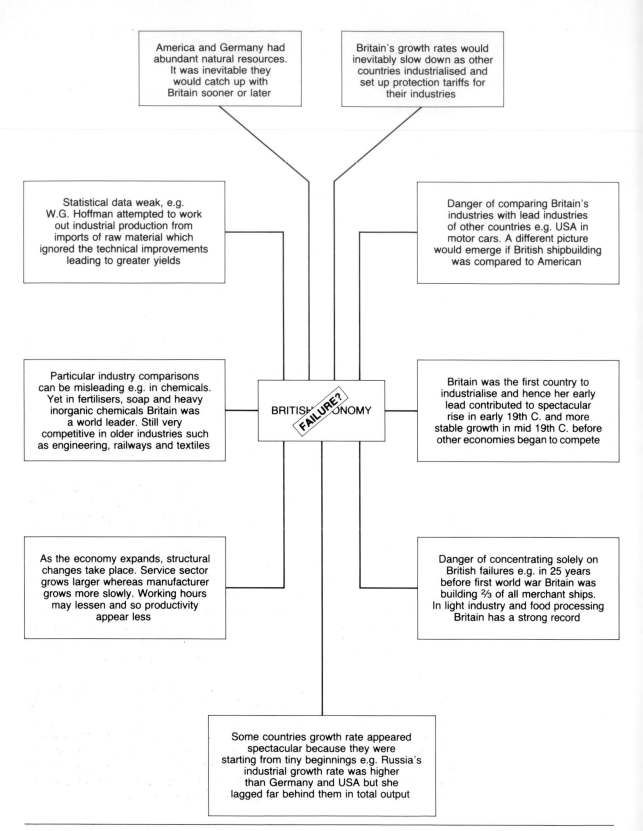

America and Germany had abundant natural resources. It was inevitable they would catch up with Britain sooner or later

Britain's growth rates would inevitably slow down as other countries industrialised and set up protection tariffs for their industries

Statistical data weak, e.g. W.G. Hoffman attempted to work out industrial production from imports of raw material which ignored the technical improvements leading to greater yields

Danger of comparing Britain's industries with lead industries of other countries e.g. USA in motor cars. A different picture would emerge if British shipbuilding was compared to American

Particular industry comparisons can be misleading e.g. in chemicals. Yet in fertilisers, soap and heavy inorganic chemicals Britain was a world leader. Still very competitive in older industries such as engineering, railways and textiles

BRITISH ECONOMY FAILURE?

Britain was the first country to industrialise and hence her early lead contributed to spectacular rise in early 19th C. and more stable growth in mid 19th C. before other economies began to compete

As the economy expands, structural changes take place. Service sector grows larger whereas manufacturer grows more slowly. Working hours may lessen and so productivity appear less

Danger of concentrating solely on British failures e.g. in 25 years before first world war Britain was building ⅔ of all merchant ships. In light industry and food processing Britain has a strong record

Some countries growth rate appeared spectacular because they were starting from tiny beginnings e.g. Russia's industrial growth rate was higher than Germany and USA but she lagged far behind them in total output

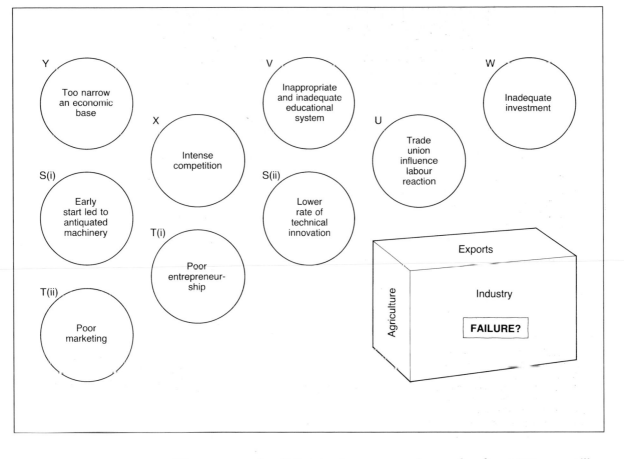

The reasons for Britain's slower rate of growth after 1870 are still a matter of debate amongst historians. Many causes are involved for no single or overriding factor can explain the complex process satisfactorily.

Source A: Britain's early start in industrialisation.

Many have suggested that Britain suffered a positive disadvantage from her early start in industrialisation ... The fact that old plant and old locations are actually in existence should be no handicap ... and if it pays the newcomer to buy certain plant it pays the older producer to scrap whatever he had and buy the new one too. The latecomer may learn from his predecessors, avoid mistakes ... This may give him a higher rate of growth but it offers no reason why the newcomer should overtake the early start technologically.

In practice there is more to it. The early start may find it harder, for institutional reasons, to break away from old methods and locations; the skills and practices of both management and trade unions may be unsuited to the new industrial environment but be deeply resistant to change. However, it is important to remember that Britain retained a wide lead in many industrial sectors to 1914. Most of these had their roots in the industrial revolution; cotton textiles, textile machinery, heavy machine tools, custom built locomotives, ships and steam engines.

... What reason could there be for not investing in cotton mills in 1905 when profits expected and realised up to the war were comparable with anywhere else.

S.B. Saul, *The Myth of the Great Depression 1873–96*

Source B: Entrepreneurial skill

Was poor entrepreneurship responsible for declining growth rates after 1870? ... British consuls abroad frequently complained that British businessmen were complacent and unenterprising compared with their rivals. The 'Economist' and other journals pointed to the slow rate at which British entrepreneurs took up new technological advances. Examples included ring spinning of cotton textiles, the Solway process in the production of soda, the use of phosphoric ores in steel production.

The Myth of the Great Depression 1873–1896 S.D. Saul

Source C: Outdated educational system

... Public schools have been criticised for teaching traditional subjects like classics rather than the more relevant subjects like applied science or mathematics. It has been claimed, too, that public schools bred an attitude of contempt for industry and trade, directing the most able of Britain's youth towards the professions, the services or the Empire.

In recent years however, historians have been less critical ... Studies of individual industries have generally concluded that where particular techniques were adopted only slowly in Britain there were sound economic reasons.

It has also been pointed out that in areas where market conditions were favourable Britain showed no lack of dynamic entrepreneurship after 1870. In shipbuilding, for example, Britain continued to dominate world markets ... in retailing too ...

Why should it be rational for entrepreneurs to use old methods? When markets are growing only slowly it may well not pay entrepreneurs to invest in expensive new machinery ... Thus the opportunities for investing in new technology were often limited by the nature of the markets facing British entrepreneurs.

M. Falkus, *Britain Transformed: An Economic and Social History 1700–1914*

Source D: A restrictive labour force

Probably the truth of the matter is that outside a few isolated pursuits ... old fashioned outright rejection of machinery was a rare occurrence ...

On the other hand it cannot be said that mechanisation was invariably greeted with enthusiasm by workers and union leaders alike ... Caution, and perhaps even some hostility, might colour their utterances but their strategy was a far cry from total rejection.

... In the end one is left with the impression that although a policy of go-slow was by and large not part of the official credo of trade unionisation, the rank and file were not immune from the attractions of such a policy ...

... It was the intrusion of unskilled workers into various British industries that prompted the more powerful dominated unions into frantic efforts to hold the line by attempting to force employers to accept the union view that every new machine or process, no matter how negligible the skill required, should remain the reserve of the skilled operative.

... rigid adherence to a specific apprentice-journeyman ratio remained a common policy of unions still trying to use apprenticeships as a protective device in the face of innovation, skill displacement and invasion by the unskilled, and hence provide the additional damning evidence for those who might demonstrate that it was trade union obstructionism that prevented the country from reaping the full benefits of technological evidence.

A.L. Levine, Industrial Retardation in Britain 1880–1914

Source E: Outmoded educational system

Public schools ... had existed long before the nineteenth century, but it was in the latter and middle parts of the century that they expanded. An important cause of this expansion was the support given them by the richer and more established entrepreneurs who increasingly sent their sons to these schools.

... the curriculum still contained the classics ... it is not that this kind of leadership taught at the schools was necessarily hostile to trading and industrial leadership, it was irrelevant.

... The small number of those undergoing a public school education at this time, in proportion to the population as a whole, might suggest that these schools could not have had the far reaching effects on Britain's economy that are being claimed. However, the extraordinary inadequacy of English education, which was revealed so clearly in the Taunton Commission, meant that the alternative to the sort of secondary education offered by the public school was, very often, no secondary education at all ...

This meant that there was no reservoir of managerial and technological talent which could supply English industry with new management, which might, even within the existing structure of ownership, have done something to mitigate the harmful effects of the 'absentee industrialist'.

D. Ward, The Public Schools and Industry in Britain after 1870 Journal of
Contemporary History II 1967

Source F: Poor investment

In less precise terms the period might be entitled 'What happened when the railways were built?' Of course, railway building went on, but never in these decades on a scale sufficient to dominate the British capital market and capital goods industries. Savings moved into other channels – channels less profitable to the investor. The expectations of 1871–73 had encouraged great expansion of plant. Cheap money, new inventions, and the need to reduce costs carried on the process in the decade that followed ... Everywhere businessmen began to search for an escape – in the insured markets of positive imperialism, in tariffs, in monopolies and employers' associations. None of these trends advanced very far in the Great Depression. But they were symptoms of the great ailment ... The mid century blandishments of the profit motive had begun to lose their force. Yet there is little evidence that British industries were starved of capital. Investment rates were low throughout the period 1873–1913 implying there was no lack of investment funds for British firms.

W.W. Rostow, *The British Economy of the Nineteenth Century*

Source G: Intensive foreign competition

Britain was finding it difficult to penetrate the rich and rapidly expanding markets of industrial Europe and America. In part this could be explained by the spread of tariff protection in these countries, but the chief factor was undoubtedly the increasing competition.

... In the more under-developed areas of the world Britain's economic performance was weakening ... Some of Britain's traditional customers were beginning to produce the goods they had once bought from Britain ... But to a large extent it was the sale of German and American products ... Germany, in particular was extremely successful and by 1913 she was exporting more than Britain to the primary producing countries. Only in the markets of the semi-industrial countries did Britain continue to maintain a substantial lead and even this was being challenged by the early twentieth century.

The extent of the foreign competition should not be exaggerated ... in 1913 Britain was still the largest exporter in the world, though only by a small margin, whilst her share of total world exports fell much less dramatically in this period than for manufactured commodities ...

D. Aldcroft, *The Development of British Industry and Foreign competition 1875–1914*

Source H: Britain's narrow economic base

The over-commitment to certain basic staple industries interferred with the growth of new industries in three main ways. In the first place it led to a scarcity of production facilities for these industries. Secondly, the long and unchallenged predominance of Britain's staple industries affected entrepreneurial psychology and lulled businessmen into making decisions and judgements based too much on past experience, which led to a misplaced emphasis on the short run as against long term benefits. Thirdly, the institutional framework against which decisions are made was so moulded by the lop-sided industrial structure than the adoption of new industries was less economic in Britain than abroad.

H.W. Richardson, *The British Economy 1870–1939*

Source I: Putting the problem in context

Between 1860–1914 Britain certainly lost the predominant position which she had held as the leading or only manufacturing nation but this was not because of the deficiencies within the British economy. It stemmed instead, from the increasing complexity of the international economy, and of the national economies within it. This brought to Britain a new role as a pivot of international trade and investment, which demanded adjustments within the domestic economy to enable Britain to carry out that role. Although some of these adjustments were difficult and painful, they were carried out sufficiently well to enable Britain to retain a commanding position in the world's economy ... Adjustments would have continued to be necessary, as the old staple industries of coal, cotton, iron and steel and shipbuilding lost their importance and were replaced by a wider spectrum of manufacturing and service industries. The advent of the first world war made it essential for these adjustments to be carried out rapidly, and the pain of the 1920s and 30s, were part of the price.

R. Floud and D. McCloskey (eds), *The Economic History of Britain. Vol II*

These sources represent fragments of historians' interpretations of the late Victorian economy, albeit the main substance of their argument. Using this information as a basis construct an answer to the following inter-related questions. The elements in your answer are arranged around the question. Your task is to prioritise the factors to produce a coherent discussion of the problem.

---

1 List all the reasons given in the sources which claim to account for Britain's industrial 'failure' in the late nineteenth century.

2 What order of priority might you place them in?

3 How would you catagorise these factors?

4 What relationships do they have to one another?

FAIR TRADE OR FREE TRADE?

The economic gospel of free trade had served Britain well whilst she had been the leading, if not the sole, manufacturing nation. As the cold wind of competition grew and economic tariff barriers were raised by competitors the appropriatness of Free Trade came increasingly under question. In some quarters the cry of 'Fair Trade' was raised and a Fair Trade League, established in 1881, demanded the imposition of reasonable tariffs on foreign manufacturers tariffs could be removed on. The goods of any country as soon as they agreed to admit British goods without duty. Others saw economic salvation in a protected Empire market. An Imperial Federation League was created in 1884. A Colonial and Indian Exhibition was staged in 1886 to popularise this view and by a series of Colonial Conferences, starting in 1887, a system of Imperial preference was worked out. Neither tariff reform organisation made much headway in the light of Britain's need for unrestricted importation of foodstuffs and raw materials. Yet the very existence of these organisations reflect the waning of British industrial confidence and the emergence of economic tensions which were to contribute to the outbreak of hostilities in 1914.

C. COMMENTS ON TRADE

The staunchest Free Trader cannot afford to overlook the advantages of the German protective system. English iron and steel, on entering Germany, are handicapped with a duty varying in amount, but reaching to over twelve and one half per cent per cwt. for tin plate. This makes it very difficult for us to compete with home-made materials. It likewise enables the Germans to raise his prices to his compatriots and screw such a profit from them that he can afford a big reduction on his export prices, so that he cuts at his English rival in two directions. The duty makes our goods too dear to sell in Germany, at the same time it makes German goods so cheap in the world market that we are being undersold therein and ousted therefrom.

E.E. Williams, Made in Germany (1896)

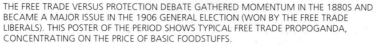

A.

THE FREE TRADE VERSUS PROTECTION DEBATE GATHERED MOMENTUM IN THE 1880S AND BECAME A MAJOR ISSUE IN THE 1906 GENERAL ELECTION (WON BY THE FREE TRADE LIBERALS). THIS POSTER OF THE PERIOD SHOWS TYPICAL FREE TRADE PROPOGANDA, CONCENTRATING ON THE PRICE OF BASIC FOODSTUFFS.

E.
Contemporary observers emphasised the failure of British entrepreneurship and the imminent dangers of German competition much as a newspaper cries up morbid aspects of the news. That was the way one sold articles or attracted the notice of officials in London. Besides there is no such thing as fashion in opinions, and this was clearly one of the popular dirges of the day.

D. Landes, The Unbound Prometheus 1969.

Questions

1 Study sources A and B.
(a) Both sources apply their propaganda to the sale of consumer goods but the intended result is meant to be different. How can they assume different results will acrue from the same tactic?
(b) Refer to the detail in source B.
How does the artist convey his message?
(c) What is the attitude to foreigners displayed in this cartoon?

2 Study sources C and D.
(a) How do they differ in the way in which they convey their point of view?
(b) Why do they differ in the way they put across their point of view?
(c) Which source might you expect to be more effective?

3 Study source E.
(a) What advantage does this secondary source have compared to the preceding sources?
(b) Because this source possesses these particular advantages does it make it more useful to an historian studying this period?

D.
LIBERAL ELECTION SLOGAN 1906.

B.

BRITAIN'S FREE TRADE POLICIES WERE BLAMED FOR GERMANY'S SUCCESS BY SOME. THIS CARTOON WAS PUBLISHED BY THE IMPERIAL TARIFF REFORM COMMITTEE. TARIFF REFORMERS, LED BY JOSEPH CHAMBERLAIN, WANTED TO END FREE TRADE AND TO PROTECT BRITISH INDUSTRY FROM FOREIGN COMPETITION.

REVIEW

Was the Great Depression of 1873–96 myth or reality?

Did the late Victorian economy fail?

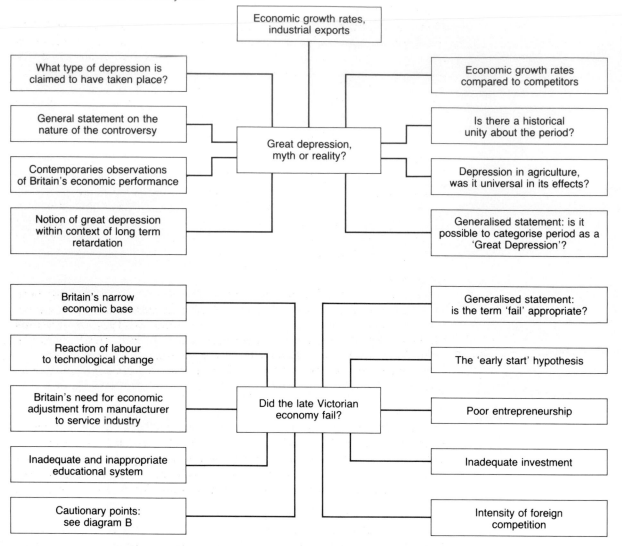

The emergence of new industries

The British economy was dominated by the old staples but alongside these giants, newer and ultimately essential industries were beginning to emerge. How successful were they and were they sufficient to provide future diversification as the old staples began to decline?

The Bicycle

Originated as an industry after 1869 and was centred on Coventry. By 1879 there were 60 firms with 700 employees. The industry experienced a boom after 1885 due to:

(a) Technological innovation – John Kemp Stanley introduced the diamond frame.

(b) Dynamic marketing – By 1913 Britain was exporting 150,000 machines compared to Germany's 89,000.

The motor car

Developed from the cycling industry with its heyday in the early 1900s. Technological innovation incuded machinery for manufacturing ball bearings, Dunlop's pneumatic tyre, the Napier cylinder engine and the Lanchester gearing and hand-brake.

Annual output reached 33,000 in 1914 but it was an American dominated industry which produced 485,000 in the same year. The American market adapted quickly to the mass manufactured market whilst Britain relied on craftsmanship.

Electrical industries

Failed to keep pace with the German and American industries for in Britain gas production was much cheaper. Standardisation of electrical fittings was only slowly achieved. Electricity powered about one-quarter of the mines and factories by 1914 and about 2000 miles of tramways. Many British electrical firms were off-shoots of giant German and American corporations.

Chemical industries

Britain led the world in glass production until 1880 when it was displaced into third position. (Soda ash was used both in glass and soap manufacture) In soap manufacture Britain led the world in 1914. In dyestuffs Germany led the world capturing nine-tenths of the world market in 1880. In superphosphates and sulphuric acid America led in the field.

Britain generally lingered behind in technological development tending to dismiss the value of research.

Retailing

Britain experienced a revolution in High St. retailing outlets and goods sold. Chain stores such as Sainsbury's and Boots made their appearance at this time. The basis of this success was due to the cheap import of raw materials from cocoa to wood pulp. In addition real wages rose as per capita consumption increased. Per capita consumption rose by 30 per cent.

Changing structure of British industry.

In 1885 almost all businesses were run by individuals or partners. By 1914 company ownership was usual although private companies, which were allowed limited liability in 1907, were still the more numerous. There was also a growth in the number of companies from 9,344 in 1884 to 62,762 in 1914, of which 77 per cent were private.

These structural changes meant;

- Greater financial reserves.
- Effective accounting methods.
- Growth of professional management.
- Growth of trade associations to control prices and production quotas.
- Growth of combines involving either vertical or horizontal integration.

18 Government and the Individual in late nineteenth century Britain

PREVIEW

FORCED FELLOWSHIP. PUNCH MAGAZINE.

'If Socialism means a wise use of the forces of all for the good of each; if it means the legal protection of the weak against the strong; if it means the performance by public bodies of duties which individuals could not perform either so well or not at all for themselves, why then, the principles of Socialism are admitted all over the field of our social activity.'

John Morley, a liberal spokesman, 1889.
Quoted in A.M. McBriar, *Fabian Socialism and English Politics 1884–1918* (1962)

Government and the individual – A changing relationship?

At first appearance it looks as though a neat division exists within the nineteenth century in respect of the relationship between the individual and government. From 1800–1830 there is a determined reluctance to legislate. From about 1825–1870 there is a growing willingness to legislate, based upon an evangelical and utilitarian rationale, to mitigate the worst effects of industrialisation. By 1870 government intervention appears to mature and collectivism to gain respectability.

It is a temptation to see the neat dividing lines in the relationship between the individual and government but one which must be carefully resisted. In the same way as government responded to the social problems of the 1830s and 1840s as exceptions to the general rule, government in the post 1870s was responding to different economic and social conditions in the firm belief that they too were legislating only where individualist action had failed to find a solution.

Individualist philosophy could condone legislation but only in so far as it regulated a problem. In no sense was it envisaged that the state should play a positive role in promoting interventionist policies i.e. the state should be reactive not proactive. The free market must be maintained and society protected only when there was a greater evil.

To understand this enables us to come to terms with what appears to be the paradox of greater collectivist action in a society which espoused an individualist philosophy. Sidney Webb's description of the individualist politician illustrates the point neatly.

'The individualist town councillor will walk along the municipal pavement, lit by municipal gas and cleared by municipal brooms with municipal water, and seeing by the municipal clock in the municipal market that he is too early to meet his children coming from the municipal school ... in the municipal reading rooms ... where he intends to consult some of the national publications in order to prepare his next speech in the municipal town hall in favour of the nationalisation of canals and the increase of the government control over the railway system. "Socialism, Sir," he will say, don't waste the time of a practical man by your fantastic absurdities. Self-help, Sir, individual self-help, that's what made our city what it is.'

S. Webb, *The Times 23 August 1902*

TALKING POINT

How did such a 'paradox' exist i.e. of collectivist action in an individualist society?

Whatever the rationale for government intervention there is little doubt that the pace of legislation after 1870 increased and the forces advocating collectivist action grew in power. Public health, housing education, enfranchisement, trade unions, railways, industry and agriculture were all areas of government attention. The 'Great Depression'; pressure to complete administration already begun; the need to win over newly enfranchised working class voters; the evidence of massive poverty were all factors which impelled the government to legislate. Some historians have identified in these initiatives the origins of the concept of the welfare state. Whether the use of this term is justified or not we will examine in the next chapter. Meanwhile decide for yourself whether there appeared distinct changes in perceptions of social problems and if there were, whether this had an effect on the role of government.

The growing awareness of poverty

So deeply imbued was the individualistic ethic in British society that the eighth annual Report of the Charity Organisation Society (1876) could confidently assert that,

'The principle is, that it is good for the poor that they should meet all the ordinary contingencies of life, relying not upon public or private charity, but upon their own industry and thrift, and upon the powers of self-help that are to be developed by individual and collective effort ... It is a harmful misuse of money to spend it on assisting the labouring classes to meet contingencies which they themselves should have anticipated and provided for.'

The Growth of charities

If the individualistic ethic failed in some instances then a host of charitable institutions could be relied upon to provide assistance. In this manner the middle class benefactors could congratulate themselves on their sense of social responsibility and, at the same time, prevent the undermining of the principle of self-help. And charitable help there was a-plenty. Housing, fallen women, drunken men, distressed gentlefolk could all find a charity to rescue them from their particular 'failing'. Many major current charities were founded at this time – the YMCA, Barnados, RSPCA and RNLI. Charity as the ideal method of assistance was encapsulated by a charity social worker C.S. Lock, when he claimed, 'Charity is a social regenerator ... We have to use charity to create the power of self-help.'

The proliferation of charities in mid- and late Victorian England provides testimony to an awareness of social problems and poverty but not necessarily to a change in attitude toward the problem. Yet the revelation that poverty was widespread should have come as no unexpected discovery. Chadwick had described the vicious cycle of poverty, ill-health and housing in his 'Report on the Sanitary Conditions of the Labouring Poor' in 1842. A host of novelists had graphically portrayed poverty in best-sellers. Henry Mayhew, a London journalist, published a series of articles exposing the misery, despair and precariousness of working life of which, 'a large body of persons of whom the public had less knowledge than of the most distant tribes of the earth.' The articles focused on particular trades and recounted the difficulties experienced by the breadwinners' families. These articles appeared in the 'Morning Chronicle' during the 1850s and were later compiled into best selling volumes.

The relative prosperity during the 1850s persuaded some that the problem of poverty was either small or diminishing. This was, of course, not the case.

TALKING POINT

To what extent should society depend upon charities?

Note

A survey in the early 1860s calculated that charitable contributions in London alone amounted to between £5.5 million and £7 million pounds annually. In the same years the total poor law expenditure amounted to less than £6 million.

TALKING POINT

If there had been so much written about poverty why had it apparently failed to improve the condition of the poor?

EXAMINING THE EVIDENCE
Changing attitudes to poverty

Re-read Chapter 17 'The Great Depression?' and bear the following questions in mind.

---

1 How might increased competition affect the government's concern about social welfare legislation during the period of the 'Great Depression'?

2 There was no reduction in national income during this period and real wages rose, yet, there was considerable poverty. How might this affect society's belief in self-help?

Source A: Extension of the vote

1867 Enfranchisement of some urban workers

1884 Enfranchisement of some rural workers

1885 A re-distribution of parliamentary seats. After this date most constituencies were single member seats with electorates of similar size.

Source B: Growth of Socialism

1881 Foundation of the Social and Democratic Federation by Henry Mayers Hyndman, a wealthy radical influenced by Marxism. The SDF espoused a political programme similar to the Peoples' Charter. They advocated free education, an eight hour day, State-aided housing schemes, public works and a graduated tax system. Despite this programme the SDF failed to attract a mass working class following.

1884 A split occurs in the SDF and a breakaway Socialist League led by Eleanor Marx, Karl Marx's daughter and William Morris, poet and artist.

1884 Foundation of the Fabian Society. This organisation took its name from the Roman general Fabius Maximus, who patiently waited and wore the enemy down rather than face them in open battle. In the same way this group of intellectuals believed it could wear down capitalism gradually by argument and propaganda. Leading Fabians included the historians Sidney and Beatrice Webb and the playwright, George Bernard Shaw.

1893 The Independent Labour Party is formed in Bradford under the leadership of an ex-Scots miner, Keir Hardie.

1901 The SDF, Fabians and trade unionists unite as the Labour Representation Committee.

Source C: Socialist belief

I believe that the whole basis of Society, with its contrasts of rich and poor, is incurably vicious ... now it seems to me that feeling this, I am bound to act for the destruction of the system which seems to me mere oppression and obstruction, such a system can only be destroyed, it seems to me, by the united discontent of numbers; isolated acts of a few persons in the middle and upper classes, which the system had bred, is the natural and necessary instrument of its destruction.

Letter from W. Morris to Mr. C.E. Maurice, a Liberal. July 1 1883. Quoted in J.W. Mackail's *Life of William Morris II*

Source D: Preventing Socialism

Social legislation, as I conceive it, is not merely to be distinguished from Socialist legislation but is its most direct opposite and its most effective antidote. Socialism will never get possession of the great body of public opinion … among the working class or any other working class if those who wield the collective forces of the community show themselves desirous to ameliorate every legitimate grievance and to put Society upon a proper and more solid basis.

A.J. Balfour in a speech in Manchester. 16 June 1895. Balfour became a Conservative Prime Minister. Quoted in E. Halevy, *Imperialism and the Rise of Labour* (1951)

Source E: Chamberlain and Liberal Interventionism

Joseph Chamberlain entered Parliament in 1876 as leader of the powerful National Liberal Foundation. This organisation was a radical wing of the Party which pioneered active interventionist municipal government. They were opposed to by the aristocratic Whig families which had dominated the Party. His social reform aspirations foundered upon the wider political stage. He opposed Gladstone's policy of Irish Home Rule and split the Liberal Party, founding his own political group, the Liberal Unionists.

Source F

Old age pensions were introduced into Germany 1889 and New Zealand in 1898.

Source G: Spread of Socialism

If Socialism means a wise use of the forces of, all for the good of each; if it means the legal protection of the weak against the strong; if it means the performance by legal bodies of duties which individuals could not perform either so well or not at all for themselves, why, then, the principles of Socialism are admitted all over the field of our social activity.

John Morley, a leading Liberal 1889. Quoted in A.M. McBriar, *Fabian Socialism and English Politics 1884–1918* (1962)

JOSEPH CHAMBERLAIN.

Source H: Unfit for war

During recruitment for the Boer War (1899–1902) it was discovered that 40 per cent, and in some areas of the country 60 per cent, of recruits had to be rejected as medically unfit.

1 Which factors appeared to have weakened the individualistic ethics?

Support your answer with reference to the sources.

2 (a) The actual number of socialists was tiny yet they were to exert a huge influence. Why should this be so?

(b) In what ways did the political parties respond to the Socialist challenge?

3 Sir William Harcourt, the Liberal Chancellor, remarking on the introduction of death duties in 1894 exclaimed, 'We are all Socialists now.'

(a) What does the term mean according to Karl Marx?

(b) Is this the same meaning as Sir William Harcourt?

4 Re-read chapter 11 on Government and the Individual in early nineteenth century Britain. What differences and similarities can you identify between the two periods?

Examining the evidence

Poverty revealed

In 1881 Henry George's 'Progress and Poverty' revived an interest in the problem of poverty and policy. A spate of books, surveys and pamphlets followed. From a variety of motives and in numerous ways, they all came to the same conclusion. Far from diminishing, poverty was frighteningly high – almost a third of the population was precariously balanced between

'OVER LONDON' – GUSTAV DORÉ. ON A BRIEF VISIT TO LONDON, GUSTAVE DORÉ PRODUCED MANY MEMORABLE AND DRAMATIC PICTURES OF LOW-LIFE LONDON.

poverty and destitution. Furthermore, the causes of poverty, appeared to have little to do with the indigence of the poor themselves.

Source A: A Christian duty

This must be to every Christian heart a loud and bitter cry, appealing for the help which it is the supreme mission of the Church to supply.

You have to penetrate courts reeking with poisonous gases arising from the accumulation of sewage and refuse scattered in all directions ... You have to ascend rotten staircases. You have to grope your way along dark and filthy passages, swarming with vermin. Then you may gain admittance to the dens in which thousands of beings who belong as much as you do to the human race for which Christ died, herd together.

Andrew Mearns, *The Bitter Cry of Outcast London* (1883)
Andrew Mearns was a Congregationalist Minister

Source B: Poverty and vice

The bastard harlot, suckled on gin, and familiar from earliest infancy, with all the bestialities of debauchery, violated before she is twelve, and driven into the streets by her mother a year or two later, what chance is there for such a girl in this world – or the next.

William Booth *In Darkest England the Way Out* (1890)
William Booth was the founder of the Salvation Army

Source C: The hidden lives of the poor

The lives of the poor lay hidden from view behind a curtain on which were painted terrible pictures of starving children, suffering women, overworked men; horrors of drunkeness and vice, monsters and demons of inhumanity; giants of disease and despair. Did these pictures truly represent what lay behind, or did they bear to the facts a relation similar to that which the pictures outside a booth at some country fair bear to the performance or show within.

Charles Booth, a Liverpool merchant set out to discover the true extent of poverty. He opened up London Offices in the 1880s. He conducted a pilot study in Tower Hamlets in 1886 and East London and Hackney in 1887. These surveys eventually appeared in a massive seventeen volume publication entitled 'The Life and Labour of the People in London' 1889–1903.

Quoted by T.S. and M.B. Simey, *Charles Booth: Social Scientist* (1960)

Source D: Charles Booth investigates poverty

The inhabitants of every street, and court, and block of buildings in the whole of London, have been estimated in proportion to the numbers of children, and arranged in classes according to the known position and condition of the parents of these children. The streets have been grouped together according to the School Board sub divisions of 'blocks', and for each of these blocks full particulars are given in the tables of the Appendix. The numbers included in each block vary from less than 2,000 to more than 30,000 and to make a more satisfactory unit of comparison. I have arranged them in contiguous groups, 2, 3 or 4 together, so as to make areas having each about 30,000 inhabitants, these areas adding up into the large divisions of the School Board Administration. The population is then classified by Registration districts, which are likewise grouped into Schoolboard divisions, each method finally leading up to the total for all London.

The classes into which the population of each of these blocks and districts is divided are the same as were used in describing East London, only somewhat simplified. They may be stated thus;

(a) The lowest class – occasional labourers, loafers and semi-criminals.

(b) The very poor – casual labour, hand-to-mouth existence, chronic want.

(c) and (d) The poor – including alike those whose earnings are small, because of irregularity of employment, and those whose work, though regular, is ill-paid.

(e) and (f) The regularly employed and fairly paid working class of all grades.

(g) and (h) Lower and Upper middle class and all above this level.

The proportion of the different classes shown for all London are as follows:

Lowest (a)	37,610	0.9%	
Very poor (b)	316,834	7.5%	In poverty 30.7%
Poor (c and d)	938,293	22.3%	
Working class, comfortable (e and f)	2,166,503	51.5%	
Middle Class and above (g and h)	749,930	17.8%	In comfort 69.3%
Inmates of Institutions	99,830		

Charles Booth *Life and Labour of the People in London Vol II* (1892)

Source E: Seebohm Rowntree investigates poverty

In this chapter it is proposed to briefly summarise the facts set forth in the preceding pages, and to consider what conclusions regarding the problem of poverty may be drawn from them.

Method of Scope of Inquiry. As stated in the second chapter, the information regarding the numbers, occupation, and housing of the working classes was gained by direct inquiry, which practically covered every working class family in York. In some cases direct information was also obtained regarding earnings, but in the majority of these cases these were estimated, the information at the disposal of the writer enabling him to do this with considerable accuracy.

The poverty line. Having thus made an estimate, based upon carefully ascertained facts, of the earnings of practially every working class family in York, the next step was to show the proportion of the total population living in poverty. Families regarded as living in poverty were grouped under two heads:

(a) Families whose total earnings were insufficient to obtain the minimum necessaries for the maintenance of more physical efficiency. Poverty falling under this head was described as 'primary' poverty.

(b) Families whose total earnings would have been sufficient for the maintenance of merely physical efficiency were it not that some portion of it was absorbed by other expenditure, either useful or wasteful. Poverty falling under this head was described as 'secondary' poverty.

... it was shown that for a family of father, mother, and three children, the minimum weekly expenditure upon which physical efficiency can be maintained in York is 21s.8d., made up as shown.

	s.	d.
Food	12	9.
Rent	4	0.
Clothing, light, fuel	4	11.
	21s.	8d.

... No expenditure of any kind is allowed for beyond that which is absolutely necessary for the maintenance of merely physical efficiency.

... A family living at the poverty line (20s.8d) must never spend a penny on a railway fare or a bus. They must never go into the country unless they walk. They must never purchase a one-half penny newspaper or spend a penny to buy a ticket for a concert ... The children must have no pocket money for dolls, marbles or sweets. The father must smoke no tobacco and drink no beer. The mother must never buy herself pretty clothes. They must never fall ill. Finally the wage earner must never be absent from his work for a single day.

... In this way 20,302 persons, or 27.84% of the total population, were returned as living in poverty. Subtracting those whose poverty is 'primary', we arrive at the number living in 'secondary' poverty, viz. 13,072, or 17.93% of the total population.

We have been accustomed to look upon the poverty in London as exceptional, but when the result of careful investigation shows that the proportion of poverty in London is practically equalled in what may be regarded as a typical provincial town, we are faced by the startling probability that from 25 to 30% of the town population of the United Kingdom are living poverty.

B.S. Rowntree Poverty: *A Study of Town Life 2nd Edition* (1901)

B. Seebohm Rowntree was a member of the famous quaker chocolate manufacturer's family of York. He wished to compare Booth's conclusions about poverty in London with that in York.

Source F: Summary of Rowntree's findings in York

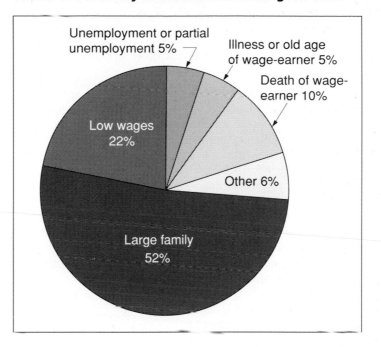

Unemployment or partial unemployment 5%

Illness or old age of wage-earner 5%

Death of wage-earner 10%

Low wages 22%

Other 6%

Large family 52%

Source G

Pauperism and Distress: Circular Letter to the Boards of Guardians

Local Government Board, Whitehall, S.W.

15 March 1886

Sir,

The enquiries which have recently been undertaken by the Local Government Board unfortunately give the prevailing impression as to the existence of exceptional distress amongst the working classes. This distress is partial as to its locality, and is no doubt due in some measure to the long continued severity of the weather.

... they are convinced that in the ranks of those who do not ordinarily seek poor relief there is evidence of much and increasing privation, and if the depression in trade continues it is to be feared that large numbers of persons usually in regular employment will be reduced to the greatest straits.

... The spirit of independence which leads so many of the working classes to make great personal sacrifices rather than incur the stigma of pauperism, is one which deserves the greatest sympathy and respect, and which it is the duty and interests of the community to maintain by all means at its disposal.

... Whatever is required in the endeavour to relieve artisans and others who have hitherto avoided poor law assistance, and who are temporarily deprived of employment is:

1 Work which will not involve the stigma of pauperism;

2 Work which all can perform, whatever may have been their previous avocations;

3 Work which does not compete with that of the other labourers at present employment;

… In districts in which exceptional distress prevails, the Board recommend that the guardians should confer with the local authorities, and endeavour to arrange with the latter for the execution of works on which unskilled labour may be immediately employed …

In all cases in which special works are undertaken to meet exceptional distress, it would appear to be necessary, 1st, that the men employed should be engaged on the recommendation of the guardians as persons whom, owing to previous condition and circumstances, it is undesireable to send to the workhouse, or treat as subjects for pauper relief, and 2nd., that the wages paid should be something less than the wages ordinarily paid for similar work, in order to prevent imposture, and to leave the strongest temptations to those who avail themselves of this opportunity to return as soon as possible to their previous occupations.

I am, etc.,

(Signed) J. Chamberlain

Joseph Chamberlian, *The Chamberlain Circular* (1886)

Source H

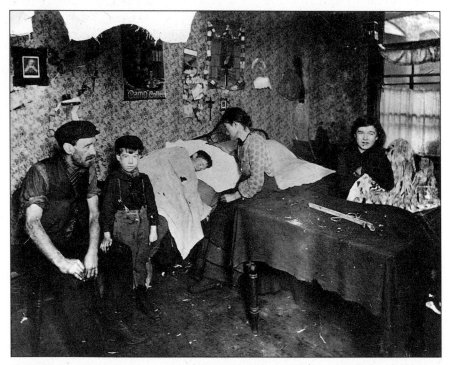

PHOTOGRAPH OF A WORKING CLASS FAMILY IN THE EAST END OF LONDON IN THE 1890s.

1 (a) Evaluate the above sources as evidence of poverty in late nineteenth century Britain?

(b) How do they attempt to persuade readers of their viewpoint?

2 What conclusions do the writers reach as to the;

(a) extent

(b) cause and,

(c) consequence of poverty?

Educating our masters

Education could provide one means of escape from poverty. The 1870 Education Act, despite its historical significance, provided neither free nor compulsory education. Nevertheless the Board schools, with which Forster was to plug 'the gaps' were soon to be of overwhelming importance. By 1880 16 per cent of children attended Board schools. This was in the same year as the Mundella Act made it compulsory for children between the ages of five and ten to attend school. By 1900 Board Schools accounted for 54 per cent of the school population. The 1891 Fee Grant Aid virtually established free elementary education and by 1895 only about 15 per cent of pupils were paying fees. Payment by results came under attack from the Cross Commission and the 1890 Revised Code abolished grants based on the results of testing in the 3Rs.

The Cross Commission also recommended the setting up of a new Standard VII for those pupils staying on beyond the new compulsory age of thirteen. Some schools had already pre-empted the decision by creating higher grade schools. These undercurrents of change were given additional momentum by the Bryce Commission on Secondary Education in 1895.

In 1900, a High Court decision disallowing the right of local authorities to levy a rate for secondary education, abruptly halted the process. By 1902, however, the forces for secondary educational provision had mustered their forces and scored a victory in the shape of A.J. Balfour's Education Act in 1902.

Examining the evidence
Educating the masses
Source A: The Bryce Report on secondary education
In dwelling on the need for a systematic organisation of Secondary Education we have more than once had occasion to explain that we mean by 'system' neither uniformity nor the control of a Central Department of government. Freedom, variety, elasticity are, and have been, the merits which go far to redeem the defects in English education, and they must at all hazards be preserved. The 'system' which we desire to see introduced may rather be described as coherence, an organic relation between different authorities and different kinds of schools which will enable each to work with due regard to the work to be done by the others, and will

therewith avoid both waste of effort and money. Of the loss now incurred through the want of such coherence and correlation, it is impossible to speak too strongly.

... Elementary education is among the first needs of a people, as appears by the fact that all, or nearly all, modern constitutional States have undertaken to provide it. But it is by those who have received a further and superior kind of instruction that the intellectual progress of the nation is maintained. But the great body of the commercial and professional classes were long forced to content themselves with a teaching which was usually limited in range and often poor in quality, and whose defects had become so familiar that they had ceased to be felt as defects.

Things have improved within the last thirty years, as may be seen by whoever compares the picture drawn by our Assistant Commissioners with that contained in the reports of the Assistant Commissioners of 1865. But the educational opportunities offered in most of our towns, and in nearly all our country districts, to boys or girls who do not proceed to the universities, but leave school at sixteen, are still far behind the requirements of our time, and far less ample than the incomes of the parents and the public funds available might well provide.

... it is not merely in the interest of the material prosperity and intellectual activity of the nation, but no loss in that of its happiness and its moral strength, that the extension and reorganisation of Secondary Education seem entitled to a place among the first subjects with which social legislation ought to deal.

The Bryce Report foreshadowed the 1902 Act.

Source B: Balfour introduces the 1902 Education Act Bill

The Act of 1870 successfully carried out this great if ... limited object ... but two unforseen consequences arose ... and three considerable omissions made themselves felt as time went on. The first of the two unforeseen consequences was the embarrasment into which the voluntary schools were thrown by the rivalry of the rate-aided Board Schools ... Mr. Forster and the Government of that day greatly under-rated the ... cost. Mr. Forster contemplated that a threepenny rate would do all that had to be done ... there was a wholly unexpected expenditure by School Boards : and the voluntary schools were subjected to a competition which, however good for education, was certainly neither anticipated nor desired by the framers of the Act of 1870. The second result was that a strain was placed upon the body responsible indeed to the community so far as regards education, but it had no responsibility for general expenditure, which was, of course, in the hands of the local authority.

Let me just enumerate hurriedly the three important omissions ... In the first place, the Act of 1870 provided no organisation for voluntary schools. Board Schools ... were organised under the School Boards. But voluntary schools ... were isolated and unconnected ...The second omission was ... that there was no sufficient provision for the education of the great staff of teachers required for our national schools. And ... third ... our primary system was put in no kind of rational or organic connection with our system of secondary education, with the University education ...

Arthur J. Balfour in a speech introducing the Education Bill of 1902

Source C: The Purpose of the Elementary Code 1904

The purpose of the Public Elementary School is to form and strengthen the character and develop the intelligence of the children entrusted to it ... to fit themselves, practically as well as intellectually, for the work of life ... It will be an important though subsidiary object of the school to discover individual children who show promise of exceptional capacity, and to develop their special gifts so far as this can be done without sacrificing the interests of the majority of children, so that they may be better qualified to pass at the proper age into Secondary Schools, and be able to derive the maximum of benefit from the education offered them.

Elementary Code 1904

Source D: Defining secondary education

... But a definition of the term 'Secondary School' – which has come to have a recognised meaning in English Education – has become indispensable in order to give to Secondary Schools a definite place in the wide and vague scheme of 'education other than elementary', with the provision and organisation of which the Local Education Authorities under the Act of 1902 have been charged, and in respect of which they obtain financial aid and administrative regulation from the Board of Education ...

Secondary Schools are of different types, suited to the different requirements of the scholars, to their place in the social organisation, and to the means of the parents of the age at which the regular education of the scholars is obliged to stop short, as well as the occupations and opportunities of development to which they may or should look forward in later life ...

Source E:

Legal school leaving age	
1880	10
1893	11
1899	12
1918	14

Questions

1 What "gaps existed" in elementary education were "plugged' by subsequent legislation?

2 Why was there reluctance to allow local authorities to provide secondary education?

3 What arguments were used by the supporters of state secondary education?

4 What unexpected results accrued from the 1870 Forster's Act?

EXAMINING THE EVIDENCE
The Royal Commission's investigation of trade unions

In 1867, after a grudging acceptance, trade unions were under the spotlight again after a number of workers had come under attack from alleged trade union officials. A government inquiry was hastily organised not only to look into the events at Sheffield but into the whole trade union movement itself.

Source A: The Sheffield Outrages

If a member refuses to pay his proportion towards the protection of his labour equally, a certain amount of force may be necessary to make him comply in a reasonable manner.

Henry Cutts, Secretary of the Sheffield Filesmith's Union.

Source B: Working conditions in Sheffield

Much of Sheffield's industry was carried on in small workshops as illustrated here. Working conditions were poor and the average life expectancy of a saw grinder was 28 years.

SAW GRINDER'S WORKSHOP.

Source C: Trade Union violence

'Sometimes they lie in wait in these dark streets, and fracture his skull; or break his arm, or cut the sinew of his wrist … or if he is a grinder they put gunpowder into his trough, and then the sparks of his own making fire it and perhaps blind him for life ... they are skilled workmen you know: well-skilled workmen at violence and all. They'll blow your house up from the cellar or let a can of gunpowder down the chimney ... and they take a chance of killing a houseful of innocent people.'

An extract from Charles Reade's novel Put yourself in his Place, which was serialised in the 'Cornhill Magazine' in 1869–70. Henry Little, a non-union saw grinder, is told by the foreman of the works what trade unionists do to their enemies.

Source D

This illustration accompanied the extract from Charles Reade's novel. The picture illustrates an incident in which trade unionists have placed gunpowder in the trough of Henry Little. He is seen hanging from the window in an attempt to escape from the resultant fire.

POLITICAL CARTOON – THE ROAD TO SHEFFIELD.

Source F

The Royal Commission on Trade Unions 1867–69

The Commission met for the first time in March 1867

The composition of the Royal Commission was:

For the Trade Unions

- Robert Applegarth (Adviser to the Commission and Leader of the Amalgamated Society of Carpenters)
- Frederic Harrison (MP and lawyer)
- Thomas Hughes (MP and lawyer)

Neutral

- Franceris Charteris, Lord Elcho (Parliamentary spokesman for the Glasgow Trades Council)
- Thomas George, Earl of Lichfield (Landowner who advocated amicable relations between employers and unions)

Against the Trade Unions

- J.A. Roebuck (MP for Sheffield)
- Sir William Erle (A judge who had not proved sympathetic in trade union cases)
- Sir Edmund Walkerhead (Retired civil servant)
- Sir Daniel Gooch (Chairman of the Great Western Railway)
- Herman Merivale (a regular writer of anti-trade union articles)
- James Booth (Retired civil servant)
- William Mathews (Chairman of the Midland Ironmasters League)

Source G: Trade Union opposition to strikes

I should say that the members are generally opposed to strikes ... we believe that strikes are a waste of money. ... Many of the other societies have taken in fact our rules and our type of management as their guide.

William B. Allen of the Amalgamated Society of Engineers in evidence to the commission

Source H: Trade Unions and justice

Everything is above board. We think as Englishmen in that everything we do shall see daylight, and therefore every rule of the Society is in that book.

... I would take the liberty of explaining that I have always held that men have no right to strike, nor masters to lock out, for I believe that the interests of the public are of much greater importance than either the masters or the men.

Edwin Coulson of the Bricklayers' Union in evidence to the commission

Source I: Trade union membership card of the Amalgamated Society of Engineers

1 Compare the image that trade unions presented in the Sheffield Outrages to that before the Royal Commission. In what ways do they differ and for what possible reasons?

Trade Unions and the Law

In 1869 the Commissioners presented their findings but as they could not agree a minority and majority report were produced. The majority report was signed by eight commissioners; the minority by Frederic Harrison, Thomas Hughes and Thomas George. The principal sticking point between them was the majority's recommendation that unions be debarred from the right to picket.

In February 1871 two laws were passed affecting trade unions. The Trade Union Act of 1871 denied the illegality of trade unions on the grounds that they were 'in restraint of trade'. Additionally the property of trade unions was protected under law and any seven members were entitled to register as a trade union.

In the same year as this apparent advance in their fortunes they were suddenly reversed by the Criminal Law Amendment Act. Under this legislation it proved almost impossible for unions to picket as they would be liable for prosecution for intimidation. It was soon clear that the legislation had teeth. In the same year as the passing of the law farm labourers' wives were imprisoned for shouting 'Bah!' to blackleg workers. Other cases soon followed.

Trade Union opposition to the Criminal Law Amendement Act

Trade unionists were furious with the Liberal government which they had thought sympathetic to the working classes. Spurred on by this desire to fight the Criminal Law Amendment Act they set about presenting a united front. Trades Councils were formed and in 1868 the Manchester Trades Council organised a Trades Union Congress, inviting delegates to attend a conference. One hundred delegates made the journey to Manchester but the Junta gave it the cold shoulder. After the passing of the Criminal Law Amendment Act in 1871, however, they saw the wisdom of joining.

Once united they recognised the need to influence members of Parliament and so set up a Parliamentary body to lobby the political parties to remove anti-trade union laws and to give support in elections to those parliamentary candidates who were friendly to their movement.

Congress's opportunity to change the law came with the 1874 election. Surprisingly, it was Disraeli, leader of the Tory party and Prime Minister, which gave them the opportunity. Once in power he invited them to participate in another Royal Commission with a view to changing the law. The unionists, fearing something underhand, refused to co-operate. Without union co-operation the Commissioners could do nothing and so the Commission was disbanded.

In spite of this the Conservatives decided to go ahead with legislation. In 1875 the Criminal Law Amendment Act was repealed and replaced by the Conspiracy and Protection of Property Act. Trade unionists would no longer be prosecuted for conspiracy or picketing, unless the criminal law was broken.

In the same year the Master and Servant Act was repealed and replaced by the Employer and Workmen Act. Under the Master and Servant Act a worker could be fined and imprisoned for breaking his or her contract, whereas the employer merely had to pay lost wages to any worker who was laid off before the end of the arranged period. Under the new Act workers and employers became equal partners in the new contract.

The Taff Vale railway incident

The law, however, was to impinge further upon trade union activity. In 1900 the Taff Vale Railwaymen complained that one of their union leaders had been demoted after asking for higher wages. This and other grievances boiled over into a strike.

Ammon Beesley, the General Manager of the railway company prosecuted the union for loss of revenue. The Taff Vale Railway Company won the legal battle and the union was faced with a crippling bill of £23,000 in compensation and a further £19,000 for legal costs. This decision appeared to reverse many of the gains made by the trade unions. It took a liberal victory and the passing of the 1906 Trades Dispute Act to restore the right of trade unions to pursue the tactic of strike action without the fear of prosecution.

Trade Unions and political contributions

One further blow came in 1909 aimed at the growing political involvement of trade unions. Walter Osborne, a branch secretary of the Amalgamated Society of Railway Servants and a supporter of the Liberal party, objected to paying the union's political fund that went toward supporting Labour members of Parliament. At this time MPs received no wages. (An annual salary was not granted until 1911.) Osborne took his complaint to the House of Lords where they declared the political levy to be illegal. In 1913, the position of the political levy was clarified in the Trade Union Act of 1913. Under this law the political levy could be charged if a majority of members agreed and every individual had the right to contract out if he so wished.

New Unionism

'New Unionism' was a catchphrase used to describe a burst of energy between 1888–91 in which workers who had never formed unions before began to mobilise their forces. Contemporaries picked out several 'new' features which they believed distinguished it from that of the old. These can be summarised in the diagram.

Older unions		New unions	
Leaders	Moderates willing to compromise with employers.	Leaders	Militants eager to fight their employers.
Membership	Largely skilled workers. The old unions kept out semi-skilled intruders who might 'water down' their craft.	Membership	Largely unskilled or low-paid workers, such as dockers and teachers.
Union dues	High dues, to pay for unemployment and sickness benefits.	Union dues	Low dues, only used to set up a strike fund.
Politics	Supported the Liberal Party.	Politics	Supported socialist, independent labour movements.

DIAGRAM OF OLD AND NEW UNIONISM.

The great dock strike summed up the mood of the times. In September 1889 the Port of London was at standstill. Ben Tillett, leader of the Tea Porters' and General Labourers' Union, had called out over 100,000 dockworkers. Their aim was to increase their wages from 5d to 6d (two and one half pence – 'A Tanner an hour'). The 'tanner'' was the nickname for sixpence.

The solidarity of the strikers was remarkable considering how poorly paid they were and the casual nature of their employment. With restrained, but highly public demonstrations, they won considerable sympathy not only at home but by contributions from abroad. After four weeks the employers agreed to talks from which they won their 'tanner', a guarantee of four hours work a day and overtime payments. A new dockers' union enrolled 30,000 members.

There were other examples of successful strikes. Will Thorne launched his National Union of Gas Workers and General Labourers' Union early in 1889, winning an eight hour day for their employees. The membership of Havelock Wilson's Seamen's and Firman's Union shot up to 65,000.

Women workers too were important in new unionism. In 1888 three hundred women at Bryant and May's match works went on strike. For low pay they did dangerous work which included the risk of catching 'phossy jaw'; a cancer of the bones caused by phosphorous. The women's campaign was skilfully directed by Annie Besant, a tremendously effective speaker on women's rights. After a fortnight the company improved wages and conditions.

WOMEN – LABOURING WORK.

Nevertheless the movement was still dominated by the male craft unions. It was not until 1885 that the TUC backed a policy of equal pay. But, in general, women remained a largely insignificant force within the labour movement.

The ranks of trade unions were also swelled by the growth of white collar unions. Clerical workers and teachers formed unions to protect their industrial conditions.

The successes of 1889 were short lived. The new unions were tiny. By 1900 they had only 200,000 members out of a total of two million. Often the employers hit back by supporting 'free' labour. In 1893 the Hull Dock Strike was broken, leading the Times to comment, 'At Hull as elsewhere the New Unionism has been defeated.'

The Power of Trade Unions

By 1914 trade unions had developed from scattered, weak, illegal groups of workers into a powerful force within the economy and society. Their newly found power caused fear in others.

Certainly there appeared to be some basis for their fears. In 1910, at Tony-y-Pandy in the Welsh coalfield, street fighting broke out during which the police were attacked and a striker was killed. Two strikers were shot dead during a riot in Liverpool in 1911.

On 1 March 1912 more than a million miners stopped work in the biggest strike to date. By 6 April the government, despairing of getting the two sides to agree passed the Miners' Wages Act which guaranteed a minimum wage to miners. Workers were not always the winners in these

ANNIE BESANT

disputes. In 1912 a huge strike in the Port of London was crushed by employers.

Meanwhile trade union power was growing as never before. Small unions began to amalgamate with larger ones. In 1913 three small railway unions joined forces to form the National union of Railwaymen, the largest and strongest union of the day. Some of these larger unions sought to co-operate with other unions. In 1913 the massive Triple Alliance was created from three giant unions: the National union of Railwaymen, the Miners' Federation and the Transport Workers' Federation.

Most trade unionists saw the Triple Alliance as a force for raising living standards of working people, others, as a powerful bully. Some feared that it might be used as a political weapon to overthrow the government.

Particularly threatening to the establishment and to the trade union hierarchy itself was syndacilism – a populist political trade unionist ideology. 'The Miners' Next Step', published by the South Wales Miners' Federation in 1912, expressed the syndacilist creed – with vigour.

'TRIPLE ALLIANCE' – POLITICAL CARTOON.

'The policy of conciliation gives the real power of the men into the hands of a few leaders – The workmen for a time look up to these men … The employers respect them. Why? Because they have the men – the real power – in the hollow of their hands. They, the leaders, become gentlemen, they become MPs …

Our objectives: alliances to be formed and trade organisations to be fostered with a view to steps being taken to amalgamate all workers into one National and International Union, to work for the taking over of all industries by the workmen themselves … we can only get what work we are strong enough to win and retain.'

Union power on this scale, the dockers' leader Ben Tillett declared, could be used as the strongest batallion in the class war. Reporting back to his union in 1912 he explained in stark terms the future class conflict.

'The class war is the most brutal of wars … The lesson is that, in future strikes, the striker must protest against the use of arms, with arms; protest against shooting with shooting; protest against violence with violence … In the 1912 strikes we had to fight with Parliament, the forces of the Crown, the judges of the law … Capitalism is capitalism as a tiger is a tiger; and both are savage and pitiless towards the weak.'

The pre-war industrial unrest was largely economic in origin and the political aspirations of syndacilism a veneer on the surface. On 2 August a crowd of trade unionists and Labour Party supporters gathered in London's Trafalgar Square shouting 'Down with class rule! Down with the war!' Two days later when war was declared working class communities flocked to the colours; their loyalties more firmly embedded to their country than in their class.

Collectivism

So much social legislation was passed in the last quarter of the nineteenth century that by 1894 the Liberal Chancellor of the Exchequer, Sir William Harcourt, on introducing death duties, declared, 'We are all Socialists now.' Of course the Chancellor did not mean that private prop-

" *Trades Union officials (to the Boy-Who-Would-Grow-Up):* '*Here, I say, think of us. This Growth has got to stop*', *(Dedicated to the Officials at Unity House and their pathetic efforts to check this modern tendency on the part of the Rank and File to outgrow Institutions.)*"

'THE WOES OF UNITY HOUSE' – WILL DYSON.

erty had been abolished but that collectivist policies had been adopted to avoid, rather than over-turn, capitalist society.

'Socialist legislation,' explained A.J. Balfour in his election campaign, 'as I conceive it, is not merely to be distinguished from Socialist legislation but is its most direct opposite and its most effective antidote. Socialism will never get possession of the great body of public opinion ... among the working class or any other class who wield the collective forces of the community show themselves desirous to ameliorate every legitimate grievance and to put Society upon a proper and more solid base.'

Arthur Balfour at Manchester, 16 January 1895, quoted by E. Halevy, *Imperialism and the Rise of Labour* (1951)

How effectively socialist principles of collectivism were used by the Liberal Party you may judge for yourselves in the following chapter.

REVIEW

To what extent had the belief in individualist ideology diminished by the latter end of the nineteenth century?

● Apparent periodisation of the nineteenth century into individualism and collectivism.

● Growing awareness of the complexity of poverty.

● Bolstering the individualist ideology – Charities and the adoption of interventionist practice – education, public health, factory legislation.

● Movements for collectivism – Trade unions – socialist organisations. Extent of impact.

19 The Origins of a Welfare State, 1905–1914?

PREVIEW

"FEE, FI, FO, FAT, I SMELL THE BLOOD OF A PLUTOCRAT;
BE HE ALIVE OR BE HE DEAD, I'LL GRIND HIS BONES TO MAKE MY BREAD."

THE GIANT LLOYD-GORGIBUSTER

"This is a War Budget. It is for raising money to wage implacable warfare against poverty and squalidness."

Lloyd George
29 April 1909

"If it is vital that the pauper should suffer the loss of personal reputation, the loss of personal freedom which is secured by detentions in the workhouse and, that the loss of political freedom by suffering disenfranchisement."

Royal Commission on the Poor Law and Relief of Distress 1909

What is a Welfare State?

Many historians contend that the breadth and depth of social reforms passed by the Liberal government between 1905–14 laid the foundations of a 'welfare state'. This process, once begun, was later completed by the post second world war Labour government between 1945 and 1951.

Other historians question this assumption and instead suggest that the process was in the tradition of nineteenth century interventionist legislation and that no new principle was involved.

A number of questions and definitions of terms need to be considered before an opinion can be expressed.

- Do the Liberal social reforms constitute a radical and revolutionary break with nineteenth century attitudes to the role of the individual and government?

- Can those welfare reforms be described as originating a welfare state?

- What were the motives of those individuals and groups who initiated the changes?

- Were they aware of the long term trends that they had set in motion?

TALKING POINT

• Is it possible, or accurate, to ascribe the vision of a welfare state to individuals who would not have such a concept to apply to their views?

TALKING POINT

• List the provisions that exist today which fall into the category of a welfare state

• What principle underlies the provision of these services?

• Why does the state provide these services?

• What appears to be the main difference in attitude between the political parties with respect to the object of these services?

• What are the possible arguments for and against this view of the welfare state?

What is a Welfare State?

There are no simple answers to the questions posed in the preview for much depends on how we define the term 'Welfare State'. In the first place the expression was not used until the 1940s so we are obliged to attach a descriptive label not in use at the time of the Liberal reforms. Our understanding is therefore heavily dependent upon our interpretation of the term 'welfare state'.

Broadly speaking, there are two definitions that may be applicable. The first and most limited use of the term is used to describe a parcel of social and educational services which the state provides.

The second definition embraces a more comprehensive notion in that the state must also redistribute income and wealth on a more equitable basis. The object of the welfare state in this instance is to produce a minimum standard of living below which no one should fall. This would create, it is believed by those that support this notion of the welfare state, a more just society in which co-operation would over-ride self interest.

As you read of the events surrounding the Liberal welfare legislation and the actual provisions of the laws decide which of these two definitions appear to be more applicable.

The election of 1905

It may seem odd that the Liberal government, which was to usher in a programme of welfare legislation, did not present social reform issues as their key electoral objective. Nor was there a coherent and general demand for radical reforms from working class organisations. Indeed many of the enfranchised working class continued to support the traditional parties. The Conservatives, in power from 1895–1905, whilst basing their principal support upon the middle classes, nonetheless attracted between one third and one half working class support.

A number of factors, however, were beginning to dent their confident assumption of power. In 1902 Lord Salisbury, who had led the Conservative Party since 1895, resigned in favour of his nephew, J. Arthur Balfour. Winston Churchill, a liberal and Balfour's political opponent, observed of the new Prime Minister that, 'had his life been cast amid the labrynthine intrigues of the Italian Renaissance, he would not have been required to study the works of Machaevelli'. Such derisive remarks can be dismissed as part of the cut and thrust for political power. From a more informed source, according to his biographer Robert Blake, he was too distant from the electorate. 'The truth was that he was too rational and that he made insufficient allowance for the unreason of the masses.' (Robert Blake, The Conservative Party from Peel to Churchill, 1970) It was becoming increasingly important, as the enfranchisement was extended, to frame policies in the context of electoral interests. Balfour was perhaps at a disadvantage in this respect.

The Boer war

Whilst the opening of hostilities against the Boers in 1899 had been greeted with considerable jingoistic enthusiasm, the later revelations of British brutality squandered this political advantage. In an attempt to destroy the Boer farmsteads as bases of supply the British had set up con-

ARTHUR JAMES BALFOUR.

centration camps for the civilian population. The camps had soon become insanitary and epidemics swept the camps, killing many civilians.

Secondary education

The promised secondary education reform had caused a religious furore. Nonconformists objected to subsidising sectarian schools and their loss of power on the School Boards incensed them. Joseph Chamberlain, who had joined forces with the Conservatives over the issue of home rule for Ireland, told the Duke of Devonshire in 1902,

'I told you that your Education Bill would destroy your own party. It has done so. Our best friends are leaving us by the scores and hundreds and they will not have us back.'

Many non-conformists backed the Liberals in the hope of the repeal of the act.

Joseph Chamberlain who had wrecked the unity of the Liberals allied his breakaway National Liberal Party to the Conservative and Unionists. His Birmingham speech of 1903 called for a rejection of free trade and its replacement with Imperial Preference and retaliation against the entry of foreign goods into Britain. The cost of Chamberlain's tariff reform would mean taxes upon foodstuffs. As Professor Asa Briggs has written, 'For some … free trade was still a religion. The principle behind it was eternal.' No other single issue was to divide the Conservative and Unionist Party and to alienate public opinion more than Chamberlain's protectionist policies.

JOSEPH CHAMBERLAIN.

Taff Vale railway incident

The Taff Vale decision had caused considerable disillusionment of the Conservative Party amongst the working classes. Apart from the Workmens' Compensation Act in 1895, social reforms were no more than a promise. Most importantly, the Boer War had postponed Chamberlain's proposal for an Old Age Pensions Scheme. The Taff Vale decision itself had alienated trade unionists and, as a consequence, the Labour Party signed an election pact with the Independent Labour Party, to oust the Tories.

Chinese 'slavery'

The reconstruction of South Africa after the Boer War with Chinese labour caused considerable criticism. 20,000 Chinese labourers entered the dominion in 1904; 47,000 the following year. They were brought in as indentured servants and segregated, without their families, in camps. To many commentators the whole exercise appeared little different from slavery.

Unemployment

High levels of unemployment in 1904–5 brought virtually no positive action from the government apart from the Unemployed Workmen's Bill (1905) which extended the public works scheme. It appeared too little, too late.

These factors soon were to produce a fissure so great in the Tory ranks that Balfour resigned, hoping that in his surprise resignation and the possible disarray of his opponents, he could be returned victorious. On 4

Note

In 1887 a Board of Trade report declared that some 20,000 workers in East London were classified as sweated labour.

Liberals 401 MPs including 24 Lib-Labs	
Conservatives	157
Labour	29
Irish Nationalists	83

December 1905 Campbell Bannerman, leader of the Liberal Party, was summoned to form a cabinet. In order to consolidate his position Bannerman called a general election for January 1906. The result was a landslide victory for the liberals.

EXAMINING THE EVIDENCE
The Liberal Party and social reform

If social reform was a minor and muddled issue in the election campaign from where was it generated, why did it come to assume major importance?

Campbell Bannerman's election addresses had acknowledged overcrowding as a social problem and suggested re-colonisation of the country and the Empire as a solution. He accepted the need for an improvement in the treatment of the poor and alleviation of conditions among the sweated trades. Yet within the same programme he promised a massive reduction in public expenditure. It was difficult to understand how these contradictions could be reconciled.

If new directions were not coming from the leadership then at least there were undercurrents that were to become significant. The majority of Liberals were new to the House and belonged overwhelmingly to the centre of the party. Yet even here there was no indication amongst them that they would support the 'New Liberalism'. As the Chief Whip of the Party, Herbert Gladstone, remarked to his leader, 'There is no sign of any violent move forward ... The dangerous element does not amount to a dozen.'

The dangerous element was indeed small, but its influence was decisive in committing the Liberal Party to a revolution in the relationship between government and its citizens. Lloyd George and Winston Churchill were the leaders of this 'dangerous element'.

Herbert Asquith, who shared their vision, became premier in 1908. Support also came from junior ministers such as Charles Masterman, social reformers like the Webbs and civil servants such as Robert Morant and William Beveridge. Were the leaders of the 'New Liberalism' inspired by a new vision of welfare reform or was it a manipulative device to retain power?

Source A: The rise of the Labour party

The emergence of a strong Labour element in the House of Commons has been generally recognised as the most significant outcome of the present election. It is out of the ordinary groove of domestic politics and will have a far wider influence than any mere turnover of party voters ... Though the Labour Party has used the Liberals in this election to help them to what they want ... they show no gratitude to the Liberal Party ... The reason is that the system of commercial organisation that now galls them is the work of the Liberals and is founded upon the ideas now outworn which gave Liberalism its period of supremacy.

The Times (30 January 1906)

ARTHUR BALFOUR AND CAMPBELL FACED WITH LABOUR.

Source C

LLOYD GEORGE.

Source D: Lloyd George's career

1867: Born in Manchester. His father dies when he is only 18 months old and Lloyd George is taken to live with his uncle near Criccieth, North Wales. He attends the local elementary school. Lloyd George's uncle is a much respected Baptist minister.

1877: He soon proved to be a quick and competent scholar which enabled him to obtain employment in a solicitor's office. After obtaining his articles he goes into partnership with his brother William.

1888: He is involved in a court case which wins him considerable fame. An Anglican clergyman refused to allow a non-conformist to be buried in his churchyard. The case was eventually taken to the High Court in London where Lloyd George won amid a blaze of glory.

1890: Lloyd George becomes a Liberal MP for Caernarvon borough by a narrow margin as a result of a local by-election. He concentrates on defending Welsh issues.

1899–1902: He is a determined opponent of the South African War. His stand on this issue nearly costs him his life during a riot at one of his meetings in Birmingham.

1905: He becomes the leading spokesman for the 'New Liberalism'.

1906–08: President of the Board of Trade.

1908–15: Chancellor of the Exchequer.

1915–16: Minister of Munitions and Secretary of State for War.

1916–22: Prime Minister.

1922–45: He loses the general election and his parliamentary seat. He is never to hold office again.

Source E: Lloyd George and the 'social question'

There is a momentous time coming. The dark continent of wrong is being explored, and there is a missionary spirit abroad for its reclamation to the realm of right ... that vast social question which must be dealt with in the future.

Lloyd George in a speech in Cardiff, February 1980

Source F

We will only be ousted from power if we fail to cope seriously with the social condition of the people, to remove the national degradation of slums and widespread poverty in a land glittering with wealth.

Lloyd George in a speech at Cardiff, 11 October 1906

Source G: 'An end to the rule of the rich'

How can you expect a healthy, sound race, with men at the end of a hard day's work going to recruit their strength, consumed in hard toil, in habitations where some of our greatest landlords would not pen their cattle ... There are about six million electors in this land at the present day, and yet the government is in the hands of one class ...

A speech by Lloyd George in Newcastle, 1903

Source H: Welfare reforms as social control

Marxists regard the welfare state as an inevitable stage in advanced capitalism when state intervention is needed both to provide industry with services (which it can no longer provide itself) and to maintain political order. Consequently they argue that the Liberal reforms were necessitated by a growing economic crisis and industrial unrest. Certainly the reforms sought to strengthen, not displace, capitalism, and many of the new policies contained surreptitious controls. For example, to encourage desireable habits, pensions would initially be denied to those who had been recently in the workhouse, goal or arrested for drunkeness.

Rodney Lowe, *Modern History Review, Vol 1 No. 1 September 1989*

---

1 (a) Does Lloyd George appear consistent in his support for social reform?

(b) After studying the actual reform measures return to this question – 'Did his actions match his rhetoric?'

2 (a) What appears to have been an equally strong political motive underlying the Liberals adoption of social reforms?

(b) Does consideration of the political factor diminish the Liberal party's motivation for reform?

3 Study source H. What examples can you quote to support the following statements?

(i) ... state intervention is needed both to provide industry with services (which it can no longer provide for itself).

(ii) ... and to maintain political order ...

(iii) ... liberal reforms were necessitated by a growing economic crisis ... and industrial unrest ...

4 After reviewing the actual liberal reforms do you consider the reform policies contained 'surreptitious controls'?

The Liberal welfare programme

Until the succession of Herbert Asquith to the premiership, the pace of reform was sluggish. The Education (Provision of Meals) Act of 1906, and the Act of 1907 which provided for medical inspection in state schools, were the first tentative steps to more comprehensive measures. In this instance government action had been prompted by a falling birth rate and the need to ensure the healthy survival of the smaller number.

EXAMINING THE EVIDENCE
The Education Acts 1906–7 – 'A Sunday dinner everyday'
Source A

CRAMMING VERSUS 'CLEMMING'! PUNCH MAGAZINE.

Source B: Provision of school meals

The Royal Commission on Physical Training in Scotland 1903 recommended that education authorities should, in conjunction with voluntary agencies, provide school meals.

Source C: Physical deterioration of children

It is the height of cruelty to subject half-starved children to the process of education.

Report of the Inter-departmental Committee on Physical Deterioration 1904.

They went on to recommend medical inspection

Source D

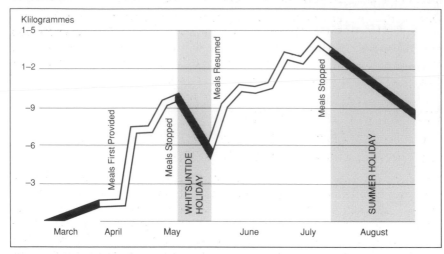

GRAPH OF CHILDREN'S WEIGHT.

The graph shows Kilogrammes on the vertical axis (1–5, 1–2, –9, –6, –3) and months March, April, May, June, July, August on the horizontal axis. Labels on the graph: Meals First Provided, Meals Stopped, WHITSUNTIDE HOLIDAY, Meals Resumed, Meals Stopped, SUMMER HOLIDAY.

Source E

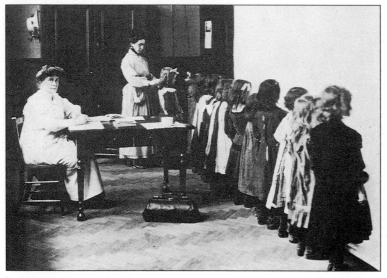

MEDICAL INSPECTION IN SCHOOLS.

---

1 Which evidence can be used to support the argument for providing school meals and medical inspection?

2 Medical treatment was not provided for in the legislation. Why was this and would it follow that children who were in need of medical treatment did not receive it?

3 Apart from a declining birth rate what other factors may have underpinned these two pieces of legislation?

4 Receiving school meals did not mean that their parents were classified as paupers. Why was this an important break with the past?

Lifting the shadow of the workhouse

One of the last acts of the outgoing Conservative premier, A.J. Balfour, was to initiate a Royal Commission on the Poor Laws. The Commission finally reported in 1909. The long delay was in considerable measure due to the deep ideological divisions within the Commission. This schism was reflected in the publication of minority and majority reports.

Examining the evidence
The Royal Commission on the Poor Laws, majority and minority Reports

Study the extracts from the majority and minority reports below. Divide into three groups. Two of the groups are to adopt the views of the majority and minority reports. Organise your arguments with your own chosen group. Deliver your reports verbally to the third group. As a member of the third group you decide how convincing you find the respective reports, in principle, and as a practical programme in the context of the time.

You may wish to react in the role of one of the major political parties of the day.

Old age pensions

By far the largest group of poor were the elderly. To many people, including the supporters of the poor law, it seemed particularly unfair that people who had lived exemplary working lives should be punished with poverty after a life of toil. As early as 1878 William Blackly proposed a scheme of contributions from which pensions could be funded. Friendly Society opposition, however, quickly ended discussion.

Charles Booth's revelations of the extent of poverty due to old age revived interest in pensions which, 'would lift from many old heads the fear of the workhouse at last.' Booth favoured a non-contributory scheme.

The introduction of pensions in Germany, as part of the bulwark against socialism, added a note of necessity to altruism, The fact that Germany was also Britain's keenest economic and imperial competitor was not lost on politicians at home.

In 1891 Joseph Chamberlain took up the cause but despite the resultant Report of the Royal Commission on the Aged Poor 1893–5, which recognised the extent of the problem, nothing was done. Whilst most interested participants admitted the need for pensions they could not agree on whether it should be contributory or non-contributory and whether a distinction should be made between deserving and undeserving poor. Meanwhile the Friendly Societies kept up a barrage of criticism against any scheme.

In 1899 New Zealand introduced old age pensions as part of a comprehensive welfare package. This action re-kindled interest and a Select Committee was appointed which included Lloyd George. The Committee was in favour of a non-contributory scheme but the massive expenditure incurred by the Boer War delayed implementation of the proposals.

The election of the Liberal Party in 1904 appeared to promise an opportunity for action but Asquith (Lord Chancellor 1906–8) was hesi-

TALKING POINT

What were the assumed advantages/disadvantages of (a) contributory (b) non-contributory pensions?

TALKING POINT

Why should Friendly Societies be opposed to Old Age Pensions?

tant. A succession of poor by-election results for the Liberals, however, eventually forced his hand. Lloyd George, Asquith's successor as Chancellor, steered the pensions scheme through the Commons. A budget surplus that year ensured a safe reception for the bill and old age pensions were to become a legislative fact.

Majority report

Workhouses

We were struck by the way in which young and able-bodied men and women, both with and without families, were admitted into the house as a matter of course. The Chairman told us there is nothing deterrent (discouraging) about their workhouse. There is no test of work, and inmates are better off and more comfortable than outside.

Pauper children

Many country workhouses are picturesque old buildings, with pleasant gardens on which the inmates are employed in raising vegetables for use in the institution. Children who are not provided for in "scattered homes" or separate schools are carefully separated from the adult paupers and sent out to the village school for their education. Those educated in these schools carry away with them a memory of happy days spent there and a real sense of gratitude to the officers.

Private charity or State services

The causes of distress are not only economic and industrial; in their origin and character they are largely moral. Government by itself cannot correct or remove such influences. Something more is required. The cooperation of the community at large, and especially of those sections of it which are well-to-do and free from the pressure of poverty, is indispensable. We have left place in the new system for all capable and willing voluntary social workers.

Dealing with unemployment

In the forefront of our proposals dealing with distress from unemployment we place labour exchanges under the control and direction of the Board of Trade. We look to them to achieve two objects:

(i) An increase in the mobility of labour (workers able to move more easily from place to place in order to find work),

(ii) The collection and distribution of information.

Associated with the labour exchange there should be, in connection with every elementary school, an intelligence bureau which would advise parents and teachers as to the branches of employment likely to give the best opening for children leaving school. By this means we hope to divert boys from the "blind-alley occupations" which so many enter at present into occupations which will lead to permanent employment.

Treatment of the poor

We will now enumerate and further describe one method of assistance which will be in future available for the treatment of the able-bodied by the Public Assistance Authority – i.e. home assistance. By home assistance we mean assistance at the home whether in money or kind, and given without requiring the recipient to live entirely in an institution. The conditions under which home assistance should be granted would be as follows:

(a) That the required assistance is not forthcoming from any other source;
(b) That the assistance be given on condition of daily work;
(c) That the assistance should be only given to an applicant with a decent home and a good industrial record;
(d) That the order for assistance should only be for a stricly limited period and subject to revision;
(e) That the applicant should be registered at the Labour Exchange, and that the relief should cease as soon as suitable occupation has been offered through the Labour Exchange.

Minority report

Workhouses

We find that these institutions have a depressing, degrading, and positively injurious (harmful) effect on the character of all classes of their inmates, tending to unfit them for the life of respectable citizenship. Their continued incarceration (imprisonment) within the General Mixed Workhouses, whether urban or rural, new or old, large or small, cannot be disqualified.

Pauper children

The system of boarding out children with foster parents or placing them in institutions is prejudiced by the fact that the Authorities are unqualified to maintain an efficient inspection of the homes, or any continuous supervision of their welfare. The children suffer from the difficulty of not getting the best teachers in Poor Law Schools, and of allocating the children to the particular types of school (e.g. mentally-defective schools, crippled schools, higher-grade schools etc.) that their individual characteristics require.

Private charity or state services

We find that the services at present administered by the Destitution Authorities (other than those connected with vagrants or the able-bodied) – that is to say the provision for:

(i) Children of school age,
(ii) The sick and permanently incapacitated, infants under school age and the aged needing institutional care,
(iii) The mentally defective of all ages,
(iv) The aged in receipt of pensions,
– should be assumed, under the directions of the County and County Borough Councils, by, respectively:
The Education Committee, Health Committee, Asylums Committee, and Pensions Committee.

Dealing with unemployment

We find that the task of dealing with unemployment is altogether beyond the capacity of authorities having jurisdiction (legal powers) over particular areas; and can be undertaken successfully only by a Department of the National Government under a Minister responsible to Parliament – a Minister for Labour.

In order to secure proper industrial training for the youth of the nation, no child should be employed at all below the age of 15; no young person under eighteen should be employed for more than 30 hours per week; and all young persons so employed should be required to attend for 30 hours per week at suitable Trade Schools to be maintained by the Local Education Authorities.

Treatment of the poor

We have therefore to report on the experience of the Poor Law in dealing with destitute able-bodied men and their dependants; of the Distress Committees in providing for labourers out of employment; of the policy in attempting to suppress vagrancy and 'sleeping out'; of the Prison Commissioners in having to accommodate in gaol large numbers of men undergoing short sentences for offences of this nature; of the Education and Public Health Authorities in feeding and medically treating the needy dependents of able-bodied men; and of the Voluntary Agencies dealing with the 'Houseless Poor' of great cities: all alike prove that any attempt to deal only with this or that section of the able-bodied and unemployed class is liable to be rendered futile by the neglect to deal simultaneously (at the same time) with the other sections of men in distress from lack of employment. Accordingly no successful dealing with the problem is possible unless provision is made simultaneously for all the various sections of the unemployed by one and the same authority.

EXAMINING THE EVIDENCE
The Old Age Pensions Act, 1908
Source A

DINNER TIME AT THE WORKHOUSE AT ST. PANCRAS.

Source B

THE WOMEN'S DAY ROOM AT THE CAMBRIDGE WORKHOUSE.

Source C: The flexibility of the Poor Law

The Poor Law is in a time of change, it is sympathetic, forward looking, reasonable and adaptable to any new sensible demand that may be made on it.

John Burns, *President of the Local Government Board, 1907*

Source D: Summary of the main points of the 1908 Pensions Act

Those entitled to a pension must have lived in Britain for at least twenty years and not been in prison for the last ten. Drunkards and malingerers could be excluded from benefits.

In 1911 the conditions were considerably relaxed but not finally abolished until 1919.

Non-contributory		
Paid to people over 70 years old		*Pensions per week*
Where their yearly means are not more than	£21. 0s. 0d.	5s.
but are not more than	£23. 12s. 6d.	4s.
but are not more than	£26. 5s. 0d.	3s
but are not more than	£28. 17s. 6d.	2s.
but are not more than	£31. 10s. 0d.	1s.
The pensions for a married couple	£0. 10s. 0d.	

Source E: In defence of Old Age Pensions

We were challenged by the member for Preston who said 'Would you declare that you are in favour of giving a pension of 5s. a week to a drunken, thriftless, worthless man or woman?' My reply is very prompt. A man of seventy with nothing in the world is not going to live a life of luxury on 5s. a week, whether his character is good or bad. Who are you to be continually finding fault? Who amongst you has such a clear record as to be able to point to the wickedness of an old man of seventy? If a man is foolish enough to get old, and if he has not been artful enough to get rich, you have no right to punish him for it. They are veterans of industry, people of almost endless toil ...

Will Crooks, MP, in a speech in the House of Commons
(Will Crooks was the first person born in a workhouse to become an MP.)

Source F: No need for alterations to the Poor Law

We are of the opinion that no fundamental alterations are needed in the existing system of poor relief as it affects the aged, and that it would be undesireable to interfere either by Statute or order with the discretion now invested in the guardians ... since it is in our view of essential importance that guardians should have power to deal on its merits with each individual case. At the same time we are convinced that there is a strong feeling that in the administration of relief there should be a greater discrimination between the respectable aged who become destitute and those whose destitution is directly the consequence of their own misconduct ...

Report of the Royal Commission on the Aged Poor, 1895, quoted in Eric Evans
Social Policy 1830–1914 (1978)

Source G: In praise of Old Age Pensions

When the Old Age Pensions began, life was transformed for such cottagers. They were relieved of anxiety. They were suddenly rich. Independent for life! At first they went to the Post Office to draw it; tears of gratitude would run down the cheeks of some, and they would say as they picked up their money, 'God bless that Lord George!' (for they could not believe one so powerful and munificient could be a plain 'Mr.') and 'God bless you miss!' and there were flowers from their gardens, and apples from their trees for the girl who merely handed them their money.

Flora Thompson, Lark Rise to Candleford
The authoress was a Post Office worker in an Oxfordshire village.

Source H: Old Age Pensions – A birthright

To the grateful recipient, pensions could never be a form of outdoor relief, it was a new birthright of an Englishmen, a part of his citizenship, not a deprivation of it. State pensions paid as of right and financed out of taxation set the Liberals firmly on a course which was to involve basic departures in social policy.

Derek Fraser, The Evolution of the British Welfare State (1973)

Source I

PHILANTHROPIC HIGHWAYMAN.

Source J: Friendly Society reaction to Old Age Pensions

The aim of the working class ought to be to bring about economic conditions in which there should be no need for the distribution of state alms. Man is a responsible being. The working class should rise to the occasion and insist upon being capable of using their own wages to their own advantage.

An official of one of the biggest Friendly societies, The Foresters. Quoted in S. Wood, The British Welfare State 1900–50 (1982)

---

1 Study sources A, B and C. In what ways can John Burn assert that the poor Law is adaptable to 'any new sensible demands made upon it'?

2 Derek Fraser (source H) asserts that pensions were 'the new birthright of an Englishman'. How valid is this claim for all English people?

3 Compare the Pensions Act with the Poor Law Amendment Act of 1834. What distinction is there in practice and in theory?

4 The Poor Law Amendment Act was not formally abolished until 1929. What role, therefore, did the provision of Old Age Pensions play in the relief of poverty?

5 To what extent is individualist and self-help principles embedded in both attitudes and policy of the liberal reforms?

Unemployment Insurance and labour exchanges

Winston Churchill, on taking office at the Board of Trade, is claimed to have remarked, 'There is nothing to do here: Lloyd George has taken all the plums!' His social reforms, however, appear to put the remark to a lie. In March 1908 in 'The Nation', he asserted 'From many quarters we may work towards the establishment of that National Minimum below which competition cannot be allowed, but above which it may continue healthy and free, to vivify and fertilise the world'.

SWEATED LABOUR.

Sweated labour

Worst of all exploited workers were the sweated labourers in the warrens of major cities. They were not protected by factory legislation nor by minimum wage rates. Nor could they protect themselves by forming trade unions. Churchill was ready to accept the argument for minimum wage rates. In 1909 the Trade Boards Act was passed providing for factory inspectors and the potential protection of 200,000 workers.

Unemployment and under-employment

The principal cause of poverty amongst the able-bodied, however, was not low wages but unemployment and under-employment. The 1907–8 depression underlined this stark truth. Unemployment rose to 7.2 per cent (800,000) in 1908. Churchill looked to Germany for a solution and suggested the laying of 'a big slice of Bismarckianism over the whole underside of our industrial system'.

He was supported in his proposition by two able advisers; Sir Hubert Llewellyn-Smith, the Permanent Secretary and W.H. Beveridge. Beveridge was to prove one of the most influential architects of social reform in post World War Two Britain. In 1909 he published his treatise, 'Unemployment: A Problem of Industry'. He argued convincingly that since men in regular work were not able to provide for their own protection against unemployment (only one-third of workers were insured through trade unions), only the State had the power to do so on such a massive scale.

The answer the Board of Trade provided was Labour Exchanges and unemployment insurance. The latter measure was delayed whilst Lloyd George attempted to formulate a combined insurance scheme for health cover. As a consequence Labour Exchanges became law in September 1909. By 1 February 1910, 83 Labour Exchanges were opened; by 1914 the number had increased to 430.

The People's Budget

The proposals for unemployment insurance were not to come without a protracted struggle and the 'winning' in 1911, of what has become popularly known as 'The People's Budget'. The conflict was focussed not on unemployment insurance but over Lloyd George's massive scheme for health insurance.

Medical provision for the vast majority of British citizens prior to 1911 relied on a patchwork of charity hospitals and dispensaries. The medical profession competed for patients; the Friendly Societies for their members. As with unemployment insurance it seemed only the power of the State could hold the ring between so many competing and powerful vested interests.

The proposals for health insurance, however, were costly. David Lloyd George's plan, in particular, was the most expensive, the most ambitious and the most controversial of the Liberal measures. The central question around which the feasibility of the plan revolved was; how was it to be paid for and, most importantly, who was to pay? Part of the scheme could be paid for by increasing the duty on beer, tobacco, spirits, petrol and an excise duty on motor cars. This alone would not be sufficient. To bridge the gap Lloyd George proposed a sliding scale of income tax contributions. Those with incomes in excess of £3,000 were required to pay a supertax of an extra 6d. in the pound bringing the total contribution of those who fell into this category to 1s. 8d. in the pound. In addition there was to be a 20 per cent capital gains tax. There was little doubt that the budget was an unequivocal attempt to re-distribute wealth through taxation. The proposals were passed in the Commons but the Lords rejected the budget and refused to compromise.

In 1911 Lloyd George had devised his strategy to move the intrangisent Lords. They were informed that if the budget proposals were not passed, then Lloyd George would recommend the creation of a further 500 life peers who would 'dilute' the opposition to his proposals. The Lords collapsed under the intended threat. Lloyd George was determined that their 'teeth' should be drawn to prevent any future disruption. From 1911 onwards they were unable to oppose budget proposals and their powers to delay bills was reduced.

On 16 December 1911, Lloyd George's bill received the royal assent. A compulsory weekly insurance levy was fixed at 4d. per employee; 3d. per employer; and a 2d contribution from the State for all workers earning less than £160 per annum for all manual labourers between the ages of sixteen and sixty. In times of need the insured worker would receive

TALKING POINT

What is 'capital' gains tax?

What might be the consequences of changing tax on capital gains?

medical treatment from a G.P., free medicine, sickness benefit of 10s. a week for thirteen weeks, 5s. 0d. a week disability benefit, for his wife maternity benefit of 30s, and treatment at a sanitorium should it be required.

Despite this apparent comprehensive scheme there were some protests from working class organisations, suspicious of the State's involvement. The British Medical Association too, had to be appeased.

Despite such protests, the reforms were put in place, representing, as they did, massive state intervention. Its significance lay in the ability of working people to avoid the Poor Law and pauperism. At the same time it must be acknowledged that it did not provide a national health service but rather a sickness insurance scheme – in other words, a means of treating the symptoms of poverty not its causes. Furthermore, the scheme operated through the cumbersome private insurance agencies.

The unemployment insurance clauses went through the Commons and took effect from the 15 July 1912. Some two and one quarter million men were assisted by a levy of two and one halfpenny each, contributed equally from the employer and employee, to which the State added one third of the total. In return, the insured worker received 7s. per week when unemployed to a maximum of fifteen weeks benefit in any one year.

TALKING POINT
What lay behind the principle of a 'three-way' contribution?

EXAMINING THE EVIDENCE
The People's Budget
Source A: The purpose of life insurance
The benefits offered in 1911 were deliberately set low to discourage malingering, but, like old age pensions, were in any case not intended to provide more than a 'lifebelt' to supplement other savings ... Unemployment insurance was intended to do no more than, in Beveridge's phrase, to average a man's earnings between good and bad times, or, as Churchill put it, to pool his luck with that of his fellow workers. It was in fact essentially insurance, socially organised and socially supplemented, to give the citizen some protection against the miseries of depression and the proved inadequacies of ad hoc relief.

Maurice Bruce, The Coming of the Welfare State (1965)

Source B: The Liberal welfare reform – a watershed?
Welfare legislation hitherto had concerned itself with the helpless, either at the beginning or the end of life ... Now the Crown provided permanent service agencies to which the mature workman might apply for aid and direction not only in an emergency ... A precedent had been sent. The departure made to prevent distress during unemployment took the state beyond the area of social welfare and into the area of social service.

B.B. Gilbert, The Evolution of National Insurance in Great Britain (1966)

Source C: Lloyd George introduces the 'Peoples' Budget'
But the Lords may decree a revolution which the people will direct. If they begin, issues will be raised that they little dream of, questions will be asked which are now whispered in humble voices, and answers will be

demanded then with authority. The question will be asked: 'Should 500 men, ordinary men chosen accidentally from among the unemployed, over-ride the judgement – the deliberate judgement – of millions of people who are engaged in the industry which makes the wealth of this country?' That is one question. Another will be, 'Who ordained that a few should have the land of Britain as a perequisite; who made 10,000 people owners of the soil, and the rest of us trespassers in the land of our birth; who is it – who is responsible for the scheme of things whereby one man is engaged through life in grinding labour, to win a bare and precarious subsistence for himself, and when at the end of his days he claims at the hands of the community he served a poor pension of eight pence a day, he can only get it through revolution; and another man who does not toil receives every hour of the day, every hour of the night, whilst he slumbers, more than his neighbour receives in a whole year of toil? Where did that table of law come from? Whose finger inscribed it?' These are the questions that will be asked. The answers are charged with the peril for the order of things the Peers represent; but they are fraught with rare and refreshing fruit for the parched lips of the multitude who have been treading the dusty road along which the people have marched through the dark ages which are now emerging in the light.

Lloyd George and the People's Budget, The Times 11 October (1909)

Source D: Welfare reforms – A beginning only

I never said this bill was the final solution. I am not putting it forward as a complete remedy. It is one of a series. We are advancing on the road, but it is an essential part of the journey. I have been now some years in politics and I have had, I think, as large a share of contention and strife and warfare as any man in British politics today. This year, this Session, I have joined the Red Cross. I am in the Ambulance Corps. I am engaged to drive a wagon through the twistings and turnings and ruts of the Parliamentary road. There are men who tell me that I have overloaded the wagon. I have taken three years to pack it carefully. I cannot spare a single parcel, for the suffering is very great. There are those who say my wagon is half empty. I say it is as much as I can carry. Now there are some who say I am in a great hurry. I am rather in a hurry, for I can hear the moanings of the wounded, and I want to carry relief to them in the alleys, the homes where they lie stricken, and I ask you, and through you, I ask the millions of good hearted men and women who constitute the majority of the people of this land – I ask you to help me set aside hindrances, to overcome obstacles, to avoid the pitfalls that beset my difficult path.

Lloyd George's 'Ambulance Wagon' speech at Birmingham, The Times 12 June 1911

Source E: Attack on unemployment

Insurance against unemployment, therefore, stands in the closest relation to the organisation of the labour market, and forms the second line of attack on the problem of the unemployment. It is, indeed, the necessary supplement thereto. The Labour Exchange is required to reduce to a minimum the intervals between successive jobs. Insurance is required to tide over the intervals that will remain. The Labour Exchange mobilises the reserves of labour for fluctuations and hastens re-absorption after changes of industrial structure. Insurance is needed to provide for the maintenance of the reserves while standing idle and of the displaced men while waiting for re-absorption. No plan other than insurance – whether purely self-supporting or with assistance from other sources – is really adequate.

William Beveridge, Unemployment: A Problem of Industry (1909)

Source F: Welfare reforms and social justice

We seek to substitute for the pressure of the forces of nature, operating by chance on individuals, the pressures of the laws of insurance, operating through averages, while modifying and mitigating effects in individual cases. In neither case is corresponding with reality lost. In neither case is risk eliminated. In neither case are pressures removed. In neither case can personal effort be dispensed with. In neither case can inferiority be protected. Chance and average spring from the same family, both are inexorable, both are blind, neither is concerned with the character of individuals or with ethics, or with sentiment. And all deviation into these paths will be disastrous. But the true economic superiority of the new foundations of averages, over the old foundation of chance, arises from the fact that the processes of waste are so much more swift than those of growth and repair, that the prevention of such catastrophies would be worth purchasing by diminution in the sense of the personal responsibility; and, further, that as there is no proportion between personal failings and the penalties extracted, or even between personal qualities and those penalties, there is no reason to suppose that a mitigation of the extreme severities will tend in any way to a diminution of personal responsibility, but that on the contrary more will be gained by an increase of ability to fight than will be lost through an abatement of the extreme consequences of defeat.

Winston Spencer Churchill, 'Notes on Malingering' 6 June 1909
Beveridge Papers D. 026

Source G

THE INCOME TAX PAYER.

Source H

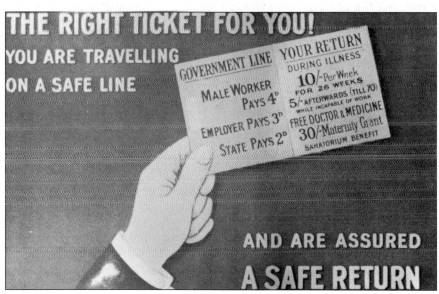

A GOVERNMENT POSTER 1911.

Source I: The Labour Party's response to the Liberal welfare reforms

And what happens when we ask for a decent minimum wage? No, say the Liberals but we will give you an Insurance Bill. We shall not uproot the cause of poverty but we will give you a sticking plaster to cover the disease that poverty causes.

Keir Hardie in a speech to the miners of Merthyr Rydfil, 1909

Source J

ELECTION POSTER – KEIR HARDIE

Source K: The need for the Poor Laws

It is vital that the pauper must suffer the loss of personal reputation; second the loss of personal freedom which is covered by detention in the workhouse; and third, the loss of political freedom by losing the right to vote … he must accept assistance on the terms, whatever they may be, which the common welfare recommends.

Evidence given by J.H. Davy, Head of the Poor Law Division to the Royal Commission on the Poor Law and the Relief of Distress, 1909

Source L: Opponents of contributory pension scheme

Any attempt to force upon the people of this country – whether for supplementary pensions, provisions for sick and invalidity, or anything else – a system of direct, personal, weekly contributions must, in our judgement, in the face of so powerful an army … prove politically disastrous.

Evidence of Sidney and Beatrice Webb in the Minority Report of the Royal Commission on the Poor Law and the Relief of distress (1909)

Source M: The need for social welfare

I hope that very soon the State will acknowledge full responsibility in the matter of making provisions for the sickness, breakdown and unemployment. It really does so now through the Poor Law, but conditions under which this system has hitherto worked have been so harsh and humiliating that working class pride revolts against accepting so degrading and doubtful a boon. Gradually the obligation of the State to find labour or sustenance will be realised and honourably interpreted.

Lloyd George, *a speech in Parliament* (1909)

1 What do these sources reveal about the tensions surrounding the introduction of unemployment and health insurance?

2 With what justification can this period of Liberal reforms be referred to as originating the welfare state?

3 What appears to have been the motivation underpinning the introduction of the welfare reforms?

4 What elements of continuity as well as change appear either explicit or implicit in the reforms?

REVIEW
Did the liberal reforms of 1905–14 constitute the origins of the Welfare State?

In 1908 Churchill told Asquith, 'I believe that there is an impressive social policy to be unfolded which would ponderously pass through both Houses and leave an abiding mark on national history.'

(Winston S. Churchill: Companion II part 2 pp. 861)

Some historians claim that the 'mark on national history' has its roots in early nineteenth century government intervention. Local Boards of Guardians, faced with the practical difficulties of relieving poverty, continued outdoor relief to the able-bodied and even provided specialist services such as hospitals. Chamberlain's 1886 circular, allowing the creation of public works to relieve distress, contravened the strict interpretation of the Poor Law Amendment Act. Compulsory vaccination 1885, compulsory education 1880, numerous and increasing public health and Factory Acts, gas and water provision by local councils, are pointed to as examples to illustrate the erosion of the individualist ideology.

Government expenditure as a percentage of the gross domestic product rose from 2.2 per cent in 1900 to 4.2 per cent in 1913. Lloyd George's 'People's Budget' had aimed at a redistribution of income to pay for welfare reforms. It may have been that Lloyd George intended to go further as is hinted in the final source in Examining the evidence above.

But did this signify an abrupt break with the past? Was the individualist ideology fundamentally and fatally undermined by Liberal legislation? Or were the architects of the reforms content to merely provide a 'lifebelt' to ensure the survival of the economy, army and capitalism?

Now return to the question which heads the review and consider the following points in your answer.

- The concept of the welfare State.
- The principles and motivation that lay behind the welfare reforms.
- The details and nature of the welfare reforms.

Did these reforms constitute a break with nineteenth century attitudes to the role of the individual and government within society?

ACKNOWLEDGEMENTS

The author and publishers wish to thank the following who have kindly given permission for the use of copyright material.

Cambridge University Press for extracts from *The Handloom weavers* by D Bythell, *The Industrial Revolution* by P Deane, *Principles of political economy and taxation 1819* by D Ricardo, *The economic history of Britain: foreign competition Vol 2* by R Flood and E McCloskey (eds);

Croom Helm for an extract from *The new economic history of railways* by P O'Brein;

HarperCollins Publishers for an extract from *The condition of the working class 1844* by F Engels;

Longman Group UK for extracts from *Origins of the Industrial revolution* by G C Thomas, by M W Flinn and *Populatrion and Society* 1700–1970 by N Tranter;

Manchester University Press for an extract from *Iron and steel in the industrial revolution* by T S Ashton;

The following photographic sources have kindly given permission for photographs to be reproduced:

British Leyland: 12.6. British Museum: 16.12. Camera Press: 15.1 The Mary Evans Picture Library: 1.1, 1.4, 1.7, 1.14, 2.11, 2.12, 2.14, 2.18, 3.1, 3.2, 3.3, 3.5, 3.6, 3.10, 3.11, 3.12, 3.14, 3.16, 3.21, 4.8, 4.16, 5.3, 6.5, 6.6, 6.8, 6.11, 7.2, 10.2, 10.20, 11.3, 11.7, 11.8, 11.9, 12.9, 13.1, 13.21, 14.6, 14.8, 14.9, 14.12, 15.17, 15.20, 18.1, 18.3, 18.6, 19.2, 19.10, 19.12. The Fitzwilliam Museum: 9.10, 9.11. The Fotomas Index: 4.5, 11.18, 14.1, 14.11, 15.6, 18.9, 19.17. The Hulton Picture Company: 1.3, 2.10, 2.13, 2.18, 3.9, 3.13, 3.17, 3.18, 3.22, 3.24, 3.25, 4.17, 5.1, 7.1, 7.6, 7.7, 7.12, 7.14, 8.1, 8.15, 8.22, 10.3, 10.13, 11.2, 11.10, 11.11, 12.2, 16.11, 18.12, 19.5. The Illustrated London News: 14.2. The Billie Love Historical Collection: 1.5, 1.6, 1.15, 1.17, 2.7, 2.8, 4.11, 4.18, 6.1, 6.3, 6.7, 6.9, 7.3, 7.4, 7.5, 7.10, 7.11, 8.3, 8.9, 8.10, 8.12, 8.24, 9.1, 9.17, 10.4, 11.4, 11.5, 11.6, 11.15, 12.1, 12.4, 12.10, 13.4, 13.5, 13.6, 13.8, 13.9, 13.10, 13.11, 13.12, 13.22, 13.24, 14.7, 14.10, 14.13, 15.3, 15.5, 15.8, 15.9, 15.10, 15.11, 15.12, 15.13, 15.16, 16.1, 16.17, 16.18, 16.19, 16.20, 17.1, 18.2, 18.5, 18.8, 19.4, 19.6, 19.14, 19.15. The Peter Newark Historical Collection: 11.12, 11.17, 12.5, 16.13. Newcastle Libraries: 13.13. C.S. Orwin: 2.2, 2.3. Oxford University: 2.9, Reading University: 2.15. The Science Museum: 8.13. Topham Picture Source: 15.4. Wiedenfeld and Nicholson: 17.23.

Index